BOOKS ARE MADE OUT OF BOOKS

Southwestern Writers Collection Series
The Wittliff Collections at Texas State University
STEVEN L. DAVIS, EDITOR

Books Are Made Out of Books

A Guide to Cormac McCarthy's Literary Influences

MICHAEL LYNN CREWS

University of Texas Press

AUSTIN

The Southwestern Writers Collection Series originates from the Wittliff Collections, a repository of literature, film, music, and southwestern and Mexican photography established at Texas State University.

Requests for permission to reproduce material from this work should be sent to:
Permissions
University of Texas Press
P.O. Box 7819
Austin, TX 78713-7819
http://utpress.utexas.edu/rp-form

♾ The paper used in this book meets the minimum requirements of ANSI/NISO Z39.48-1992 (R1997) (Permanence of Paper).

LIBRARY OF CONGRESS CATALOGING DATA

Names: Crews, Michael Lynn, author.
Title: Books are made out of Books : a guide to Cormac McCarthy's literary
    influences / Michael Lynn Crews.
Other titles: Southwestern Writers Collection series.
Description: First edition. | Austin : University of Texas Press, 2017. | Series:
    Southwestern writers collection series, The Wittliff collections at Texas State
    University | Include bibliographical references and index.
Identifiers: LCCN 2017003553| ISBN 978-1-4773-1348-0 (cloth : alk. paper) |
    ISBN 978-1-4773-1469-2 (library e-book) | ISBN 978-1-4773-1470-8
    (non-library e-book)
Subjects: LCSH: McCarthy, Cormac, 1933–
Classification: LCC PS3563.C337 Z64 2017 | DDC 813/.54—dc23
LC record available at https://lccn.loc.gov/2017003553
doi:10.7560/313480

For Denise, Jane, and Danny
And for James Barcus,
Requiescat in Pace

Table of Contents

Chapter 8. The Stonemason   *218*

Chapter 13. Correspondence 276

Acknowledgments

I am grateful to my wife, Denise, and our children, Jane and Danny, for keeping my spirits up.

From Baylor University, Sarah Ford, Luke Ferretter, and Richard Russell all provided helpful feedback on the book. Richard, in particular, has been a source of encouragement and inspiration. He has served as a model of scholarly integrity, one I have tried to emulate.

James Barcus, also from Baylor, and sadly no longer with us, deserves special thanks. This book was launched from a conversation over coffee with him, and he helped shepherd it through its first iteration. His enthusiasm for the book, for the work of Cormac McCarthy, and his generous support of my endeavors were invaluable to me. I miss him and wish he could have seen the book in print. He was its first champion.

Thanks to Katie Salzmann and Steve Davis at the Southwestern Writers Collection, Texas State University–San Marcos. Without Katie's exceptional work, my own would not be possible. Thanks to Rick Wallach, for very kind words, and for his contribution to McCarthy studies.

I would also like to thank everyone at the University of Texas Press who worked on the publication of this book, especially Casey Kittrell, who shepherded it through its second iteration. And thanks to Katherine H. Streckfus, whose keen eye helped me to make this a better book.

BOOKS ARE MADE OUT OF BOOKS

CHAPTER 1

Introduction
Books Out of Books

In 1992, Cormac McCarthy granted his first lengthy interview in a career spanning three decades. Asked to comment on his literary influences, he told the interviewer, Richard B. Woodward, that "the ugly fact is books are made out of books.... The novel depends for its life on the novels that have been written." In the same interview, Woodward informs us that "McCarthy would rather talk about rattlesnakes, molecular computers, country music, Wittgenstein—anything—than himself or his books." Critics interested in the question—one inevitably asked about a writer whose work one admires—of McCarthy's literary interests and influences have had to sustain themselves on scraps. We know that *Moby-Dick* is his favorite book, and that he admires Joyce, Faulkner, and Dostoyevsky. These names make up the litany that he can be counted on to volunteer. Digging through the nooks and crannies of his meager offerings to literary journalists, we could add Tolstoy, Flannery O'Connor, and Shakespeare. These are nutritious enough hors d'oeuvres, but hardly satisfy the appetites of those who are fascinated by the ways in which, to borrow McCarthy's formulation, books are made out of books. To call this an *ugly* fact suggests that something like Harold Bloom's anxiety of influence haunts McCarthy's creative efforts. But, for the critic, this fact is a tantalizing invitation to research.

However reticent McCarthy may be in interviews about discussing his books—or the influence of other books on them—by making his literary papers available to scholars, he has made it possible to begin research into his influences in earnest. In December 2007, the Southwestern Writers Collection (SWC), which is part of the Wittliff Collection of the Alkek Library at Texas State University, in San Marcos, Texas, purchased a sizable collection of McCarthy's papers, which became available to scholars in the spring of 2009. The collection includes notes, correspondence, and drafts. The acquisition of correspondence between McCarthy and J. Howard Woolmer, a rare book dealer and publisher, added another source of information about McCarthy's reading habits. It is now possible to offer a tentative answer to the following question: What books, what writers, were on McCarthy's mind during the composition of his novels? In his notes, in letters to Woolmer and others, and often in holograph marginalia found in early drafts of the novels, McCarthy tells us himself. And by examining the way in which these books went into the making of his own, we can learn something about the way influences shape McCarthy's own imaginative endeavors. What follows will be an extended study of Cormac McCarthy's reading interests and influences, but only those that can be identified through direct references in the archives. Writers that McCarthy has mentioned in interviews, or who can be identified through clear literary allusions in his published works, are outside my province.

For instance, McCarthy's interest in Emily Dickinson is signaled by the following allusion in *Child of God*. Lester Ballard, upon waking up in the hospital to discover that his arm has been amputated, is described as noting the ghastly absence "apparently with no surprise" (175). The poem to which this alludes begins with the following lines: "Apparently with no surprise / To any happy Flower / The Frost beheads it at its play" (Poem 1668). Any reader acquainted with the poetry of Dickinson could identify the source of the allusion. The focus of my research is on references to other writers that do not appear in any publication, references that can only be found in the Wittliff archives. Since no reference to Dickinson appears in the archives, I do not include an entry for her. The following project is the fruit of exclusively archival research, and my purpose is to provide readers with information that was not available until McCarthy's papers became available.

The main body of this work is comprised of alphabetized entries corresponding to the names of writers or thinkers to whom McCarthy clearly refers in his papers. These entries consist of a description of the location of the reference within the archives, and some context, such as biographical information about the author, or the location in the source text of a quotation that McCarthy has copied into his notes or margins. I then establish a connection between these references to other writers and McCarthy's own work. In some cases, I draw out some interpretive conclusions on the basis of that connection. The entries explore McCarthy's influences and interests as revealed by the books he was reading during the composition of his novels.

This introduction will provide an account of McCarthy's career and of how five decades' worth of a writer's accumulated papers ended up at Texas State University. I will then describe the contents of the ninety-eight boxes housed in the Wittliff Collection as well as the process—a kind of scholarly hunting and pecking, magnifying glass in hand—by which I located and then explicated McCarthy's references to other writers. Finally, I will discuss the way McCarthy "borrows" from other writers (or is it stealing—the preferred approach, according to T. S. Eliot, of the masters?), and from that discussion, draw some conclusions about his approach to composition.

T Is for Texas, T Is for Tennessee:
Cormac McCarthy's Literary Journey

Cormac McCarthy was born in Rhode Island on 20 July 1933.[1] At the age of four his family moved to Knoxville, Tennessee, where his father, Charles McCarthy, worked as a lawyer for the Tennessee Valley Authority. Many of McCarthy's early southern novels are set in and around Knoxville, and *Suttree*, which he worked on for nearly two decades, is steeped in his firsthand knowledge of Knoxville in the 1950s. McCarthy was raised Roman Catholic and attended a Catholic high school. He was a student at the University of Tennessee in 1951 and 1952; served in the US Air Force, where he was stationed in Alaska, from 1953 to 1957; and returned to the University of Tennessee from 1957 to 1960. His first published works, the stories "Wake for Susan" and "A Drowning Incident," were published in the student literary journal during this time. He left the university without taking a degree and began what would become a peripatetic lifestyle for the next two decades. Besides Knoxville and its environs, he has lived in New Orleans, Chicago, and Lexington, Kentucky. In the 1960s he traveled in England and France, and he briefly lived on the island of Ibiza in the Mediterranean. He married Lee Holleman, with whom he had a son,

Cullen, in 1961. That marriage was short-lived, and in 1966 he married Anne DeLisle, whom he met on a ship sailing to England in 1965.

His first novel, *The Orchard Keeper*, was published in 1965 under the guidance of the eminent editor Albert Erskine, who worked with such luminaries as Malcolm Lowry and Ralph Ellison. *Outer Dark* appeared in 1968, followed by *Child of God* in 1973. *Suttree*, which vies with *Blood Meridian* for the status of magnum opus in McCarthy's oeuvre, was published in 1979, though his work on the novel dates back to the early 1960s. My own surmise is that it was the first novel he ever worked on. Much of the early excised fragments housed at Texas State reveal an amateurish quality that is not present in the already mature craftsmanship of *The Orchard Keeper*. McCarthy seems to have originally envisioned his protagonist as a kind of tortured artist figure, more Stephen Dedalus than Cornelius Suttree.

That ur-*Suttree*, as I have come to think of it, exists in fragments in the archives, as does an ur–*Blood Meridian*, which McCarthy began writing in the mid-1970s. His notes for *Suttree* often contain notes for *Blood Meridian* as well. The early versions of that novel suggest something more like a raucous, picaresque buddy adventure than the metaphysical horror/western novel that many critics regard as his crowning achievement. The 1970s also saw the fruits of McCarthy's interest in screenplay writing. *The Gardener's Son*, directed by McCarthy's friend Richard Pearce, aired on PBS in January 1977.

McCarthy and DeLisle divorced, and McCarthy relocated to the Southwest in the late 1970s in order to research *Blood Meridian*. El Paso, Texas, became his home base for much of the 1980s and 1990s, and the Tennessean became a Texan. During that time he traveled to locations in both the United States and Mexico that provide settings for both *Blood Meridian* and *The Border Trilogy*. The former was published in 1985, and though the novel met with critical acclaim, a large audience continued to elude McCarthy. He was financially buoyed by the award of a Genius Grant by the MacArthur Foundation, which also led to McCarthy's friendship with the physicist Murray Gell-Mann, which would eventually lead to McCarthy's association with the Santa Fe Institute.

McCarthy finally found a large audience with the publication of the first installment of *The Border Trilogy* in 1992. *All the Pretty Horses* was a literary best-seller and garnered for McCarthy a National Book

Award. *The Crossing* followed in 1994, and *Cities of the Plain* completed the trilogy in 1998. At around this time, McCarthy married his third wife, Jennifer Winkley, with whom he had his second son, John. They relocated to Santa Fe, New Mexico, where McCarthy, through his friendship with Gell-Mann, became a research fellow at the Santa Fe Institute. The couple later divorced. He published *No Country for Old Men*, later adapted into an Oscar-winning film by the Cohen brothers, in 2005. In 2006, he published *The Road*, which won the Pulitzer Prize and became an Oprah Winfrey book club selection.[2]

In 2013, a second McCarthy screenplay was produced. *The Counselor*, directed by Ridley Scott, opened in November of that year to a fairly cold critical reception, though the screenplay itself, published shortly before the release of the film, is much longer than the filmed version, and will probably need to be evaluated in its own right after the dark cloud hanging over the film dissipates. McCarthy still lives in Santa Fe, and is, by his own account, working on several novels. A much anticipated novel, *The Passenger*, exists in an early draft housed at Texas State, though it is unavailable to scholars until after publication. Like *Suttree* and *Blood Meridian*, its composition has extended over a long period. In fact, we know from an anecdote, told by Michael Dirda, that he was doing research for it as long ago as 1999. Dirda, former editor of the *Washington Post*'s *Book World*, in an essay entitled "Excursion" from his collection *Readings*, tells of meeting Joseph DeSalvo, owner of the Faulkner House Bookshop in New Orleans, in 1999. He informed Dirda that "A few weeks earlier, Cormac McCarthy came in. 'I recognized him,' Joe recounted, 'and asked if he would sign a couple of his books.' The famously reclusive novelist just said, 'No, Joe, I don't do that anymore.' Apparently McCarthy was spending some time [in New Orleans] researching the lives of deep-sea divers on offshore oil rigs" (210). Rick Wallach, one of McCarthy's early critical champions, has stated that insider reports on *The Passenger* indicate a connection with offshore oil rigs in the Gulf of Mexico. Rumors abound about when this novel will see the light of day, but most of them are hopeful about a release date in the near future. Happily, Cormac McCarthy's literary journey does not appear to be complete.

The Wittliff Collection

Texas State University acquired McCarthy's papers in December 2007. This impressive coup was facilitated by Bill Wittliff, who, with his wife Sally, founded the Southwestern Writers Collection at Texas State in 1986 (Todd 34). Bill Wittliff, a screenwriter best known for his screenplay adaptation of *Lonesome Dove*, first became interested in McCarthy after reading, in the mid-1980s, a McCarthy screenplay at the Sundance Institute (34). This may have been either *Whales and Men*, which Wittliff acquired for the SWC several years before the purchase of the larger collection, or *Cities of the Plain*, which McCarthy was also working on in the mid-1980s. Wittliff and McCarthy met and became friends in 1987, and after years of discussions with McCarthy, Wittliff negotiated an agreement for the purchase of the papers in 2007 (34). The collection was later enhanced by the purchase, from J. Howard Woolmer, a book collector and bibliographer, of over one hundred letters exchanged between Woolmer and McCarthy between 1969 and 2005. The SWC continues to seek correspondence to add to the collection. Letters from McCarthy to Robert C. Cumbow, author of *The Films of Sergio Leone*, and Peter Greenleaf, an acquaintance of McCarthy's, are currently available to researchers.

The Cormac McCarthy Papers consist of notes, early drafts—some complete, some in fragments, and often containing holograph corrections and marginal notes—as well as setting copies and proofs. All of McCarthy's published works, excepting *The Counselor*, are represented, including the screenplay *The Gardener's Son* and the two stage plays, *The Stonemason* and *The Sunset Limited*. In addition, the collection contains correspondence from McCarthy's editors, copy editors, and experts that he consulted on technical questions. For instance, in the papers for *The Crossing*, McCarthy consulted a doctor, Barry G. King, for information about gunshot wounds—no shortage of which will be found in McCarthy's corpus.

The papers are housed in ninety-eight boxes, each of which contains several folders. I have documented my findings by referencing both the box and the folder numbers for the pages I refer to. The boxes are labeled by the title of the work that the enclosed material represents, and then by the content of each folder. For instance, Boxes 1–7 contain material related to *The Orchard Keeper*. The first folder of the first box, which features correspondence between McCarthy and his editors at Random House, is labeled "Correspondence, 1964–1965, n.d." The second folder contains McCarthy's notes for *The Orchard Keeper*. The third folder contains a complete draft of the novel, labeled "Late Draft," the fourth contains the container box for the draft, and folder five contains another complete draft, labeled "Late Draft." Boxes 2–7 contain proofs of the novel. Each of McCarthy's works is represented by a similar arrangement. My focus has been on the boxes that contain correspondence, notes, and early drafts containing McCarthy's handwritten corrections and marginalia. That is where researchers can find McCarthy's references to writers and books that were on his mind during the composition of his novels and plays. Such references can be found throughout the collection, but there are three gold mines: *Suttree*, *Blood Meridian*, and the three drafts of the unpublished screenplay *Whales and Men*.

I have found direct references to nearly 150 writers in the archives. My search has been for direct references to the names of authors, the titles of books, or clearly attributable quotations. Two examples will illustrate both the occasional difficulties of tracking down McCarthy's references and how I have gone about sleuthing for them.

The first example is of a reference to Melville's *Moby-Dick* contained in McCarthy's notes for *Suttree* (see entries for Melville in *Suttree* and *The Stonemason*). The notes are found in Box 19, Folder 13. The typed page on which the reference appears is, like all of McCarthy's notes, a real hodge-podge, but it is typical of what we find in the boxes for other novels. The page contains lists of words and fragments of prose from the novel itself, including bits of dialogue and description. The page in question also contains the lyrics to several hillbilly songs, including the words to "Don't That Road Look Rough and Rocky." All of this is interesting, but I look for names and quotations, and on this particular page I found one. A single line of type, unrelated to anything else on the page, features the following quotation from *Moby-Dick*: "'Federated along one keel' Melville." Short, fragmentary quotations like this appear from time to time in the McCarthy papers. He does not always, as he did in this case, supply the name of the author of the quotation. In the age of Google, that is usually not a problem, but it cuts down on time to have the name in hand. A Google search took me to the location of the quotation: chapter 27, "Knights and Squires." The chapter describes the ragamuffin crew of the *Pequod*, and features the following passage, from which McCarthy culled the quotation copied into his notes: "They were nearly all Islanders in the Pequod, *Isolatoes* too, I call such, not acknowledging the common continent of men, but each *Isolato* living on a separate continent of his own. Yet now, *federated along one keel*, what a set these Isolatoes were!" (107, emphasis added). Finding the source completes step one of the process.

Step two involves figuring out the relationship between the quotation and McCarthy's published works. This cannot always be done, and I began to think that this fragment from Melville, along with the hillbilly songs and lists of long-dead archaisms to be found on the same page, never found its way into *Suttree*. However, something about the quotation sounded familiar, and I was sure that McCarthy had used it somewhere. Giving up on *Suttree*, I turned to *Blood Meridian*, since I had discovered that McCarthy's notes for *Suttree* often contained notes for McCarthy's first western novel, the composition of which overlapped, in the second half of the 1970s, with the last stages of the composition of *Suttree*. I looked for the word "federated" in John Sepich's online concordance to McCarthy's novels, a resource that has been indispensable to this project. And there it was, on page 226. Here is McCarthy's subtle, sneaky theft from Herman Melville, in a description of another ragamuffin crew, the Glanton gang: "Each man scanned the terrain and the movements of the least of creatures were logged into their collective cognizance until they were *federated with invisible wires* of vigilance and advanced upon that landscape with a single resonance" (226, emphasis added). Step two was complete. Having established, through his own literary papers, a connection between McCarthy and another writer, I then explored the significance of that connection for our understanding of McCarthy's work. Each entry in the work that follows chronicles these three steps in the process.

Literary allusions typically bear enough phraseological similarity to the source that most educated readers can make the connection, but McCarthy's appropriation of Melville would likely go unnoticed. Gregory Machacek, in an illuminating discussion of literary allusion in the *PMLA*, highlights, as a feature of literary allusion, the often covert nature of one writer's appropriation of another: "The fact that a phraseological appropriation can be covert, then, the fact that its derivation can go unnoticed, distinguishes it from learned or indirect reference, where readers tend to be aware that they are missing something if the referent is unknown" (527). McCarthy's appropriation of Melville falls into this class of covert allusions.

Machacek suggests that a more precise term for the kind of allusion McCarthy is making is "phraseological appropriation," since the inherent possibility that the reference will go unnoticed suggests that such references become almost seamless elements within the work in which they are incorporated. For Machacek, this means that phraseological appropriations display an "almost ontological" difference from other language in a literary work: "An integrated verbal repetition treats preexisting phraseology almost as a sort of physical raw material that can be cut, reworked, and incorporated into a new setting—like scraps of paper glued to a collage or fragments of stone set into a mosaic" (527). That is a fitting metaphor for McCarthy's appropriation of the work of other writers. In fact, Machacek's figure of stones in a mosaic calls to mind Edwin Arnold and Dianne Luce's report that McCarthy once used stones from James Agee's Knoxville home in an annex he built onto a house he lived in with his second wife Anne DeLisle. McCarthy's phraseological appropriation of Melville is a verbal analogue to his appropriation of the stones from Agee's house. Quotations and references to other writers that appear in the McCarthy archives are so many stones in the extended building project that McCarthy began with the publication of *The Orchard Keeper* in 1965.

A second example of my research process involves a misattributed reference to a writer found in McCarthy's notes for *Blood Meridian*. Box 35, Folder 4, containing handwritten notes for the novel, includes the following attribution: "The ground and the unground—see Herrigel Way of Zen 1st few pp." Searching for a discussion of the ground and the unground in Eugen Herrigel's book yielded nothing, so I concluded that McCarthy had misattributed the quotation to the German scholar of Buddhism. However, I had come across the term "unground" some years ago in Nicolas Berdyaev's introduction to a 1958 edition of Jacob Boehme's *Six Theosophic Points*. We know of McCarthy's interest in Boehme because a quotation from the German mystic serves as an epigraph to *Blood Meridian*. That quotation, it turned out, comes from *Six Theosophic Points*. McCarthy had been reading both Herrigel and Boehme during the composition of *Blood Meridian*, and he mixed them up in what looks, on the page, to be a hastily written reminder to go back and look at a source. In this case, the source is Berdyaev's introduction (the first few pages), which features a lengthy discussion of Boehme's concept of the unground (see entry for Boehme in *Blood Meridian*).

Although a great many of the references were easy enough to track down, relating them to McCarthy's published works can be difficult. Boehme's particular brand of Christian dualism seems to have impinged on McCarthy's thinking while he was creating the nightmarish character Judge Holden, and, more importantly, while he was thinking through the relationship between the judge and the kid, characters he likely thought of as archetypes of a quasi-Gnostic metaphysics that informs the novel.

In the next section I will discuss one of the conclusions that I have drawn from studying the relationships between McCarthy's influences and his published work, and say something about his approach to composition.

Literary Influence and the Novels of Cormac McCarthy

One thing we learn from a study of influence is that critics do not approach reading in the same way that an artist does, or at least not in the way the artist Cormac McCarthy does. For instance, Rick Wallach, in an essay exploring kinships between *Blood Meridian* and *Beowulf,* discusses how both works depict martial codes. As a critic, he is interested in particular in how *Beowulf* gives rise to ideas in McCarthy's novel. However, looking at the references to the poem in McCarthy's notes, we find nothing about martial codes, no notes-to-self about exposing the "contagion of systematized violence" (201) in *Beowulf.*

Here are two quotations from the Francis Gummere translation of *Beowulf* as they appear in a short, ultimately excised fragment from an early draft of *Suttree*. They are in quotation marks, which are also in McCarthy's draft:

> Apace apace heart's blood bright on the lampkept walk. Helm up thy gorestained shortsword, he is surely done. Darkflecked and welling blood and pale blue tubers pouching from his sectored gutbag. A perilous journey with peril done. A black screechowl (Black howlet in a

black tree ordains the dead with sooty cantata) "and nicors that lay on the ledge of the ness" B/wulf, "mere-wife monstrous. Brinewolf

In all times man's noblest work has been to take arms against his enemies, to defend that with which he is charged. My wife my land my aged. (Infirm elders)

Where is the enemy? What is the shape of him? Where kept and what the counter of his face? (Box 30, Folder 1)

The three questions that conclude this passage, which does not otherwise resemble anything in *Suttree*, should sound familiar to those who have read the novel. They appear in the italicized opening pages. The quotations from *Beowulf* come from the poet's description of the nightmarish lake within which Grendel's mother dwells, and from names ascribed to her during Beowulf's fight with the "Brinewolf." The line "A perilous journey with peril done" probably evokes the Perilous Chapel episode of the Grail legend, which McCarthy was interested in at the time. References in his papers to Jessie L. Weston's *From Ritual to Romance* make the association likely. What McCarthy finds in both the epic poem and the medieval legend is a tense, gothic mood that he aims to duplicate.

Here is the relevant passage from *Suttree*. The echoes of *Beowulf* are clear enough, though I never noticed them until I read the early draft of the novel quoted above:

The night is quiet. Like a camp before battle. The city beset by a thing unknown and will it come from forest or sea? The murengers have walled the pale, the gates are shut, but lo the thing's inside and can you guess his shape? Where he's kept or what's the counter of his face? (4–5)

Here we see McCarthy imagining Knoxville, Tennessee, as a version of Hrothgar's mead hall, menaced by monsters roaming a nightmare gothic landscape.

Knowing that McCarthy was interested in Weston's book provokes interesting questions about its influence on McCarthy's thinking. There is no doubt that he was thinking about the book, but the archives suggest that in addition to ideas, the substance of an artist's thematic concerns, he found what can only be described as raw material to be shaped into aesthetic form. A marginal note from an early draft of *Suttree* contains the following quotation from chapter 13 of Weston's book: "Many knights have been slain there, none know by whom" (Box 30, Folder 1). This line comes from a discussion of the Perilous Chapel episode of the Grail legend, the subject of the chapter. Here is the quotation with some context added: "When Perceval asks of the Chapel he is told it was built by Queen Brangemore of Cornwall, who was later murdered by her son Espinogres, and buried beneath the altar. Many knights have since been slain there, none know by whom, save it be by the Black Hand which appeared and put out the light" (133). The quotation, which appears in McCarthy's notes for *Suttree*, actually shows up in *Blood Meridian*, the composition of which overlapped with the writing of the former. Here is how Weston's line works its way into McCarthy's novel: describing the bloody aftermath of a bar fight involving the kid and two other young men who have joined Captain White's filibuster, the narrator tells us that "the boy lay with his skull broken in a pool of blood, *none knew by whom*" (40, emphasis added). It is, for the critic, simultaneously frustrating and fascinating to consider that what McCarthy liked about the Weston quotation was the sound of the words.

This is not to say that McCarthy was merely mining Weston for striking turns of phrase. Knowing that he was interested in her book, and knowing that McCarthy's original title for *The Road* was *The Grail*, ought to open up a whole new path in McCarthy criticism (the pathbreaker here is Lydia Cooper, whose "Cormac McCarthy's *The Road* as Apocalyptic Grail Narrative" discusses Weston's work in relation to McCarthy). However, what we discover in the archives, in instance after instance, is that ideas are, for McCarthy, material, just as images, metaphors, and striking turns of phrase are. Looking at the way McCarthy records the influence of other writers in his notes tells us much about how he uses their work as material to be incorporated into his own. And what we find, when we find references to other writers, looks more like colors on a painter's palette than ideas indexed for later development. Even when we find McCarthy appropriating the work of thinkers, it is difficult to draw a line between intellectual and aesthetic appropriation, so suffused with the latter is the former.

A good example of this blurring of lines can be found in an examination of McCarthy's interest in Michel Foucault during the composition of *Suttree*. In his notes, McCarthy copied out several very brief quotations from the first chapter of Foucault's *Madness and Civilization*. Madness was on McCarthy's mind when writing the novel. More precisely, he was interested in nonrational states of consciousness and their potential for illumination. His notes make it clear that in Foucault's book he found a fruitful intellectual inquiry into this matter. However, he also found raw matter for composition, colors on a palette to mix and mingle; ideas, yes, but ideas clothed in the bright colors of words that create the right kind of frisson in both the writer and the reader.

One of the quotations from *Madness and Civilization* is "Thing [*sic*] become so burdened with meaning that their forms are dimmed" (Box 19, Folder 13). The quotation comes from Foucault's discussion of how perceptions of visual art began to change during the Renaissance. He argued that the fragmentation brought about by the dissolution of the unified Christian culture of the Middle Ages led to an interest in the artistic expression of madness, or folly, as well as a renewed understanding of the images found in medieval art. He saw this as liberation. Here is Foucault (I have italicized the sentence from which McCarthy quoted):

> Paradoxically, this liberation derives from a proliferation of meaning, from a self-multiplication of significance, weaving relationships so numerous, so intertwined, so rich, that they can no longer be deciphered except in the esoterism of knowledge. *Things themselves become so burdened with attributes, signs, allusions that they finally lose their own form. Meaning* is no longer read in an immediate perception, the figure no longer speaks for itself. (18–19, emphasis added)

There is no question that McCarthy is interested in the content of this paragraph. But he is equally interested in the form, in what Robert Frost called "the sound of sense." As I have indicated, McCarthy's notes for *Suttree* often overlap with early notes for *Blood Meridian*, which he began writing in the mid-1970s. Foucault's influence can be detected in both books, but the following quotation from *Blood Meridian* shows us how much emphasis McCarthy places on the sound half of the sound/sense continuum. The passage describes the appearance of the judge and the fool as they cross the desert:

It was the judge and the imbecile. They were both of them naked and they neared through the desert dawn like beings of a mode little more than tangential to the world at large, their figures now quick with clarity and now fugitive in the strangeness of that same light. Like things whose very portent renders them ambiguous. *Like things so charged with meaning that their forms are dimmed.* (281–282, emphasis added)

McCarthy is fairly shameless about this kind of literary theft, but he covers his tracks well.

The following quotation from John Dewey's *Art as Experience* describes the artistic process in a way that resembles my description of McCarthy's interest in the sound of sense. After drawing a distinction between subject and substance, Dewey explains the significance he attaches to these different aspects of a work of art:

The distinction may, I think, be paraphrased as that between matter *for* and matter *in* artistic production. The subject or "matter for" is capable of being indicated and described in other fashion than that of the art-product itself. The "matter in," the actual substance, *is* the art object itself and hence cannot be expressed in any other way. The subject for Milton's "Paradise Lost" is, as Bradley says, the fall of man in connection with the revolt of the angels—a theme already current in Christian circles and readily identifiable by any one familiar with the Christian tradition. The substance of the poem, the esthetic *matter*, is the poem itself; what became of the subject as it underwent Milton's imaginative treatment. (110, emphasis in original)

Dewey goes on to say that "the artist himself can hardly begin with a subject alone. If he did, his work would almost surely suffer from artificiality" (111). That McCarthy's borrowings from novelists, poets, writers, and thinkers do not feel artificial is a testament to his artistic abilities.

As we see in the examples of *Beowulf*, Weston, and Foucault, McCarthy finds *matter for* his novels in the writers who have influenced him. But he also shapes those influences into *matter in* his novels. He thinks through and with the materials of fiction, and the echoes of precursors and sources serve, for McCarthy, perhaps for all imaginative writers, *as* material. In fact, McCarthy's sources are so seamlessly woven into the fabric of the novels that they are often hard to find, though insightful critics, such as Dianne Luce and John Sepich, have a gift for discovering them. For the rest of us, the McCarthy archives in San Marcos are a real treasure.

I will conclude with a note about how to read this book. Given the alphabetical arrangement of the material, one way to approach it is as a reference work, in which case readers will "enter" the text at the point of immediate interest—call it a vertical entry point. However, some readers will prefer a horizontal approach and read it from start to finish. To those who approach it in that fashion, I should note that they will encounter some repetition, since the book is written both for them and for those who prefer to dip a toe in at different points along the shore. What will sound repetitious to the former will be new to the latter. Also, references to some authors appear in the papers for more than one work. Readers who are using the book as a reference guide will find cross-references to the chapters where additional entries on a single author can be found.

I should also note that this volume contains chapters on all but two of McCarthy's published works, *All the Pretty Horses* and *The Sunset Limited.* While the archives contain material for both of them, I could not find therein any references to authors or books, which were my exclusive interests for this volume.

CHAPTER 2

The Orchard Keeper

McCarthy's first novel, begun in 1959 and published in 1965, tells the intertwined stories of three characters, a young boy named John Wesley Rattner, a bootlegger named Marion Sylder, and an old mountain-man named Arthur Ownby. Set in eastern Tennessee in the 1930s, it follows the coming-of-age of John Wesley, whose no-account father lies moldering in a spray pit where Sylder hid his body after killing him in a vicious fight. Ownby watches over the body in a kind of quasi-ritualistic fashion. Neither Ownby nor Sylder know that the corpse in the spray pit is John Wesley's father, and the chief irony of the narrative is that the two men, who are linked in different ways to John Wesley's father, become surrogate fathers to the boy.

What they have in common is an outlaw status that the young boy admires and emulates. Each resists, in his own way, the encroachment of modernity into the rural community of Red Branch. Sylder models a fierce independence that takes the form of smuggling unlicensed liquor into Knoxville, while Ownby models a way of life lived close to and in harmony with the natural world. John Wesley witnesses the fall of both men as the modern world, ably represented by law enforcement, catches up with them. His coming-of-age must take place against the shadow of these defeats, and he must puzzle out his place in a world that he cannot resist, but that cannot completely be his home. The novel ends with the sober reflection that the heroes of the old world are now "myth, legend, dust" (246).

McCarthy's archived papers for *The Orchard Keeper* contain few references to other writers, but those who are named are all significant influences: William Faulkner, Robert Frost, Nathaniel Hawthorne.

One feature of particular interest in the early drafts of the novel is the presence of holograph marginal comments that provide direct evidence of authorial intention, almost like stage directions. This sort of thing becomes increasingly rare in later novels. *Outer Dark* contains similar authorial meta-comments, but after that they are almost nonexistent. The presence of such comments in the drafts of his first two published novels reveals a young writer thinking through plot, character, and symbolism in an overt way. If McCarthy told Oprah Winfrey the truth, he does not plan out his novels, and the drafts and notes contained in the archives bear this out. But these stray marginal comments give us a glimpse of what such planning would look like and suggest that early on he may have done more of it.

McCarthy's papers contain hundreds of references to other writers, and in some cases one can trace the lines of influence with some ease, but not because McCarthy traces them for us. However, it is remarkable to find, in a marginal comment, McCarthy identifying Hawthorne's "Ethan Brand" as the source of his idea for the spray pit, and the graveyard scene in *Hamlet* as an inspiration for the corpse that McCarthy placed in that spray pit. Partly owing to McCarthy's own evasions when interviewed (he is a novelist who claims that he no longer reads novels), there is something strange about him showing his overtly literary preoccupations in so forthright a fashion. The feeling of surprise testifies to McCarthy's success at crafting a certain kind of persona, one not unlike Mark Twain's—Twain often played the part of the Socratic *eiron*, but, as Alan Gribben has shown in his two-volume *Mark Twain's Library*, he was a studiously well-read man. So, too, is Cormac McCarthy, and his archived papers show that his reading is hardly confined to physics tomes and nonfiction. The traces of a reader deeply immersed in literature are everywhere in his papers. Though explicit authorial commentary disappears from the margins of his drafts after his 1960s novels, his literary interests are well recorded. Absent the archives, the novels themselves make this clear. Like White in McCarthy's late work *The Sunset Limited*, Cormac McCarthy is a "culture junky." The evidence is in.

Faulkner, William (1897–1962)

SEE ALSO *THE STONEMASON*

William Faulkner has the distinction of being the most obvious of McCarthy's many influences, and critics have duly noted it, at times with irritation. Harold Bloom, though an ardent partisan for *Blood Meridian*, finds McCarthy's southern novels to be too heavily freighted with Faulknerian cargo (which, for Bloom, is not the problem — not hiding it well enough is). Whether one counts that as a fatal aesthetic flaw, à la Harold Bloom, or not, Bloom is surely right about Faulkner's ghostly presence in McCarthy's prose. Unsurprisingly then, one of the first references to another writer in McCarthy's papers is to William Faulkner. Box 1, Folder 2, which contains notes for *The Orchard Keeper*, features notes on Faulkner's novels *Intruder in the Dust* and *The Hamlet*.

The handwritten page on which the notes appear contains, on the left side, page numbers corresponding to the manuscript (pages 82–157), and next to these are words and phrases about which McCarthy needed to make stylistic and spelling decisions. Included among the manuscript pages numbered on this sheet are those corresponding to the scene in which Marion Sylder takes John Wesley out raccoon hunting. Next to the page numbers for this section of the novel, McCarthy wrote, "Intruder in the Dust p 6." Beneath that he wrote, "redbone," and beneath that, "black & tan," the names of dogs mentioned on the page McCarthy cites. Below the second name, McCarthy wrote, "but: (17) Shetland pony." A similar list several lines up from this one makes clear that McCarthy was trying to decide whether or not to capitalize the names of dog breeds, and was using Faulkner as a guide. The other list looks like this: "caps Bluetick Walker, Redbone, Beagle, Plott," and next to this note he wrote, "see *Hamlet*," which at first I took to mean Shakespeare's play, but the reference is definitely to Faulkner's novel, which contains references to these dog breeds. McCarthy seems to have been stumped by Faulkner's decision not to capitalize the names of dogs while capitalizing the name of the horse. McCarthy also seems to have been using a collection of Robert Frost's poems as a style manual, because next to the citation of *Intruder* is the following: "see Morgan colt in Frost's poem." The poem is "The Runaway," and takes as its subject a Morgan colt observed by two passersby (see entry for Frost in this chapter). As with the dogs in Faulkner, McCarthy's interest here is in Frost's capitalization of the "M" in the horse's name. To capitalize or not to capitalize was McCarthy's question. In the published novel, the names are not capitalized.

McCarthy's use of Faulkner as a guide even to minute stylistic decisions reinforces the fact of his deep indebtedness to his literary master, a Virgil guiding him into the underworld. Some critics find that the debt nearly bankrupts the borrower. Harold Bloom's reservations have been noted. Orville Prescott's *New York Times* review of *The Orchard Keeper* features the title "Still Another Disciple of William Faulkner" (qtd. in Arnold and Luce 1). Though Prescott's review is mostly favorable, he wrote that McCarthy "half submerges his own talents beneath a flood of imitation" (qtd. in Arnold and Luce 2). Patrick Cuttrell, reviewing *Outer Dark* for the *Washington Post*'s *Book World*, wrote that "the shadow of Faulkner lies very dark—proving once again what a disastrous model for lesser men that writer is. Mr. McCarthy has got from him the interminable shapeless sentence and the trail of very literary epithets which look impressive" (qtd. in Jarrett 23).

The stylistic echoes of Faulkner do not require fine tuning to hear. Here is a passage, taken at random from *The Orchard Keeper*, that could have come right out of a Faulkner novel: "Rocking quietly in her chair she had the appearance of one engaged in some grim and persevering endeavor in which hope was the only useful implement. Not even patience. As if perhaps in some indistinct future the chair itself would rise and bear her away to glory with her sitting fiercely sedate and her feet maybe tucked under the rung, her skirt gathered about her" (73).

"Fiercely sedate" is pure Faulkner, resembling the italicized phrase appearing in the following description of Rosa Coldfield in *Absalom, Absalom*, which sounds very similar to McCarthy's description of John Wesley's mother. Sitting across from Quentin Compson, she is "so bolt upright in the straight hard chair that was so tall for her that her legs hung straight and rigid as if she had iron shinbones and ankles, clear of the floor with that air of impotent and *static rage* like children's feet" (7, emphasis added). In the description of Mrs. Rattner, McCarthy limns Faulkner's style, but at times he simply cuts and pastes. When Arthur Ownby discovers the fire in the spray pit where he has interred

the corpse of Kenneth Rattner, we are told that "he stopped for a moment and he could feel the *old fierce pull of blood* in power and despair"
(158, emphasis added). In Faulkner's short story "Barn Burning," the
protagonist, a boy named Colonel Sartoris Snopes, attempts to escape
his father's malign influence, which is described as "the old fierce pull
of blood" (3). This is an early example of what I call phraseological
appropriation, though here, as saturated with Faulkner's language as
The Orchard Keeper is, one wonders if this instance is deliberate or
unconscious.

McCarthy's use of appropriation and allusion suggests that he is very
much aware of the pressure of literary influence—books are made out
of books. Rather than evade the ugly fact, McCarthy openly (although
sometimes very covertly) riffs, like a jazz musician, on tunes composed
by others. He is aware of literary tradition and respectful of the canon,
and he deliberately situates himself in a knowing relationship to precursors. During the writing of *The Orchard Keeper*, McCarthy was very
much aware of T. S. Eliot, whose sewer-like Thames (see entries for
Eliot in *Suttree* and *The Road*) in *The Waste Land* runs to the environs
of Knoxville, Tennessee, in *Suttree*, which McCarthy was working on at
the same time. Perhaps his strong sense of indebtedness derives in part
from Eliot's "Tradition and the Individual Talent," in which Eliot writes
that "no poet, no artist of any art, has his complete meaning alone.
His significance, his appreciation is the appreciation of his relation to
the dead poets and artists. You cannot value him alone; you must set
him, for contrast and comparison, among the dead" (38). Given the
centrality of allusion and appropriation in Eliot, it makes sense that
McCarthy, in exploring his own version of a wasteland, would employ
a similarly freighted style.

However, it should be noted that McCarthy's novels, despite their
obvious similarities to Faulkner's works, are also noteworthy for their
differences. In fact, the stylistic ventriloquism places the differences
in sharp relief. As Robert Jarrett points out, much of McCarthy's
early fiction "takes place against the background of the urbanized
New South whose emergence is satirized through Faulkner's Comp-
sons and Snopeses" (25). Jarrett argues that Faulkner's novels focus
on the weight of history—the searing legacy of slavery and the Civil
War—and its role in shaping the lives of contemporary southerners.
Consequently, his novels are primarily set in the Delta regions where

the plantation culture of the Antebellum South continued to haunt the present, regions quite different from the Appalachian south of McCarthy's novels (24–26).

Frost, Robert (1874–1963)

SEE ALSO *THE ROAD*

McCarthy refers to Robert Frost in notes for *The Orchard Keeper* and in the margin of an early draft of *The Road*, where he quotes from Frost's apocalyptic musings in the poem "Fire and Ice." Allusions — almost always a form of homage for McCarthy — to Frost's poetry in *Suttree*, as well as the early and late references to his work in both early and late notes and manuscripts, suggest that the New England master has been a significant literary influence on McCarthy. Both writers explicitly evoke pastoral conventions, but in an American vein that emphasizes nature's harshness. Both eschew the pathetic fallacy, either through Frost's playful skepticism and mockery or through what Georg Guillemin, describing McCarthy's pastoralism, calls "melancholy equanimity," which "bestows an egalitarian existential status on all terrestrial phenomena" (8), whether human or nonhuman.

The reference to Frost in *The Orchard Keeper* can be found in Box 1, Folder 2, which contains notes for the novel. It appears alongside a reference to William Faulkner on a page of copy-editing queries keyed to manuscript pages (see entry for Faulkner in this chapter). McCarthy was trying to decide whether or not to capitalize the names of dog breeds and was using Faulkner and Frost as stylistic models. The note reads: "Walker? Redbone? (see Morgan colt in Frost's poem)." Frost capitalizes the "M," though McCarthy, following Faulkner, chose not to capitalize the names. The poem is "The Runaway," about two characters who encounter a young colt in a pasture just as the first snow of the year is setting in. Much of the poem is composed of the folksy anthropomorphisms of one of the characters as he worries about the colt, which seems to be separated from its mother. McCarthy's interest in this case seems to have been strictly stylistic, though the poem explores the mysterious continuum encompassing the impersonal coldness (he presents coldness on a literal, rather than an anthropomorphic level—

Frost's irony undermines the speaker's front-porch vernacular version of the pathetic fallacy) of nature, the opaque (to us) sentience of animals, and the human consciousness of these foreign elements in our terrestrial ambience, and McCarthy is also interested in this continuum. In *The Orchard Keeper*, he imagines his way, with really bold audacity, into the point of view of a cat. In *All the Pretty Horses*, he attempts the same trick in his depiction of the continuum that connects raw nature, humanity, and a kind of in-between state occupied by the horses that John Grady breaks. Early drafts of *The Crossing* reveal McCarthy's efforts to depict the consciousness of the wolf captured by Billy Parham. In the end, he eliminated all the passages containing the wolf's point of view, and the published novel emphasizes the frightening otherness of the wolf.

A vision of the frightening otherness of the natural world is what McCarthy's pastoralism shares with Frost's, though the two writers employ radically different tones in expressing that vision. One of Frost's most disturbing meditations on nature, "Design," a wicked little *reductio ad absurdum* of the theological Argument from Design, focuses on a spider's capture of a moth, but somehow it manages to be both ghastly in its imagery and jovial and light in tone. Frost's poems, even at their darkest, give us the comforting perspective of a human observer or speaker. McCarthy, as Guillemin points out in his excellent *The Pastoral Vision of Cormac McCarthy*, frequently adopts a tone of "melancholy equanimity" in an effort to eliminate such comforts. According to Guillemin, he does this through abrupt shifts in focus that create a sense of parity between human and nonhuman elements in a given scene. Guillemin points to the haunting image in *Suttree* of the train on fire while going up a mountain in a snowy forest. Guillemin argues that McCarthy creates a "nonhierarchical" set of relationships in which "man, machine, and nature seem to be in perfect harmony in an aesthetic that is based on the relatedness of things, and not on the incongruity of the machine in the garden" (16). In effect, McCarthy makes both nature and human artifacts, perhaps human nature itself, radically *other*.

However, despite Frost's sometimes comforting tone, the matter of his poems is often as fiercely alienating as anything in McCarthy. Frost's "Desert Places," for instance, offers a dispiriting nihilism that McCarthy (contra Guillemin), through the unironic, un-Frost-like evocation of religious motifs and imagery, largely avoids, though he certainly skirts the borderlands of nihilism. In "Desert Places," the speaker, who resembles, in some respects, the speaker in Wallace Stevens's "The Snow Man," reflects, while looking into a field rapidly filling up with snow, on the radical emptiness of the cosmos. In doing so he discovers the "melancholy equanimity" that Guillemin finds in McCarthy's pastoral vision: "They cannot scare me with their empty spaces / Between stars—on stars where no human race is. / I have it in me so much nearer home / To scare myself with my own desert places" (lines 13–16). We can hear exacerbated echoes of this kind of metaphysical despair in the voice of Cornelius Suttree, or—pick any Cormac McCarthy novel at random—in the voice of what Guillemin calls "the melancholy narrator" (9) whose voice haunts all of McCarthy's work.

Hawthorne, Nathaniel (1804–1864)

McCarthy refers to Nathaniel Hawthorne in a holograph marginal note in an early draft of *The Orchard Keeper.* The note appears at the upper right corner of a typed page containing the scene in which Arthur Ownby discovers that John Wesley Rattner and Warn Pulliam have set a fire in the spray pit in which the bones of Kenneth Rattner are interred. The note proposes several possible plot developments: "gone to white ashes as Ethan Brand? or: Boy plays with skeleton of his father? or skull" (Box 1, Folder 3, emphasis in original).

The note on Hawthorne provides support for Steven Frye's suggestion that McCarthy's novels should be read as exemplars of American Romance. Frye describes the genre in *Understanding Cormac McCarthy*: "Its major practitioners are Hawthorne, Melville, Poe, and later Faulkner. One can associate many of their works with the high gothic romance in the ambiguous mode, involving novels and short stories that explore densely psychological, metaphysical, and religious issues, always with an emphasis on a darkness that implies not pessimism but radical skepticism, the notion that there are boundaries to the human intellect, realms beyond which the human mind cannot travel" (12). McCarthy's interest in Melville and Faulkner is well documented, but he also mentions Hawthorne and Poe in his papers. All of these writers explore the dark side of humanity's spiritual nature, but they also employ techniques drawn from the allegorical mode, another propensity McCarthy shares with them.

This was recognized early on by the critic Guy Davenport. In a review of *Outer Dark*, he wrote, "Mr. McCarthy is unashamedly an allegorist. His responsibility as a storyteller includes believing with his characters in the devil, or at least in the absolute destructiveness of evil." The use of allegory allows McCarthy to write two-tiered narratives; on one level he employs the techniques of literary naturalism, which gives the novels their surface grittiness; on another level he imbues them with spiritual meanings that give them their distinctively moral or religious feel. He gets to have things both ways. Readers who find McCarthy's novels to be nihilistic are right, but so, too, are those who find them to be nearly religious in character. We know from early drafts of *The Road* that the original title was *The Grail*. This provides a perfect illustration of McCarthy's approach. On one level the novel is a story about a boy and his father on a dangerous journey. On another it is a kind of Everyman quest narrative chronicling a spiritual journey. The brief note on Hawthorne written at the very beginning of his career as a writer indicates how early this interest in allegory appears.

Although McCarthy's papers only mention "Ethan Brande," two other stories by Hawthorne contain characters and scenes that bear a strong resemblance to aspects of *Blood Meridian*. In "Young Goodman Brown," the Satanic figure that Brown meets in the woods is described in a way that sounds remarkably similar to a description of Judge Holden: "And yet, though the elder person was as simply clad as the younger, and as simple in manner too, he had an indescribable air of one who knew the world, and would not have felt abashed at the governor's dinner-table, or in king William's court, were it possible that his affairs should call him thither" (621). Here is Tobin's description of the judge in *Blood Meridian*: "He's been all over the world. Him and the governor they sat up till breakfast and it was Paris this and London that in five languages, you'd have give something to of heard them. The governor's a learned man himself he is, but the judge . . ." (123). Like Hawthorne's devil, the judge is worldly wise and comfortable at the governor's table.

The second instance strongly suggestive of Hawthorne's influence is in McCarthy's description of the "legion of horribles" who attack the filibusters in the desert, which resembles Hawthorne's description of the riotous mob tarring and feathering Major Molineux at the climax of "My Kinsman, Major Molineux." Here is Hawthorne's description of the mob:

> A mighty stream of people now emptied into the street, and came rolling slowly towards the church. A single horseman wheeled the corner in the midst of them, and close behind him came a band of fearful wind-instruments, sending forth a fresher discord, now that no intervening buildings kept it from the ear. Then a redder light disturbed the moonbeams, and a dense multitude of torches shone along the street, concealing by their glare whatever object they illuminated. The single horseman, clad in a military dress, and bearing a drawn sword, rode onward as the leader, and, by his fierce and variegated countenance, appeared like war personified.... In his train, were wild figures in the Indian dress, and many fantastic shapes without a model, giving the whole march a visionary air, as if a dream had broken forth from some feverish brain, and were sweeping visibly through the midnight streets. (617)

While Hawthorne's evocation of violent chaos differs in details, the resemblances are remarkable, right down to the wind instruments that herald the rioters, the Indian dress, and the visionary character of the whole thing. Hawthorne's likening the scene to a dream that has "broken forth from some feverish brain" finds an echo in McCarthy's description of the Comanche attackers as "wardrobed out of a fevered dream" (52). If Hawthorne is the source in each of these cases, that would mean that his influence on McCarthy should be reckoned among the most important. Both are what Bryan Giemza would call "dead ringers."

CHAPTER 3

Outer Dark

*O**uter Dark* follows the separate journeys of a brother and sister, Culla and Rinthy Holme, through a landscape that is vaguely Appalachian, but owes more to fairy tale and folktale for its locales and characters. It is the one Cormac McCarthy novel that does not take pains to locate events in an actual place. The novel, first published in 1968, is an American Gothic Romance, owing as much to Hawthorne as to Faulkner. Culla sets the story in motion when he leaves the pair's incestuously conceived child in the woods to die. A traveling tinker finds the baby, and Rinthy, who does not believe Culla's claim to have buried the child, sets off in search of the tinker, whom she correctly believes has taken the baby. Culla leaves soon after, though the purpose of his journey is more ambiguous. Rinthy is motivated by her love for the child, and her travels, though full of travail, are also marked by signs of grace. Culla, by contrast, is dogged by three malign beings, a kind of unholy trinity, who function as Furies summoning Culla to a reckoning for his evil action. The father-figure of this trinity is McCarthy's first go-round with the devil (right down to a cloven boot), a character who bears comparisons with the judge of *Blood Meridian* and even Anton Chigurh in *No Country for Old Men*. The climax features the ghastly murders of the tinker and the child by the trinity; the denouement leaves Culla and Rinthy on their separate roads, Culla's shadowed by his own darkness, and Rinthy's lighted by grace.

I have located one clear reference to another writer, Albert Camus, in the archives for *Outer Dark*, and its presence is significant, as it verifies the intuition of many McCarthy critics that French existentialism is one of the earliest and most profound influences on McCarthy's art and life. Perhaps the most interesting feature of the archived papers for this novel is the presence of holograph marginal notes that show McCarthy stating in bald language themes and meanings that the published novel leaves to the reader to discover through interpretation. For instance, one such note confirms the fundamentally allegorical nature of the narrative: "In order for this book to make sense the events must assume the shape of a character and the characters themselves become mere moves, mere manifestations of the perfect, coherent, logical, and immutable deformation of evolving fate" (Box 8, Folder 2). No reader is likely to take Culla and Rinthy as examples of "rounded" characters, but the marginal note makes clear that their flatness is by design. McCarthy reveals his designs in another marginal comment: "THEME: The triune kill all that Holme <u>wants</u> to kill—ending with child. ?" (Box 8, Folder 1). This is the only time McCarthy supplies his own CliffsNotes in a draft, and the question mark suggests that he was not sure, at that point, what the theme of the novel was.

Camus, Albert (1913–1960)

SEE ALSO *WHALES AND MEN*

Albert Camus's morally engaged and heroically stoic brand of existentialism has been an abiding influence on McCarthy. The archives contain a reference in an early draft of *Outer Dark* and another in the screenplay *Whales and Men*. Camus informs both McCarthy's philosophical pessimism and his strong sense of moral responsibility. Long acknowledged among critics, McCarthy's debt to Camus has occasioned sharp disagreements about the nature of McCarthy's pessimism as readers attempt to situate him along a spectrum of responses to the often absurd predicament of humanity. Is McCarthy a nihilist, or does his tragic sense of the human condition entail some form of Gnostic spirituality, or does it entail a quasi-Christian sense of the fall and an attendant need for redemption (as opposed to Gnostic enlightenment)? Despite Camus's respectful rejection of religion as a fully authentic response to life, discussions of his influence on McCarthy tend, when they do not align him with Camus's atheism, to emphasize McCarthy's interest in spirituality, whether Gnostic or Christian (McCarthy has clearly contemplated Eastern spirituality as well, though Christianity and its heretical cousin Gnosticism seem to dominate his imagination). Camus asks us to contemplate life in the raw, to be honest about its tragic dimensions, and to respond in good faith, bravely and authentically, to its grim but morally bracing reality. He invites questions about final things. Hence, critical reflections about his influence on McCarthy tend to move in the direction of such questions.

In an early draft of *Outer Dark*, McCarthy wrote the following in a handwritten marginal note. He prefaced the note with "On Camus," but it is unclear whether he is quoting from a source or it is his own commentary. If the former is the case, I cannot find that source. The note reads as follows: "Because the highest aspirations of man are spiritual therefore it demeans him to say that his highest purpose is simply to eliminate pain" (Box 8, Folder 2). Above "eliminate," McCarthy wrote "minimize" as an alternative (adding support for the possibility that he is the author of this commentary on Camus). The note makes plain that the critical tendency to link discussions of Camus with McCarthy's spiritual and metaphysical predilections is sound. Clearly the French existentialist (though Camus sometimes bristled at the word, it has become an unavoidable shorthand) inspired McCarthy's commitment to plumbing the depths of human experience in his fiction. However valuable this brief bit of marginalia to an understanding of Camus, it is invaluable for an understanding of McCarthy.[1]

Critics noted the influence of Camus long before the archives confirmed it. John Lewis Longley, in his "Suttree and the Metaphysics of Death," discovers an "existential consciousness" (82) in *Suttree*, and Frank Shelton, in "Suttree and Suicide," which brings Camus's *Myth of Sisyphus* to bear on his reading of McCarthy's novel, finds in Suttree an example of "existential man facing the absurd" (74). According to Shelton, McCarthy endorses Camus's response to the absurd, which, according to Shelton, is a "life of flight and revolt, unreconciled to death and absurdity" (82).

William Prather shares Shelton's assessment of McCarthy's philosophical stance, arguing that Suttree rejects both suicidal despair and religion as authentic responses to the absurd in favor of the commitment to action recommended by Camus. He describes Camus's ideal comportment as "an enhanced state of consciousness, clear freedom of thought and action, and a whetted appetite for life," which are "of sufficient worth to warrant continuing to live in the absurd universe and not attempting to escape from it, as tantalizing as other alternatives may appear" (149). Prather is pointed in his insistence that "like Camus, Suttree clearly rejects the recourse to religion" (142).

Prather is working a vein first opened by Vereen Bell, who, without explicitly evoking Camus, sees McCarthy's heroes, such as Arthur Ownby, as heroic because they are "anomic," a word Bell quotes from a social worker's assessment of the cantankerous mountain man in the denouement of *The Orchard Keeper*. The mountain man is a Camusian rebel in the face of absurdity. Bell's judgment about the McCarthy universe remains the bleakest. According to Bell, McCarthy's metaphysics can be summarized as follows: "none, in effect—no first principles, no foundational truth, Heraclitus without Logos" (9). This would almost be a conversation killer, but Bell is generous enough to allow that "the pressure of meaningfulness remains even where meaning will not separate out" (9), which leaves readers with something to talk about.

Bell's seminal work was published prior to the publication of *The Border Trilogy* and the plays *The Stonemason* and *The Sunset Limited*, which foreground theological and moral issues in ways that suggest that Bell's thesis may, at the very least, require severe qualifications. For instance, the following passage, quoted from one of Ben's meditations on the gospel of Freemasonry in *The Stonemason*, might be hard to square with Bell's antimetaphysical McCarthy:

> According to the gospel of the true mason God has laid the stones in the earth for men to use and he has laid them in their bedding planes to show the mason how his own work must go. A wall is made the same way the world is made. A house, a temple. This gospel must accommodate every inquiry. The structure of the world is such as to favor the prosperity of men. Without this belief nothing is possible. What we are at arms against are those philosophies that claim the fortuitous in mens' inventions. For we invent nothing but what God has put to hand. (10)

McCarthy's ironies are subtle, and he does suggest that Ben is, to some degree, an unreliable spokesman for the gospel of Freemasonry. That is simply to say that McCarthy is a creator of fictions, and not preaching any sort of gospel. In calling Ben's reliability into question, he leaves other doors open. Nevertheless, it is hard to deny that McCarthy seems deeply invested in the philosophical and theological musings found in the play. Whatever this gospel is, it is not absurdist, and it is not derived from Camus. *Pace* Bell, it does not suggest an antimetaphysical skepticism about foundations and first principles. Pessimism is not nihilism (a happy thought). Surely none would deny that McCarthy is the former, but the claim that he is also the latter seems increasingly untenable in the light of his complete corpus. The passage should remind us that McCarthy's influences are richly varied and not easy to tally with each other, though there are obvious areas of overlap. Camus's existentialism is one; Jacob Boehme's Christian theosophy is another (see entry in *Blood Meridian*); T. S. Eliot's Anglican Christianity would be another (see entries for Eliot in *Suttree* and *The Road*)—not exactly oil and water, but significantly different. All must be reckoned with.

Dianne Luce attempts to reconcile different philosophical streams in her discussion of Camus's influence in *Reading the World*. Specifically, she identifies points of congruity between Camus and Gnosticism, which many critics have rightly identified as an influence on McCarthy's metaphysical speculations. She applauds the work of Dale Cosper and Ethan Cary for its focus on McCarthy's indebtedness to Gnostic thought. Of particular relevance to this discussion, Luce notes that Cosper and Cary "dispute the tendency to read *Suttree* as strictly existentialist or absurdist, arguing that the book does not fit Camus's criteria for the absurd novel" (199). Instead, they argue that the novel centers around a Gnostic metaphysical dualism of good and evil (199). While Luce is generally positive in her assessment of this view, she argues that Cosper and Cary create an unnecessary either/or dilemma in their rejection of an existentialist reading. Luce argues that McCarthy draws from both existentialism and Gnosticism in *The Gardener's Son* and *Suttree*. Speaking of the former, she claims that "the screenplay may be read as a Gnostic/existentialist allegory, revealing McCarthy's full awareness that Gnosticism informs and is revivified in the thought of Heidegger, Camus, and other existentialists, in which post–Industrial Revolution dread of the urbanized and mechanized collective functions as a modern analogue of the ancient gnostic dread of cosmos" (176). She also notes that Camus himself took Gnostic thought seriously while rejecting its bias against the natural world, an aspect of the tradition that McCarthy also rejects (177).

Luce makes a strong case for the influence of both Camus and Gnosticism on *The Gardener's Son*, but most critics find Camus's influence most pronounced in *Suttree*. However, not all agree with the centrality of a reading that views Suttree as a Camusian rebel defying an absurd cosmos. As Luce points out in her study, Cosper and Cary reject the absurdist reading in order to highlight what they see as Suttree's turn to Gnostic spirituality. Indeed, they claim that Suttree, by the novel's end, "has become a Gnostic" (qtd. in Luce 199). Though archival material conclusively verifies McCarthy's interest in Gnosticism during the composition of *Suttree* (see entry for Flaubert in *Blood Meridian*), the suggestion of a Gnostic "conversion" sounds an odd note. The phrase "becoming a Gnostic" is discordant in a way that the phrases "becoming a Christian" or "converting to Islam" are not. To use William James's useful categories for beliefs, a Gnostic conversion does not seem like a live option. Gnosticism functions as a storehouse of symbols and metaphysical tropes that often usefully map onto a number of modern philosophies—it sorts with the pessimistic *Weltanschauung* of existentialism, as Hans Jonas persuasively argued in his epilogue to *The Gnostic Religion*. However, it does not function as, to borrow from William James again, a "variety of religious experience." Existentialist and Gnostic readings, while undeniably useful for an understanding of *Suttree*, may obscure a less sexy reading of Suttree's spiritual development, one that finds in the concluding pages of the novel a kind of Christian "dying to self and rising to new life," exemplified by the corpse in the houseboat, Suttree's encounter with the water boy, and the car that stops unheralded to pick him up and carry him away from the slavering hellhounds on his track. Gnostic and existentialist readings emphasize the badness of the world and contrast this with Suttree's "enlightenment," whether we read that as Camusian revolt or a kind of pneumatic awakening. A more Christian reading of Suttree's "conversion" emphasizes the badness of Suttree and the perils of a world full of temptation. The former sees enlightenment where the latter sees redemption or grace.

That all of these readings "work" is a testament to McCarthy's artistry as well as a reminder that, however philosophical he may be, McCarthy is not a philosopher but a novelist, and he is finally interested in Suttree's sole talisman, "the human heart" (468). Nevertheless, the possibility of a more Christian reading of Suttree's character—a reading emphasizing the dying of the "old man" and a rising to new life through a process of redemption—has been unduly neglected given McCarthy's pervasive use of Christian imagery and symbols. One of the most significant readings of *Suttree* to appear is that of James Watson, whose study of what he calls "Catholic Existentialism" properly draws attention to those images and symbols. He acknowledges the usefulness of the Camusian reading, but highlights its limitations: "This reading of the existential philosophy undergirding *Suttree* is helpful, but not complete. What has gone unnoticed in the criticism on *Suttree* is the way that McCarthy uses precisely performed Roman Catholic sacraments to mete out the existential revelations that Suttree experiences" (7). Specifically, Watson demonstrates that Baptism, the Eucharist, and Last Rites are all administered to Suttree. He recognizes that the novel features an often scathing criticism of the Roman Catholic Church, but points out that the critique of the institution of the church does not imply a critique of its sacramental spirituality. He notes that the efficacy of the sacraments is not a function of the spiritual vitality of this or that priest in this or that church: "We may take this even further: even grave sin on the part of the priest performing the sacrament would not invalidate the *de facto* performance of it. It seems that the educated, post-Catholic Suttree would be aware of it; McCarthy surely is. And so in maneuvering Suttree into the correct partaking of the various sacraments—in spite of his animosity toward the Church—McCarthy is setting up a framework or grammar for the dispensing of some sort of grace" (9).

Watson's appeal to McCarthy's personal background seems appropriate in the light of Bryan Giemza's research into McCarthy's relationship to Catholicism. He records the Jesuit priest Patrick Samway, in remarking upon a lengthy conversation he had with McCarthy, saying that he "knew things that only a Jesuit would know" (220). Christian readings of McCarthy risk tendentiousness, as do readings that emphasize Camusian existentialism, but the Samway quotation lends extratextual support to Watson's superbly textual argument.

A quotation from McCarthy's correspondence with a student of Robert Coles lends additional credibility to the reading Watson proposes. In particular, what he says about Flannery O'Connor, a Catholic writer for whom McCarthy has expressed great admiration (see entry for O'Connor in *Blood Meridian*), is of great relevance. In light of the discussions of Gnosticism that inform so much of McCarthy criticism, his take on "knowledge" in the letter should also be noted: "An intellectual is a person who feels that his learning—and it may be pitifully little—entitles him to status.... People who really do *know* are inevitably returned to the common ground of man. I think too that O'Connor is a better writer than [Ignazio] Silone or [Georges] Bernanos for the simple reason that she is able to dramatize love and grace strikingly in their absence" (qtd. in Giemza 221, emphasis in original). Gnosticism has always appealed to spiritual and intellectual elites (like Cormac McCarthy, for instance). Here McCarthy appears to reject elitist *knowing* in favor of the more common experience of grace, which he believes O'Connor depicts with rare artistry.

When Watson claims that McCarthy, in his reference to the sacraments, is "setting up a framework or grammar for the dispensing of some sort of grace," he is describing the method of Flannery O'Connor. Her characters are often recipients of grace even when they would like to take a pass on the offer—see, for example, Hazel Motes in *Wise Blood*, or Hulga Hopewell in "Good Country People." Grace, in O'Connor's fiction, is not always graceful; at times it comes in painful ways. The grandmother in "A Good Man Is Hard to Find" enters a state of grace only by having a gun pointed at her head. O'Connor's characters flee God's grace and get it anyway. If it comes in a rough form, it is not less necessary. Typhoid fever turns out to be just the thing that Suttree needs. When, during his recuperation, the priest, whom Suttree does not suffer gladly, pours a few drops of wine down Suttree's throat, Suttree says, simply, "That works" (461). According to Roman Catholic belief, it does indeed.

Camus should be regarded as a major influence on McCarthy, and certainly one source for his philosophical pessimism, but that pessimistic view, which accords in many respects with Gnostic metaphysics, needs to be understood within the broadest possible context. McCarthy's metaphysics draw from many streams, some of which flow from less exotic spiritual sources. At least, they flow from more familiar sources—What could be more exotic than eating the flesh and drinking the blood of God?

CHAPTER 4

Child of God

One of McCarthy's most disturbing novels, *Child of God* (1973) follows the descent of Lester Ballard from community outcast to cave-dwelling serial killer and necrophiliac. Set in Sevier County, Tennessee, in the 1960s, the novel opens with Ballard being dispossessed of his family home, which sets his decline in motion. Not the kind of guy who can readily get a date, Ballard's sexual awakening is with the body of a young woman whom he finds dead alongside her lover in a car hidden off the main road. Having awakened this taboo desire, he begins murdering women to add to what will become an underground harem of corpses. After an attempt to murder the new owner of his family home—dressed in women's clothes taken from his victims—he is hunted down by the community. He narrowly escapes a lynch mob, but is finally captured and sent to a mental institution. Surprisingly, McCarthy grants flashes of dignity to his grotesque protagonist. The narrator insists that he is "a child of God much like yourself perhaps" (4). McCarthy manages to elicit sympathy for Ballard, whose longings—for home, love, community, family, companionship—are the universal longings of all human beings. Ballard's insanity twists these longings into demented actions. McCarthy, in one of the great tightrope acts of American fiction, manages to create both pathos and moral revulsion in his depiction of Ballard. In its own horrific fashion, *Child of God* is a novel about what it means to be human.

McCarthy's papers for this work are scanty, though the archives do contain an early draft of the novel that includes material McCarthy later excised. The only artistic figure McCarthy mentions in his notes is Alfred Hitchcock, which provides additional support for Dianne Luce's already strong case in *Reading the World* that McCarthy likely had the serial killer Ed Gein—Norman Bates, the antagonist in *Psycho* (1960), is loosely modeled on Gein—in mind when he created Lester Ballard.

The early draft of the novel is unique in that it contains marginal comments written by McCarthy's editor Albert Erskine. Noteworthy among those comments are some scathing criticisms of a scene that McCarthy cut from the final draft. In it Lester Ballard, in a fit of guilt, castrates himself. The scene is gruesome even by McCarthy's very liberal standards. Like a few scenes from *Suttree* that were also cut, the descriptions cross the line into sadism; combined with sexual overtones, the violence of these cut scenes feels pornographic. In the margin next to McCarthy's description, Erskine wrote, with unmistakable exasperation, "No! Talk to me about this" (Box 16, Folder 5). An additional note at the bottom of the page castigates McCarthy for the gratuitous nature of the scene: "Mac, it seems to me arbitrary; not set up. Ok if you motivate it earlier, somehow, but as it comes it is unprepared for. He has haunting guilts for what he did? Ok, but foreshadow it, or you'll lose the reader." This sounds like a diplomatic way of reining in a tendency in McCarthy toward excess in the depiction of violence and depravity, an excess that requires consummate aesthetic—and, surely, moral—balance between the violence and other elements within the narrative. Erskine, quite rightly, calls him out for failing to achieve that balance here. McCarthy, quite rightly, cut the scene, thereby sparing Lester (and the reader) a different kind of cut altogether.

Hitchcock, Alfred (1899–1980)

McCarthy's papers for *Child of God* do not contain references to other writers, but one reference to the filmmaker Alfred Hitchcock confirms the influence of *Psycho* on McCarthy's novel, an influence long suspected and substantially confirmed by Dianne Luce in her study *Reading the World: Cormac McCarthy's Tennessee Period*. The reference appears in Box 16, Folder 1, which contains handwritten manuscript notes keyed to page numbers. McCarthy's note in the margin seems to address the question of whether or not to keep the grisly depiction of Ballard's murder of one of the dumpkeeper's daughters. The scene is indicated by the word "shell" and a snippet from the scene, "but he did not find it." Here is the relevant passage from the published novel: "The crack of the rifle was outrageously loud in the cold silence. Through the spidered glass he saw her slouch and stand again. He levered another shell into the chamber and raised the rifle and then she fell. He reached down and scrabbled about in the frozen mud for the empty shell but he could not find it" (118–119). Underneath the word and quotation McCarthy used to indicate the scene, he wrote, "or: work it into Hosp. conversation." The question seems to be whether to describe the murder in graphic detail or mention it in secondhand fashion during Lester's stay in the hospital. McCarthy chose to keep it, and the marginal note indicates that the decision was motivated in part by the influence of Hitchcock. The note reads, "Hitchcock would just leave it." Indeed, the depiction of violence in *Psycho*, while restrained by McCarthy's standards, was designed to (and did) shock audiences. *Child of God* is McCarthy's first foray into true gore, and it is matched only by *Blood Meridian* in its grisly aesthetic (though *Outer Dark* hints at things to come—most notably, McCarthy's penchant for dead babies).

Dianne Luce argues that McCarthy's aim was similar to Hitchcock's in that both artists implicate the reader/viewer in the voyeurism of fictional characters. Luce's chapter on *Child of God* makes a detailed case for her claim that Lester Ballard, child of God though he may be, is also very much the child of McCarthy's interest in two real murder cases—those of Ed Gein and James Blevins—and the fictionalized version of Gein in Robert Bloch's novel *Psycho* and Hitchcock's film adaptation of the same: "*Child of God* engages Hitchcock's film so significantly as to suggest that McCarthy's very idea to write a novel exploring man's darkest impulses—and his tendency to repress and deny them—through the story of a murderous voyeur/necrophile originated at least partly in his encounter with *Psycho*. Hitchcock's experimentation with cinematic techniques to heighten the audience's awareness of the ways in which viewers are implicated in Norman's voyeurism is answered in *Child of God* by McCarthy's narrative strategies toward the same end" (152–153).

However, Luce stresses that "all these sources are completely absorbed into McCarthy's vision for his novel. It is a measure of McCarthy's success that despite his planting a sequence of rather obvious traces of *Psycho* near the end of *Child of God*, readers failed to notice them for over twenty years" (153). Luce's noticing is another instance of her keen ability to locate McCarthy's sources. The reference to Hitchcock in McCarthy's notes verifies her already carefully argued claim about his influence on McCarthy, and an early draft of *Suttree* contains a marginal note that verifies her belief that Donald Davidson influenced McCarthy as well (see entry for Davidson in *Suttree*).

The note also highlights McCarthy's interest in film. According to Edwin Arnold and Dianne Luce in their introduction to *Perspectives on Cormac McCarthy*, Richard Pearce approached McCarthy about writing the script for *The Gardener's Son* in part because of the cinematographic quality of *Child of God* (5). Though Hitchcock's is the only artist's name to appear in the archived papers for this novel, his influence on McCarthy appears to have been profound, and maybe even pivotal. The cinematographic style of *Child of God* marks the first real departure for McCarthy from the tether of William Faulkner, and, in many respects, the first of his novels to bear his original stamp. Leaner than Faulkner's, McCarthy's prose in *Child of God* appears less indebted to the lush southern gothic of his literary hero. The turn toward the narrative strategies of film may account for the shift.

CHAPTER 5

The Gardener's Son

*T*he *Gardener's Son* is a screenplay written for the PBS series
Visions. McCarthy wrote the screenplay in 1976, and the
show aired on 16 December of that year. McCarthy based
the story on historical events that took place in the mill town of
Graniteville, South Carolina, in 1876. Two families are the focus of the
drama, the Greggs, who own the mill, and the McEvoys, who work for
the Greggs. Patrick McEvoy is the gardener of the title; his son Robert
is a young man whose sense of the injustices his family must endure as
mill workers boils over into an act of murder.

The screenplay begins with the amputation of Robert's leg, which
had become infected after a severe break. The indignity of the amputation deepens Robert's alienation from his circumstances in life and
fuels the anger that drives him throughout much of the narrative.
When the paternalistic but caring William Gregg dies, his cruel son
James takes over the mill. His offer to pay Robert's sister Martha for
sexual favors infuriates Robert, who leaves the town in disgust. He returns two years later to find that James has run roughshod over the
lives of the mill workers. Almost immediately upon his return, he murders James, and the remaining scenes follow the court trial. Robert is
found guilty and hanged.

McCarthy's papers for *The Gardener's Son* contain a number of references to works that he consulted during his research into the historical events behind the story; other references are part of his research
into folkways and traditions. Only two cultural references appear, one
to Joyce's *Ulysses*, and another to the Beat poet Allen Ginsberg. The
relevance of either writer to the screenplay is hard to determine, but I
have included an entry for Ginsberg, partly because very little criticism

has examined the influence of the Beat movement on McCarthy, and partly because allusions to Ginsberg in *Suttree* indicate that McCarthy had read his poetry. McCarthy's historical research took him to *Paternalism and Protest: Southern Cotton Mill Workers and Organized Labor, 1875–1905*, by Melton Alonza McLaurin. He also consulted *The Child That Toileth Not*, by Thomas Robinson Dawley, a study of child labor practices. Other books and writers listed in McCarthy's papers are *Old Ways of Working Wood*, by Alex Bealer; *Foxfire 2*, edited by Eliot Wigginton and his students; and *House, Form, and Culture*, by Amos Rapoport, a study of how the environment affects architecture. Aldous Huxley's travel book *Beyond the Mexique Bay* is mentioned, but without any clear connection to the screenplay, as is *Person and God in a Spanish Valley*, by William Christian, a study of religious customs in a small Spanish community. McCarthy also lists the names of several films, although, beyond the names, he offers no hints as to his specific interests. They include *Black Orpheus*, *In Cold Blood* (the film, not the book), *La Dolce Vita*, and *The Great Gatsby* (again, the film, not the book—that is, the 1974 film with Robert Redford).

Bealer, Alex (1921–1980)

Alex Bealer wrote several books about old-fashioned methods of woodworking and blacksmithing. In his handwritten notes for *The Gardener's Son*, McCarthy wrote down the title of Bealer's *Old Ways of Working Wood* (Box 18, Folder 3), a book that explores the ancient craft of woodworking, and one that contrasts the craft, the "old ways," with modern mechanized methods. Bealer expounds on this contrast in his introduction:

> In olden times, roughly from the Middle Ages until around 1840 in America and 1900 or later in Europe, the artisan was more important than his tools. He was, of course, dependent on the special tools of his trade, but he used his tools to shape wood as he desired rather than design his work to fit the limitations of his machines as is common in modern industry. Also, the old time artisan had no compunction about designing new tools to do special jobs. Each of his tools was but an extension of himself. His individuality became immortal in his work. (11)

The contrast between modern technological means of production and organization and old traditions marked by an organic relationship between the worker and his world and traditions embodied in a craft—for instance, stonework in *The Stonemason*—is one that finds expression throughout McCarthy's corpus: hunting, woodworking, stonemasonry, wolf hunting, ranching, blacksmithing, and horse breaking, to name a few, are treated with loving reverence by McCarthy, an admirer of honest work and devoted craftsmanship. He laments the encroachment of the modern world into the old traditions and crafts from his first work, *The Orchard Keeper*, in which both Marion Sylder and Arthur Ownby exemplify, in very different ways, aspects of the dying old world. *The Border Trilogy*, in which McCarthy laments the passing of the cowboy life exemplified by John Grady Cole, continues the theme.

Christian, William (b. 1944)

In handwritten notes for *The Gardener's Son*, McCarthy wrote down the title of William Christian's religious and sociological study of a small Spanish community, *Person and God in a Spanish Valley*. According to Emanuel de Kadt in his review of the book for *Religion*, quoted on the back cover of a revised edition of the book, in *Person and God* the "reader somehow experiences the passing of the generations and the centuries, the succession of priests with different views, each a representative of the Catholicism of his time, the propagation and then institutionalization of ever-changing forms of worship, and the tension set up between innovating priest and conservative community." McCarthy was likely interested in Christian's book as a model for depicting a small, homogeneous community confronting historical change.

Dawley, Thomas Robinson (1862–1930)

McCarthy wrote down the title to Thomas Robinson Dawley's *The Child That Toileth Not: The Story of a Government Investigation That Was Suppressed* (1912) in his handwritten notes for *The Gardener's*

Son (Box 18, Folder 3). As Cara A. Finnegan noted, Dawley based the book on his investigations of southern cotton mills for the US Bureau of Labor. In it Dawley argues against child-labor reform, claiming that life in the cotton mills is better for children than farm labor. According to Finnegan, Dawley believed that "life on the farm damages children physically and morally; life in the textile mills offers children education, good health, positive moral development, and wages in exchange for what Dawley suggests is only 'light' work.... [T]he mill saves children rather than dooms them." McCarthy would have used Dawley's book for historical background on life in textile mills, as a source of examples of the rhetoric of betterment used to prop up communities like the one described in the screenplay, and for the wealth of photographs (more than one hundred) Dawley includes, which would have helped both McCarthy and the director, Richard Pearce, visualize such a community with accuracy.

Ginsberg, Allen (1926–1997)

McCarthy mentions Allen Ginsberg in Box 18, Folder 3, which contains holograph research notes for his television screenplay *The Gardener's Son*. On the upper right corner of a page of notes, McCarthy wrote: "'Jail's honed him down to rib and soul'—Ginsberg on Leary." The quotation comes from Ginsberg's introduction to Timothy Leary's *Jail Notes*, an account of Leary's numerous run-ins with the law for drug offenses: "Dr. Leary has taken the burden of giving honest report of LSD and Cannabis in terms more accurate and harmless than the faked science of the Government Party Hacks and therefore his imprisonment is an act of insult to Science, Liberty, Common Sense, Freedom, Academy, Philosophy, Medicine, Psychology as an Art, and Poetry as a tradition of human mind-vision. Well, jail's honed him down to rib and soul" (13–14).

An interest in Leary's explorations of psychotropic drugs is unsurprising, given comments McCarthy made to Garry Wallace about his own explorations: "McCarthy commented that some cultures used drugs to enhance the spiritual experience, and that he had tried LSD before the drug was made illegal. He said that it had helped to open his eyes to these kinds of experiences" (G. Wallace 138). This statement accords with McCarthy's interest in nonrational experience as a source of wisdom, an interest that manifests itself most overtly in *Suttree* (see entry for Foucault in *Suttree*).

McCarthy alludes to Ginsberg's notorious poem "Howl" twice in *Suttree*. The first allusion is to line 8: "who cowered in unshaven rooms in underwear, burning their money in wastebaskets and listening to the Terror through the wall." The allusion occurs when Suttree is recuperating at the home of J-Bone's parents after his "vision quest" in the mountains, during a period of disturbing dreams: "Even the community of the dead had disbanded into ashes, those shapes wheeling in the earth's crust through a nameless ether no more men than were the ruins of any other thing once living. *Suttree felt the terror coming through the walls.* He was seized with a thing he'd never known, a sudden understanding of the mathematical certainty of death" (295, emphasis added).

The second allusion is to the last line of the first section of "Howl": "with the absolute heart of the poem of life butchered out of their own bodies good to eat a thousand years." The allusion appears near the end of the novel in Suttree's reflections on the new roads going through McAnally Flats: "He knew another McAnally, *good to last a thousand years*" (463, emphasis added). McCarthy's interest in the Beat writers of the 1950s is documented by Don Williams in his article "Cormac McCarthy Crosses the Great Divide," in which he writes that McCarthy, after leaving the Air Force, traveled to San Francisco to see "the haunts of the famous Beat writers of the day" (9). Though largely unexplored by critics, this influence, along with that of Henry Miller, often thought of as a precursor to the Beats, seems worth exploring. McCarthy's work shows a greater overall maturity and sophistication than that of writers like Jack Kerouac and Allen Ginsburg, and yet there is something decidedly "Beat" about Cornelius Suttree.

Gurdjieff, George (1866–1949)

On a page of his handwritten notes for *The Gardener's Son*, McCarthy wrote the name "Gurdjieff" (Box 18, Folder 3). The significance of the Russian spiritual guru George Gurdjieff for McCarthy is unclear, but the appearance of his name reminds us that McCarthy's interests range into esoteric mysticism.

Huxley, Aldous (1894–1963)

McCarthy wrote down the title to Aldous Huxley's 1934 travel book *Beyond the Mexique Bay* in his handwritten notes for *The Gardener's Son*. Huxley's book records his travels through the Caribbean, Guatemala, and Mexico during the early 1930s. The note verifies McCarthy's interest in Huxley, but its significance, if any, for the screenplay is unclear.

Joyce, James (1882–1941)

SEE ALSO *SUTTREE*; IN ADDITION, SEE
ENTRIES FOR JOSEPH GERARD BRENNAN
AND PETER DE VRIES IN *SUTTREE*

A reference to James Joyce's *Ulysses*, which McCarthy has listed among his favorite books, provides a glimpse into the composition of *The Gardener's Son*. In his handwritten notes for the screenplay, McCarthy wrote "stills comprise an <u>overture</u> as in <u>Ulysses</u>" (Box 18, Folder 3). The overture to which he is referring is a series of seemingly disconnected fragments that preface Episode 11 of Joyce's novel, "The Sirens." Here is a sample:

> Bronze by gold heard the hoofirons, steelyringing.
> Imperthnthn thnthnthn.
> Chips, picking chips off rocky thumbnail, chips.
> Horrid! And gold flushed more.
> A husky fifenote blew.
> Blew. Blue room is on the
> Gold pinnacled hair. (221)

According to Stuart Gilbert, these fragments are meant to function in much the same way that a leitmotiv functions in the overture to an opera: "These fragmentary phrases appear almost meaningless to the reader till he has perused the chapter to its end; nevertheless, they should not be skipped. They are like the overtures of some operas and operettes, in which fragments of the leading themes and refrains are introduced to prepare the hearer's mood and also to give him, when these truncated themes are completed and developed in their proper place, that sense of familiarity which, strangely enough, enhances for most hearers their enjoyment of a new tune" (242–243).

Of course, Joyce's fragments in no way resemble the fragmentary introduction of a musical leitmotiv—for starters, unlike the opera leit-motiv, Joyce's fragments give no pleasure, a significant difference—but their distant structural resemblance served Joyce's goal of getting the kitchen sink into his encyclopedic novel. From Joyce's "overture" McCarthy got the idea of using still shots at the beginning of the film as a means of introducing themes that would be worked out by story's end. Here are McCarthy's directions: "Series of old still shots of the town of Graniteville and of the people. These are to have the look of old sepia photographs and may look stiff or posed. They comprise an overture to the story to follow, being shots of the characters in the film in situations from the film itself, so that they sketch the story out in miniature to the last shot of an old wooden coffin being loaded into a mule-drawn wagon and a shot of the town" (5). Unlike Joyce's over-ture, McCarthy's actually does achieve a similar aesthetic effect to that of the briefly introduced leitmotiv that is so important to some operas, particularly those of Wagner, whose work McCarthy admires.

McLaurin, Melton Alonza (b. 1941)

McCarthy cites Melton Alonza McLaurin's book *Paternalism and Protest: Southern Cotton Mill Workers and Organized Labor, 1875–1905,* in his handwritten notes for *The Gardener's Son* (Box 18, Folder 3) as the source for information about technological developments in the textile industry in the late nineteenth century that McCarthy recorded in his notes. McLaurin, now a retired professor at the University of North Carolina in Wilmington, is the author of numerous historical works on the American South.

Rapoport, Amos (b. 1929)

McCarthy lists Amos Rapoport's book *House, Form, and Culture* in his handwritten notes for *The Gardener's Son*. Rapoport describes his work in the following quotation: "I am one of the founders of the new field of man-environment studies, which deals with how people and environments interact. In this field my special interests are theory-synthesis, cross-cultural studies, socio-cultural variables, meaning and symbolism. An important additional interest is vernacular architecture" (qtd. in "Rapoport, Amos"). He is a kind of anthropologist of housing, as is McCarthy in some of his own work, most notably *The Stonemason*, though Rapoport's work would have been of interest as McCarthy attempted to imagine life in a "planned" worker's community for his screenplay.

CHAPTER 6

Suttree

*S*uttree, along with *Blood Meridian*, is at the center of McCarthy's corpus. Though most assessments of his achievement give the palm to the latter, a good case can be made for *Suttree* as McCarthy's true magnum opus. In addition to being his funniest book, revealing McCarthy to be one of the masters of comic writing in American literature, it possesses a fecund richness found nowhere else in his work—*Suttree* is large, it contains multitudes. The allusion to Walt Whitman's "Song of Myself" is apposite. While many critics have noted the debt to James Joyce's *Ulysses*, the novel exhibits, in a more American vein, similarities to Whitman's capacious poem. Like Joyce with Dublin, McCarthy makes Knoxville a living presence. Like Whitman, he gives us a protagonist who is "one of the roughs," one fascinated by the often bizarre diversity of characters and types who live outside the circle of polite society, a circle Cornelius Suttree has fled by design.

Suttree, estranged from his affluent family—like McCarthy's, Suttree's father is a powerful attorney—lives on a houseboat on the Tennessee River eking out a spartan living as a rather desultory fisherman. Episodic rather than plot-driven, the novel depicts Suttree's often comic, sometimes bizarre, frequently grotesque relationships and encounters with the denizens of McAnally Flats. Most important among these relationships is his friendship with Gene Harrogate, the notorious "moonlight melonmounter" whom Suttree encounters during a stint in a prison work camp. Harrogate, whose entrepreneurial spirit leads him into often outrageous dilemmas, often supplies the comedy. McCarthy's artistic audacity finds full expression in him, and Harrogate also supplies much of the novel's pathos. Suttree's companions include drunks, the homeless, petty criminals, a taciturn Native American named Michael, and African Americans living in precarious proximity to a racist white society. He has two romantic interests in the novel: Joyce, a prostitute, and Wanda, the daughter of a mussel fisherman who dies in a landslide shortly after Suttree joins her family on the river.

The novel ends after Suttree undergoes a series of hallucinations, brought on by typhoid fever, that take the form of a Kafkaesque tribunal. Afterward, he leaves the river. The moldering corpse of a homeless man who died in Suttree's houseboat is taken to be him, and the denouement of the novel reads like a symbolic enacting of a death, burial, and resurrection. The novel is a comedy not merely because it contains lots of funny incidents. *Suttree* is a comedy in the sense that it ends on a happy note. The novel is freighted with melancholy, despite the humor, which is often grim in its implications, but it is hard to read the finale as anything other than hopeful.

What holds the episodic novel together is Suttree's spiritual journey. His exile from his affluent family has a faintly monastic character. Like St. Anthony in the desert in Gustave Flaubert's treatment of the legend—*The Temptation of St. Anthony*, a book McCarthy was keenly interested in during the composition of *Suttree* and *Blood Meridian*—Suttree is beset by temptation, but unlike the saint, Suttree often gives in to it. Suttree's drunkenness, despite the comic pratfalls it makes possible, is treated as a spiritual problem that he often repents of—"my life is ghastly," he observes after a binge—but frequently returns to, like the scriptural dog to its vomit. His relationship with the prostitute, Joyce, is depicted as a descent into soft, flabby decadence. His wanderings in the mountain take the form of a spiritual vision-quest, and the hallucinations that hunger and thirst provoke are, like those induced by his later bout with fever, glimpses into his inner spiritual turmoil. Suttree knows dark nights of the soul, but the trajectory of his story is away from the slavering hellhounds that the narrator urges all of us to fly—devil dogs that still pursue him at the novel's end, but that he seems to have eluded as he gets into a car with a stranger who stops for him without being hailed. McCarthy ends what is arguably his greatest novel on a note of spiritual triumph. McCarthy does write happy endings. Critics have taken insufficient notice. However, the oversight is understandable; with the *possible* exception of *Child of God* (yes, *Child of God*), this is the only novel that follows the narrative arc of comedy rather than tragedy.

McCarthy worked on *Suttree* for roughly twenty years. According to a chronology in *The Cambridge Companion to Cormac McCarthy*, he began working on it in the late 1950s at about the same time he began *The Orchard Keeper*. Throughout his career, McCarthy has maintained this pattern of working on more than one book at a time. During the composition of *Suttree*, he published *The Orchard Keeper*, *Outer Dark*, and *Child of God*. He began work on *Blood Meridian* in 1974, and his notes for *Suttree* often contain notes for what he was then just calling his "Western." According to the Cambridge chronology, he began working on *The Passenger* in 1980, soon after the publication of *Suttree* in 1979 and while deep into his first western novel.

McCarthy cut a great deal from the early drafts of the novel. The archives contain fragments of scenes and entire episodes. A comic visit to a cockfight did not make the cut, though with revision it would not be out of place in the published novel. However, his editor, Albert Erskine, seems to have insisted that the novel was bogged down by too many characters, many of whom remained flat, playing entirely for broad comedic effect. A letter dated 27 May 1977 from Erskine to McCarthy pleads for streamlining (Box 19, Folder 1). The slightly exasperated tone of the letter suggests that McCarthy was pushing back, but the excised material in the archives shows some willingness on McCarthy's part to bend.

Along with *Blood Meridian*, McCarthy's *Suttree* papers provide the richest trove of cultural references. The entries that follow reveal a novelist fully engaged with literary and philosophical precursors.

Abbey, Edward (1927–1989)

McCarthy's notes for *Suttree* contain the following reference to Edward Abbey, the American naturalist, ecological crusader, and all-around provocateur: "Butterfly dream in Chuang Tzu (Communal soul) Abbey??" (Box 19, Folder 14). The answer to the question posed by the interrogatory punctuation is *Desert Solitaire*. That book, compiled from journals Abbey kept while working as a seasonal ranger at Arches National Park, near Moab, Utah, became his most popular nonfiction work. His most famous work of fiction is the infamous *Monkey Wrench Gang*, about the efforts of what would now be called eco-terrorists to blow up a dam. The passage from *Desert Solitaire* referenced by McCarthy was a direct influence on Suttree's hallucinogenic spirit-quest in the mountains. Here is the passage from Abbey:

> I went native and dreamed away days on the shore of the pool under the waterfall, wandered naked as Adam under the cottonwoods, inspecting my cactus gardens. The days became wild, strange, ambiguous—a sinister element pervaded the flow of time. I lived narcotic hours in which like the Taoist Chuang-tse I worried about butterflies and who was dreaming what.... I slipped by degrees into lunacy, me and the moon, and lost to a certain extent the power to distinguish between what was and what was not myself: looking at my hand I would see a leaf trembling on a branch. (200)

McCarthy borrowed three elements from this passage: going native in a wilderness, the inability to distinguish between dream and reality, and the inability to distinguish self from world. The last element probably lies behind McCarthy's equation, in his note, between the butterfly dream and the notion of a communal soul, which finds expression in Suttree's delirious pronouncement to a nurse during his bout of typhoid fever: "I know all souls are one and all souls lonely" (459). We also find it in the following description of the Glanton gang in *Blood Meridian*: "For although each man among them was discrete unto himself, conjoined they made a thing that had not been before and in that communal soul were wastes hardly reckonable more than those whited regions on old maps where monsters do live and where there is nothing other of the known world save conjectural winds" (152).

It would be useful to begin with the quotation from the famous butterfly dream, one of the key texts in Chinese philosophy, as translated by Burton Watson in *Chuang Tzu: Basic Writings*:

> Once Chuang Chou dreamt he was a butterfly, a butterfly flitting and fluttering around, happy with himself and doing as he pleased. He didn't know he was Chuang Chou. Suddenly he woke up and there he was, solid and unmistakable Chuang Chou. But he didn't know if he was Chuang Chou who had dreamt he was a butterfly, or a butterfly

dreaming he was Chuang Chou. Between Chuang Chou and a butterfly there must be *some* distinction! This is called the Transformation of
Things. (45, emphasis in original)

This trope, the ontological ambiguity of dream and reality, seems well-
nigh universal among human beings. In the West we have Shakespeare's "We are such stuff as dreams are made on," and even children
must contemplate the insubstantiality of things while singing "Row
Your Boat." The notion has been one that has exercised McCarthy's
imagination throughout his career. The epilogue to *Cities of the Plain*
is an extended meditation on Chuang-tzu's anecdote.

The idea, mediated through Abbey, finds expression in Suttree's
mountain vision-quest:

He had begun to become accompanied.
    First in dreams and then in states half wakeful.... Before two days
more had gone he hardly knew if he dreamt or not.... Old distaff Celt's
blood in some back chamber of his brain moved him to discourse with
the birches, with the oaks. A cool green fire kept breaking in the woods
and he could hear the footsteps of the dead. Everything had fallen from
him. He scarce could tell where his being ended or the world began nor
did he care. (285–286)

McCarthy's borrowings from other writers are often difficult to trace,
but given the presence of all three elements in the Abbey passage, there
seems to be a clear line of influence from *Desert Solitaire* to *Suttree*.

At some point in his career, McCarthy met and became friends with
Abbey. According to Richard Woodward's *New York Times Magazine*
profile, McCarthy favors the company of scientists to other writers, but
"one of the few he acknowledges having known at all was the novelist
and ecological crusader Edward Abbey. Shortly before Abbey's death
in 1989, they discussed a covert operation to reintroduce the wolf to
southern Arizona." McCarthy mentioned Abbey's death in a letter to
J. Howard Woolmer dated 8 April 1989: "I also lost another writer
friend [he had just mentioned the death of Bruce Chatwin] two weeks
ago—Ed Abbey. I think he came across in his writing as something of
a curmudgeon but he was a kind and a generous man—qualities, sad
to say, not common to writers" (Box 1, Folder 7). A published collection

of Abbey's letters contains a short congratulatory note from Abbey to McCarthy dated 15 June 1986:

> Have just read *Blood Meridian*. A beautiful terrible splendid book. You must have made a compact with the Judge Hisself to write such a book. I envy you your powers, salute your achievement and dread not a little for the safety of your soul.
>
> Luckily, altho' wholly true, your book is not the whole truth—which you know as well as I. Now I must read your other books while looking forward to your next. (184–185)

Abbey's qualified endorsement of McCarthy's grim vision, and his confidence that McCarthy would endorse the qualification, seems prescient in the light of the meditative conclusion of *The Road*, a novel that otherwise lets very little light in, either literally or figuratively. I suspect that the whole truth to which Abbey alludes would include the hum of mystery in the deep glens where "all things were older than man" (*The Road* 287). Abbey, the cantankerous eco-anarchist, heard the same hum, and many readers hear it in passages like the one quoted above from *Desert Solitaire*.

Agee, James (1909–1955)

James Agee is one of McCarthy's literary heroes. He is referred to twice in McCarthy's notes for *Suttree*, and the italicized prose poetry of the first few pages of that novel is an homage to the poetic, italicized opening of Agee's *A Death in the Family*. Both are lyrical responses to Knoxville, though Agee's prose poem is a fond and sentimental childhood reminiscence, while McCarthy's is darker, the reflections of a melancholy flaneur writing in the register of Charles Baudelaire. Rick Wallach, in his essay "Ulysses in Knoxville," argues that "*A Death in the Family*'s long meditation on death and the crisis of the absent father, and the supportive if sometimes conflicted response of family and community, shadows every step that Buddy Suttree and his unintended protégé Gene Harrogate take" (51). It is fairly well established that McCarthy used bricks from Agee's childhood home in a wall he built when renovating a barn near Louisville, Tennessee, where he lived with his second wife, Anne DeLisle (Arnold and Luce 4). Agee's masterpiece, *Let Us Now Praise Famous Men*, contains portraits of the types of poor, rural southerners featured so prominently in McCarthy's southern fiction. Agee's eye for detail in describing their physical existence influenced McCarthy's dedication to verisimilitude in his own fiction.

McCarthy's notes for *Suttree* in fact contain a direct quotation from *Let Us Now Praise Famous Men*. The typed line reads, "To 'veer so wide of the ordinary as to …' Agee" (Box 19, Folder 14). Agee's book, which features now famous photographs by Walker Evans, was the culmination of work that began as a commission from *Fortune* to write about the condition of Alabama tenant farmers during the Depression. Though *Fortune* eventually dropped the project, Agee continued to write about the three families he interviewed—the Woods, the Gudgers, and the Ricketts. The quotation comes from a description of the Gudgers' "safe," the name rural southerners used for a cupboard: "The ordinary safe is a tall, dark, flimsy wood cabinet with several shelves, with double doors faced in rusted tin pierced in ventilative patterns of geometry and of radiant flowers, and smelling stuffily yet rather sweetly of hens, butter, and fried pork and of the cheap metals of its forks. I speak of this because the Gudgers' safe *veers so wide of the ordinary as to* seem comic or even surrealist in this setting, as a Frigidaire might" (179, emphasis added). Although I cannot find any direct use of this quotation in *Suttree*, the novel, like all of McCarthy's southern fiction, revels in grotesque descriptions of rural life; both characters and their environs veer awfully wide of the ordinary.

It is easy to see why this description would appeal to McCarthy: he had an appreciation for the material culture of those living outside polite society. The following description of Suttree's observations of a rural scene, picked at random, has the same flavor of Agee's descriptions: "Out there a jumbled shackstrewn waste dimly lit. Kindling-wood cottages, gardens of rue. A patchwork of roofs canted under the pale blue cones of lamplight where moths aspire in giddy coils. Little plots of corn, warped purlieus of tillage in the dead spaces shaped by constriction and want like the lives of the dark and bitter husbandsmen who have this sparse harvest for their own out of all the wide earth's keeping" (29).

Reese's skiff, comic and surreal like the Gudgers' safe, is another example of veering wide of the ordinary. It is described as "a patchwork shack composed of old slats and tarpaper and tin snuff signs all mounted in wild haphazard upon a derelict barge and turning with the keelless rotations of a drunken bear" (306–307). Veering from the ordinary might be a good description of McCarthy's aesthetic, and Agee's book is a major influence on that aesthetic.[1]

Algren, Nelson (1909–1981)

On a page of holograph notes for *Suttree*, McCarthy wrote "try old doors (Algren)" (Box 19, Folder 13). This comment refers to Nelson Algren's poem "Tricks Out of Times Long Gone," which serves as the epilogue to his travel book *Who Lost an American?* The quoted words are in the third stanza: "Hepghosts made of rain that softly *try old doors* / Forever trying to get down one last bet" (267, emphasis added). The poem, in its rhythm, diction, and atmosphere, appears to be a direct influence on the italicized opening pages of *Suttree*. The poem, like McCarthy's text, is a guided tour through the derelict warrens of a city, perhaps Algren's native Chicago, places where the downtrodden, so much the focus of Algren's work, live. Here are some of the lines that inspired McCarthy:

Again that hour when taxies are deadheading home
Before the trolley-buses start to run
And snow dreams in a lace of mist drift down
When asylum, barrack, cell and cheap hotel
All those whose lives were lived by someone else
Who never had a choice but went on what was left
Return along old walks where thrusts of grass
By force of love have split the measured stone.

I think hep-people leave small ghosts behind
For haunting of winter ball parks and locked bars
That ghosts of old time hookers walk once more
That no ghost follows where a square has gone.

Tonight when chimneys race against the cold
Tricks out of times long gone, forgotten marks
Come seeking chances lost, and long-missed scores
Faces once dear now nameless and bereft
Hepghosts made of rain that softly try old doors
Forever trying to get down one last bet....
... Drifters of no trade whose voices, unremembered,
Speak in the city wires overhead—
Now is the victims' hour where they go
Where winoes used to drink themselves to death (267)

Here is the opening paragraph of *Suttree*:

*Dear friend now in the dusty clockless hours of the town when the
streets lie black and steaming in the wake of the watertrucks and now
when the drunk and the homeless have washed up in the lee of walls in
alleys or abandoned lots and cats go forth highshouldered and lean in
the grim perimeters about, now in these sootblacked brick or cobbled
corridors where lightwire shadows make a gothic harp of cellar doors
no soul shall walk save you.* (3)

While the significance to McCarthy of "try old doors" is unclear, what
is evident is that the poem finds an echo in McCarthy's prose poem.
We can see those echoes in its repetitions indicating a late hour ("Again
that hour," "Tonight when chimneys," "Now is the victims' hour"), in
its descriptions of the underbelly of a city, in its focus on outcasts—on
what Leslie Fiedler, in describing Algren's work, called the "stumble-
bum" (qtd. in Cox 17)—and in parallel images ("Now is the victims'
hour where they go / Where winoes used to drink themselves to
death"—Algren; "now in the dusty clockless hours ... when the drunk
and the homeless have washed up in the lee of walls"—McCarthy).

Another source for the italicized passage in McCarthy is the itali-
cized opening of James Agee's *A Death in the Family*, "Knoxville:
Summer, 1915," also a prose poem, also about Knoxville. However,
Agee's reminiscence is idealized and nostalgic.[2] This is an example of
McCarthy's appropriation of a form for the purpose of imbuing it with
original content (see Agee).

Bellow, Saul (1915–2005)

McCarthy typed three short quotations from Saul Bellow's 1961 novel *Herzog* at the top of an early manuscript page left out of the final draft of *Suttree*. The page is in a folder labeled "Left from Suttree." A holograph note next to the typed quotations identifies their source as *Herzog*. Bellow's novel chronicles the breakdown of Moses Herzog, a college professor whose disillusionment with the modern world takes the form of letters addressed but never sent to political, artistic, scientific, and philosophical figures. The letters are often critiques of twentieth-century nihilism, utilitarianism, and materialism. The novel's action follows Herzog's attempt to get custody of his daughter June from his ex-wife Madeleine, who left him for Herzog's close friend Valentine Gersbach.

The first quotation is, "What view of things was he advancing?" (Box 19, Folder 13). It is taken from a scene in which Herzog is waiting for his attorney, Simkin, in the Chicago courthouse where he plans to initiate custody proceedings. While waiting for Simkin, Herzog observes several criminal cases going before a magistrate. One involves a male prostitute named Aleck who attempted to rob a store. The quotation comes from Herzog's reflections on Aleck (the part McCarthy copied is in italics):

> Herzog tried to guess the secret of this alert cheerfulness. *What view of things was this Aleck advancing*? He seemed to be giving the world comedy for comedy, joke for joke. With his dyed hair, like the winter-beaten wool of a sheep, and his round eyes, traces of mascara still on them, the tight provocative pants, and something sheeplike, too, even about his vengeful merriment, he was a dream actor. With his bad fantasy he defied a bad reality, subliminally asserting to the magistrate, "Your authority and my degeneracy are one and the same. (280–281, emphasis added)

As is often the case with McCarthy's references to the work of other writers, the relationship between McCarthy's novel and the source is difficult to determine precisely, but two observations suggest themselves.

The first is that the male prostitute Aleck, an insouciant sexual transgressive, might be a model for the character Tripping Through the Dew, the always good-humored transvestite who moves among Suttree's African American friends in McAnally Flats. Second, Herzog, in his disillusionment with the modern world, expresses an appreciation for someone on the margins of the society with which he is at odds, much as Suttree is at odds with the "polite" society his father wants him to be a part of. Suttree rejects his father's claim that life is found "in the law courts, in business, in government. There is nothing occurring in the streets. Nothing but a dumbshow composed of the helpless and the impotent" (13–14). Herzog's perception of a moral equivalence between the prostitute and the magistrate makes Herzog and Suttree kindred spirits.

The second quotation is a fragment: "As I sat naked . . ." It comes from a scene in which Herzog remembers a navy psychiatrist who examined him in 1942 "and told me I was unusually immature" (394). The psychiatrist, whose rational reduction of the human being to psychological categories, is one of the figures with whom Herzog quarrels in his unsent correspondence. The fragment is difficult to correlate precisely with anything in *Suttree*, and it appears in the following passage: "However, *as I sat naked*, pale, listened to the sailors at drill in the dust, heard what you told me about my character, felt the Southern heat, it was unsuitable that I should wring my hands" (394, emphasis added). But the paragraph that expands upon Herzog's memory sounds very much like a key moment in *Suttree*. Herzog, in his letter, says that he followed Dr. Zozo's career "in the journals" (394). He then addresses himself to the doctor:

> I am really in an unusually free condition of mind. "In paths untrodden," as Walt Whitman marvelously put it. "Escaped from the life that exhibits itself . . ." Oh, that's a plague, the life that exhibits itself, a real plague! There comes a time when every ridiculous son of Adam wishes to arise before the rest, with all his quirks and twitches and tics, all the glory of his self-adored ugliness, his grinning teeth, his sharp nose, his madly twisted reason, saying to the rest—in an overflow of narcissism which he interprets as benevolence—"I am here to witness. I am come to be your exemplar." (394)

The passage from *Suttree* that this calls to mind is one in which Suttree has a kind of spiritual epiphany about himself, one that involves a rejection of "the life that exhibits itself." In the scene, Suttree addresses himself in the form of a "quaking ovoid of lamplight on the ceiling." He repents, in this conversation with his double, of one thing, that "I spoke with bitterness about my life and I said that I would take my own part against the slander of oblivion and against the monstrous facelessness of it and that I would stand a stone in the very void where all would read my name. Of that vanity I recant all" (414). Though Suttree expresses his epiphany with an existentialist heaviness foreign to the lightness Herzog finds in his freedom from the snares of the ego, the sentiment of spiritual peace seems similar.

The last quotation, even more difficult to link to McCarthy's novel, is "He tapped one, two, three times with his pencil." The scene is one in which Herzog, having just taken his daughter June to an aquarium, is involved in a traffic accident. A police officer is investigating the accident: "The senior policeman pointed two, three, five times with the rubber tip of his pencil before he spoke another word; he made you consider the road (there Herzog seemed to see the rushing of the Gadarene swine, multi-colored and glittering, not yet come to the cliff)" (348). Obviously, something about this image sparked something in McCarthy's mind, though the relationship is unclear. What is clear is that Bellow's novel, as a whole, was on McCarthy's mind when he was composing some of the early sections of *Suttree*.[3]

Bellow was an early admirer of and advocate for Cormac McCarthy. As Richard B. Woodward points out, Bellow was a member of the committee that awarded McCarthy a Genius Grant in 1981 from the MacArthur Foundation (Woodward 2), and according to Bellow's biographer James Atlas, his support was enthusiastic (493). Woodward quotes Bellow's praise for McCarthy's "absolutely overpowering use of language, his life-giving and death-dealing sentences" (2). Woodward also records Bellow's description of McCarthy's physical presence: "He gives an impression of strength and vitality and poetry"; he is "crammed into his own person" (3). Perhaps Bellow saw in Cornelius Suttree a literary affinity with his own alienated, but spiritually searching, Moses Herzog—as, perhaps, did McCarthy.

Beowulf *(ca. eighth century)*

SEE ALSO *BLOOD MERIDIAN*

Beowulf was on McCarthy's mind during the composition of both *Suttree* and *Blood Meridian*. The first reference comes from a very early draft of *Suttree*, probably composed in the mid to late 1960s. Further references appear in McCarthy's notes for both novels. Peter Josyph, in his essay "Blood Music," rightly names *Beowulf* as a literary "grand-father" (26) to *Blood Meridian*, and Rick Wallach's essay "From *Beowulf* to *Blood Meridian*" explores that connection in detail. His thesis is that "the two texts are really most alike in their detailed depiction of martial codes, by which I mean structured social systems that justify and promulgate conflict, represent violence as craft, and convention-alize destructive activity in a craftsmanly way" (199). He notes that the Wild West setting of *Blood Meridian* allows McCarthy to explore the "contagion of systematized violence" in a cultural milieu hospitable to martial codes (201).

However, the earliest reference to *Beowulf* suggests that McCarthy envisioned the violent world of the poem as analogous to the darker regions of the mind. It appears in an excised passage from a very early draft. The scene bears no resemblance to anything in the published novel; it belongs to what we might call the ur-*Suttree*, a novel that exists, happily, only in fragments housed in McCarthy's archives. Here is the fragment containing the reference to *Beowulf*: "He knows his own dark lake that lies in a silence where the winds [*sic*] forbidding fingers are not even heard and deep and cold these waters and the caves she covers where Grindel lurks" (Box 30, Folder 1). Notes from the same box and folder contain two quotations from the Francis Gummere translation of the poem: "and nicors that lay on the ledge of the ness B/wulf," and "mere-wife monstrous. Brinewolf." The first quotation comes from line 1427. Beowulf and Hrothgar's warriors are gazing down at the lake inhabited by Grendel's mother:

> ... The band sat down,
> and watched on the water worm-like things,
> sea-dragons strange that sounded the deep,
> *and nicors that lay on the ledge of the ness—*

such as oft essay at hour of morn
on the road-of-sails their ruthless quest. (Gummere trans.,
    lines 1424–1429, emphasis added)

The second note references two names the poet gives to Grendel's mother during Beowulf's underwater combat with her. In line 1506 she is called a "brine-wolf," and lines 1518–1519 read, "Then the warrior was ware of that wolf-of-the-deep, / *mere-wife monstrous*" (emphasis added).

When McCarthy quotes from other works in his notes, the quotations usually stand alone. Here, they seem to be integrated into a longer passage, some of which McCarthy used in the italicized opening of *Suttree*. The passage describes a gothic scene featuring a warrior much like Beowulf, and the scene contains a proclamation of a martial code like the one Wallach finds in *Blood Meridian*. As the passage bears no resemblance to anything in *Suttree*, and as quotations from *Beowulf* also appear in the notes for *Blood Meridian*, they may be early seeds of that novel. Another reason to think so is that McCarthy's notes for *Blood Meridian* reveal an interest in Jessie L. Weston's *From Ritual to Romance*, her study of the Grail legends that T. S. Eliot cited as an influence on *The Waste Land* (see entry for Weston in this chapter). In particular, McCarthy was interested in the chapter describing the Perilous Chapel episode of the Grail legend, and the haunted gothic mood of the excised passage resonates with that episode. Here is the passage, with the section McCarthy salvaged for *Suttree* in italics:

Apace apace heart's blood bright on the lampkept walk. Helm up thy gorestained shortsword, he is surely done. Darkflecked and welling blood and pale blue tubers pouching from his sectored gutbag. A perilous journey with peril done. A black screechowl (Black howlet in a black tree ordains the dead with sooty cantata) "and nicors that lay on the ledge of the ness" B/wulf) "mere-wife monstrous. Brinewolf

In all times man's noblest work has been to take arms against his enemies, to defend that with which he is charged. My wife my land my aged. (Infirm elders)

Where is the enemy? What is the shape of him? Where kept and what the counter of his face? (Box 30, Folder 1, emphasis added)

An additional reason for thinking of this passage as a kind of ur-text for *Blood Meridian* is the line about man's noblest work, which sounds a bit like the judge. The phrase "to take arms against" echoes Hamlet's "to take arms against a sea of troubles," but it also sounds very much like the judge's words to the kid in Fort Griffith: "You of all men are no stranger to that feeling, the emptiness and the despair. It is that which we take arms against, is it not?" (329).

However, the influence on *Suttree* is also evident in the three questions that end the passage, which are also present in the italicized opening of *Suttree*. They appear in McCarthy's eerie description of a city besieged by something monstrous outside the walls, which certainly recalls the atmosphere of paranoia in Hrothgar's mead hall induced by the predacious Grendel and his mother. Here is the quotation, with the relevant portion italicized: "The night is quiet. Like a camp before battle. The city beset by a thing unknown and will it come from forest or sea? The murengers have walled the pale, the gates are shut, but lo the thing's inside and *can you guess his shape? Where he's kept or what's the counter of his face?*" (4–5, emphasis added). Given the manuscript evidence of the influence of *Beowulf* on the passage in which these words were originally written, we can say with confidence that McCarthy is deliberately echoing the dim, frightening, and violent atmosphere of *Beowulf* in the opening pages of the novel.

Brennan, Joseph Gerard (1910–2004)

Joseph Gerard Brennan was a philosopher and literary critic who taught philosophy at Barnard and at the US Naval War College. His work often explores the influence of philosophy on literature, as in *Thomas Mann's World* and *Three Philosophical Novelists* ("Brennan, Joseph Gerard"). McCarthy refers to the latter—a study of Joyce, Mann, and André Gide—in a typed note on a page from an early draft of *Suttree* (see also entries on Joyce in *The Gardener's Son* and this chapter; in addition, see entry for Peter De Vries in this chapter). The note reads "Gogarty on Joyce Brenan [*sic*] 3 Phils. Nov" (Box 30, Folder 1). This reference provides an interesting and rare example of McCarthy identifying the source of a deliberate literary theft. The typed note appears in the right margin next to the following lines:

You met?
The Logos extabernacled.
Who was?
Turned muttering and maudlin into the street

McCarthy took the second and fourth lines almost verbatim from Brennan's book. In the passage from *Three Philosophical Novelists*, Brennan quotes Oliver St. John Gogarty, an Irish physician, politician, and writer who was the inspiration for Joyce's Buck Mulligan, on *Finnegans Wake*: "Gogarty ... presses a charge of deliberate irrationalism against Joyce, 'This arch-mocker in his rage would *extract the Logos*, the Divine Word or Reason *from its tabernacle*, and turn it *muttering and maudlin* into the street'" (49, emphasis added). The first appropriation from the Gogarty quotation appears in *Suttree*, at the end of the scene in which Suttree, in one of his frequent funks, takes a melancholy trolley ride. The scene ends with the following sentence (a double theft, with its allusion to Frost): "Suttree with his miles to go kept his eyes to the ground, *maudlin and muttersome* in the bitter chill, under the lonely lamplight" (179, emphasis added). The second quotation shows up in one of the surreal descriptions of Suttree's hallucinations during his bout of typhoid fever:

> Seized in a vision of the archetypal patriarch himself unlocking with enormous keys the gates of Hades. A floodtide of screaming fiends and assassins and thieves and hirsute buggers pours forth into the universe, tipping it slightly on its galactic axes. The stars go rolling down the void like redhot marbles. These simmering sinners with their cloaks smoking *carry the Logos itself from the tabernacle* and bear it through the streets while the absolute prebarbaric mathematick of the western world howls them down and shrouds their ragged biblical forms in oblivion. (457–458, emphasis added)

The first "borrowing" seems to be a clear case of McCarthy finding something musical in another writer's phrasing and, with minor transliteration, weaving into his own work. McCarthy liked the alliterative "maudlin and muttering," though his "maudlin and mutter*some*" does give it a McCarthyesque touch.

The second quotation demonstrates the appealing wordplay that

McCarthy enjoys in other writers, but it also provides him with an arresting image that conveys the sense of chaos, of unreason, that characterizes Suttree's occasional descents into the more savage purlieus of the unconscious. Brennan takes issue with Gogarty's characterization of *Finnegans Wake*, arguing that "Joyce's fault, if it is fault, lies not in irrationality, but in his excessive, almost theological rationalism" (49). This sounds right, but I suspect, given the way McCarthy incorporates the work of other writers into his own, that what struck him about this quotation was not the rightness or wrongness of Gogarty or Brennan on Joyce, but the sound of the words and the vivid image of chaos in the "Logos extabernacled." McCarthy wanted to verbally approximate Suttree's vertiginous tilting at the edge of madness, and he found a model in Brennan's book.

Brown, Christy (1932–1981)

McCarthy's notes for *Suttree* contain a single reference to Christy Brown's first novel, *Down All the Days*. McCarthy typed the title and "P34" next to it (Box 19, Folder 14). Brown, an Irish writer and artist, was most famous for his autobiography *My Left Foot*, made internationally famous because of the 1989 film starring Daniel Day Lewis in the lead role. Due to cerebral palsy, Brown was paralyzed from birth, but he was able to write and paint with his left foot, the only part of his body over which he retained control ("Brown, Christy"). *Down All the Days* is a fictionalized autobiography about growing up in Dublin's slums in the 1930s and 1940s. The novel's depiction of the boisterous and seedy underbelly of Dublin may very well have influenced McCarthy's own efforts at depicting the night side of a large American city.

The page McCarthy references recounts the main character's delirium after being hit in the head by a rock during a conflict between neighborhood boys over rights to cinders the boys would sell after gathering them from the train yard. The description of the character's delirium while in the hospital sounds very much like the descriptions of Suttree's hospitalization with typhoid fever. Here is page 34 of *Down All the Days* from the edition McCarthy would likely have read:

He was crawling down a long, dark tunnel of pain; the walls seemed about to collapse, to fold in upon him; everything seemed to be breaking up, dissolving, disintegrating; he seemed to be stuck, submerged in a sort of gum mucilage; sharp brittle points of light flashed before his eyes; into the loud confusion of his mind things swam.... When he awoke it was still dark, but a different sort of darkness now, permeated by a dim unlocated effulgence; a circle of light shone remotely through a green bamboo screen; voices from behind it, subdued: "Some difficulty with urine," a man's voice said; "You know what to do, sister."

Here is McCarthy's description of Suttree's bout with typhoid delirium:

Another door closed, door closed, door closed softly in his skull. Light bloomed rose, lime green. He was going out by a long tunnel attended by fading voices and a grainy humming sound and going faster and past gray images that clicked apart in jagged puzzle pieces. Down a corridor that opened constantly before him and dissolved after in iron dark. (452)

When Suttree wakes to a woozy half-consciousness, it is, as for Brown's protagonist, to the voice of attending nurses and doctors. While no fingerprints could indict McCarthy for theft here, the page number in the notes, and the similar moods and images (both characters feel they are in a tunnel) in the two passages suggest that this is one of those instances when McCarthy was struck not by an idea or theme in a book he admired but by purely aesthetic techniques of description (see, for instance, the entry for Tom Wolfe and his arthritic trees in *Blood Meridian*).

Of interest to McCarthy scholars is the presence of another novel recounting life in Dublin impinging on McCarthy's imagination, taking its place on the same shelf as *Ulysses*. In this case, the novel shares with *Suttree* a street-level depiction of the grit, slime, and sleaze of a city's underbelly. It also sits on the same shelf as two other influences on McCarthy: Nelson Algren and Henry Miller (see entries for Algren in this chapter, and for Miller in this chapter and in the chapter on correspondence).

Cooke, Ebenezer (ca. 1667–ca. 1732)

A holograph marginal note on a page of fragments from an early draft refers to the little known English poet Ebenezer Cooke, whose satirical poem "The Sot-Weed Factor, Or, a Voyage to Maryland" (1708) inspired the American novelist John Barth's 1960 novel *The Sot-Weed Factor*. McCarthy's note-to-self clearly refers to the former: "ck out Sot Weed Factor early Eng. works" (Box 30, Folder 1). McCarthy's interest in the poem is in keeping with his off-the-beaten-track approach to reading, but Robert D. Arner's description of the work and its author's significance also help to explain McCarthy's interest. Arner claims that "Cooke initiated a tradition of Southern humor that eventually spawned Mark Twain and William Faulkner and that remains vitally alive today. His portraits of what he called the 'planting rabble' of Maryland, his deflation of the contradictory American dreams of pastoral innocence and unlimited economic advancement, and his irreverent handling and comic mythologizing of history are also very much in the mainstream of American literary traditions and entitle him to more careful critical attention than he has hitherto received" (n.p.). The poem satirizes the get-rich-quick schemes of Englishmen seeking their fortunes in America, specifically, a tobacco merchant (sot-weed factor) who "encounters a gallery of rogues and scoundrels who eventually cheat him of the goods he has brought and send him raging back to England" (n.p.) McCarthy may have learned about Cooke from another book he read during the composition of *Suttree—Maryland: A Guide to the Old Line State* (see entry in this chapter). There "Sot-Weed Factor" is described as a "shrewd, if somewhat fantastic, picture of life in the colony at the turn of the eighteenth century" (132).

Dante Alighieri (1265–1321)

McCarthy's notes for *Suttree* contain the following stand-alone sentence, one that does not appear in the published novel: "Sweating before the furnace door in his cleric's robes like one of Dante's stoker popes" (Box 19, Folder 14). It is not clear what scene, if any, this was cut from, but it is in keeping with the novel's anticlerical bent. Here is one of the more ferocious examples, taken from a scene in which Suttree recalls playing hooky from church with J-Bone when they were children: "Grim and tireless in their orthopedic moralizing. Filled with tales of sin and unrepentant deaths and visions of hell and stories of levitation and possession and dogmas of semitic damnation for the tacking up of the paraclete" (254). Suttree's reminiscence takes place in his childhood church, to which, in spite of his hostility, he has repaired during a period of spiritual anguish (are there any periods free from spiritual anguish for Suttree?), suggesting that beneath the antipathy nostalgia lurks. When a priest approaches him, Suttree assumes his posture of defiance, telling the priest that the church is "not God's house" (255).[4]

While McCarthy likely took some inspiration for his own attacks on the clergy from Dante's attacks in *The Divine Comedy*, the influence of the poet's horrific images of hell and purgatory surely impinged upon McCarthy's own imagination. The attack of the Comanches on the filibusters in *Blood Meridian* possesses some of Dante's genius for hellish grotesquerie. Dante's vision of man's life as a fraught spiritual journey would also be appealing to McCarthy's vision of the human condition. In fact, a clear allusion to Dante invites a reading of Suttree as a pilgrim, and, like Dante, his journey necessarily takes him through hell. The allusion occurs during Suttree's vision quest in the mountains: "In these silent sunless galleries he'd come to feel that another went before him. . . . [S]ome othersuttree eluded him in these woods and he feared that should that figure fail to rise and steal away and were he therefore *to come to himself in this obscure wood* he'd be neither mended nor made whole but rather set mindless to dodder drooling with his ghostly clone from sun to sun across a hostile hemisphere forever" (287, emphasis added). Not insignificantly, what follows this evocation of Suttree's ghostly double is a phantasmagoric hallucination that evokes medieval images of hell, a hallmark of Suttree's haunted consciousness.

Davidson, Donald (1893–1968)

Dianne C. Luce, like John Sepich, has a genius for discovering McCarthy's influences. In her 2009 study of McCarthy, *Reading the World: Cormac McCarthy's Tennessee Period*, she correctly identifies

Donald Davidson's two-volume history of the Tennessee River, *The Tennessee*, as an influence on McCarthy. She rightly associates his fictional critique of the forces of modernity at play in rural Tennessee with Davidson's similar critiques in his history of the river. A marginal note from an early draft of *Suttree* reads: "VII—The Tennessee—Davidson" (Box 30, Folder 1). This note could be referring to chapter 7 of either volume 1 or volume 2 of *The Tennessee*, or could be specifying volume 2 if the "V" stands for "Volume." The page on which the note appears, a description of Suttree's journey upriver to meet up with Reese's family, does not seem to owe anything to either of the chapters, so the note likely refers to the second volume.

Davidson, a poet, a critic, and a historian, is now mostly remembered for his association with the Fugitives, a group that included among its members John Crowe Ransom, Allen Tate, and Robert Penn Warren.[5] One of the authors of the notorious *I'll Take My Stand: The South and the Agrarian Tradition*, Davidson's defense of traditional folkways against the encroachment of modernity finds echoes in McCarthy's southern fiction. According to Luce in *Reading the World*, "in his river history, Davidson defended the traditional cultures of the entire Tennessee Valley, including that of East Tennessee, sympathetically chronicling what was lost with the TVA's introduction of progressive culture; McCarthy seems to have found this compatible with his own aims in *The Orchard Keeper*" (271). Ironically, Cormac McCarthy's father, Charles McCarthy, was on the legal staff of the TVA from 1934 to 1967, serving as chief counsel from 1958 to 1967 (Arnold and Luce 3). Though reading biography into a writer's works is always a precarious venture, it is fascinating to consider the degree to which the tensions between Suttree and his father mirror similar tensions in McCarthy's own life, tensions that may have been related to McCarthy Sr.'s involvement with the kinds of government agencies that McCarthy critiques throughout his southern fiction. Knowing that McCarthy's outlook was influenced to some degree by Davidson, staunch critic of the TVA, lends credibility to the biographical reading.

Luce, though careful to avoid labeling McCarthy a "latter-day Agrarian," points out several affinities between McCarthy's outlook and the philosophy of *I'll Take My Stand*: "A value placed on individualism; a value placed on ties to the land and the understanding that nature is not to be conquered; an emphasis on structuring time through awareness of natural cycles rather than through the artificial, fast-paced schedules of the mechanized world; a perception of the industrial, progressive economy as a threat to social bonds; and a perception of the spiritual deadness of those caught up in 'progress'" (271).

The appeal of Davidson's *The Tennessee* to McCarthy, a man whose own work celebrates wilderness, is evident in the first pages. For Davidson, the river symbolizes a way of life threatened on all sides: "Until the advent of the Tennessee Valley Authority it defied every human attempt at conquest. It could be used, but only at great hazard and on terms forbidding to commerce and industry. So it remained a wild river, cherishing its wildness while civilization rushed across it or away from it" (1:6). *Suttree*, like *The Orchard Keeper*, is heavy with the keen awareness that "civilization" is, like the railroad in Faulkner's novella *The Bear*, always making inroads into spaces where both nature and human societies are either pristine and untainted or more authentic. And like Faulkner, and like Davidson in his ecological speculations, McCarthy also finds something deeply religious in this untainted quality of wilderness. The introduction to *I'll Take My Stand*, quoted in the introduction to *The Tennessee*, makes this understanding of the natural world plain: "Religion is our submission to the general intention of a nature that is fairly inscrutable; it is the sense of our role as creatures within it" (1:vi). McCarthy's heroes, Arthur Ownby, Suttree, John Grady Cole, all exhibit a sense of piety in their relationships to the natural world that McCarthy would have found in the beautiful prose of Davidson's books.

As I have suggested, the marginal note in the *Suttree* draft probably refers to Davidson's second volume, and in it we find a woodcut illustration of a flatboat ferry that Dianne Luce, in a real scholarly coup, identifies as McCarthy's source for the ferry that Culla encounters in *Outer Dark*: "Donald Davidson's river history, *The Tennessee*, which mentions the locations of many ferries along its course, prints an illustration by Theresa Sherrer Davidson that seems a better model of the flatboat ferries with cable rigging described by . . . McCarthy" (126). Luce notes three points of similarity between the illustration and the scene McCarthy describes: the ferryman, wearing a hat "vaguely nautical" (McCarthy 159), a man waiting for the ferry, and another man approaching the river on horseback (Luce 126–127). The illustration appears in volume 2, page 146, of *The Tennessee*, and, given Luce's argument, and the knowledge provided by the archives that McCarthy did, indeed, know Davidson's book, it is surely a source for the scene in *Outer Dark*.

Luce finds Davidson's influence to be very pronounced in *The Orchard Keeper*. Perhaps we can see an echo of the following passage from *The Tennessee* in the last sentence of that novel: "The Indians are gone, and the Indian river wears the manacles and dress of civilization. How all this came about is a long story and a strange one. It begins with legend. It ends with statistics" (18). And here is the closing paragraph of *The Orchard Keeper*: "They are gone now. Fled, banished in death or exile, lost, undone. Over the land sun and wind still move to burn and sway the trees, the grasses. No avatar, no scion, no vestige of that people remains. On the lips of the strange race that now dwells there their names are myth, legend, dust" (246). Davidson's elegiac history of the Tennessee River, which is almost a character in *Suttree*, exerted a powerful influence on Cormac McCarthy's imagination.

De Vries, Peter (1910–1993)

An early, excised passage from *Suttree* contains a holograph marginal note: "See Tents of Wickedness for Joyce parody" (Box 30, Folder 1). Peter De Vries, the author of *The Tents of Wickedness*, was a comic novelist who wrote for *The New Yorker*. Though largely unread today, he was at one time regarded as a master satirist of American life. Kingsley Amis called him "the funniest serious writer to be found on either side of the Atlantic" (qtd. in Higgins n.p.). D. G. Myers, writing in *Commentary*, describes De Vries as writing "a special kind of humor, filled with puns and plays on words and inversions of popular clichés and famous sayings" (n.p.). De Vries was a religious man with a background in the Dutch Reformed Church. Myers quotes Terry Teachout's description of *The Blood of the Lamb* as a "furious tract about the impossibility of religious faith written by a man who wanted desperately to believe."[6] *The Tents of Wickedness* (1959), De Vries's satire on artists, contains parodies of James Joyce, William Faulkner, Ernest Hemingway, and Thomas Wolfe, all writers McCarthy admires and emulates.

McCarthy's note references the Joyce parody, and the page on which the note appears contains what looks like McCarthy's own parody of the master (see entries on Joyce in *The Gardener's Son* and this chapter; in addition, see the entry for Joseph Gerard Brennan in this chapter). The presence of the marginal note and the Joyce parody, along with a comic poem McCarthy wrote in another section of his *Suttree* papers containing the line "Je crois c'est trop Joycean" (Box 19, Folder 14), suggests that McCarthy was very much aware of Joyce's influence on him and that, in order to avoid slavish imitation, he sometimes engaged in parodic homage. Rick Wallach suggests something similar in his "Ulysses in Knoxville": "From James Joyce's *Ulysses*, the masterpiece of Cormac McCarthy's Appalachian canon derives its very motor power: the intersecting peregrinations through Knoxville and environs of its two principal figures, Buddy Suttree and his hapless would-be protégé Gene Harrogate, inflect the wanderings of Leopold Bloom and Steven Dedalus through Dublin, another city one could navigate successfully with its most illustrious book in hand" (54). Wallach goes on to say that "McCarthy's pilferage from both Agee and Joyce, and the spirit in which he revises his stolen material, are *quintessentially parodical*" (54, emphasis added). The archival marginalia confirm this insight.

McCarthy, in fact, loves literary parody, the mode that his very subtle allusiveness most often takes. McCarthy co-opts the elevated diction of literary precursors and transplants it into the sordid purlieus of his fictional worlds. For instance, during a freeze in Knoxville, Suttree visits a homeless shelter to check up on the ragpicker. While there, he overhears the following conversation among the derelicts in the house. A parody of W. H. Auden's "In Memory of W. B. Yeats," the conversation between them concerns the death of their fellow drunk Cecil. I have italicized the line that gives it away:

> Where'd he die?
> Uptown. He got too drunk to come in and I reckon he passed out.
> He was froze, they said. I don't know.
> He froze, said Mauve man. Old Cecil did.
> Cecil froze.
> Old Cecil froze from head to toes
> And stiffer than a tortoise
> In spite of drinking strained canned heat
> And dilute Aqua Fortis

Suttree waved away these things from his ears. Cecil was being discussed by the company. *All agreed that the day of his death was a cold one.* Today even colder. It's colder than a welldigger's ass said one, another said A witch's tit. A nun's cunt said a third. On Good Friday.(175, emphasis added)

Here is the first stanza of Auden's poem:

He disappeared in the dead of winter;
The brooks were frozen, the airports almost deserted,
And snow disfigured the public statues;
The mercury sank in the mouth of the dying day.
What instruments we have agree
The day of his death was a dark cold day.
        (lines 1–6, emphasis added)

Poor Yeats. Poor Cecil. Juxtaposing the dignified Auden elegy with the vulgar language of a group of homeless alcoholics huddling from the cold simultaneously parodies Auden and elevates poor old Cecil. Something similar happens when McCarthy parodies the father/son dynamic of Bloom and Dedalus through the analogous pairing of Suttree and Harrogate. One of the most beautiful things about *Suttree* is the strange (because of the lack of whitewashing) nobility with which McCarthy graces lovable lowlifes like Gene.

Other instances of such parody abound. Thomas D. Young Jr. identified several such appropriations in *Suttree* ("Imprisonment" 108), citing instances in *Suttree* where McCarthy appropriates Frost (179), cummings (195), and Faulkner (453–454). A marginal note on a page from an early draft of the novel indicates that McCarthy was aware of the strong influence of Thomas Wolfe on his prose (Box 30, Folder 1, see entry for Wolfe in this chapter). *Child of God* parodies Emily Dickinson (who is also parodied in De Vries's novel). When Lester Ballard awakes in the hospital after narrowly escaping a lynch mob, his reaction to the loss of his arm is described in this way: "He pulled the sheet from about his neck and studied the great swathings of bandage at his shoulder *apparently with no surprise*" (175, emphasis added). Here is Dickinson: "*Apparently with no surprise* / To any happy flower / The Frost beheads it at its play" (emphasis added). The burden of redeeming

Ballard is a heavy one, but McCarthy pulls it off, and in his distinctive approach to literary allusion shows the same kindness to Ballard that he shows to Harrogate and Cecil.

In *Ulysses*, Joyce famously parodies the entire sweep of English literature. McCarthy's devotion to that novel, and his interest in De Vries's *The Tents of Wickedness*, suggests that he gives great thought to "the ugly fact [that] books are made out of books" (qtd. in Woodward). Perhaps this indicates something like Bloom's anxiety of influence at work in McCarthy's writing, but if so, that anxiety finds release in humorous allusions and parodic appropriations. It suggests, happily, that McCarthy, so often regarded as the prince of darkness in American literature, knows how to *play*. Parody, like irony, is a mode that teaches humility, since it reveals the way that shifts in context change the meanings we like to believe are fixed and stable; received in the right spirit, parody offers a model for taking in the world with a lightness of spirit that welcomes laughter at the human condition. Much of what makes *Suttree* such a bracing, even uplifting, reading experience might be accounted for by the presence of this lightness of spirit, a counterbalance to the book's melancholy.[7]

Eliot, T. S. (Thomas Stearns) (1888–1965)

SEE ALSO *THE ROAD*

An allusion to T. S. Eliot in McCarthy's notes for *Suttree* (Box 19, Folder 14) highlights his interest in *The Waste Land*, a poem widely acknowledged by critics as an influence on McCarthy's exploration of spiritual decay as mirrored in the physical decay of a river city: Knoxville is to London as the Tennessee is to the Thames. The allusion appears in a brief fragment of two sentences not found in the published novel: "An embryonic earth of scoria and seething meld. This handful of dust in the lode of the firmament." The allusion is to Section One of *The Waste Land*, "The Burial of the Dead": "Only / There is shadow under this red rock, / (Come in under the shadow of this red rock), / And I will show you something different from either / Your shadow at morning striding behind you / Or your shadow at evening rising to meet you; / I will show you fear *in a handful of dust*" (lines 24–30, emphasis added). Though this allusion does not make it into the novel, another allusion to the poem does, as does the general atmosphere of Eliot's poem.

We find an allusion to *The Waste Land* in Suttree's reflections on the corpse of a suicide he sees early in the novel: "He turned heavily on the cot and put one eye to a space in the rough board wall. The river flowing past out there. Cloaca Maxima. Death by drowning, the ticking of a dead man's watch" (13). This passage alludes to the title of Eliot's Section Four, "Death by Water," and the figure of the drowned Phoenician sailor. As for the influence of the poem on the general atmosphere of *Suttree*, Steven Frye argues that the italicized opening of the novel, by "weaving the present moment of the city's degeneration with the remote past," evokes "the wasteland of medieval legend and more particularly the modern and urban 'Waste Land' of T. S. Eliot's poem" (*Understanding Cormac McCarthy* 53). McCarthy's grotesque descriptions of urban blight and of a river choked with human waste do recall the London and Thames of the poem. Eliot's image of a river full of "empty bottles, sandwich papers, / Silk handkerchiefs, cardboard boxes, cigarette ends / Or other testimony of summer nights" ("The Fire Sermon" lines 177–179) finds echo in *Suttree*: "With his jaw cradled in the crook of his arm he watched idly surface phenomena, gouts of sewage faintly working, gray clots of nameless waste and yellow condoms roiling slowly out of the murk like some giant form of fluke or tapeworm" (7). The last clause in that inventory may even be a subtle allusion to Eliot's "testimony of summer nights." More importantly, the novel exhibits an affinity with the poem's anguished mourning over a civilization in spiritual ruin, and, in tracing Suttree's path toward some kind of redemption, with the poem's yearning for spiritual renewal as figured in references to the legendary Fisher King. Edwin Arnold draws attention to this parallel in his "Naming, Knowing, and Nothingness," where he asserts that "we should remember that Suttree is a fisherman, although the river he fishes runs out of Eliot's *Waste Land* and he more often resembles the wounded Fisher King than ... the Christian fisher of men" (59).

Since McCarthy was working on *Blood Meridian* while completing *Suttree*, it is not surprising to find allusions to Eliot in that novel as well. Though the setting of McCarthy's western differs greatly from the urban *Suttree*, it also functions as a spiritual wasteland, one where the protagonist is pursued not by hellhounds on his trail, but by the devil himself. The following allusion to *The Waste Land*, which appears during the kid's wandering journey with Sproule, affirms such a reading of the novel's setting: "Climbing up through ocotillo and pricklypear where the rocks trembled and sleared in the sun, *rock and no water and the sandy trace* and they kept watch for any green thing that might tell of water but there was not water" (62, emphasis added). In Section Five, "What the Thunder Said," Eliot describes the modern wasteland as a desert landscape: "Here is no water but only rock / *Rock and no water and the sandy road* / The road winding above among the mountains / Which are mountains of rock without water" (lines 331–334, emphasis added). Such allusions bolster a reading of both novels as spiritual explorations of the dark night of the soul rather than expressions of nihilistic despair.

McCarthy's use of both literary allusion and phraseological appropriation suggest an awareness of Eliot's essay "Tradition and the Individual Talent," the thesis of which might be crudely crystallized by McCarthy's observation that "books are made out of books." Steven Frye gets this aspect of McCarthy's work exactly right in his reflections on McCarthy's relationship to literary predecessors: "Eliot suggests that literary history is dynamic, and the contemporary writer actively participates in the tradition that precedes him. . . . McCarthy is very much this 'traditional' author in the terms Eliot articulates. He evokes the past in all its forms and connotations, and he 'builds' his works out of a life-long reading practice that absorbs and reenvisions, apprehends and recontextualizes" (*Understanding Cormac McCarthy* 7). Our awareness of the way McCarthy builds on the work of Eliot highlights the spiritual gravity of McCarthy's purposes in exploring the degradation and evil to be found in human life. His tips of the hat to Eliot remind us of the rich soil he is working.

Blood Meridian features a subtle allusion to Eliot during a description of the Glanton gang's travels through the desert: "At night the wolves in the dark forests of the world below called to them as if they were friends to man and Glanton's dog trotted moaning among the endlessly articulating legs of the horses" (188). The allusion is to the final lines of "The Burial of the Dead" section of *The Waste Land*, when the speaker addresses "Stetson," and asks about the corpse he planted in his garden last year, warning him, "Oh keep the Dog far hence, that's friend to men, / Or with his nails he'll dig it up again!" (lines 74–75).

Ericson, Eric B. (dates unknown), and Goesta Wollin (1912–1995)

McCarthy references the authors of *The Ever-Changing Sea* and *The Deep and the Past* in notes and marginalia for *Suttree*. Box 19, Folder 13, labeled "Left from Suttree," contains a page on which McCarthy typed a quotation from the former of the two books: "The extraordinary similarity between the human eye and the squid's eye is a brilliant example of evolutionary convergence; they are alike in almost every detail. Both have a transparent cornea, an iris diaphragm, a clear lens, a chamber filled with liquid, and muscles to control the focus of the lens and movement of the eyeball. Etc …" This observation, conveyed in the dry reportage of popular science, is transmuted into a macabre image of madness and horror in the novel. It occurs during Suttree's hallucinations after he is drugged by Mother She, when he has this vision: "He saw an idiot in a yard in a leather harness chained to a clothesline and it leaned and swayed drooling and looked out upon the alley with eyes that fed the most rudimentary brain and yet seemed possessed of news in the universe denied right forms, like perhaps the eyes of squid whose simian depths seem to harbor some horrible intelligence" (427). The Ericson and Wollin quotation, ironically enough, seems to connect with McCarthy's interest in Michel Foucault's book *Madness and Civilization*, which also helped shape the above quotation from *Suttree* (see entry for Foucault in this chapter). Foucault's book is about how the *episteme* of scientific rationality seeks to control madness (the idiot chained to the clothesline).

Farrell, James T. (1904–1979)

Box 19, Folder 11, contains a 3″×5″ spiral notebook with holograph notes for *Suttree*. The ruled lines list words keyed to manuscript page numbers. These kinds of checklists are standard practice for McCarthy. His purpose appears to be to review the words for spelling, style, and aesthetic appropriateness (McCarthy's copy editors often question his tendency to combine words that are normally separated into one, his use or lack thereof of hyphens, and his propensity to use lowercase when uppercase is standard—see Box 2, Folders 2–10, for correspondence with copy editor Bert Krantz). On a line without a manuscript page number, McCarthy wrote, in parentheses, "James T. Farrell—send copy?" I am unfamiliar with any source that would indicate a relationship between the two writers, but the note suggests that McCarthy was an admirer and believed that Farrell might appreciate *Suttree*. Farrell, author of the *Studs Lonigan* novels, is widely regarded as one of the masters of American naturalism. His gritty brand of verisimilitude owed much to his upbringing in Chicago's South Side ("Farrell, James T."). Though McCarthy can be described as a practitioner of a kind of naturalism, his penchant for allegory, symbolism, and lyricism make his novels unorthodox within that tradition. However, what Joseph Warren Beach said of Farrell—"There is no reason why the squeamish or tender-minded should put themselves through the ordeal of trying to like his work" (qtd. in "Farrell, James T.")—could surely be said of McCarthy.

Flaubert, Gustave (1821–1880)

Gustave Flaubert's *The Temptation of St. Anthony* was a significant influence on McCarthy during the mid to late 1970s when he was working on both *Suttree* and *Blood Meridian*. It ought to be regarded as a formative influence on *Blood Meridian*, perhaps even precipitating the shift away from the conventional genre western that McCarthy began writing to the philosophical novel we now know.[8] References to Flaubert's book appear in McCarthy's notes for both *Suttree* and *Blood Meridian*. Box 19, Folder 14, containing notes for the former, features three quotations from *The Temptation* on a page McCarthy labeled with a handwritten heading: "Sut—Mtns." Suttree's "vision quest" was also deeply influenced by Foucault's *Madness and Civilization*. Both Flaubert and Foucault were inspired in their reflections on the potential for wisdom in visionary and nonrational states of consciousness by Brueghel's painting of the temptation of St. Anthony, and Foucault cited Flaubert's work as a major influence on his thinking. These two writers are nodes within a nexus of thinkers and theological systems that McCarthy was exploring in order to shape the nightmarish metaphysics of *Blood Meridian*.

The three quotations from McCarthy's *Suttree* notes are as follows. I have numbered them for convenience:

1. "Those who traverse the desert meet animals passing all conception." P159 The Temptation of Saint Anthony
2. "All the fearful pictures on the wall started into hideous life."
3. Nous allons au nord. Le cote d la & le niege. Dan le plateau blanc le hippopodes veugle coupon avec les termines de sont pieds le plant ultramarine (*Le Tentation de St. Antoine*).

The third quotation is translated by Kitty Mrosovsky as "We go north, to the land of swans and snow. On the white plain, the blind hippopods are breaking the ultramarine plant with the ends of their feet" (157). The first quotation also appears on a page of handwritten notes for *Blood Meridian*: "Flaubert creatures surpassing description" (Box 35, Folder 4). McCarthy alludes to it in the passage from the novel in which the survivors of the attack by the Yumas on the ferry controlled by the Glanton gang encounter the judge in the desert. Interestingly, the scene also contains an allusion to Foucault's *Madness and Civilization* (18–19) that emphasizes the closeness of these two texts in McCarthy's mind. I have italicized the allusions, with the Foucault appearing first. The passage describes the appearance of the judge and the imbecile; it also features an allusion to *King Lear*, another work that explores both the madness and the wisdom to be found in wandering desert places:

> Like things whose very portent renders them ambiguous. *Like things so charged with meaning that their forms are dimmed.* The three at the well watched mutely this transit out of the breaking day and even though there was no longer any question as to what it was that approached yet none would name it. They lumbered on, the judge a pale

pink beneath his talc of dust like something newly born, the imbecile much the darker, lurching together across the pan at the very extremes of exile like some scurrilous king stripped of his vestiture and driven together with his fool into the wilderness to die.

Those who travel in desert places do indeed meet with creatures surpassing all description. (*Blood Meridian* 281–282, emphasis added)

The subtle but tangible frisson that McCarthy achieves by nesting allusions to Foucault, Flaubert, and Shakespeare in a single passage is a testament to both his indebtedness to his influences and his strikingly original appropriation of their words and ideas.[9]

The Flaubert quotation also serves as a reminder that for McCarthy ideas are often of secondary importance to sounds and images. McCarthy loved the ring of that line from Flaubert, so much so that he was still stealing from the French author as late as the composition of *The Road*. In an early draft of that novel, McCarthy wrote, "In his dreams the cold blind oculous of the sun was always falling away like the moon in a lake. Because the world was so divested of mental provender his dreamlife had become rich and strange indeed and he understood how *travelers in the desert meet with creatures surpassing all understanding*" (Box 87, Folder 6, emphasis added). McCarthy must have realized that he was not only borrowing from Flaubert, but also from his own previous borrowing, and so in revision he changed the passage dramatically: "He'd been visited in a dream by creatures of a kind he'd never seen before" (153). Needless to say, it would take a textual Schliemann to excavate this passage, absent McCarthy's notes, down to the strata that contains Gustave Flaubert's *The Temptation of St. Anthony*. However, it is there, raising questions about what else might be there. As revelatory as the McCarthy papers often are, the revelations are surely just the tip of the iceberg.

I have been unable to find correlations between the second and third quotations in the *Suttree* notes, though the second resonates with quotations from Wyndham Lewis and Giuseppe Tomasi di Lampedusa that are also found in McCarthy's *Suttree* papers (see entries for Lewis and Lampedusa in this chapter). The entry for Lewis discusses their relationship in greater detail. The third exemplifies the phantasmagoric quality of much of *The Temptation*—and, as the heading referring to Suttree in the mountains would indicate, McCarthy, in describing Suttree's visionary hallucinations in that section of the novel, evokes Flaubert's surreal descriptive strategies for those scenes.

The second quotation appears at the beginning of *The Temptation*, when St. Anthony recalls his early years as an ascetic, and, in particular, a period of residency inside "a Pharaoh's tomb." Here is Mrosovsky's translation (which I use throughout the discussion): "But witchery winds through those underground palaces, where the aromatic smoke of long ago seems to thicken the shade. From the depths of sarcophagi I heard a doleful voice rising and calling me; or I saw, all of a sudden, *the abominable things painted on the walls start into life*; and I fled to a ruined citadel on the edge of the Red Sea" (62, emphasis added). The third quotation appears in section four, in which Anthony converses with a "parade of heretics, thinkers, philosophers, wise men, martyrs, sinners, and saints who represent a dizzying array of theological truths," as William J. Berg and Laurey K. Martin explain in their book *Gustave Flaubert* (112). Among them is Apollonius of Tyana, who is taking his leave from Anthony in the lines McCarthy quoted. Though I have been unable to link the quotation to anything in either *Suttree* or *Blood Meridian*, the relationship between the characters Apollonius and Anthony bears a striking resemblance to the relationship between the kid and the judge. Other characters, who may all, ultimately, be the same Satanic being—at one stage named as The Devil—also resemble the judge, which strongly suggests that Flaubert's work was a vital source of inspiration for McCarthy. As I have suggested, it may very well be the chief inspiration for McCarthy's decision to "go metaphysical"; early drafts, from which the judge is conspicuously absent, do not exhibit this philosophical predilection.

A brief summary of *The Temptation* will help clarify the similarities between Flaubert's work and McCarthy's *Blood Meridian. The Temptation*, which is difficult to classify in terms of genre, resembles more than anything else the second part of Goethe's *Faust*, which Mrosovsky identifies, in the introduction to her translation, as a "giant predecessor" (10). Written as a play, it centers around a dialogue between a diabolic tempter and his human prey, and it features, like Goethe's work, a host of fantastic creatures and characters from mythology, folklore, and classical literature. Flaubert adds figures from the unorthodox fringes of Christianity, as well as eastern sages and saviors. Freud was fascinated by *The Temptation*, writing, in a letter from 1883, that "it calls up not only the great problem of knowledge ..., but the real riddles of life, all the conflicts of feelings and impulses; and it confirms the awareness of our perplexity in the mysteriousness that reigns everywhere" (qtd. in Mrosovsky 21). *The Temptation* explores the contradictory systems of religion and philosophy that seek to answer life's riddles as well as the manifold forms and expressions of human desire—for sex, knowledge, power—that drive these searches. Freud's enthusiasm for the book is not hard to fathom.

Divided into seven sections, *The Temptation* chronicles the desert ascetic St. Anthony's experiences as his doubts and desires plunge him into a series of temptations, both of the flesh and of the mind, that pull him away from his vocation. The first section leads us through the first stirrings of doubt that precipitate the phantasmagoria that follows in the other six. In the second section, as Berg and Martin put it, "the seven capital sins—gluttony, greed, envy, wrath, lust, sloth, and pride—appear in the form of hallucinations" (112). In the third section, Anthony encounters a former disciple, Hilarion, who analyzes "his privations as perverse forms of desire," and "tempts Anthony with knowledge held by heretic wise men" (112). In the fourth section, Anthony encounters the heretic wise men called up by Hilarion. Their contradictory claims also contradict Anthony's orthodox beliefs, intensifying his doubt. In the fifth section, the gods of ancient pagan religions appear. The section concludes with Hilarion's revelation that he is "the possessor of all knowledge, the devil, and Hilarion offers to show Anthony the wonders of the universe" (113). In the sixth section, Anthony is tempted by the wonders of science and metaphysics. The final section shows Anthony being tempted by Death and Debauchery, women who extol, respectively, suicide and pleasure (113), and by the Sphinx and the Chimera, "one representing reason and immobility, the other imagination and change, each expressing the desire to be the other" (113). The temptations come to an end when Anthony has a vision of Jesus in the sunrise, after which he seems to resume his religious vocation, though the abruptness of the shift makes his final spiritual state ambiguous.

The most striking similarity between *Blood Meridian* and Flaubert's work is that of the judge and the devil who tempts Anthony, who appears in different guises in different sections. However, there are two other similarities that stand out, one in the horrific depiction of violence in Flaubert's section two, when Anthony is tempted to the sin of wrath, and the other in the exploration of Gnosticism, a religious system that, as Leo Daugherty has shown, also figures in *Blood Meridian* (see "Gravers False and True: *Blood Meridian* as Gnostic Tragedy").

The violent scene from section two is set in Alexandria. Anthony, tempted to the sin of wrath, envisions the slaughter of Arian heretics at the hands of Christian monks. Given McCarthy's interest in *The Temptation*, it seems likely that this scene, with its *Grand Guignol* theatricality, influenced his depiction of violence in *Blood Meridian*: "One after another, Antony comes upon all his old enemies. He recognizes some whom he had forgotten; he commits atrocities on those before he kills them—disemboweling, slitting throats, beating out brains, dragging old men by the beard, crushing children, hacking the wounded. ... [B]lood spurts up to the ceilings, spills back down the walls, wells up from the decapitated trunks of corpses, fills the aqueducts, collects on the ground in large red puddles" (78–79).

The following passage from *Blood Meridian*, describing the carnage inflicted by the Glanton gang on an Indian encampment, bears a striking resemblance to the passage from Flaubert: "The dead lay awash in the shallows like the victims of some disaster at sea and they were strewn along the salt foreshore in a havoc of blood and entrails. Riders were towing bodies out of the bloody waters of the lake and the froth that rode lightly on the beach was a pale pink in the rising light. They moved among the dead harvesting the long black locks with their knives and leaving their victims rawskulled and strange in their bloody cauls" (157). At one point during the massacre, "a young woman ran up and embraced the bloodied forefeet of Glanton's warhorse" (156), which echoes the following from *The Temptation*: "To make the Solitaries relent, they clasp them round the knees" (78–79). The resemblances are striking enough to suggest that in Flaubert's text we are looking at a primary influence on McCarthy's depiction of violence in *Blood Meridian*.

In section four of *The Temptation*, Anthony, having undergone the temptations of the flesh, is subjected to spiritual temptations as he encounters figures representing conflicting and heretical religious systems. Many of these figures represent Gnostic heresies. Knowing that Flaubert's work influenced McCarthy lends weight to Leo Daugherty's argument in favor of a Gnostic reading of *Blood Meridian*. Though the presence of Gnostic ideas and symbols is undeniable, it is worth recalling that McCarthy's papers show us a writer willing to draw inspiration from others, but hardly one who paints by the numbers when inspiration is transmuted into his own art. I think it would be a mistake to read *Blood Meridian* as the expression of a systematic philosophy or theology. McCarthy's use of these ideas serves aesthetic ends. Nevertheless, their presence in the work provides another fascinating layer of meaning to our reading of this riddle of a book.

According to Hans Jonas, widely regarded as one of the foremost scholars of Gnosticism, five broadly shared tenets characterize the disparate schools of thought that fall under this shared heading:

> The typical Gnostic system starts with a doctrine of divine transcendence in its original purity; traces the genesis of the world from some primordial disruption of this blessed state, a loss of divine integrity that leads to the emergence of lower powers who become the makers and rulers of this world; then, as a crucial episode in the drama, it recounts the creation and early fate of man, in whom the further conflict becomes centered; the final theme—in fact, the implied theme throughout—is man's salvation, which is more than man's, since it involves the overcoming and eventual dissolving of the cosmic system and is thus the instrument of reintegration for the impaired godhead itself, the self-saving God. ("Gnosticism" n.p.)

Daugherty argues that the judge should be read as one of the lower powers that Jonas describes as rulers of this world (163). This is certainly a valid way of reading his character, but because McCarthy's depiction of the judge resonates with Milton's Satan, Goethe's Mephistopheles, and Boehme's Devil in *Six Theosophic Points*, the book from which McCarthy took one of his epigraphs, we must accept it as one among many possible readings (see entry for Boehme in *Blood Meridian*). Surely the judge is meant to confound our efforts at "placing" him in a philosophical or theological schema. But Daugherty is also surely right that the Gnostic schema makes sense of some aspects of the judge. Flaubert's explorations of Gnostic thought add another angle from which to contemplate McCarthy's interest in this ancient countercurrent in the Christian stream.

Anthony, in the course of his temptations, converses with the Manichaean prophet Mani, who lays out four doctrines that are paralleled
in *Blood Meridian*. They are as follows: "The celestial earth is at the
upper extremity, the mortal earth at the lower extremity.... At the top
of the highest heaven dwells the impassible Divinity; beneath, face to
face, are the Son of God and the Prince of Darkness.... There is one
soul only, universally poured out, like the water of a river divided into
several branches.... The aim of every creature is to release the celestial
ray locked in matter" (102–103).

The first doctrine, common to all forms of Gnosticism, asserts that
human beings inhabit a fallen realm of being, the realm of matter,
often characterized as a botched creation effort—an effort attributed,
in Gnosticism's more deliberately antinomian forms, to the God of the
Old Testament. Daugherty draws attention to a passage that invites an
understanding of the realm inhabited by human beings as one resembling the fallen world of Gnostic cosmology. The text reads as follows:
"The survivors ... slept with their alien hearts beating in the sand like
pilgrims exhausted upon the face of the planet Anareta" (46). Daugherty cites *The Oxford English Dictionary* (*OED*) as defining Anareta as
"the planet which destroys life" (qtd. in Daugherty 163), according to
Renaissance belief. He notes that McCarthy's punctuation of the sentence invites a particular reading: "The implication is clearly that our
own Earth is Anaretic," and that "in *Blood Meridian*, the Earth is the
judge's" (163). This reading accords with the peculiar Gnostic inversion
of traditional theodicy, which, according to Daugherty, does not seek
an account of the presence of evil in the world, but rather of how good
gets into such an evil place (162). For the Gnostics, Daugherty writes,
"evil was simply everything that *is*, with the exception of the bits of
spirit emprisoned here" (162, emphasis in original). With the caveat
that McCarthy is not graphing his fiction onto a static schema, there is
no question that the image of Earth as Anareta fits the mood of alienation that marks McCarthy's exploration of good and evil.

The divine spark, those "bits of spirit" that Daugherty mentions,
originate in the "impassable Divinity" who inhabits the "highest
heaven." The hidden God that Flaubert evokes in the words of Mani
finds a place in *Blood Meridian*. Following a discussion of the judge's
myriad talents, including the ability to "outdance the devil himself,"
Tobin tells the kid about "how little store [God] sets by the learned"

(123). He elaborates by sketching out a kind of apophatic theology: "He's an uncommon love for the common man and godly wisdom resides in the least of things so that it may well be that the voice of the Almighty speaks most profoundly in such beings as lives in silence themselves" (124). When the kid tells him that he has not heard God's voice, Tobin replies that "when it stops ... you'll know you've heard it all your life" (124). This, significantly, is all we hear about the God who dwells in silence, but it is also of great significance that Tobin cannot answer the kid when he asks if the voice speaks to the judge, who may be the "Prince of Darkness" that Flaubert's Mani mentions. Tobin suggests as much by calling him a "sootysouled rascal" (124).

However, Mani tells Anthony that beneath the highest heaven of the pure Divinity, the Prince of Darkness stands "face to face" with the Son of God (102). Throughout *Blood Meridian*, the kid and the judge are paired in such a way that they seem to stand, in some allegorical fashion, face to face with each other as metaphysical polarities. The kid's silence contrasts so sharply with the judge's loquacity that we can only make this inference from his words and from McCarthy's use of symbolism to delineate characters. Of course, the contrast between silence and verbosity may very well be one of those symbols. John Sepich, in *Notes on Blood Meridian*, finds a symbolic pairing of the judge and the kid in the scene involving the tarot cards. In the scene, the gypsy woman reading the cards is described as being "like that blind interlocutrix between Boaz and Jachin inscribed upon the one card in the juggler's deck that they would not see come to light, true pillars and true card, false prophetess for all" (94). The card, according to Sepich, is the High Priestess (109). Using Richard Cavendish's *The Tarot* as his source, Sepich explains that Jachim and Boaz are two pillars framing the entrance to the Temple in Jerusalem. On the tarot card, they flank the High Priestess and represent stability (109–110). He quotes Cavendish as follows: "The pillars stand for the balance of opposites of which reality is made—fire and cloud, light and darkness, positive and negative" (110). In addition, they represent "Mercy and Severity" (110). Sepich believes that "these opposites are in many instances represented in the world of the kid and judge" (110). In a footnote, he also suggests that this notion of the world's order being based upon a balance of opposites accords with McCarthy's interest in Boehme's *Six Theosophic Points*. In fact, McCarthy has loosely borrowed from both Flaubert and Boehme in order to construct a fictional universe in which the judge and the kid stand in relation to each other as doubles (for a further discussion of the kid and the judge as doubles, see the entry for Kierkegaard in *Blood Meridian*).

In *Blood Meridian*'s deserts, readers encounter many strange things. Some of the strangeness derives from Flaubert's metaphysical phantasmagoria, a defining work for McCarthy's first foray into the western genre.

Foucault, Michel (1926–1984)

Box 19, Folder 13, labeled "Left from Suttree," contains a typed page of notes referring to Michel Foucault's *Madness and Civilization* (I have numbered the lines as they appear in McCarthy's notes):

1. Gryllos grotesque faces set in the bellies of monsters (Comanches)
2. Thing [*sic*] become so burdened with meaning that their forms are dimmed.
3. "Bird wings avid and disturbing as hands" Foucault
4. Dulle Griet
5. Pitiless
6. The madman and the murderer are few among us and the saint as well.
7. But the seeds of their being lie dormant in all men.

Foucault's book represents his ongoing project of demonstrating the historical contingency of forms of knowledge, *epistemes*, regarded as transcendent by thinkers who accept the Enlightenment vision of Reason as normative. Foucault describes how the concept of madness, or folly, freed from strictly religious understandings during the Renaissance, became a subject of fascinated interest among intellectuals and artists during that period. However, he goes on to chronicle the West's conceptual transformation of madness into the rational terminology of medicine, and of the concomitant need for political and institutional control.

McCarthy's notes refer to the first chapter, "Stultifera Navis," in which Foucault describes the historical movement from the late

Middle Ages to the Renaissance in terms of how it produced a liberation of possible meanings to be found in medieval gothic images
absent the constraints of the homogeneous "network of spiritual
meanings" associated with a unified Christian culture (18). From this
discussion McCarthy gets the second quotation: "Things themselves
become so burdened with attributes, signs, allusions that they finally
lose their own form. Meaning is no longer read in an immediate perception, the figure no longer speaks for itself" (18–19). McCarthy, with
a slight modulation, imports the first sentence of the quotation into
Blood Meridian.

 According to Foucault, images, "freed from wisdom and from the
teaching that organized it," become signifiers not of demonic powers,
but rather of madness and folly within the human psyche, fields of
inner experience that are frightening, but also rich with the possibility
for esoteric knowledge (18–19). Foucault offers, as an example, the
figure of the gryllos, and McCarthy's first note refers to Foucault's description: "These *grotesque faces set in the bellies of monsters* belonged
to the world of the great Platonic metaphor and denounced the spirit's
corruption in the folly of sin. But in the fifteenth century the gryllos,
image of human madness, becomes one of the preferred figures in the
countless *Temptations*" (20, emphasis added). Foucault is referring
to one of the most popular subjects among Renaissance painters: the
saint being tempted by demons, which, according to Foucault, represented for Renaissance artists dark psychic exploration rather than
religious experience (20).

 According to Foucault, in these Renaissance depictions of medieval
figures, who often combine human and animal attributes, "animality
has escaped domestication by human symbols and values; and it is animality that reveals the dark rage, the sterile madness that lie in men's
hearts" (21). It is from this part of Foucault's text that the third quotation derives: "Impossible animals, issuing from a demented imagination, become the secret nature of man; ... these are the screech owls
whose toad bodies combine, in Thierry Bouts's *Hell*, with the naked-
ness of the damned; these are Stephan Lochner's winged insects with
cats' heads, sphinxes with beetles' wing cases, *birds whose wings are as
disturbing and as avid as hands*" (21, emphasis added).

 Foucault's influence on McCarthy can be found in the sections of
the novel in which Suttree teeters on the edge of madness, his three

hallucinatory episodes. The first occurs during his "vision quest" in the mountains, the second during his bout with typhoid fever, and the third when he is drugged by the old witch Mother She. Suttree's visions in the mountains resemble the *Temptation* paintings that Foucault refers to in the above quotation, as well as Renaissance visions of hell found in artists such as Brueghel and Bosch:

> Suttree heard laughter and sounds of carnival. He saw with a madman's clarity the perishability of his flesh. Illbedowered harlots were calling from small porches in the night, in their gaudy rags like dolls panoplied out of a dirty dream. And along the little ways in the rain and lightning came a troupe of squalid merrymakers bearing a caged wyvern on shoulderpoles and other alchemical game, chimeras and cacodemons skewered up on boarspears and a pharmacopoeia of hellish condiments adorning a trestle and toted by trolls with an eldern gnome for guidon. . . . A mesosaur followed above on a string like a fourlegged garfish heliumfilled. (287)

Foucault suggests that human beings can access a certain kind of knowledge in such visions, a knowledge silenced by the modern world's institution of rational techniques of control over mental illness. Like Foucault, McCarthy explores the possibility that extreme states of consciousness are not to be despised, however stark the risks they pose, but rather should be seen as instructive.

The fifth quotation, the single word "Pitiless," comes from a passage in which Foucault discusses the frightening but necessary knowledge of those psychic regions that medieval religion, on the one hand, and rational science, on the other, suppress or control: "When man deploys the arbitrary nature of his madness, he confronts the dark necessity of the world; the animal that haunts his nightmares and his nights of privation is his own nature, which will lay bare hell's *pitiless* truth" (23, emphasis added). That madness might lead to a useful knowledge of the dark side of human nature, a knowledge the civilized world seeks to repress, is an idea also present in Suttree's visit to the witch Mother She. In fact, he willfully undergoes a hallucinatory drug trip for the purpose of seeking the knowledge that comes from a psychic liberation from sanity, civilization, and rational order.

The fourth line of McCarthy's notes refers to Peter Brueghel the Elder's 1564 painting *Dulle Griet*, a painting mentioned by Foucault in the same section of the book from which McCarthy has taken the other quotations. The painting depicts Dulle Griet, or Mad Meg in Flemish folklore, "forcing her way through the myrmidons of hell," as Brueghel scholar Robert L. Delevoy has described it (70). In Delevoy's words: "Through a throng of monstrous creatures, spawn of the atavistic fears that haunt the mental underworld, Dulle Griet strides boldly forward, carrying the long sword of the giants of mythology, wearing a helmet and breastplate, her eyes flashing fire, while from her gaping lips issues the song of the eternal tyrant, *wil je niet je moet wel* ('whether you like it or not, you *shall*')" (70, emphasis in original). Delevoy claims that Dulle Griet "incarnates the spirit of oppression and brutality—elemental malevolence without a spark of pity" (71). However, Foucault sees in the image a symbol of the Renaissance fascination with the potential for esoteric knowledge found in the exploration of madness and folly (14–15). He associates Brueghel's painting with other contemporary works of art, such as Desiderius Erasmus's *Praise of Folly* and the paintings of Hieronymus Bosch and Albrecht Dürer, in which "Madness or Folly was at work, at the very heart of reason and truth" (14).

McCarthy seems to have associated Brueghel's Dulle Griet with the witch Mother She. On an ultimately excised page from an early draft of *Suttree*, he wrote in pencil both "Dulle Griet (witch?)," and near that note the name "Mother She," which makes the association probable. Indeed, Mother She is a kind of macabre wisdom figure in the novel, able to predict futures, and, through the administration of hallucinogens, she helps Suttree open his doors of perception.[10] At the end of the experience, he has been reduced to a kind of primal being, "floating like the first germ of life adrift on the earth's cooling seas, formless macule of plasm trapped in a vapor drop and all creation yet to come" (430). At one point in his delirium, he has a vision of "an idiot in a yard in a leather harness," an image of madness constrained, the theme of Foucault's book. The idiot, in keeping with Foucault's equation of madness and knowledge, possesses "some horrible intelligence ... of things known raw, unshaped by the constructions of a mind obsessed with form" (427). This passage also resonates with the second quotation in McCarthy's notes. Both McCarthy and Foucault suggest that from the disintegration of forms comes a kind of primal, death-haunted, but pristine understanding of the human condition.

Interestingly, McCarthy wrote, in parentheses, the word "Comanches" next to the first of the Foucault quotations. His work on *Suttree* overlapped with what he was calling in the mid and late 1970s his "Western," and the scene in which the filibusters are attacked by Comanche warriors also suggests a preoccupation with the formless madness that lies beneath the carapace of civilization.[11] The description of the motley attire of the Indians echoes Foucault's claim that a "proliferation of meaning ... a self-multiplication of significance" can lead to a condition in which "things themselves become so burdened with attributes, signs, allusions that they finally lose their own form" (18–19). The clothing of the Comanches constitutes a proliferation of forms that in their chaotic and contextless multifariousness instantiate a disintegration of form and meaning. The scene is worthy of Bosch or Brueghel, whose work, through his reading of Foucault, would have been on McCarthy's mind when writing it:

> A legion of horribles, hundreds in number, half naked or clad in costumes attic or biblical or wardrobed out of a fevered dream with the skins of animals and silk finery and pieces of uniform still tacked with the blood of prior owners, coats of slain dragoons, frogged and braided cavalry jackets, one in a stovepipe hat and one with an umbrella and one in white stockings and a bloodstained weddingveil and some in headgear of cranefeathers or rawhide helmets that bore the horns of bull or buffalo and one in a pigeontailed coat worn backwards and otherwise naked and one in the armor a Spanish conquistador ... a horde from a hell more horrible yet than the brimstone land of Christian reckoning, screeching and yammering and clothed in smoke like those vaporous beings in regions beyond right knowing where the eye wanders and the lip jerks and drools. (52–53)

Here we see what Foucault calls "hell's pitiless truth; the vain images of blind idiocy" (23).

In addition to the scene involving the Comanches, McCarthy alludes to Foucault's text in a description of the judge and the fool. In this case, he paraphrases the second quotation—"Things themselves become so burdened ... that they finally lose their own form"—when we are told that the judge and fool are "Like things so charged with meaning that their forms are dimmed" (282). This is deft, literary theft, but it would take a keen eye to catch it without the archival record of McCarthy's interest in *Madness and Civilization*, which should be regarded as a significant source of inspiration for both *Suttree* and *Blood Meridian*. McCarthy's work often resembles a long descent into the underworld, and into the hopefully refining fires that the artistic exploration of such realms might bring. McCarthy's interest in Foucault underscores that interest.[12]

Graves, Robert (1895–1985)

In his notes for *Suttree*, McCarthy refers to Robert Graves's *The White Goddess*, a work very much in line with McCarthy's interest in religion and myth. The typed note reads: "periwinkles, blue gallows flowers (Wh Gds p 211)" (Box 19, Folder 14). *The White Goddess* is a dizzying synthesis of mythology, esoteric philosophy, religious symbolism, and archaic ritual, all in the service of a theory of poetry that makes the Muse-goddess of the title central to poetic inspiration. Randall Jarrell, in his *Third Book of Criticism*, summarizes Graves's project: "All that is finally important to Graves is condensed in the one figure of the Mother-Mistress-Muse, she who creates, nourishes, seduces, destroys; she who saves us—or, as good as saving, destroys us—as long as we love her, write poems to her, submit to her without question, use all our professional, Regimental, masculine qualities in her service" (111). McCarthy's note refers to Graves's discussion of flowers sacred to the White Goddess: "the erotic briar-rose and primrose and the baleful blue *vincapervinca*, or periwinkle, which the Italians call the 'flower of death' and with which, in medieval England, condemned men were garlanded on their way to the gallows" (201).

I cannot find a correlation with *Suttree*, unless it is with Mother She's "dark flowers in the old coalscuttle [which] swayed like paper cobras" (425). However, McCarthy's interest in Graves is unsurprising, given his fascination with esoteric religious thought: myth, Gnosticism, hermeticism, alchemy. His interest in Graves may, in fact, be quite significant for our understanding of some of the obscure aspects of McCarthy's most philosophical novel, *The Crossing*. The ex-priest that Billy encounters in the ghost town of Huisiachepic offers Billy a religious view couched in a theory of narrative: "Things separate from their stories have no meaning. They are only shapes. Of a certain size and color. A certain weight. When their meaning has become lost to us they no longer have even a name. The story on the other hand can never be lost from its place in the world for it is that place. And that is what is to be found here. The corrido. The tale. And like all corridos it ultimately told one story only, for there is only one to tell" (142–143). This passage echoes the opening line of Graves's poem "To Juan at the Winter Solstice": "There is one story and one story only / That will prove worth your telling, / Whether as learned bard or gifted child; / To it all lines or lesser gauds belong / That startle with their shining / Such common stories as they stray into" (137). The final stanza of the poem refers to the White Goddess, or Mother-Muse, of Graves's personal mythology. If this poem is the source of McCarthy's apothegm about the equation of life and narrative in *The Crossing*, that, combined with our knowledge that he has read *The White Goddess*, may account for the presence of the idea of the *matrix* that lies at the heart of *The Crossing*'s philosophical vision.

We are first introduced to the idea when Billy encounters the old wolf-trapper and heretical mystic Don Arnulfo. He goes to the old man to seek advice about catching the wolf that is killing cattle on his father's ranch. Billy asks about a bottle labeled Number Seven Matrix that he retrieved from the abandoned home of another wolf-trapper, Echols. The old man, switching to Spanish, calls it *la matriz*. The Spanish word emphasizes a meaning largely absent from its English equivalent: womb. Don Arnulfo, continuing, "said that the matrix was not so easily defined. Each hunter must have his own formula. He said that things were rightly named its attributes which could in no way be counted back into its substance. He said that in his opinion only shewolves in their season were a proper source" (45). The shewolf that Billy captures and attempts to return to Mexico is pregnant. After the wolf dies, McCarthy uses the word "matrix" again in his description of Billy's mystical vision of the wolf: "He ... closed his own eyes that he could see her running in the mountains, running in the starlight where the grass was wet and the sun's coming as yet had not undone the rich matrix of creatures passed in the night before her" (127).

The vision mounts to an appreciation of the wolf that transcends her earthly existence: "He took up her stiff head out of the leaves and held it or he reached to hold what cannot be held, what already ran among the mountains at once terrible and of a great beauty, like flowers that feed on flesh" (127). This association with both life and death, and the wolf's apotheosis into a kind of ultimate creative principle, suggest that the shewolf be read as an avatar of the figure Graves celebrates. In fact, Graves claims that the White Goddess, in the figure of the Celtic Cerridwen, "was a Wolf-goddess too, like Artemis" (222). Whatever we make of the shewolf, what is clear is that she functions as the mystical center of a novel that is as much a dark religious vision as it is a picaresque tragic adventure. And at the heart of that vision is the matrix, the womb of being.[13]

Hoagland, Edward (b. 1932)

McCarthy's notes for *Suttree* contain several quotations from Edward Hoagland's first nonfiction work, *Notes from the Century Before*, a chronicle of the writer's travels in a region of Northwest British Columbia near the Yukon Territory. The genre of the book, American naturalism, which combines detailed and vivid landscape description with earthy philosophical reflection on humanity's relationship with the natural world, is one McCarthy favors, and a vital source for his own brand of landscape word-painting. Hoagland is recognized as one of the most accomplished writers in this genre, and his work has garnered the praise of luminaries such as Annie Dillard and Edward Abbey (see entry for Dillard in *Blood Meridian* and for Abbey in this chapter).

The page of notes (Box 19, Folder 12) on which the quotations appear contains Hoagland's name and the title of the book. Clustered around them are the following fragmentary quotations (I have numbered them for convenience):

1. "lupine and yarrow"
2. Cows bowels "like going through the objects of someone recently deceased" actually "He might have been going through an old persons [*sic*] last possessions."

3. "wrapped in motives and notions unknown to us, like the street-sweeper humped over his broom one meets at dawn in a foreign city." (grizzly)

The first fragment comes from an entry (the book is composed of dated journal entries) in which Hoagland describes his experiences at a mining camp. Caribou gather in large numbers near the camp, and Hoagland recalls that "I walked up the caribou mountain through an old burn, with the willows and aspen head-high and *lupine and yarrow* and fireweed growing. A few spruce were left alive on knolls and in hollows which the fire skipped by" (167, emphasis added). Near the quotation, McCarthy typed "black and jagged burnt spruce forest," which is not a quotation from Hoagland, but clearly refers to Hoagland's description of the "old burn." McCarthy's notes often record landscape descriptions that strike him (see Tom Wolfe in *Blood Meridian*), though it is not always evident that the note correlates with a descriptive passage in his own work. What is evident is that vivid word-painting of scenery is one of the artistic techniques that McCarthy admires in other writers, and that nature writing in general is one of the most powerful influences on his novels.

The second quotation is Hoagland's figurative description of a farmer cutting up a cow he has just slaughtered. The passage is striking for its matter-of-fact grotesquerie: "He began to loosen and strip off the skin, mainly by pushing down on it with his elbows. Opening the body, he sawed through the brisket, handling the organs familiarly, turning them over, examining the uterus to confirm that she had been barren, and let them slide down on the ground in their dull, various colors. He was gently respectful about this. *He might have been going through an old person's last possessions*; the sense was the same" (151, emphasis added). In the same paragraph, a "neighbor boy" who witnesses the slaughter "laughed because the *cow's bowels* had moved when she was shot, and at the dismal-sounding exhalations from her dead lungs" (151, emphasis added).

Although it is difficult to say why this passage found its way into McCarthy's notes, or whether it inspired anything in his novel, one candidate might be the scene in which Gene Harrogate slaughters a hog belonging to a black neighbor who lives across the viaduct from Harrogate's "home." The goofy kid laughing about the cow's postmortem bowel movement has something of Harrogate's personality about him. Here is Harrogate with the deceased shoat: "Finally he raised the pig's leg and stuck the blade into the pig's stomach. Then he had another thought and seized one ear and wrested the head up and hacked open the throat. Blood poured out and ran over the dirt.... Now he sliced the pig open and hauled forth the guts, great armloads of them, he'd never seen so many. What to do with them" (140). Whether the "cow's bowels" scene from Hoagland is a direct influence or not, McCarthy's quoting of the scene in his notes, and his comic reveling in Harrogate's attempt to prepare the hog for consumption, both tell us something about McCarthy's interest, not so much in *the grotesque*, though he is certainly interested in that, but in *the gross*.

In Hoagland, such descriptions emphasize the matter-of-fact quality of much nature writing, as well as a willingness to gaze without flinching upon the harsh realities of life lived outside the prophylactic comforts of a bourgeois existence. Presumably, such writers discover a greater authenticity in such steely vision. McCarthy's purposes would seem to overlap here with those of nature writers like Hoagland, but McCarthy, to his great credit, knows how to play these things for laughs, and "Harrogate and the Hog" is one of the great comic moments in *Suttree*.

The third quotation appears in Hoagland's description of a trip down the Dawson River into a valley "so new and strange that I wasn't even particularly nervous. It seemed that if we met a bear he would not take exception to us, but would go on about his business *wrapped in motives and notions unknown to us, like the streetsweeper humped over his broom one meets at dawn in a foreign city*" (178, emphasis added). The passage evokes the strangeness of a natural landscape largely untouched by human beings, a place "rather like *The Wizard of Oz*, unimaginable, jungly, fantastic country that had its own logic and that, except perhaps for a man named Dawson or an occasional Indian like Alec Jack, we were the first human beings to see" (178). McCarthy's landscape description often aims for the same sense of nature as *alien*. Despite the homeliness of Hoagland's streetsweeper simile, this kind of parity, in which both the human and nonhuman worlds are linked, and thereby shown to be equally strange, equally foreign, is a commonplace feature of McCarthy's imagination. Georg Guillemin suggests that this parity characterizes McCarthy's "narrative perspective," a perspective that reveals a fundamental ontological indifference in the world. However, Guillemin says, "its pessimistic indifference bestows an egalitarian existential status on all terrestrial phenomena alike" (8). Consequently, it is unsurprising that McCarthy would enjoy Hoagland's pairing of the bear and the streetsweeper.

Hunting in the Old South: Original Narratives of the Hunters *(1967)*

McCarthy refers to this book, an anthology of hunting stories compiled by Clarence Gohdes, on a page containing an excised scene featuring the Knoxville cop Tarzan Quinn (Box 30, Folder 1). At the top of the page, McCarthy copied words and quotations from one of the hunting stories, "Wild Cattle Hunting on Green Island," by Charles Hallock. This material does not appear to be related to the scene involving Tarzan. Hallock (1834–1917), according to Gohdes's introduction to the hunting sketch, was a nineteenth-century journalist and outdoorsman best known as the editor of the periodical *Forest and Stream.* He also wrote the book *The Recluse of the Oconee*, which McCarthy refers to on the same page. The piece, which was originally published in *Harper's Magazine*, gives a raucous account of a hunt for wild cattle on an island off the coast of Georgia where a plantation has been abandoned to the slaves who used to work it, and where the once domesticated Devon cattle have become wild and dangerously ornery.

The often comic account reads like something out of one of McCarthy's southern novels, but what really caught his interest was the language used by the slaves who participate in the hunt with the white sportsmen in search of dangerous prey. Here are the references as McCarthy typed them (and one reference to a *Playboy* sex guide interspersed with the hunting material):

> Scurry and scrubrace (hunting in old south p67)
> predessicated / "you irridiscible old sootbag"
> other neologisms se P/boy's sxguide
> conflutious "but that dont go down with this child"
> See: The Recluse of the Oconee Chas Hallock 1854 (ed of Fst & strm)

It is not clear if those "other neologisms" were *in* the *Playboy* sex guide, or, if they were, *what* in the sex guide required fresh linguistic resources. But the other words come from the Hallock hunting sketch, mostly in the fairly racist depiction of the slaves. The words in the second line come from the following snippet of dialogue: "Oh, go 'way, you irridiscible soot-bag! What ye want come luff foolin' round heah for, makin' sich a noise? Afeard de cattle, does ye? 'Tink you must be prediwessicated. Keah!" (68). McCarthy's notes frequently contain, and in fact are often nothing more than, lists of archaic and obscure words, local color slang, and the argot of social outcasts and outsiders. He obviously took delight in the outlandish verbal motley found in Hallock's representation of the slaves' speech.

Joyce, James (1882–1941)

SEE ALSO *THE GARDENER'S SON*; IN ADDITION, SEE ENTRIES FOR JOSEPH GERARD BRENNAN AND PETER DE VRIES IN THIS CHAPTER

James Joyce is, by McCarthy's own admission, one of the major influences on his work. When asked to name the novels that mean the most to him, he invariably names *The Sound and the Fury*, *The Brothers Karamazov*, *Moby-Dick*, and *Ulysses* (Kushner 46). *Suttree*, in particular, owes both stylistic and thematic debts to *Ulysses*, as Rick Wallach has argued in his "Ulysses in Knoxville." According to Wallach, "From James Joyce's *Ulysses*, the masterpiece of Cormac McCarthy's Appalachian canon derives its very motor power: the intersecting peregrinations through Knoxville and environs of its two principal figures, Buddy Suttree and his hapless would-be protégé Gene Harrogate, inflect the wanderings of Leopold Bloom and Steven Dedalus through Dublin, another city one could navigate successfully with its most illustrious book in hand" (54). In fact, McCarthy is very much aware of the debt. In the first line of a poem that appears in an early, excised fragment of *Suttree*, McCarthy wrote, "Je crois c'est trop Joycean." This shows genuine insight, for McCarthy is not immune from the charge of at times writing too much like his literary influences, particularly Joyce and Faulkner.

Box 19, Folder 13, containing notes for *Suttree*, features a short bit of doggerel composed by McCarthy. It begins with an acknowledgment of Joyce's influence on his own style. The poem appears at the end of a paragraph describing Gene Harrogate, the "moonlight melonmounter," sneaking through the fields toward his assignation. The first line of the poem reads "Je crois c'est trop Joycean" (I think it's too Joycean). The other lines are as follows:

> Qui ou est l'homme qu'il passé le nuit
> Dans le foret tout sans le bruit
> C'est lui qui dorme cela
> Brouille comme les homes la bas

McCarthy's notes for *Suttree* (Box 19, Folder 14) also contain a quotation from *Ulysses*: "'A hoary pandemonium of ills.' JJ 555." The quotation is from chapter 14, which describes Leopold Bloom's encounter with a group of ribald medical students while waiting for the birth of his friend Mrs. Purefoy's child. The medical students make obscene jokes about matters gynecological. The narrator, in language parodying Thomas Carlyle's, addresses what Stuart Gilbert calls "a roaring panegyric" to "Theodore Purefoy, the polyphiloprogenitive" (310–311). In the passage, which celebrates human fecundity, the narrator compares the Purefoys with a "modern" childless couple. The sentence McCarthy quotes is a savage description of a woman who is hip, all too hip, for children. Joyce describes her in the following way: "She is *a hoary pandemonium of ills*, enlarged glands, mumps, quinsy, bunions, hayfever, bedsores, ringworm, floating kidney, Derbyshire neck, warts, bilious attacks, gallstones, cold feet, varicose veins" (345–346, emphasis added). Unfortunately, I have been unable to find a connection between this quotation and anything in *Suttree*. McCarthy's notes often resemble a pastiche of words, phrases, and occasional quotations that represent possibilities. Much of what we see in these notes winds up on the cutting floor, and this may be an example of McCarthy's compositional detritus.

Jung, Carl Gustav (1875–1961)

SEE ALSO ENTRY FOR *TABULA SMARAGDINA*
IN THIS CHAPTER

Numerous references to Carl Gustav Jung in McCarthy's notes for both *Suttree* and *Blood Meridian* indicate that McCarthy had a serious interest in Jung's work during the period when the composition of these two novels overlapped during the late 1970s. This fact, as well as frequent quotations from Gustave Flaubert's *The Temptation of St. Anthony* (see entry for Flaubert in this chapter), confirms that Gnosticism was very much on McCarthy's mind at this time, and lends weight to Leo Daugherty's thesis, argued in his seminal "Gravers False and True: *Blood Meridian* as Gnostic Tragedy," that "gnostic thought is central to Cormac McCarthy's *Blood Meridian*" (159). In fact, Dianne C. Luce makes a persuasive case that Gnostic thought is central to McCarthy's early Tennessee novels as well. For instance, she finds that McCarthy's preoccupation with shadows in *Outer Dark* derives from Jung's concept of the shadow as a projection of an inner darkness. She claims that for McCarthy, shadows "seem a literal manifestation of Jung's concept of the shadow, that archetypal dark side of the self deriving from the collective unconscious that complements yet is not acknowledged by the ego" (*Reading the World* 76). Rick Wallach, in "Judge Holden, *Blood Meridian*'s Evil Archon," notes similarities between the Satan of Jung's *Answer to Job* and Judge Holden (6). And John Sepich devotes an entire chapter of *Notes on Blood Meridian* to correspondences between Jungian ideas and Judge Holden. According to Sepich, "Holden comes out of the archetypes" (141). Early in the chapter entitled "Why Believe the Judge?," Sepich quotes, as proof of the case he goes on to make with his usual rigor, from Jung's "Approaching the Unconscious": "Life is a battleground. It always has been, and always will be; and if it were not so, existence would come to an end" (qtd. in Sepich 142). The McCarthy papers offer manuscript evidence for the prescience of these critics.

Box 19, Folder 13, labeled "Left from Suttree," contains a reference to Jung on a page of typed notes. The reference is unclear, as the name appears by itself; however, the line beneath it, "this gnostic, this shabby shapeshow that masks the higher world of form," certainly confirms McCarthy's interest in Jungian Gnosticism. The line in the notes appears in *Suttree* in a description of construction workers building a highway through McAnally Flats: "Gnostic workmen who would have down this shabby shapeshow that masks the higher world of form" (464). That reference to the higher world of form conflates Gnostic cosmology with Platonic idealism. The former often features a mythical hierarchy of being that locates the true God, or *pleroma*, at the highest level, and the earthly plane of being at the bottom. Both Gnosticism and Platonism share a belief that the physical world of form is, indeed, a "shabby shapeshow."

Box 19, Folder 13, contains notes for *Suttree* that feature a short philosophical observation that is loosely drawn from Jung's *Memories, Dreams, Reflections*. McCarthy precedes the observation, which does not appear in any published work, with a citation: "Jung MDF 347 #2." The F in the abbreviated title is a typo, and should be R. The first number refers to the page, the second to the paragraph. Here is what McCarthy wrote as a reflection on the cited passage from Jung: "We are caught in appreciations of things by endowing them with names, but the nature of the world is non verbal, has nothing to do with words at all. We cannot apprehend the true nature of reality beyond the veil of the nominal."[14] This idea, that language inhibits our direct apprehension of reality, that it is, in fact, a sign of spiritual alienation, becomes something of an obsession during the years that McCarthy turned to writing westerns and screenplays. Here is the passage, in the second paragraph of page 347, from Jung's *Memories, Dreams, Reflections*, in which he discusses the relationship between language and the archetypes of the unconscious: "The real facts do not change, whatever names we give them. Only we ourselves are affected. If one were to conceive of 'God' as 'pure Nothingness,' that has nothing whatsoever to do with the fact of a superordinate principle. We are just as much possessed as before; the change of name has removed nothing at all from reality" (347). Although McCarthy's citation preceding his comments about language verify Jung as a source for his ideas, McCarthy's view of language seems darker than the one Jung adopts in the passage McCarthy was contemplating.

McCarthy says that language cuts us off from "the true nature of reality." He sees an existential rupture. However, Jung is merely qualifying the limitations of language, making the less controversial point that language is often capable of pointing us in the direction of "the true nature of reality" without necessarily encapsulating that reality. Language functions heuristically, as a means to an end, rather than as an end in itself. In the passage quoted above, after making the observation that language and reality, particularly divine reality, are not mirror images of each other, Jung goes on to discuss the way in which language does help us to understand that reality:

> On the other hand, a positive name for the unknowable has the merit of putting us into a correspondingly positive attitude. If, therefore, we speak of "God" as an "archetype," we are saying nothing about His real nature but are letting it be known that "God" already has a place in that part of our psyche which is pre-existent to consciousness and that He therefore cannot be considered an invention of consciousness. We neither make Him more remote nor eliminate Him, but bring Him closer to the possibility of being experienced. (347–348)

Jung acknowledges the difficulties involved in naming ultimate or divine things, but he does not conclude on the basis of those difficulties that language is a barrier.

For McCarthy, language not only is a barrier, but is a barbed-wire fence surrounding a concentration camp. This is not an exaggeration, but precisely the description offered by one of the characters in the unpublished screenplay *Whales and Men*. The character Peter Gregory, described as a "titled Irish aristocrat," claims, during a long philosophical discussion about the alienation produced by language, that humanity has, through our preference for the ersatz reality of our linguistic world, turned a garden "into a detention center" (Box 97, Folder 5). According to Peter, this rather shocking conclusion emerged from teenaged meditations on the nature of good and evil provoked by a bout of measles: "I began to see all symbolic enterprise as alienation. Every monument a false idol. Language had conditioned us to substitute our own creations for those of the world. To replace the genuine with the ersatz. The living with the dead" (Box 97, Folder 5). This kind of heavy-handed, adolescent existentialism sinks the screenplay. It is, in fact, a strange sentiment coming from a writer.

I am not confusing the character with the author here. This idea is recurrent in McCarthy's fiction, a commonplace of the various roadside and armchair philosophers whose portentous, leaden diction, un-varied from one interchangeable wise man to the next, often punctuate the action in McCarthy's western novels. For instance, in *The Crossing*, the old wolf-trapper and *brujo* Don Arnulfo makes the same claim about the alienating effects of language: "Between [men's] acts and their ceremonies lies the world and in this world the storms blow and the trees twist in the wind and all the animals that God has made go to and fro yet this world men do not see. They see the acts of their own hands or they see that which they *name* and call out to one another but the world between is invisible to them" (46, emphasis added). Later in the novel Billy has a conversation with the Yaqui Indian Quijada, who had earlier restored Billy's stolen horses to him. Quijada, employing McCarthy's stock philosophical diction, makes the same point as Don Arnulfo: "The world has no name, he said. The names of the cerros and the sierras and the deserts exist only on maps. We name them that we do not lose our way. Yet it was because the way was lost to us already that we have made those names. The world cannot be lost. We are the ones" (387). In *The Road*, the father remembers being in "the charred ruins of a library," and the narrative comment on this memory is charged with the same acid judgment about language: "Some rage at the lies arranged in their thousands row on row" (187). The reference to Genesis (from garden to detention center) in *Whales and Men* re-minds us that McCarthy's work has always evoked a kind of truncated Christian vision, one in which signs of the Fall are everywhere, signs of redemption scarce (though certainly not entirely absent). Language, the whole network of symbolic and coded existence, is, for McCarthy, one of the chief signs of that fallen condition.

Presumably, McCarthy would not count his own books among the lying tomes the father encounters in the burned-out library. Perhaps McCarthy's view is not so different from Jung's, though the harshness of his (linguistic!) critique of language makes it seem quite different. Like Jung, McCarthy would acknowledge that language can work to overcome our fallen condition, but that redemption requires a re-deemed language, a language more in tune with the unconscious and ancient origins of our being. The enigmatic figure that Billy encoun-ters in the epilogue to *Cities of the Plain* suggests something like this in his attempts to explain the content of dreams: "It is not the case that there are small men in your head holding a conversation. There is no sound. So what language is that? In any case this was a deep dream for the dreamer and in such dreams there is a language that is older than the spoken word at all. The idiom is another specie and with it there can be no lie or no dissemblance of the truth" (281). And Quijada, in the same discussion quoted above, speaking of a type of Mexican folk song, the *corrido*, tells Billy that "the corrido is the poor man's history. It does not owe its allegiance to the truths of history but to the truths of men. It tells the tale of that solitary man who is all men" (386). The languages of dream and poetry function truthfully because, as Jung has it in the passage quoted above, they emerge from "that part of our psyche which is pre-existent to consciousness and that ... therefore cannot be considered an invention of consciousness." McCarthy eschews the rejection of truth typical of poststructuralism and deconstruction. His critique is ultimately not of language, but of the fallen, tragic animal that substitutes the symbol for the real.

Koestler, Arthur (1905–1983)

In his notes for *Suttree* McCarthy typed the following reference to Arthur Koestler's *The Sleepwalkers: A History of Man's Changing Vision of the Universe*: "Sleepwalkers p396 Unspeakable polygons of discord." The note refers to Koestler's discussion of Johannes Kepler's Renaissance riff on the Pythagorean notion of the music of the spheres, and although I cannot find a corresponding allusion in either *Suttree* or *Blood Meridian*, to which some of the notes on the same page refer, Koestler's philosophical concerns in his history of Western cosmology tally with McCarthy's interests in science, and, in particular, in the relationship between science and a desacralized modern world of nuclear power in which human beings have become alienated from their cosmic milieu.

Koestler is best known for his novel *Darkness at Noon*, a now classic indictment of Soviet totalitarianism, but his oeuvre encompasses explorations of science, psychology, history, and aesthetics. Koestler's precocious engagement with the intellectual movements of his time — communism, anticommunism, Freudianism, and Zionism, to name a few — led to encounters with the intellectual movers of his time. Anne Applebaum, in her review for *The New York Review of Books* of Michael

Scammell's biography of Koestler, mentions Langston Hughes, W. H. Auden, Bertolt Brecht, Walter Benjamin, Thomas Mann, Dylan Thomas (with whom he got drunk), Mary McCarthy, George Orwell, Cyril Connolly, Noel Coward, Jean Paul Sartre, Simone de Beauvoir (with whom he slept), Timothy Leary (with whom he got high), and Sidney Hook. Koestler's illustrious life ended with a notorious death: a double-suicide with his wife Cynthia. He was seventy-seven and dying of leukemia, she fifty-five and healthy. This unseemly parting arrangement, as well as his bequest of a large portion of his estate to the funding of research into parapsychology—in his final years he was fascinated by ESP—have not served his posthumous reception well. However, *Darkness at Noon* retains its place, along with Orwell's *1984*, as a classic repudiation of totalitarianism.

The Sleepwalkers, which McCarthy was reading during the writing of *Suttree* and *Blood Meridian*, is a history of astronomy and cosmology from Pythagoras to Isaac Newton. George Steiner, writing about Koestler in *The New Yorker*, describes the book as "one of the rare feats of convincing imaginative re-creation of great science, of the poetic logic of discovery" (270). The philosopher Stephen Toulmin, in a review published in *The Journal of Philosophy*, summarizes the thesis as follows: "The conclusion he puts forward at the end of the book is that modern science is trying too hard to be rational. Scientists have been at their best when they allowed themselves to behave as 'sleepwalkers,' instead of trying too earnestly to ratiocinate" (502). Toulmin, like Steiner, gives high marks to Koestler's treatment of Kepler in the passage that McCarthy quotes.

According to Koestler, Kepler found harmonious geometrical proportions throughout the natural world. These harmonies were "the archetypes of universal order, from which the planetary laws, the harmonies of music, the drift of the weather, and the fortunes of man are derived" (394–395). Kepler believed that some geometrical ratios were concordant, while others were discordant. The harmonies are discovered through geometrical reasoning. Here is Koestler's explanation: "Thus the pure archetypal harmonies, and their echoes, the musical consonances, are generated by dividing the circle by means of construable, regular polygons; whereas the 'unspeakable' polygons [according to Koestler, polygons that cannot be constructed with a compass and ruler] produce discordant sounds, and are useless in the scheme of the universe" (396). These are the "unspeakable polygons of discord" in McCarthy's notes. Four lines up from this note, McCarthy wrote "G major clashes with purple," which, if it belongs in the thought-cluster recorded on this page, suggests that McCarthy was reflecting on aesthetic harmony and discord, both in sensual and cosmic terms. We also see such reflections in his interest in Wyndham Lewis and Michel Foucault (see entries for Lewis and Foucault in this chapter), writers whose work touches on aesthetic problems related to dynamism and stasis (Lewis), and order and chaos (madness and folly) in art. Here McCarthy seems to be recording his interest in the contrast between harmony and discord as both aesthetic and metaphysical polarities.

In addition, this note is an early indication of McCarthy's now well-known interest in science, and in particular his interest, revealed during his interview with Oprah Winfrey, in the psychology of scientific discovery. In a clip that was not aired on her regular broadcast, but was posted on her website, McCarthy commented on the relationship between the unconscious and scientific discovery, noting the famous story of the German chemist Friedrich Kekulé, whose discovery of the ringlike structure of benzene was prompted by a dream of the ouroboros—the mythical snake eating its own tail. McCarthy's linking of scientific discovery with the unconscious accords with Koestler's thesis in *The Sleepwalkers*, which is that scientific breakthroughs, like artistic inspiration, often emerge as much from nonrational intuitions as from rational procedures, from the "unconscious, pre-rational layers of the self" (531). Koestler thus claims that it is "a perverse mistake to identify the religious need solely with intuition and emotion, science solely with the logical and rational," since "both branches of the cosmic quest originate in the same source" (531). Although it is unclear whether those discordant polygons found their way into McCarthy's published works—and if they did, in precisely what way—his interest in Koestler's foray into cosmology and creativity is not hard to fathom.

Lampedusa, Giuseppe Tomasi di (1896–1957)

McCarthy typed a quotation from this Italian novelist's *The Leopard* in his notes for *Suttree*: "2 'gleamed motionless as those of statues and like them a little cruel'" (Box 30, Folder 1).

The Leopard is a novel about the response of its protagonist, Don Fabrizio Corbera, prince of Salina, to the decline of the Italian aristocracy and the shift toward liberalism in politics and economics. According to Augustus Pallotta, in his entry on Giuseppe Tomasi di Lampedusa for the *Dictionary of Literary Biography*, Don Fabrizio warily contemplates the changes occurring around him but cherishes the stability and traditions of the aristocracy. The fragment McCarthy quotes comes from a description of the beautiful Angelica, the daughter of an "aggressive and socially ambitious entrepreneur who symbolizes Italy's new ruling class." The courtship of Angelica by Don Fabrizio's nephew offers an instance of the conflict between the old and new orders. McCarthy's quotation comes from a sentence in *The Leopard* that reads, "Under a mass of raven hair, curling in gentle waves, her green eyes *gleamed motionless as those of statues, and like them a little cruel*" (Lampedusa 77, emphasis added).

According to Pallotta, Don Fabrizio echoes Lampedusa's own views, and although "he believes in the desirability of social progress ... he does not believe in the attainment of genuine equality and a classless society. His pessimism is nurtured by the realization that individuals are motivated by selfish interests, not egalitarianism or a sense of community, even as they seemingly strive for social justice." This conclusion sounds very much like McCarthy's comments in a 1992 interview with Richard B. Woodward: "I think the notion that the species can be improved in some way, that everyone could live in harmony, is a really dangerous idea." In addition to its concerns with historical change, *The Leopard* also touches on many of the themes that were prominent in the literature of midcentury existentialism, which would also have appealed to McCarthy. Pallotta noted that "the final three chapters of *Il Gattopardo* [the original title for *The Leopard*] are permeated with a sense of alienation, impending death, and insistent, underlying questions about the meaning of existence." These concerns also permeate *Suttree*, and they account for McCarthy's interest in *The Leopard* (for a discussion of the significance of those statue-like eyes, see the entry for Wyndham Lewis in this chapter).

The Leopard may have also influenced the organization of *Blood Meridian*, a possibility made plausible by the frequent overlap between notes for that novel and *Suttree*. Like *Blood Meridian*, *The Leopard* delineates sections within each chapter below its chapter headings. For instance, chapter 1 of *The Leopard* features, among several others, the following section breaks: "Rosary and introduction to the Prince—The garden and the dead soldier—Dinner—A carriage to Palermo" (13). Obviously, this is a common feature of many books from Lampedusa's era—it was a popular convention among nineteenth-century writers— but it is interesting that a novel that we know McCarthy was interested in at the time he was writing *Blood Meridian* makes use of it.[15]

Lewis, Wyndham (1882–1957)

McCarthy's notes for *Suttree* contain a reference to Wyndham Lewis's *Time and Western Man* (1927): "Time & Western Man (Speng.: Classical man & timelessness—the eyes of the statues)" (Box 19, Folder 14). The quotation refers to Lewis's discussion of Oswald Spengler's distinction, in *The Decline of the West*, between classical (Greek) and Faustian (modern European) understandings of time.

Lewis is probably best known as the founder of the Vorticist movement in the visual arts during the 1920s, for his status as one of the key figures of the modernist movement in both the visual and literary arts, and for his often savagely satirical novels. A brief dalliance with Fascism in the 1930s, which Lewis abandoned when his grasp of the movement became better informed, tainted his reputation, which has never quite recovered ("Lewis, Wyndham"). T. S. Eliot called him "the most fascinating personality of our time" (qtd. in "Lewis, Wyndham"), and W. B. Yeats, commenting on Lewis's irascible contrarianism, wrote, "I do not always hate what he hates and yet I am always glad that he hates" (qtd. in Pritchard 66–67). *Time and Western Man*, a book that Yeats admired (167), is Lewis's gloves-off attack on the obsession with time among contemporary philosophers. Though philosophers are his chief target—Henri Bergson and Alfred North Whitehead are not treated kindly—writers such as Gertrude Stein, James Joyce, and Marcel Proust also call forth Lewis's ire. He critiques the tendency of the "Time-Mind" to replace the classical mentality. The latter privileges space as the root metaphor of intelligence, whereas "the Time-view, the flux" (Lewis xix), is exemplified in philosophies like Whitehead's that privilege time and process. Lewis's purpose is to criticize this view "from the position of the plastic or the visual intelligence" (xix). He devotes a long chapter to Spengler, who is singled out as an especially egregious exemplar of the "Time-mind."

It would be interesting to discover McCarthy's reaction to this book. Greatly admired by one of his literary heroes, Yeats, it offers withering criticisms of another, Joyce (see entries for Joyce in *The Gardener's Son* and this chapter; see also entries for Joseph Gerard Brennan and Peter De Vries in this chapter). Furthermore, Spengler, whom Lewis sets out to eviscerate in his highly entertaining and entirely undiplomatic style, has been a rich source of inspiration for McCarthy. Whatever McCarthy's final verdict on Spengler's organic philosophy of civilizations and their cycles of birth and death, there is no question that his imagination has been shaped by Spengler's brand of historical pessimism and apocalyptic prophecy. The title of his first western, *Blood Meridian: Or the Evening Redness in the West,* is nothing short of an homage to Spengler's *Decline of the West.*

Lewis, despite his critical stance toward Spengler, shared the German historian's pessimistic assessment of the West's prospects. McCarthy also shares it. He told David Kushner, in an interview for *Rolling Stone,* that rather than suffering slow extinction through ecological catastrophe, "we're going to do ourselves in first" (52). So while McCarthy's broad agreement with Spengler's dark vision seems assured, the question of his agreement with details remains open, and McCarthy's interest in Lewis's highly critical evaluation of Spengler suggests a certain flexibility in his own thinking about him.

McCarthy's note on *Time and Western Man* references two passages from Lewis's discussion of Spengler's preference for dynamic—and, more importantly, organic—Faustian art over static classical art. Note the reference to the "eyes of the statues": "Whenever a Classical "thing" *comes to life,* then it immediately becomes 'Musical.' When the greek statue, for instance, came to life in Byzantium or Alexandria by receiving soulful eyes that '*entered into*' the onlooker—then it is Faustian and non-Classical" (269, emphasis in original). Throughout this section, Lewis criticizes Spengler's suggestion that there is something lifeless about classical art, with its emphasis on space and static form, as opposed to Faustian art, which, with its awareness of the dynamic flux of existence, imbues life into artistic forms. Lewis identifies the representation of eyes as one of the ways Spengler marks the distinction. The following passage, in which Lewis describes Spengler's contrast between classical and Faustian art, made a deep impression on McCarthy:

> The attic statue "neither speaks nor looks." The sculptor makes its eyes *blind*. It is a *thing*, really, an object among other objects. It is, in short, "the individual thing," without a "soul." The Greek regarded himself as surrounded by static and soulless "things"; whereas we, and our "Faustian" brothers, regard ourselves as surrounded by "forces," and as dynamically involved in a World-Soul.
>
> In contrast to the "Classical," the byzantine artist supplied his human figures with enormous eyes: "the beholder's sphere is invaded by an action-at-a-distance," emanating from the picture, by means of these fixed and hypnotic, almost living, *eyes*. Art has come to life." (276, emphasis in original)

McCarthy would likely reject both Spengler's invidious comparison between classical and romantic (or Faustian) art and Lewis's equally vociferous partisanship on behalf of classical modes. Both writers rehearse the standard trope of Western criticism of the bifurcation of these two sensibilities, with all the binary oppositions that entails: the spatial versus the temporal, emotion versus reason, static harmony versus kinetic dynamism, to name a few of the ways in which this knife cuts. McCarthy is more interested in these distinctions as poles bracketing a psycho-spiritual continuum.

However, there is no question that his fascination with extreme dissociative states of consciousness (*Suttree*), with chaotic violence (*Blood Meridian*), and with wilderness as a pristine foil to the excessive forms of rational and mechanical order that threaten rural, traditional, and natural orders (*The Orchard Keeper*) all point to an aesthetic prioritizing of the tensions between the two poles of a continuum rather than a vindication of one over the other.

Other references to different writers in McCarthy's notes from the same period suggest that the idea of an aesthetic continuum between, to use the rough-and-ready distinction, classical and romantic sensibilities was of great interest to McCarthy during the period in the mid-1970s when the composition of *Suttree* and *Blood Meridian* overlapped. Specifically, he was drawn to images of art as either formally static or dynamic. For instance, McCarthy's notes for *Suttree* contain a

reference to Lampedusa's *The Leopard* that quotes a passage in which
the eyes of statues feature as a metaphorical description of a character
(see entry for Lampedusa in this chapter for the context of this passage). The italicized portion is what McCarthy quotes in his notes (Box
30, Folder 1): "Under a mass of raven hair, curling in gentle waves, *her
green eyes gleamed motionless as those of statues*, and like them a little
cruel" (Lampedusa 94, emphasis added). Here is an image of art as
static. By contrast, McCarthy also copied into his notes for *Suttree* a
quotation from Flaubert's *The Temptation of St. Anthony* that records
an image of art as dynamic, and as *entering into* the beholder (see
entry for Flaubert in this chapter). The quotation comes from a scene
describing the ascetic monk's time living in a pharaoh's tomb: "All the
fearful pictures on the wall started into hideous life" (Box 19, Folder
14). This image resonates with Lewis's account of Spengler's description of Faustian art as somehow entering into the beholder. Compare
the last sentence of the long quotation from Lewis above with the short
quotation from Flaubert—Lewis: "Art has come to life"; Flaubert: "All
the fearful pictures on the wall started into hideous life." McCarthy
was clearly fascinated by the two artistic polarities explored in differing ways by Lewis, Spengler, and Flaubert.

The third source for McCarthy's speculations on the difference between static and dynamic forms of art, and the psychological states
that correspond to each, is Foucault's *Madness and Civilization* (see
entry for Foucault in this chapter), in which Foucault discusses Brueghel's painting of St. Anthony's temptation as an exemplar of how
Renaissance artists opened themselves up to psychological explorations of nonrational states of consciousness, an exploration not available to medieval artists or to the post-Renaissance neoclassical art of
the Enlightenment. Flaubert's *Temptation*, a major influence from
this period, records the desert saint's descent into disordered states
of mind. Clearly, McCarthy was deeply interested in how art functions
as a catalyst for psychological exploration and in its relationship to
both order and chaos. *Blood Meridian* descends into the vertiginous
purlieus of the latter pole of consciousness with an abandon that led
McCarthy's friend Edward Abbey to write, in a letter, that the book
caused him "to dread not a little for the safety of your soul" (see entry
for Abbey in this chapter).

McCarthy's deep fascination with science indicates that he places great stock in the rigorous and rational search for knowledge, and his strong belief in a moral order, at least as a desiderata, suggests that he espouses an ethical comportment that sheds light into the darkness of the world. However, there is no question that he sees great value in brave excursions into the darker regions of the mind and of human experience. The father and his son in *The Road* are "carrying the fire," the same fire, one supposes, that Sheriff Bell's father is carrying in the horn in the dream that concludes *No Country for Old Men*. But one gets the sense that, for McCarthy, that fire is always in danger of going out, that it is a fragile inheritance that must survive in the midst of great darkness.

The fragility of goodness is related to McCarthy's tragic sense of the transience of all things. This melancholy preoccupation with transience, in the final analysis, puts him in the camp of Lewis's despised "Time-philosophers." McCarthy believes, like Bergson and Whitehead, and like Spengler, that the unstable flux of time carries all along with it, that process, rather than stasis—becoming, rather than being—constitutes the fundamental reality. Suttree, for instance, tells the priest who administers the Eucharist to him during his recovery from typhoid fever that "nothing ever stops moving" (461). The wise gypsy that Billy encounters near the end of *The Crossing* is also a time-philosopher, one who rejects humanity's attempt to hold the flux of experience at bay. Commenting on the power of photographs, he tells Billy that "what he came to see was that as the kinfolk in their fading stills could have no value save in another's heart so it was with that heart also in another's in a terrible and endless attrition and of any other value there was none. Every representation was an idol. Every likeness a heresy. In their images they had thought to find some small immortality but oblivion cannot be appeased" (413).

This is not nihilism. Value is real. The light men and women carry in their hearts is real. But "oblivion cannot be appeased." McCarthy is often most poignant when he evokes this motif of the inevitable diminishment of all good things as time marches on in its endless flux. There is genuine pathos in this vision, requiring as it does a kind of stoic resolve before the grim realities of humanity's condition. The values McCarthy celebrates are spiritual values, but the image of the matrix, the *matriz*, or cosmic womb, that seems so significant in *The Crossing*, is not an image of a static, Platonic order, but of a dynamic reality that is more like the Taoist notion of a pregnant emptiness that is the womb and tomb of all that comes to be and of all that passes away. The recognition of this metaphysical reality explains why the gypsies, as the leader tells Billy, "were men of the road" (413). Nothing ever stops moving. The peripatetic philosopher, generous of heart, but alive to the transience of his condition, makes transience his guiding principle as he stays on the move (see the entry for Bruce Chatwin in the chapter on correspondence for a discussion of the virtues of a nomadic life).

Lissner, Ivar (1909–1967)

Ivar Lissner, known to English-speaking readers as the author of several books about ancient history and culture, including *The Living Past*, *The Silent Past*, and *Man, God, and Magic*, was known in Germany as a journalist—he edited the periodical *Kristall*—and, more notoriously, as a Nazi spy during World War II (Corleis 59–60). McCarthy mentions him in his notes for *Suttree* (Box 19, Folder 14). On a typed page, which also contains references to Oswald Spengler and Arthur Koestler (see entries for Spengler and also for Koestler in this chapter), McCarthy wrote: "Lissner p36 The Ram in the blossoming tree." This is a reference to Lissner's book *The Living Past* (1957), a sweeping global history of the ancient world, both east and west. The passage McCarthy noted appears in Lissner's discussion of Leonard Woolley's excavation of the royal cemetery in the ruins of Ur, where the remains of kings, queens, and their sacrificed servants were found alongside valuable artifacts. The passage reads, "Woolley found many other objects: golden daggers, axes, lance heads, carriage shafts and bridle rings, and, finally, the famous 'Ram in the Blossoming Tree,' a magnificent work of art made of precious metals and colored stones" (page 34 in the edition cited in the bibliography). The page from McCarthy's notes on which this reference appears contains material related to both *Suttree* and *Blood Meridian*, though I cannot find a direct correlation between the Lissner note and either of those novels. We know that the notes also refer to *Blood Meridian* because one line from them contains a simile—"Willow leaves like jade dace"—that appears on page 193 of *Blood Meridian*—"The Vandiemendlander raised and cocked the pistol. In the clear waters of the pool willow leaves turned like jade dace" (next to the note McCarthy typed "ck," which often serves as a reminder to check whether he has already used a word or phrase in another novel that he is working on simultaneously). McCarthy's interest in Lissner's book is in keeping with his efforts to create a sense that contemporary events take place against a backdrop of deep time, a sense that the past, even the archaic past, profoundly informs the present.

The italicized opening of *Suttree* provides a striking example of this evocation of the archaic past in his descriptions of Knoxville: "*Old stone walls unplumbed by weathers, lodged in their striae fossil bones, limestone scarabs rucked in the floor of this once inland sea*" (3). The buildings are "*like a rampart to a farther world forsaken, old purposes forgot*" (3). The river is "*afreight with the past*," and the ancestors of those who now live by its side, "*old teutonic forebears*," reenact the "*dramas and parables*" of their "*semitic chapbook*" (4). In *Blood Meridian* the judge is something of an archaeologist: "In his lap he held the leather ledgerbook and he took up each piece, flint or potsherd or tool of bone, and deftly sketched it into the book.... His fingers traced the impression of old willow wicker on a piece of pottery clay and he put this into his book with nice shadings, an economy of pencil strokes" (140). At the site of the Anasazi ruins, in one of his periodic Chautauqua meetings, he tells his audience that though long gone, the ancient tribe is "not so dead" (142). Referring to the ancient dwellings, he tells them, "Here are the dead fathers. Their spirit is entombed in the stone. It lies upon the land with the same weight and the same ubiquity," for "who builds in stone seeks to alter the structure of the universe and so it was with these masons however primitive their works may seem to us" (146).

The power of the past, its insistent pressures on the present, even if only as "myth, legend, dust," is one of McCarthy's thematic touchstones, and his interest in Lissner accords with what we see in his fiction.

Mailer, Norman (1923–2007)

Norman Mailer, author of, among many other works of both fiction and nonfiction, *The Naked and the Dead* and the Pulitzer Prize-winning *The Executioner's Song*, is cited once in a holograph marginal note in an early draft of *Suttree*. McCarthy was contemplating the mot juste for the male ejaculate and wrote down three possibilities: gyzm, jissom, and gism. He wrote Mailer's name next to the last one, and, indeed, Mailer prefers that spelling in his 1967 novel *Why Are We in Vietnam?*, about a teenage boy's hunting trip prior to his departure for the war. Mailer's work — rough, vulgar, masculine, and violent — would likely have appealed to the young McCarthy, who was much impressed by writers like Henry Miller, Nelson Algren, and J. P. Donleavy. This particular bit of marginalia demonstrates how minutely McCarthy considers word choices and reveals a novelist attentive to the work of contemporaries. The curious reader will want to know that McCarthy chose jissom.

The Malleus Maleficarum *(1487)*

In *Suttree*, McCarthy's love of the gothic finds expression in the frightening Mother She, the witch Suttree consults for insight into his own spiritual condition, and whose magical philter induces one of his hallucinogenic trips. His notes for *Suttree* (Box 19, Folder 14) show that he consulted *The Malleus Maleficarum*, or *The Witch's Hammer*, as part of his research for the character. At the top of a page of notes related to Mother She, McCarthy wrote "The Witch's Hammer — 1487," and underneath that, "Her philtres, the appurtenances to her trade" (Box 19, Folder 14). *The Malleus Maleficarum* is a manual for those tasked with the official investigation and prosecution of witches following a papal bull of 1484. The authors, Heinrich Kramer and James Sprenger, were Dominican priests who served as the chief inquisitors for Germany during the fierce persecution of witches following the church's directive to tamp down on heresy and various forms of sorcery (P. Hughes 178). According to Pennethorne Hughes, in his history of witchcraft, the book is "a most hideous document" that sent "to a writhing death thousands of misguided, superstitious, and ignorant souls, of whom only a few were perhaps actuated consciously by the motives and beliefs it sought to destroy" (180).[16]

The notes that follow the reference to *The Witch's Hammer* contain trial runs at the scene in which Ab Jones, accompanied by Suttree, visits Mother She in order to seek guidance in his quest for vengeance against the abusive, racist cop Tarzan Quinn. Mother She pulls out a bag of small animal bones and casts them on the table to read the pattern, only to discover that the message is for Suttree, who later returns to seek insight into his own anguished and alienated spiritual condition. What is interesting about McCarthy's notes for this scene is how much they reveal his thinking about the subject of witchcraft and divination, which both the novel and notes suggest he takes seriously. One note, a sentence excised from the published work, reads, "There are lacunae in the nights dakr [*sic*] archives which account for her effects" (Box 19, Folder 14). Another contains an excised description of the scattered bones that is wordier, and probably thereby less effective, than the published description: "He waited for her to fetch down her purse of bones to see what Rorschach constructions might his story tell, a figure in a carpet, a figure dug from a cave floor composed of tiered fossils sunk in improbable juxtaposition, taxonic absurdities, enemies of order."

Finally, on the same page we find actual commentary on the scene, philosophical speculation on the nature of Mother She's "magic." This kind of direct commentary is exceedingly rare in McCarthy's notes, which are usually composed of lists of words, phrases, sentences, and occasionally whole paragraphs that he is contemplating for use in the work at hand. The absence of direct commentary, outlines, planning, notes-to-self, and other techniques for organizing ideas suggests that when McCarthy is writing fiction he *thinks fictionally*, which is to say that he thinks in the voice of the imagined narrator or in the voice of imagined characters, not in the voice of Cormac McCarthy. It suggests that for Cormac McCarthy the act of creation involves a kind of immersion in the work and concomitant effacement of his own consciousness that is not far removed from his description of the creative process to Oprah Winfrey in 2007: "Some people say do you, do you plot everything out? And I said no. That would be death. I mean, you can't, you can't plot things out. You just, you just have to trust in, you know, wherever it comes from."

Later in the same interview he described the inspiration for *The Road*. According to McCarthy, he and his son John were in a hotel in downtown El Paso, and while looking out the window he had a vision of the town reduced to a wasteland: "I just had this image of these fires up on the hill and everything being laid to waste and I thought a lot about my little boy. And so I wrote those pages and that was the end of it. Then about four years later, I was in Ireland and I woke up one morning and I realized that it wasn't two pages of notebook. It was a book. And it was about that man and that little boy." If this account is accurate, the novel never existed in any kind of schematic form. From vision to narrative, McCarthy describes a seamless, and to a great extent unconscious process, but one that unfolded entirely through the forms of the imagination. This *is* thinking, but through images, scenes, and dialogue, rather than through premises and propositions.

Consequently, it is surprising to find a note that comments on some aspect of the narrative from outside of the rhetorical elements native to storytelling. But contained within the notes on Mother She is what appears to be McCarthy's voice, a voice surprisingly discordant in what is, after all, his own writing. Here is Cormac McCarthy's explanation of Mother She's witchcraft: "Her interpretation of the boneblot is a (manifestation of her psyche), but in her the psychic and pneumatic elements are interchanged by virtue of her gift so that she has delved into the soul of the earth and picked out Jones to be (as object) subsumed into her vision and to serve as surrogate of her MOHP. Hence her trance a mechanics for the cessation of her will" (Box 19, Folder 14).

The psychologist Gregory Bateson distinguishes between what he calls First Order and Second Order Thinking. First Order thinking is immediate and intuitive. Second Order thinking is conceptual and abstract, operating at a remove from, and as a commentary upon, the contents of First Order thinking (see Bateson's *Steps to an Ecology of Mind*). Mother She is, to use McCarthy's terminology, a MOHP, a manifestation of *his* psyche, and like the fires on the hills above El Paso, a First Order phenomenon. The explanation of Mother She's powers is decidedly Second Order, and it's not the kind of thing McCarthy does very often in his notes. He doesn't think about writing a story, he thinks through and in the story.[17]

Maryland: A Guide to the Old Line State *(1940)*

McCarthy cites this book in Box 30, Folder 1, which contains photocopied fragments from an early *Suttree* manuscript. Part history and part travel guide, the book was compiled by the Writers' Program of the Work Projects Administration in the State of Maryland. The reference is contained in the following fragment: "At this time Knoxville suffered the periodic visits of a demented person known as ..." Next to the fragment, he typed "Maryland Write[ers'] Project." The passage from the Maryland book describes an incident that took place in Cumberland, Maryland, and appears in the chapter dedicated to that city: "For several years Cumberland suffered from time to time the visits of a demented Virginian named Harris, who would walk naked through the streets prophesying the wrath of heaven. On one occasion he paraded up the aisle of a church. At last his relatives were prevailed upon to keep him home. Shortly afterwards, however, the city met with a visitation that some regarded as a fulfillment of Harris' prophecies" (266). The visitation was a disastrous fire that destroyed seventy-five buildings. "Fears of celestial wrath" briefly abated, but were "roused to fever pitch by the unusually splendid showers of Leonids of that year" (266).

In *Suttree*, Cumberland becomes Knoxville, and the harbinger of wrath is no longer fire, but bats falling from the sky. The "demented Virginian" becomes a rabid madman. It is fascinating to consider, apart from the truly delicious variety of McCarthy's reading habits, that this short paragraph from a guide to Maryland, a product of New Deal largesse, would become the seed from which one of McCarthy's funniest episodes (call it "Harrogate and the Bats") would grow. While McCarthy has dramatically changed the story, the demented Virginian, like a palimpsest, is there in the opening sentences of the episode: "It is told first by Oceanfrog Frazer to idlers at the store. How a madman came down from the town and through the steep and vacant lots above the river" (207). Something about this short anecdote from the Maryland travel guide stayed with McCarthy and worked its way, consciously or unconsciously, into *Suttree*.

Massinger, Philip (1583–1640)

Philip Massinger was an English playwright known for his politically charged and morally didactic stage dramas. He wrote for the King's Men during the reign of Charles I, composing over fifty plays in his lifetime, many in collaboration with John Fletcher. Never widespread, interest in Massinger has fluctuated over time, but T. S. Eliot, a great maker and breaker of literary reputations, seems to have finished him off with a 1920 hit piece (Edwards n.p.). McCarthy refers to Massinger on a page of notes for *Suttree* pertaining to the motif of doubleness that haunts the novel. Suttree's frequent encounters with apparitional doppelgangers (during his "vision quest" in the mountains, for instance), and his anxious consciousness of his stillborn twin as a counterpart to his own broken psyche, his sense of being a "gauche carbon" (14), are examples of this motif. The Massinger reference appears on a page labeled "Dexter—Sinister—Coriolis" (Box 19, Folder 14) that features notes on leftwardness in nature (see the entry for Joseph Wood Krutch in *Blood Meridian* for a longer discussion of this theme). McCarthy typed a quotation from Massinger's play *The Virgin-Martyr* (written in collaboration with Thomas Dekker): "Left-ey'd knight of the antipodes Philip Massinger." The subject of the play is religious persecution, driven on in this case by a devil manipulating events in the guise of a powerful political adviser (Harpax).

In the scene McCarthy quotes from, Harpax is in conversation with his two servants in evil, Hircius, a whoremaster, and Spungius, a drunkard. Asking them how they like serving him elicits the following reply from Hircius: "I would not give up the cloak of your service, to meet the splayfoot estate of any *left-eyed knight above the antipodes*; because they are unlucky to meet" (84, emphasis added). McCarthy no doubt enjoyed the phrasing, but appearing as it does alongside scientific observations about Coriolis forces and dextral phenomena, it seems more like a research note on the subject of leftwardness than a record of aesthetic appreciation. (The Coriolis force, a concept in physics, has to do with the forces that affect rotating masses.)

Melville, Herman (1819–1891)

SEE ALSO *THE STONEMASON* AND *WHALES AND MEN*

Box 19, Folder 13, labeled "Left from Suttree," contains a typed page of notes, one line of which reads, "'Federated along one keel' Melville." This is a quotation from chapter 27 of *Moby-Dick*, titled "Knights and Squires." The chapter describes the ship's mates and their harpooneers as analogous (though the irony is pronounced) to the medieval figures of the chapter title. The quotation comes from a paragraph describing the diverse crew of the *Pequod*: "They were nearly all Islanders in the Pequod, *Isolatoes* too, I call such, not acknowledging the common continent of men, but each *Isolato* living on a separate continent of his own. Yet now *federated along one keel*, what a set these Isolatoes were!" (107, emphasis added). The connection to *Suttree* is unclear, but McCarthy was likely thinking about his "Western" when he copied this quotation. It becomes a muted allusion in *Blood Meridian*: "Each man scanned the terrain and the movements of the least of creatures were logged into their collective cognizance until they were *federated with invisible wires* of vigilance and advanced upon that landscape with a single resonance" (226, emphasis added). The presence of the quotation in both his notes and in the novel itself confirms the sense of so many readers that McCarthy had *Moby-Dick* very much in mind when writing *Blood Meridian*.

Notes for *Suttree* do sometimes contain notes for *Blood Meridian*, which McCarthy was working on simultaneously in the late 1970s. For instance, Box 19, Folder 12, contains a typed sheet of notes labeled "Suttree Check List." McCarthy wrote "WESTERN" in the margin, though the reference is unclear. The same box and folder contain a page of handwritten notes for *Suttree* with two references to McCarthy's western novel. The first is "Ck [check] West?" and is followed by "things become so burdened with meaning that their forms are dimmed," which is a quotation from Michel Foucault's *Madness and Civilization* (see entry for Foucault) and is in fact used in *Blood Meridian*. When the kid and Tobin encounter the judge and the fool in the desert, they are described as being "like things whose very portent renders them ambiguous. Like things *so charged with meaning that their forms are dimmed* (281–282, emphasis added). On that same page, he wrote, "Stars jostled on a black and seamless sea See West," which does appear in *Blood Meridian* as, "They moved on and the stars jostled and arced across the firmament and died beyond the inkblack mountains" (46).

A holograph note at the top of an excised fragment from the Reese episode of *Suttree* also refers to *Moby-Dick*—chapter 89, "Fast Fish and Loose Fish." The note reads: "Trover (Melville Whale—Trover)" (Box 30, Folder 1). I cannot find a referent for this. The fragment is from a very early draft of *Suttree*, and consequently could have been written during the composition of any of McCarthy's first three novels. However, John Sepich's invaluable concordances to McCarthy's works do not show the word "trover" appearing in any of the novels. The word appears in *Moby-Dick* in a discussion of proprietary laws related to the capture of whales: a loose fish is potentially anyone's catch, even if one ship has already wounded the whale in an initial attempt at capture, while a fast fish belongs to the ship that has the whale fast against it.

The account in *Moby-Dick* is a humorous critique of man's desire for ownership: "Some fifty years ago there was a curious case of *whale-trover litigated* in England, wherein the plaintiffs set forth that after a hard chase of a whale in the Northern seas, they (the plaintiffs) had succeeded in harpooning the fish" (308, emphasis added). The plaintiffs had to abandon the whale, only to see it captured by another boat. The *Oxford English Dictionary* defines a trover as "an action at law to recover the value of personal property illegally converted by another to his own use." Melville cynically suggests that much of human life can be understood following the legal principle of fast and loose fish: "What is the great globe itself but a Loose-Fish? And what are you, reader, but a Loose-Fish and a Fast-Fish, too?" (310). Melville's aside on a principle of maritime law turns out to be a comic turn on Hegel's master and slave.

Miller, Henry (1891–1980)

SEE ALSO CORRESPONDENCE

McCarthy's admiration for Henry Miller is evident in the numerous references to the notorious writer in his notes, in letters to J. Howard Woolmer, and in admiring comments McCarthy made about Miller during his interview with Oprah Winfrey in 2007. *Suttree* is often cited as evidence of McCarthy's artistic indebtedness to Joyce and Faulkner, but given McCarthy's admiration for Miller, the writer of the infamous *Tropic of Cancer* should be considered an influence on the novel as well. In fact, excised early drafts and fragments suggest that Miller loomed large in McCarthy's imagination when he first conceived the idea for the novel. As bawdy as *Suttree* can be, earlier versions were much racier, featuring a robustly obscene spirit that nettled McCarthy's editor, Albert Erskine. Erskine's efforts to clean up the final work appear to have been mostly fruitful.

In fact, *Suttree* is in some respects Henry Miller *manqué*. The kind of grotesque sexual comedy for which Miller is known is mostly absent from the final version of *Suttree*, but it is very much in evidence in earlier drafts.[18] Suttree's interlude with the prostitute (Joyce) is almost an homage to Miller, and he kept these scenes despite Erskine's fervent wish that he cut them: "I know by now that for reasons of your own (and they may be better than I can see) that you are determined to keep the whore-keeping-Suttree bit and the mussel-gathering bit ... but I'd like to repeat that I believe they not only don't pull their weight but might even sink the boat—a boat that deserves to float" (letter to McCarthy, 27–29 May 1977, Box 19, Folder 1).

Erskine's protestations were one curb on McCarthy's imitations of Miller, but the final, published version of *Suttree*, a work that McCarthy labored over for two decades, is one that is far removed from anything in Miller's oeuvre. The difference lies in McCarthy's serious commitment, evident in all of his work, to addressing the moral and spiritual potential of human beings even in the midst of evil and squalor. Edwin Arnold was one of the first critics to appreciate this aspect of McCarthy's work. In an essay that reads McCarthy's works as moral parables, he makes a strong case for understanding *Suttree* as a spiritual journey: "Religion, Faith, God, Death, Grace are constant topics of conversation between Suttree and such figures as the ragpicker, the goatman, Daddy Watson, the street evangelists and numerous strangers he encounters.... By the end he has entered [the] world of the spirit and has acknowledged its power" (60).

Indeed, the Christian iconography of death and resurrection (the body in the houseboat, the waterboy, the car that stops even though Suttree has not flagged a ride) confirm the fundamentally spiritual nature of Suttree's journey. Although Miller's work also addresses humanity's spiritual condition, McCarthy's novels foreground these issues in ways that preclude the full adoption of Miller's aesthetics. None of this diminishes McCarthy's clear enthusiasm for Miller. Influence is always filtered through intellectual, moral, spiritual, and aesthetic dispositions that may be quite foreign to the source of inspiration. I have located two references to Miller in the McCarthy papers and two in the Woolmer letters.

The first reference from the papers is on a leaf titled by McCarthy "Suttree Check Sheet," located in Box 19, Folder 12. At the top of the page a holograph note reads: "Tues H. Miller 1 December / ?." I have not been able to determine what McCarthy is referring to here.

The second reference to Miller is located in Box 19, Folder 13, marked "Left from Suttree." On a typed page of notes, a holograph note in the upper right corner reads "Miller 'gnomic aorist' 1st person histor[ic?]." Though the note references Miller, McCarthy is actually citing a letter written to Miller from the novelist Lawrence Durrell. Composed in 1937, the letter describes the style in which Durrell's novel *The Black Book* was written: "In order to destroy time I use the historic present a great deal—not to mention the gnomic aorist" (55). In discussing McCarthy's holograph note, Bryan Giemza explains that "the gnomic aorist is used in Greek to present timeless, general facts, and one sees it in *Suttree* with a shift from past action to present tense timeless" (212). Giemza provides, as an example, the following quotation from the novel: "Somewhere in the gray wood by the river is the huntsman" (471).

Durrell's strategy to destroy time through the use of an unusual tense must have been appealing to McCarthy, whose own work often seems to function on two levels, one deeply imbued with the modes of realism and naturalism, the other employing archetypical and allegorical modes. That second level often carries the spiritual meanings that are central to McCarthy's novels. The line that Giemza quotes is instructive. The huntsman with his hounds compels a reading of *Suttree* as spiritual allegory, and of his journey as one from death to life, fall to grace, sin to redemption. Suttree's exit from Knoxville, read allegorically, resembles a death, burial, and resurrection.[19]

Montaigne, Michel Eyquem de (1533–1592)

SEE ALSO *WHALES AND MEN*

McCarthy quotes Montaigne quoting Seneca in the scene where Suttree is hit over the head with a floor buffer during a bar fight pitting McAnally Flats boys against rival neighborhood toughs. McCarthy identifies the source as the great French essayist in a holograph marginal note in an early draft of the scene (Box 20, Folder 1). It reads, "Roman philosopher after Montaigne." Here is the passage as it appears in the early draft with the quotation italicized:

> He swayed. What he toppled toward was not the black of nothing but an enormous livercolored cunt with prehensile lips that breathed like some warm enormous bivalve. He took a small step, stiffly fending. How to elude this confusion. Work of libidinous deities, and so unlike the Madonna of his desires. Or mother of eternal attendance, maid of dark rain and lamps against the night. Plump softly cloven powdered breasts and fragile claviclebones alabastrine above the rich velvet of her gown. *What man is such a coward he would not rather fall once than remain forever tottering?* (Box 20, Folder 1, emphasis added)

The published version is roughly the same, despite some streamlining and cleaning. The quotation comes from Montaigne's essay "To Flee from Sensual Pleasures at the Price of Life," in which he considers both Stoic and Christian admonitions to reject the sensual pleasures of life, and in some cases life itself, in favor of higher ideals of the good life. He quotes Seneca as advising a young man of power and status to "either quit that life you lead, or quit life altogether. I do indeed counsel you to follow the milder way, and untie rather than break the knot you have so badly tied; provided that if it cannot be otherwise untied, you break it. No man is such a coward that he would not rather fall once than remain forever tottering" (162).

If we are aware of the origin of the epigrammatic maxim, its lofty presence in the midst of one of Suttree's most sordid moments becomes an inside joke, a bit of comic juxtaposition.

Nordau, Max (1849–1923)

McCarthy's notes for *Suttree* contain a reference to Max Nordau with the word "degeneracy" written next to the name (Box 19, Folder 14). Nordau published the international best-seller *Entartung* (*Degeneration*) in 1892. The book, following up on the work of the criminologist Cesare Lombroso, expands the nineteenth-century concept of a degeneration of the human species by charting that degeneration among artists and writers. Everyone from Charles Baudelaire and Oscar Wilde to Leo Tolstoy and Friedrich Nietzsche make the list of degenerate authors (Herman 125). However, the focus of the idea of degeneration was on a perceived increase in industrial societies of criminals, prostitutes, and lunatics. At the heart of the idea is the belief that modern societies were producing human beings who represented a "morbid deviation from an original type" (110). Consider, in this light, the following quotations from the italicized opening of *Suttree*:

> *This city constructed on no known paradigm, a mongrel architecture reading back through the works of man in a brief delineation of the aberrant disordered and mad....*
>
> *We are come to a world within the world. In these alien reaches, these maugre sinks and interstitial wastes that the righteous see from carriage and car another life dreams. Illshapen or black or deranged, fugitive of all order, strangers in everyland.* (3–4)

Or consider this description of Suttree's McAnally companions, which appears during his hallucinated mock trial:

> Mr. Suttree it is our understanding that at curfew rightly decreed by law and in that hour wherein night draws to its proper close and the new day commences and contrary to conduct befitting a person of your station you betook yourself to various low places within the shire of McAnally and there did squander several ensuing years in the company of thieves, derelicts, miscreants, pariahs, poltroons, spalpeens, curmudgeons, clotpolls, murderers, gamblers, bawds, whores, trulls, brigands, topers, tosspots, sots and archsots, lobcocks, smellsmocks, runagates, rakes, and other assorted and felonious debauchees. (457)

That is a delineation of the aberrant disordered and mad.

However, McCarthy's interest in Nordau may have had more influence on *Blood Meridian*, and, as is so often the case, the notes from that novel often overlap with notes for *Suttree*. The same typed page on which the reference to Nordau occurs also contains the name Grannyrat Chambers, a character who makes an appearance in *Blood Meridian*. The best evidence that McCarthy was reading Nordau in his research for his western is Judge Holden, a true believer in the theory of degeneracy. The concept of degeneracy was closely allied with pseudo-scientific physiological notions (Herman 109–110). When Holden first encounters "the idiot," whom he later adopts as his "fool," he conducts a phrenological exam on the man's brother, "holding him by the fore-head while he prodded along the back of his skull with the ball of his thumb" (239). The judge's fascination with the idiot seems in keep-ing with his "point of view" as a scientist, or pseudo-scientist. His ac-count of Black Jackson to the Mexican officer, Sergeant Aguilar, is full of the kind of racist speculations about mankind that often form the backdrop to degeneration theory, particularly as laid out by Arthur de Gobineau, who believed that "all European culture was drawn from a single biological type, the white Aryan or Indo-German," and that mis-cegenation leads to degeneration (Herman 58–59):

> He sketched for the sergeant a problematic career of the man before them, his hands drafting with a marvelous dexterity the shapes of what varied paths conspired here. . . . He adduced for their consideration references to the children of Ham, the lost tribes of Israelites, certain passages from the Greek poets, anthropological speculations as to the propagation of the races in their dispersion and isolation through the agency of geological cataclysm and an assessment of racial traits with respect to climatic and geographical influences. (*Suttree* 84–85)

The overtly racist form of degeneration theory also finds a voice in Cap-tain White, the leader of the filibuster expedition, who laments the re-turn of territory to Mexico after the Mexican War: "And then by God if we didn't give it back. Back to a bunch of barbarians that even the most biased in their favor will admit have no least notion in God's earth of honor or justice or the meaning of republican government" (33). Their degenerate status is underlined by his claim that "the Apaches wont even shoot them. Did you know that? They kill them with rocks" (33).

Although McCarthy's novels, in their sympathy for outcasts and those deemed degenerate or beyond the pale by society, eschew any-thing like the views espoused by Gobineau, Lombroso, or Nordau, it is clear that McCarthy familiarized himself with these nineteenth-century theorists in order to provide proper shading to characters, such as Captain White and Judge Holden, who espouse similar views. It should be noted that the narrative voice that predominates in *Suttree* often expresses something like the horror of human degeneracy found in Nordau and others, and that McCarthy's historical pessimism, which owes so much to Spengler (see entry for Spengler in this chapter), seems open to theories of decline. McCarthy's compassion for suffering humanity distances him, however, from the more virulent forms that philosophies of decline can take.[20]

Pater, Walter (1839–1894)

McCarthy alludes to the English essayist, critic, and champion of aestheticism Walter Pater in an excised fragment from a very early draft of *Suttree* (Box 30, Folder 1). Pater's famous exhortation to burn like a "hard, gemlike flame" echoes in a passage in which McCarthy's protagonist, sometimes called "The Poet" in the earliest drafts of the novel—drafts likely dating to the early 1960s—reflects on the role of the artist in transmuting the tragic materials of life into art. This early protagonist, forerunner of Cornelius Suttree, resembles Stephen Dedalus from Joyce's *Portrait of the Artist as a Young Man* and *Ulysses* more than he does the character found in McCarthy's mature, finished novel. Pater was a major influence on two of McCarthy's literary heroes, Yeats and Joyce, and the latter looms large in both the early and late versions of *Suttree*. It appears that McCarthy set out to write *A Portrait of the Artist* and ended up writing *Ulysses* in Tennessee, since these very early fragments (very few of which remain) reflect an interest in the burgeoning aesthetic consciousness of an artist, whereas the latter reflect a more panoramic interest in the dynamic, sprawling life of an urban metropolis, with a keen eye on its underbelly.

Pater's famous reflections on "success in life," as gauged by the intensity of aesthetic perception and experience, provide the philosophical underpinning for both the allusion and the passage in which it appears—though McCarthy's narrator suggests that the artist's role as witness to the aesthetic vibrancy of life alienates him from its most profound depths. Here is the well-known passage from Pater's conclusion to *The Renaissance*:

Not the fruit of experience, but experience itself, is the end. A counted number of pulses only is given to us of a variegated, dramatic life. How may we see in them all that is to be seen in them by the finest senses? How shall we pass most swiftly from point to point, and be present always at the focus where the greatest number of vital forces unite in their purest energy.... To burn always with this hard, gemlike flame, to maintain this ecstasy, is success in life. (152)

And here is the passage from McCarthy's ur-*Suttree*, composed in the shades of Paterian purple that mar his early forays into the novel:

He must be the hero, the tragic one, a role forever denied me. Whether mortality be stone or star I the chronicler have not to choose. Fate picks her own heroes and the tellers of legend in which these *gemlike figures burn so limpid and brief,* the pursuers at a safe distance of their weblike accretion of failings, bleak turns of fortune, all those minute drags toward perdition which conspire against and inevitably over-whelm the hero and his final expiration in the flooded pyrotechnics of which he alone in death is capable, of these things is the teller barred, for in tracking fate like a stylus he only eludes her. He can never be her child, the darling of her wrath. He is forever deprived of a noble—that is a tragic—life. (Box 30, Folder 1, emphasis added)

In other words, The Poet is no John Grady Cole.

Unsurprisingly, McCarthy's take on Pater's image of life lived to the full emphasizes the tragic nature of such a life. Pater's exhortation to cultivate an exacerbated sensibility in the midst of the Heraclitean flux of sensation has a more stirring ring to it, but the crystallization of ex-perience in the hard, gemlike flame is not possible without a poignant sense of transience, and a note of melancholy hangs over his celebra-tions of aesthetic ecstasy. That melancholy note sounds throughout McCarthy's work. McCarthy's aestheticism, like Pater's, emphasizes the ephemeral quality of beauty. McCarthy cares deeply about beauty, but he seems perpetually sorrowful at how rare and fragile it is, and how vulnerable to time's depredations. His reflections on beauty ex-press what Pater calls the "sense of the splendour of our experience and of its awful brevity" (61).

We find that sense in the following observation from *All the Pretty Horses*: "He thought that in the beauty of the world were hid a secret. He thought the world's heart beat at some terrible cost and that the world's pain and its beauty moved in a relationship of diverging equity and that in this headlong deficit the blood of multitudes might ultimately be exacted for the vision of a single flower" (282). In *The Counselor*, Westray tells the Counselor that "time is not going to stop. ... It's forever. And everything that exists will one day vanish. Forever. And it will take with it every explanation of it that was ever contrived. From Newton and Einstein to Homer and Shakespeare and Michelangelo. Every timeless creation. Your art and your poetry and your science are not even composed of smoke" (61–62). As bleak as Westray's pronouncements are, they affirm rather than deny truth, beauty, and excellence.

Poe, Edgar Allan (1809–1849)

McCarthy wrote "Ulalume?" in the margin of a page from a very early draft of *Suttree* (Box 30, Folder 1). The page on which the reference to Poe appears belongs to the earliest strata of the novel, and though it is impossible to date precisely, it was likely composed in the 1960s, when McCarthy was writing a very different book, one much more self-consciously poetic, even lyrical, whose protagonist appears to have been an artist figure (he is called, in some early fragments, "The Poet"). Even a cursory reading of these early fragments indicates that McCarthy was writing a very bad book. Like *Blood Meridian*, which began as a rather light western, *Suttree*, which McCarthy worked on for two decades, became a different novel at some point during the composition. In the case of both novels, the differences indicate an imaginative gestalt shift. In some of the worst passages of the early *Suttree*, McCarthy took forays into pretentious purple prose.

"Ulalume" is certainly a literary precursor to the passage next to which McCarthy wrote the title of Edgar Allan Poe's poem. The scene describes a kind of dream journey in which an unspecified number of characters ("*Their* path led through a honeysuckle jungle" [Box 30, Folder 1, emphasis added]) travel through a haunted, gothic landscape on a path leading through a cemetery. All of this does echo "Ulalume," with its "dim lake of Auber" and "misty mid region of Weir," and a protagonist whose path leads to the tomb of his lost love. The passage describing the cemetery ends with this reflection: "He knows his own dark lake that lies in a silence where the winds [sic] forbidding fingers are not even heard and deep and cold these waters and the caves she covers where Grindel lurks." (The reference to *Beowulf* is interesting insofar as it is one of several references to the Anglo-Saxon epic in McCarthy's notes for *Suttree* and *Blood Meridian*—see entries for *Beowulf* in this chapter and *Blood Meridian*.) So, like Poe's poem, the early *Suttree* describes a gothic journey that is actually an inward journey, a consultation with Psyche. Like a palimpsest, the published *Suttree* carries faint traces of the *poet*aster stylings of the earliest drafts, but it is difficult to imagine something like the above quotation in the final version of the novel.

McCarthy's devotion to the gothic mode is one of the defining characteristics of his work, and gothic elements are present to some degree in nearly all of his novels, so it is unsurprising that Poe might count among McCarthy's influences.[21] One of the gothic elements in McCarthy's first novel, *The Orchard Keeper*, Arthur Ownby's nightmarish fear of cats, is an homage to Poe's story "The Black Cat."

In one scene Ownby sees a cat in his window during the night, "black in the paler square of the window, a white mark on its face like an inverted gull wing. And the window frame went all black and the room was filling up, the white mark looming and growing" (60). That growing white mark parallels the ghostly cat of the Poe story, which is also black with a white spot, in this case on its chest. The white mark on Poe's cat, like the one on McCarthy's, becomes an object of horror because of its ability to seemingly change shape: "The reader will remember that this mark, although large, had been originally very indefinite; but, by slow degrees . . . it had, at length, assumed a rigorous distinctness of outline" (Poe 602)—the outline of a gallows. The similarities between the two scenes are too close to be coincidence, but the reference to "Ulalume" in a draft of *Suttree* that would have been nearly contemporaneous with *The Orchard Keeper* indicates a literary kinship between the two authors.[22]

Shakespeare, William (1564–1616)

SEE ALSO *BLOOD MERIDIAN* AND *THE ROAD*

In a 2007 interview for *Rolling Stone*, when McCarthy was asked about the writers he admired, he named the usual suspects: Melville, Joyce, Dostoyevsky, and Faulkner. David Kushner, the author of the article, then says that "when [McCarthy] talks of writers he admires, like Shakespeare, there's one quality he says they share in common: soul. 'You can't write good poetry unless you have a soul to express,' he says. And he holds the highest regard for those who express 'the soul of the culture,' as he puts it" (46). Whatever the state of our *geist*, it seems clear that McCarthy aspires to paint on a wide canvas, and there is no question that Shakespeare has been one source of inspiration for McCarthy's sweeping aesthetic vision. From the revenge motif of *The Orchard Keeper* to the echoes of Gloucester in the story of the blind man in *The Crossing*, McCarthy pays homage to the master in big and small ways, and the McCarthy papers contain several references to Shakespeare.

Box 19, Folder 14, which contains notes for *Suttree*, includes a leaf on which McCarthy has typed a quotation from *Hamlet*: "Hamlet (invocation) Nymph on thy orisons be all my sins remembered." The quotation comes from Act 3, Scene 1, when Hamlet has just finished his "To be or not to be" soliloquy and Ophelia enters the room. McCarthy's interest in *Hamlet* is evident throughout *Suttree*, which McCarthy's editor Albert Erskine noted in a letter dated 27 May 1977. Erskine's letter is an impassioned plea for greater economy in the composition of the novel, the elimination of characters who serve no clear purpose, and, most importantly, for clarification of Suttree's character and motivations. In addressing this last point, Erskine notes the novel's *Hamlet* obsession. A viewing of Laurence Olivier's film of the play prompted Erskine's comments:

The reason for the Hamlet aside is that I was brooding about Suttree when I was watching the Dane, and I was struck by what they have in common and what they don't. Both are fascinated by maggots, excrement, decay; but beyond fascination, Suttree seems to relish this constellation. Both are at odds with family, but with a difference: Hamlet has a reason beyond the self-pity the two share. Hamlet is a tragic figure; Suttree only pitiful, and chiefly to himself. Goaded enough, Hamlet puts on quite a heroic performance at the end; Suttree performs the Homeric act (when he is goaded) of sending a squad car into the river, like a true juvenile delinquent, and shortly thereafter takes off on a bus for parts unknown for reasons unspecified. Hamlet is rich and kind to inferiors; Suttree is poor by choice (and oh so proud of the choice), but offer him money from any source and he'll take it and blow it on the symbols of what he has piously rejected, dropping a buck or so into a blind man's hat to show how good, deep down, he is, how generous, how unlike his evil father or his evil uncle, whose addiction to drink (God save us) Suttree is somewhat disapproving of. (Box 19, Folder 1)

I quote the letter at length because it seems passionately just about the shortcomings of Cornelius Suttree. Whether these are *aesthetic* shortcomings in the novel, as Erskine seems to imply, is another question, but who could disagree with the evaluation of Suttree's deep flaws?

However, *Suttree*, despite McCarthy's obvious homage (the italicized opening quotes Act 5, Scene 2, line 342, when the narrator, describing the decay of the West, says, "The rest indeed is silence" [5]), is a very different work from *Hamlet*, one with a very different purpose, something Erskine's otherwise astute letter seems to miss. *Suttree* is not a tragedy, but rather a comedy, in both senses of the word. In the colloquial meaning, it is a funny book, full of ribald, often grotesque humor worthy of Geoffrey Chaucer, Mark Twain, or even George Washington Harris. The numerous characters who come and go without leaving a deep impression on the reader—one of Erskine's objections to the book—are comic grotesques. They leave just the impression they are meant to leave. But the novel is a comedy in a more literary sense as well. *Suttree* is a story about a man moving from sin to salvation, from hell to heaven, a pilgrim like Dante (whose *Divine Comedy* McCarthy alludes to during Suttree's vision quest in the mountains). We have to see Suttree in all his flawed degradation in order to see the depths from which the sinner must rise, but the novel is punctuated by moments of grace, moments of insight, and—more often—by dark nights of the soul whose ultimate end is spiritual awakening. That this pilgrimage ends as a comedy rather than a tragedy is signified by the dreamlike ending of the novel. A dead body in Suttree's abandoned houseboat is mistakenly identified by the denizens of McAnally Flats as Suttree himself. "Suttree" lies dead while Suttree moves on, encountering the mysterious waterboy, and a car that stops to pick him up though he has not flagged a ride. These are images of redemption, of death, burial, and resurrection, a highly charged network of soteriological symbols. Hamlet arrives at a kind of stoic serenity by the end of Shakespeare's play; Suttree is redeemed.[23]

I have located one other reference to Shakespeare in McCarthy's notes for *Suttree*. Box 19, Folder 14, contains a handwritten note on a page of otherwise typed fragments: "disease 'beyond my practice'— Mbeth." The words "all mine" appear above the quotation. I cannot find a place where McCarthy makes use of the quotation, which is from Act 5, Scene 1, of *Macbeth*. The line is spoken by a doctor who is clinically observing Lady Macbeth as, in a seeming trance, she struggles with her guilt: "This disease is beyond my practice, yet I have known those which have walked in their sleep, who have died holily in their beds" (lines 65–67).

Spengler, Oswald (1880–1936)

SEE ENTRY FOR WYNDHAM LEWIS IN *SUTTREE*

Oswald Spengler looms large in Cormac McCarthy's imagination. Spengler's monument to historical pessimism, *The Decline of the West*, informs McCarthy's own deeply pessimistic philosophy of history, and it is one—perhaps even the main—source of McCarthy's apocalyptic vision of humanity's fate. In fact, the full title of McCarthy's first western, *Blood Meridian: Or the Evening Redness in the West*, echoes the German title of Spengler's book, *Der Untergang des Abendlandes*, which, according to Spengler, was meant to suggest a slow decline akin to sunset (H. S. Hughes vii).

In *The Decline of the West*, Spengler argues that cultures and civilizations, like organisms, come into being, grow into maturity, and decline into old age and death. He distinguishes between culture, which begins to form early in the life of a people, and civilization, the sclerotic old age of a people, when the vital life force of the culture begins to atrophy (Herman 236–240).[24] Spengler identifies eight world civilizations, though his focus is on the declining "Faustian" civilization of Europe, a civilization that "restlessly pursues knowledge and change," and whose "chief product, science, is merely the concretization of this indomitable Western will, which it then projects onto the rest of the world in mechanical, rather than organic, terms" (240). The Faustian civilization is characterized by the domination of the will, the mechanization of time and space—the former symbolized most acutely by the mechanical clock (240)—and an imperialistic drive to enlarge the space dominated by the state (240).

Judge Holden is a Faustian figure, one who has acquired much knowledge, and who ceaselessly searches for new knowledge, and does so with the express purpose of imposing his will on the organic order of nature. On the subject of the judge's nearly limitless knowledge, Tobin at one point lists (for the kid) Holden's prodigious range of expertise:

> God the man is a dancer, you'll not take that away from him. And fiddle. He's the greatest fiddler I ever heard and that's an end on it. The greatest. He can cut a trail, shoot a rifle, ride a horse, track a deer. He's been all over the world. Him and the governor they sat up till breakfast and it was Paris this and London that in five languages, you'd have give something to of heard them. The governor's a learned man himself he is, but the judge ... (*Blood Meridian*, 123)

Tobin does not finish the sentence, but the quotation establishes the judge's bona fides as a practical man of the world, a man of skill who is also knowledgeable about law (239), plants and animals (198), history (140), and, of course, warfare. It is tempting to call the judge a Renaissance man, but McCarthy has Spengler's Faustian man in mind, a much more ambiguous and sinister character altogether. What makes the Faustian spirit sinister is the Baconian (and Foucauldian) equation of knowledge and power. In one of the genuinely chilling moments of the novel, the judge makes this equation explicit: "Only nature can enslave man and only when the existence of each last entity is routed out and made to stand naked before him will he be properly suzerain of the earth" (198). In elaborating on this claim to suzerainty, the judge articulates the Faustian credo:

The man who believes that the secrets of the world are forever hidden lives in mystery and fear. Superstition will drag him down. The rain will erode the deeds of his life. But that man who sets himself the task of singling out the thread of order from the tapestry will by the decision alone have taken charge of the world and it is only by such taking charge that he will effect a way to dictate the terms of his own fate. (199)

He concludes this lyrical celebration of the Western will-to-power by explaining his motivation for recording the natural world in his ledger: "The freedom of birds is an insult to me. I'd have them all in zoos" (199).

Faustian man is Satanic in his desire to impose his untrammeled will on creation and in his restless desire to transgress boundaries once thought inviolate or sacred. The judge embodies the Faustian spirit, and he does so in the role of Mephistopheles. What makes *Blood Meridian* something of a classic of horror literature is the fact that the main character may be the devil, though McCarthy leaves room for a host of other possibilities. McCarthy's novel is, in some respects, an homage to Christopher Marlowe, John Milton, and Johann Wolfgang von Goethe.

Shades of Milton's Satan are present in the scene in which the judge extracts from the earth the ingredients for gunpowder, thereby rescuing Tobin and his companions from a band of Comanche warriors. In this scene the judge delivers a sermon that echoes a similar speech delivered by Satan in *Paradise Lost*. In the judge's sermon, he tells his listeners that "our mother the earth ... was round like an egg and contained all good things within her" (130). The good things, of course, provide the implements of war. Here is Satan extolling his minions to take from the earth the elements necessary for what we might call Faustian warfare:

Which of us who beholds the bright surface
Of this ethereous mold whereon we stand,
This continent of spacious Heaven, adorned
With plant, fruit, flower ambrosial, gems and gold,
Whose eye so superficially surveys
These things, as not to mind from whence they grow

Deep under ground, materials dark and crude,
Of spirituous and fiery spume, till touched
With Heaven's ray, and tempered, they shoot forth
So beauteous, opening to the ambient light?
These in their dark nativity the deep
Shall yield us, pregnant with infernal flame;
Which into hollow engines long and round
Thick-rammed, at the other bore with touch of fire
Dilated and infuriate, shall send forth
From far with thundering noise among our foes
Such implements of mischief as shall dash
To pieces and o'erwhelm whatever stands
Adverse, that they shall fear we have disarmed
The Thunderer of his only dreaded bolt.
  (*Paradise Lost*, Book Six, lines 472–491)

If Tobin's description of the judge as a "sootysouled rascal" (124) were not enough, the deliberate echoes of his Miltonic precursor cement the Satanic reading of his character, and his overweening will-to-power confirms his Faustian pretensions: both Satan and the judge wish to be suzerains.

The first reference to Spengler in McCarthy's papers is in Box 19, Folder 14, where we find the following:

Grace comes in the absence of will
    see spnglr on Job

This fragmentary note alludes to Spengler's discussion, in *The Decline of the West*, of what he calls the Magian culture, one of the eight world civilizations identified in the book. The Magian culture, best exemplified in the monotheistic religions of the Near East, contrasts strongly with the Faustian culture whose decline Spengler's book chronicles. The Faustian will-to-power contrasts, specifically, with the defining characteristic of the Magian, "a *will-less* resignation, to which the spiritual 'I' is unknown" (Spengler 302, emphasis in original). Spengler then links this will-less comportment of the Magian with the idea of Grace, which "underlies all sacraments of this culture" (303). He identifies Augustine, "the last great thinker of early-Arabian Scholasticism," as one of the primary exponents of this idea, which is anti-Western in its implications (303). From Augustine, Spengler moves to the Book of Job as another exemplar of the Magian worldview. McCarthy's note on Spengler and Job refers to the following passage from Spengler:

> For him [Augustine] grace is the substantial inflowing of something divine into the human Pneuma, itself also substantial.... From Augustine, as from Spinoza so many centuries later, the notion of force is absent, and for both the problem of freedom refers not to the Ego and its Will, but to the part of the universal Pneuma that is infused into a man and its relation to the rest of him. The conception that the idea of Grace excludes every individual will and every cause but the One, that it is sinful even to question why man suffers, finds an expression in one of the most powerful poems known to world-history, a poem that came into being in the midst of the Arabian pre-Culture and is in inward grandeur unparalleled by any product of that Culture itself—the Book of Job. It is not Job but his friends who look for a sin as the cause of his troubles. (303–304)

This contrast between the dominating will and a will-less attunement to the divine underlies McCarthy's understanding of humanity's spiritual nature, as well as his implicit critique, made most forcefully in *Blood Meridian*, of the modern West's domineering will-to-power over the organic world. McCarthy's notes for *Suttree* and *Blood Meridian* often overlap, and it is clear that his reading of Spengler influenced both books.

The connection between spiritual redemption and a surrendering of the will is evident in Suttree's moments of epiphany. In a key scene for interpreting Suttree's spiritual journey, he has a conversation with his own innermost self, envisaged as a "quaking ovoid of lamplight on the ceiling" of his houseboat (414). The conversation ends with a resignation toward suffering and a renunciation of self that echo Spengler:

> What do you believe?
> I believe that the last and the first suffer equally. Pari passu.
> Equally?
> It is not alone in the dark of death that all souls are one soul.
> Of what would you repent?

> Nothing.
>
> Nothing?
>
> One thing. I spoke with bitterness about my life and I said that I would take my own part against the slander of oblivion and against the monstrous facelessness of it and that I would stand a stone in the very void where all would read my name. Of that vanity I recant all.
>
> Suttree's cameo visage in the black glass watched him across his lamplit shoulder. He leaned and blew away the flame, his double, the image overhead. (414)

The last third of the novel is punctuated by these moments, saving moments within the spiritual pilgrimage of a character who is, literally, a "son of Grace" (432).

The final pages of the novel, in which Suttree undergoes a symbolic death and resurrection (a motif McCarthy also employs at the end of *Child of God*) reveal the end of the pilgrim's journey as a selfless state of grace: "Walking down the little street for the last time he felt everything fall away from him. Until there was nothing left of him to shed. It was all gone. No trail, no track. The spoor petered out down there on Front Street where things he'd been lay like paper shadows, a few here, they thin out" (468–469). Blessed by the mysterious child waterbearer, and carried away from Knoxville by the car that stops without having been flagged down, the "child of grace" finally seems to transcend the depredations of a life ruled by the will.

Spengler's reflections on Job influenced much of the philosophical material in *The Crossing*, and in particular the meditations of the ex-priest in Huisiachepic on free will, determinism, and suffering. The ex-priest tells Billy the story of a man who loses his family in a terrible earthquake and in his grief sets out on a religious quest to understand the suffering nature of man. The grief-stricken pilgrim eventually reaches a resignation resembling that of Job's after his rejection of the ministrations of his three well-meaning but misguided counselors, Eliphaz, Bildad, and Zophar. The wisdom that is the fruit of his resigned state takes grace as foundational to a true vision of human nature. As the ex-priest explains it to Billy, "It is God's grace alone that we are bound by this thread of life" (156). The old man of the ex-priest's story, like Suttree, has surrendered his will ("Grace comes in the absence of will"); in Spengler's terms, he has abandoned the Faustian desire to bring nature into submission, to give reasons and rationales for what in our fraught condition of suffering seems chaotic and meaningless. We learn that the ex-priest knew the old man, and as an "advocate of priestly things" sought to counsel him to a more rational understanding of man's place in the world and his relationship to God. He is a one-man Eliphaz, Bildad, and Zophar: "He believed in a boundless God without center or circumference. By this very formlessness he'd sought to make God manageable. This was his colindancia" (152–153).

The old man's response to the priest constitutes a rejection of the will, which he characterizes as an adversarial stance toward God. The final sentence of this passage recalls Suttree's epiphany following his self-interrogation on the houseboat, when he repents of his desire to "stand a stone in the very void where all would read my name" (414). And Suttree's epiphany is echoed in the words that I have italicized: "He understood what the priest could not. That what we seek is the worthy adversary. For we strike out to fall flailing through demons of wire and crepe and we long for something of substance to oppose us. Something to contain us or to stay our hand. Otherwise there were no boundaries to our own being and we too must extend our claims until we lose all definition. Until we must be swallowed up at last by *the very void to which we wished to stand opposed*" (153, emphasis added). The similarity is unmistakable and confirms that the passage from Spengler remained fixed in McCarthy's imagination.

Steele, Wilbur Daniel (1886–1970)

A photocopy of Wilbur Daniel Steele's short story "How Beautiful with Shoes," taken from the anthology *50 Great Short Stories*, edited by Milton Crane, appears among the collection of excised material from *Suttree* contained in Box 19, Folder 13. The story explores the emotional awakening of a simple young country girl, Amarantha, who is kidnapped by a psychotic but poetic ex-teacher, Humble Jewett. Jewett has recently escaped from an insane asylum, where he had been sentenced to go for attempting to murder the principal of his school. A lover of beauty, he was inspired to his murderous rage when the principal forbade teaching *The Song of Songs* as erotic poetry rather than spiritual allegory. Jewett meets a bad end at the wrong end of a shotgun, but before that he recites a lot of poetry to Amarantha, who undergoes an aesthetic variation on Stockholm Syndrome by blossoming into a sensitive soul as a result of her kidnapping. Steele wrote close to two hundred short stories, but this is the only one McCarthy is likely to have come across. Outside of the Crane anthology from which McCarthy copied the story, his work had been essentially forgotten by the time McCarthy was working on *Suttree*.

Almost unknown today (though the anthology McCarthy owned is still in print—Steele's one toehold on literary fame), Steele was a prolific and esteemed short story writer and novelist in the 1920s and 1930s, earning four O. Henry Awards, among other literary prizes. Mel Seesholtz describes his stories as "impressionistic, romantic yarns, which combine exotic escape with reaffirmation of traditional American values" (n.p.). The collapse of his literary reputation seems to have been precipitous. According to Seesholtz, F. Scott Fitzgerald, in a 1938 letter to an editor planning an anthology of contemporary literature, wondered "Why Wilbur Daniel Steele, who left no mark whatever, invented nothing, created nothing except a habit of being an innocuous part of the O'Brien anthology?" (n.p.) We might well ask of McCarthy, "Why Wilbur Daniel Steele?" Steele's story, which Martin Bucco calls "hill-billy fiction" (125), features a murderous psychotic with a taste for poetry ("He quotes from poets whose names are now lost"), who escapes the asylum and kidnaps a "cloddish Carolina girl" (Bucco 125), whom he regales with ancient verse before being blown away by a hick lout with a shotgun. Why not Wilbur Daniel Steele?

Steinbeck, John (1902–1968)

McCarthy's notes for *Suttree* contain a quotation from John Steinbeck's *The Log from the Sea of Cortez*, a nonfiction account of a specimen-gathering boat expedition Steinbeck conducted with his marine biologist friend Ed Ricketts. The work is a travel journal very much in the tradition of American naturalist writing, one of McCarthy's favorite genres. McCarthy typed the quotation as, "'The sky sucks up the land, a dream hangs over everything' Sea of Cortez" (Box 19, Folder

14). This version leaves out part of the actual text, taken from a paragraph in which Steinbeck reflects on the difficulty Jesuit missionaries must have faced when trying to persuade the native Indians to accept the Christian mystery, when their land was already charged with religious mystery: "The very air here is miraculous, and outlines of reality change with the moment. The sky sucks up the land and disgorges it. A dream hangs over the whole region, a brooding kind of hallucination" (84). The influence of this passage on McCarthy's own writing is unclear, but to my ear this sounds like the kind of descriptive writing McCarthy employs in *Blood Meridian*, a novel in which landscapes are often rendered with both naturalistic precision and hallucinatory mystery. Since the composition of *Blood Meridian* overlapped for several years with that of *Suttree*, it is entirely possible that McCarthy's note pertains to his "Western," as he called it in the late 1970s (see the entry on Foucault in this chapter for another example of McCarthy's notes for *Suttree* overlapping with notes for *Blood Meridian*).

Stephenson, Carl (1893–1954)

McCarthy's notes for *Suttree* contain a quotation from Carl Stephenson's famous adventure tale "Leiningen Versus the Ants": "'A vapor instinct with horror' Carl Stephenson" (Box 19, Folder 14). Stephenson's story, often anthologized in collections of the Amazing Adventure type, and made into the film *The Naked Jungle*, starring Charlton Heston, in 1954, tells of a plantation owner in Brazil who must protect his land and workers from an onslaught of army ants, and does so through his boldness and ingenuity. The sentence that caught McCarthy's attention is one in which Stephenson describes the growing awareness of the approaching ants among the plantation's animals: "Their approach was announced by the wild unrest of the horses, scarcely controllable now either in stall or under rider, scenting from afar a vapor instinct with horror" (346). The connection to *Suttree* is unclear, but McCarthy's interest in the story is noteworthy because it reinforces Michael Chabon's contention, voiced in a 2007 review of *The Road* for *The New York Review of Books*, that McCarthy can be profitably read as a writer of genre fiction. Chabon argues that McCarthy's novels employ the conventions of gothic horror and adventure, often in the same novel, as in *Blood Meridian*.

Chabon's recognition of McCarthy's indebtedness to the adventure tale is insightful, and the reference to the Stephenson story in the *Suttree* notes bears it out. In his article, Chabon identifies the elements of the adventure genre that appear in *The Road*, along the way identifying Jack London as a source, an insight supported by marginalia in an early draft of that novel: "It is the adventure story in both its modern and epic forms that structures the narrative. There are strong echoes of the Jack London–style adventure, down to the novel's thematic emphasis on the imperative to build a fire, in the father's inherent resourcefulness, in his handiness with tools and guns, his foresight and punctilio, his resolve—you can only call it pluck—in the face of overwhelming natural odds, savage tribesmen, and the despair of solitude" (Chabon, "Apocalypse" n.p.). While some might shudder to think of an artist of McCarthy's caliber finding inspiration in a boy's adventure tale (I, like Chabon, am decidedly not among them), the McCarthy papers confirm an influence that readers can see without them, as Chabon did in his astute review.

Tabula Smaragdina

SEE ALSO ENTRY FOR CARL
GUSTAV JUNG IN THIS CHAPTER

McCarthy's *Suttree* papers contain two references to this major work of Hermetic mysticism, one of the foundations of Renaissance alchemy. It was also an influence on the thinking of Jung, whose impact on McCarthy is considerable (see *Memories, Dreams, Reflections* 170–172). The *Tabula Smaragdina*, or "Emerald Tablet," provides "a comprehensive explanation of the world," according to the scholar of hermetic philosophy Florian Ebeling. It provides an account of creation, describes "the material essence of the world" using Aristotelian categories, and, most importantly for Renaissance esoteric philosophy, establishes the correspondence between Heaven and Earth through the maxim "as above, so below" (Ebeling 49–50). McCarthy wrote the title of the work in a holograph page of notes for *Suttree* (Box 19, Folder 13) and in the margin of an early draft of the novel. The marginal note appears next to a discussion of the caves under Knoxville:

> Aint that right Suttree?
> What's that?
> About there bein caves all in under the city.
> That's right.
> What all's down there in em?
> Blind slime. *As above, so it is below.* Suttree shrugged. Nothing that
> I know of, he said. They're just some caves. (Emphasis added)

McCarthy reformulates the mystical doctrine of the correspondence of the macrocosm and microcosm into an ironic reflection on the sad human condition, but that is typical of McCarthy's approach to philosophical and religious issues, which is to have things both ways. By evoking the hermitic tag, he situates his work within one of the main currents (or maybe undercurrents) of Western spirituality, a tradition he takes seriously, but introduces a note of irony that emphasizes the more humble, fallen, searching side of man's spiritual journey, even a sense of angst and anxiety, though the tone is gentle and humorous rather than despairing.

Jung mentions the *Tabula Smaragdina* in *Memories, Dreams, Reflections*, a book that McCarthy references several times in his papers, and one that clearly influenced McCarthy's thinking about humanity's spiritual nature (see Jung in this chapter). In that book, Jung describes a period shortly after his break from Freud during which he felt spiritually and intellectually disoriented. He sought guidance, as always, through attention to his rich and vivid dreams. One dream had a dramatic effect on Jung's development of his theory of archetypes. In it he is in "a magnificent Italian logia," and he is sitting in "a gold Renaissance chair" placed in front of an emerald table. His children are sitting around the table. A dove lands on the table and transforms into a little girl, who, after playing with the children for a while, transforms back into a bird and delivers a cryptic message (171–172).

Jung associated the table in the dream with "the story of the Tabula Smaragdina ... the emerald table in the alchemical legend of Hermes Trismegistos. He was said to have left behind him a table upon which the basic tenets of alchemical wisdom were engraved in Greek" (172). McCarthy's familiarity with Jung's work in general, and this book in particular, indicates that it is one source for McCarthy's interest in Hermetic philosophy, alchemy, and occult lore (see Jung). Another connection between Jung's account of his emergence from his post-Freud disorientation and McCarthy's work lies in Jung's description of how he turned to doing stonework as a form of spiritual therapy. Like the poet Robinson Jeffers, whom McCarthy also admired, Jung later built a stone tower on his property (see entry for Jeffers in *Whales and Men*).

Like the poet Jeffers and the psychologist Jung, McCarthy finds that stonework exemplifies a life lived in spiritual harmony with the order of the cosmos itself. In McCarthy's play *The Stonemason* the character Ben Telfair explains the mystical relationship between stone and the builder in describing his grandfather's philosophy: "He says that to a man who's never laid a stone there's nothing you can tell him. Even the truth would be wrong. The calculations necessary to the right placement of stone are not performed in the mind but in the blood. Or they are like those vestibular reckonings performed in the inner ear for standing upright" (66–67). He goes on to say that the plumb bob points "to a blackness unknown and unknowable both in truth and in principle where God and matter are locked in a collaboration that is silent nowhere in the universe" (67). McCarthy uses the image of the vestibular reckonings in the inner ear in *The Road* as well: "He rose and stood tottering in that cold autistic dark with his arms outheld for balance while the vestibular calculations in his skull cranked out their reckonings. An old chronicle. To seek out the upright" (15).

In *No Country for Old Men*, Sheriff Bell, in recounting a memory of combat from World War II, recalls his admiration for a stone water trough he discovered on an old farm. Imagining the builder, Bell attributes a spiritual purpose to this simple act of creation: "But this man had set down with a hammer and chisel and carved out a stone water trough to last ten thousand years. Why was that? What was it that he had faith in?" (307). He concludes that "there was some sort of promise in his heart" (308). In both *The Stonemason* and *No Country for Old Men*, stonework is directly linked to humanity's spiritual place in the cosmos.

According to Lyndy Abraham's *A Dictionary of Alchemical Imagery*, stone is "the place where the prima materia is found," ("Rock" 172), and the philosopher's stone is one of the core ideas in medieval and Renaissance alchemy. It is able to "transform the earthly man into an illumined philosopher" ("Philosopher's Stone" 145). The enigmatic figure in the epilogue to *Blood Meridian* who strikes fire from the rocks is surely, however we may interpret his significance, a hermetic figure. On one of McCarthy's pages of notes for *Blood Meridian*, he wrote "Jung—stone" (Box 35, Folder 4). McCarthy draws heavily from these esoteric analogies between stone and humanity's spiritual nature, and the *Tabula Smaragdina* is one of the primary sources for the understanding of correspondences that undergirds the analogies.

Thompson, Francis (1859–1907)

McCarthy copied a phrase from Francis Thompson's poem "The Poppy" in his notes for *Suttree*. The handwritten page of notes (Box 19, Folder 13) contains the quotation "'laving meres,'" followed by a question mark. Thompson, considered one of the major figures in the English Catholic Revival, included "The Poppy" in his *Poems on Children*. It describes a man walking with a small child. The child picks a poppy and hands it to the man, an act that provokes a long melancholy reflection on his own mortality. The phrase McCarthy quotes comes from the sixth stanza, which describes the man's grateful response to the child's innocent gesture:

> And his smile, as nymphs from their *laving meres*,
> Trembled up from a bath of tears;
> And joy, like a mew sea-rocked apart,
> Tossed on the waves of his troubled heart. (6, emphasis added)

Nothing specific in the poem suggests a direct connection with *Suttree*, but its melancholy tone and death-haunted diction certainly accord with the prevailing mood of McCarthy's novel. McCarthy's notes often reveal an artist's interest in the aesthetic feel of certain words and descriptions, but no apparent interest in the thematic content conveyed by the words. My best guess is that there was something about "laving meres" that caught his attention. I cannot find evidence that it found its way into the novel; though he does use the word "laving" to describe Gene Harrogate ladling sugar out of a bowl (172), the meaning of the word is different in that context.

What might be more significant is the revelation of McCarthy's reading of Thompson, whose most famous poem, "The Hound of Heaven," might be one source of inspiration for the hound sniffing along behind Suttree at the end of the novel:[25] "An enormous lank hound had come out of the meadow by the river like a hound from the depths and was sniffing at the spot where Suttree had stood. Somewhere in the gray wood by the river is the huntsman and in the brooming corn and in the castellated press of cities. His work lies all wheres and his hounds tire not. I have seen them in a dream, slaverous and wild and their eyes crazed with ravening for souls in this world. Fly them" (471).

The context suggests that these hounds have a demonic provenance. The hunter would then best be viewed as the figure of death, or perhaps the devil. This last seems likely, since the devil keeps showing up in McCarthy's novels in one form or another (the leader of the unholy trinity in *Outer Dark*, *Blood Meridian*'s Judge Holden, Anton Chigurh). That would make the Thompson influence problematic, because the hound in his poem is a metaphor for God's pursuit of the fleeing sinner. However odd the image (surely what makes the poem so striking and memorable), its subject is God's grace and his tireless efforts to save souls. The speaker in the last paragraph of *Suttree*, enigmatically addressing the reader in the first person, seems to be offering good advice when he tells us to flee these hounds. They first appear, however, in the italicized opening of the novel: "Is he ... a hunter with hounds or do bone horses draw his deadcart through the streets and does he call his trade to each? Dear friend he is not to be dwelt upon for it is by just suchwise that he's invited in" (5). The arc of the novel does in fact show Suttree fleeing, in however desultory a fashion, these hounds.

Trumbo, Dalton (1905–1976)

On a page of holograph notes for *Suttree* (Box 19, Folder 13), McCarthy quotes a phrase from a letter from Dalton Trumbo to his son Christopher. McCarthy's note reads "'howling his bill of particulars' Trumbo." Trumbo was best known as a screenwriter, though his

1939 novel *Johnny Got His Gun* was a critical and commercial success. He was blacklisted in the 1940s and 1950s for his association with the Communist Party. The humorous letter from which McCarthy quotes urges Christopher Trumbo to read *Sex Without Guilt* by Albert Ellis, a "manual for masturbators" (443), and what follows is an extended comic routine on the subject. At one point he describes going with his father to "one of those Calvinist fertility rites disguised as a father-and-son banquet" (446). The speaker, he writes, was "an acrid old goat named Horace T. McGuinness" who hypocritically (he kept a "doxy") denounced youthful sexual desire, and in particular masturbation: "By closing my mind and abandoning all sanity I can still hear that demented old reprobate *howling his bill of particulars* against poor Onan, shaking his fist at us all the while and sweating like a diseased stoat" (448, emphasis added).

As is so often the case, McCarthy's highly elliptical way of quoting sources (see Algren), combined with the lack of context in the arrangement of his notes, makes it difficult to know what kind of significance to ascribe to the Trumbo quotation. However, one possibility is that the fiery preacher McGuinness served as a model for the old man in *Suttree* who howls moral excoriations down on passersby from his window. Trumbo describes McGuinness as frenzied, harshly judgmental, and physically grotesque: "When speaking—and he always spoke—he displayed the carious ruin of what in his youth had been a gaggle of strong yellow teeth" (446). Here is the old man from *Suttree*, "howling his bill of particulars" against Gene Harrogate, who gives onanism a whole new name:

> Half out from a housewindow high up the laddered face of soot-caulked clapboards hung some creature. Sprawled against the hot and sunpeeled siding with arms outstretched like a broken puppet. Hah, he called down. Spawn of Cerberus, the devil's close kin.
> Harrogate clutched his lower teeth.
> A long finger pointed down. Child of darkness, of Clooty's brood, mind me.
> Shit, said Harrogate.
> The window figure had raised itself to address some other audience.
> See him! Does he not offend thee? Does such iniquity not rise stinking to the very heavens? (105)

However likely this association may be between Trumbo's preacher and the old man in *Suttree*, another possibility might account for the presence of the quotation. McCarthy may have simply liked the sound of the phrase "bill of particulars," which shows up in *Blood Meridian*, whose composition overlapped with *Suttree*. In fact, several notes from the same two sheets on which the Trumbo quotation appears contain references to his "Western." In the town of Ures, Glanton's gang is approached by "impromptu sutlers crying out each his *bill of particulars*" (201, emphasis added). The archaic phrasing would have been appealing to McCarthy, given his penchant for anachronisms. The Trumbo letter is, in fact, full of a kind of Joycean wordplay that would have delighted McCarthy.

West, Nathanael (1903–1940)

Fragments excised from *Suttree* feature characters and scenes that McCarthy's editor, Albert Erskine, considered unnecessary or detrimental to the novel's overall design. A letter dated 27 May 1977 fairly begs McCarthy to trim what Erskine clearly regards as fat (Box 19, Folder 1). McCarthy kept the scenes that Erskine so deplored in that letter, but he cut others that we can assume met with the same censure. One such scene involves a character called Duckman, whom McCarthy describes as a "flagrant homosexual" who "has taken up chickenfighting" (Box 19, Folder 13). An early version of the novel features an extended comic scene at a cockfight that goes awry when a character called Primrose (absent from the published novel, prominent on Erskine's hit list) pours whiskey on a cat that then catches fire under a stove. Comic pandemonium ensues when the building catches on fire. The scene is reminiscent of George Washington Harris's Sut Lovingood tales, which are a likely influence on McCarthy largely neglected by critics.

The page on which the reader is introduced to Duckman contains a holograph marginal note: "This is impossible—see Day of the Locust!" (Box 19, Folder 13). McCarthy is referring to a scene in Nathanael West's novel in which the male characters' conflicting desires for the want-to-be actress Faye Greener are symbolized by a vicious cockfight that takes place in the character Homer Simpson's garage. The novel explores the latent and often overt violence engendered by lust and jealousy in a Hollywood culture of tinsel desires and false hopes. The cockfight foreshadows both the actual violence that later breaks out between the main characters and a riot that presages the darker apocalypse hinted at in West's darkly comic vision of twentieth-century America.

It is unclear what the cockfighting scene in *The Day of the Locust* renders "impossible" in McCarthy's description of the Duckman scene, but the note verifies the source of McCarthy's interest in cockfighting. Duckman is a grotesque very much like the ones readers encounter in the novels of Nathanael West, whose appeal for McCarthy is not difficult to understand. West's novels feature a liberal use of the literary grotesque, shocking scenes of violence, black comedy, and apocalyptic foreboding. However, McCarthy plays the cockfighting scene for almost slapstick comic effects. West also plays the violence of cockfighting for laughs, but with a satirical edge and artistic vision lacking in McCarthy's raucous scene. McCarthy's own artistic vision is evident in his decision to cut it.

Weston, Jessie L. (1850–1928)

McCarthy refers to Jessie L. Weston's *From Ritual to Romance* in his notes for both *Suttree* and *Blood Meridian*. Weston's book is perhaps best known today for its influence on T. S. Eliot's *The Waste Land*, and in particular on the legend of the Fisher King that Eliot employs as he works out his poetic mythology of the spiritual crisis of modern humanity. Weston's book explores medieval Grail legends and relates them to the archaic rituals of vegetative cults that feature a god who dies and is resurrected. McCarthy was particularly interested in chapter 13, which discusses the Perilous Chapel episode of the Grail legend. In that episode, the Grail knight—in some versions Gawain, in others Percival—encounters an eerie deserted chapel in which he undergoes some kind of trial. According to Weston, "the details vary: sometimes there is a Dead Body laid on the altar; sometimes a Black Hand extinguishes the tapers; there are strange and threatening voices, and the general impression is that this is an adventure in which supernatural, and evil, forces are engaged" (132).

The first reference appears at the top of a page of typed notes for *Suttree*, where McCarthy wrote in pencil: "Fenestrae of the Perilous Chapel compared to that of L&N depot" (Box 30, Folder 1). Weston does not mention the fenestrae of the Perilous Chapel, nor does McCarthy mention the fenestrae of the L&N depot, so it is difficult to sort out this tantalizing, because rare, instance of McCarthy offering meta-commentary on his own fiction. Here is the allegorizing habit of mind that Guy Davenport noticed early in McCarthy's career (see "Outer Dark"). McCarthy is imagining a train depot as the Perilous Chapel of Grail romance. However, none of the passing references to the L&N depot in the novel invite symbolic or allegorical readings. One possibility is that the train depot became the bus depot, where the following scene, one that evokes Weston's supernatural and evil forces, takes place: "In the long arcade of the bus station footfalls come back like laughter. He marches darkly toward his darkly marching shape in the glass of the depot door. His fetch come up from life's other side like an autoscopic hallucination. Suttree and Antisuttree, hand reaching to the hand" (28). The gothic doppelganger motif makes this a plausible, if muted, analogue to the equally gothic Perilous Chapel episode (Mallory's version is often cited as an early instance of English Gothic). Lending more plausibility to the reading is the "hand reaching to the hand," which might suggest the mysterious Black Hand that features in some versions of the story. If it is meant to be an allusion, it is so opaque as to remain a private one, which is actually in keeping with McCarthy's approach to literary allusion. Without the archives as a guide, many of them would remain private, almost like inside jokes.

The second quotation appears at the bottom of the same page as the one quoted above. Also handwritten, it is a direct quotation from Weston's book: "'Many knights have been slain there, none know by whom'—Weston p 176" (Box 30, Folder 1). The quotation refers to the fate of the many knights who have visited the chapel prior to Percival. McCarthy's interest in this quotation appears to be, as is often the case, purely aesthetic. He liked the sound of it. In particular, he liked the sound of the final clause of the sentence, which shows up in *Blood Meridian*, a book McCarthy was working on during part of the composition of *Suttree*. It shows up at the end of chapter 3, after the kid and two other recruits for the filibuster get into a bar fight. One of the two, Earl, is killed in the fight, and McCarthy's description, straight out of

Weston, is as follows: "He lay on his side in the dust of the courtyard. The men were gone, the whores were gone. An old man swept the clay floor within the cantina. The boy lay with his skull broken in a pool of blood, *none knew by whom*" (40, emphasis added). We could call this a coincidence; perhaps the phrase was lodged in his unconscious and emerged spontaneously. But this is not likely. McCarthy wrote it down for a reason, and that reason appears to be that he liked the sound of the phrasing and wanted to use it. We know he works this way, because his notes are little more than congeries of potential material to be worked into the novels, from words to paragraphs, and occasionally to whole passages.

None of this is to suggest that McCarthy was not interested in the thematic and symbolic potential of the Grail legend. In fact, he was still thinking about the Holy Grail as late as the writing of *The Road*, which was originally titled, in the early manuscripts, *The Grail*. However, it is significant that McCarthy dropped that title. He told Oprah Winfrey that he thought of the novel as a story about a boy and a man on a road, rather than a symbol of mankind's spiritual journey. No reader can buy this, and the original title gives the game away, which is why McCarthy took care to cover his tracks. However, the heavy-handedness of deliberately inviting comparisons with the medieval quest for the Holy Grail is what makes McCarthy's decision to change the title the right one. The story *is*, after all, about a man and a boy on the road, whatever else it may be. If it is not that, first and foremost, it would fail as a work of art.

The final reference to Weston appears in McCarthy's notes for *Blood Meridian*, in which he typed "Parsifal—the village that disappears on being approached (Weston?)" (Box 35, Folder 7). The question mark after Weston's name indicates that he did not have the book handy when he typed this—and, in fact, his memory is slightly off. Here is the passage he is trying to recall: "He rides by moonlight through the forest, till he sees before him a great oak, on the branches of which are lighted candles, ten, fifteen, twenty, or twenty-five. The knight rides quickly towards it, but as he comes near the lights vanish, and he only sees before him a fair little Chapel, with a candle shining through the open door" (133). McCarthy misremembers the vanishing candle lights as a village that disappears. This image made an impact, because he wrote this same note about the disappearing village in pencil in several other places throughout his notes for *Blood Meridian*.

Wolfe, Thomas (1900–1938)

Thomas Wolfe was a serious influence on McCarthy during his formative years as a writer. His name appears twice in *Suttree* marginalia, and McCarthy mentions him in a 1988 letter to J. Howard Woolmer that makes his enthusiasm clear. Stylistic similarities between Wolfe and McCarthy are evident in early drafts of *Suttree*. Fragments written in the early or mid-1960s suggest a very different novel altogether, one centered around a character referred to as The Poet, perhaps a literary offshoot of Wolfe's Eugene Gant, who is also an artist figure who translates the experience of a particular time and place into lyrical expression. Wolfe's style can be self-indulgent and undisciplined. Early drafts of *Suttree* suffer from a similar tendency toward self-indulgent lyricism and a kind of treacly and mawkish quality that is happily absent from the final work (after two decades of writing and revision), but perhaps were a hangover from McCarthy's desire to write his own version of the artist's journey, à la *Of Time and the River*.[26]

In the 1988 letter to Woolmer, dated 5 January 1988 McCarthy wrote: "My sister-in-law was in Asheville the other day and passed up a chance to buy a 1st edition of *Look Homeward Angel* in very good condition for $200.00. This sounds cheap to me is it?" Woolmer's response (9 January 1988) indicates how low Thomas Wolfe's star had sunk since his midcentury heyday: "About your query about Look Homeward Angel. That's a very high price for Mr. Wolfe" (Box 1, Folder 7). McCarthy's estimation for a writer who impacted him in his formal years as an author was obviously much higher than what Woolmer believed was warranted. Wolfe was, at one time, regarded as a major American novelist, and he was often placed in company with Faulkner and Hemingway. Faulkner, in a Q&A session with students at the University of Virginia, said of Wolfe that among his contemporaries "he had failed the best because he had tried the hardest, he had taken the longest gambles, taken the longest shots" (*Faulkner in the University* 206). McCarthy may have been aware of these remarks, and others in which Faulkner rated Wolfe very highly among American novelists.[27] McCarthy's enthusiasm for Faulkner, one of his most significant influences, may have led him to Wolfe.

Another reference to Wolfe appears in a holograph marginal note on a fragment of an early manuscript containing a scene in which Gene Harrogate is being taken to prison. The fragment is in Box 19, Folder 13, and reads "see: s. story: "Joe"/also Time and the River." I am unaware of a Thomas Wolfe short story with that title, though several feature minor characters with that name. The reference to *Of Time and the River* may be to a scene in which the protagonist, Eugene Gant, takes a train to New York. The description is touched with a sense of melancholy about things left behind, a mood that also characterizes McCarthy's description of Harrogate's train ride to prison. The following image from the draft of *Suttree* echoes a similar passage in Wolfe's novel: "A grimly lit tavern reared above the reek of coke and dust in the cinderblown yard, rapid and staccato multiplication of faces protean and blurred and stunned with passage in the windowlights of speeding coaches swept in a rush and clatter down and gone and the desolate howl of the engine hanging in the air damned of all deliverance." Here is the similar passage from *Of Time and the River*: "And then the slow toiling train has passed these lives and faces and is gone, and there is something in his heart he cannot say" (53). The tone in the second quotation is more maudlin and sentimental, but much of the description of Harrogate in McCarthy's early draft bears the same trait. The following passage from that draft would be quite foreign to any scene involving Gene Harrogate in the published novel:

> Harrogate had nothing to leave behind because he had never had anything. When they took him away he heard the sad and lonesome moan of the fouroclock bearing upon the crossing and he said that a goodbye. It hung in the air like the sound of his name called out in anguish. The things of his childhood were too perishable to need putting away. Things made of stone and wood that he had for companions in his lonely youth and which the earth took back into their primal anonymity. The pocketknife with its brass bolsters shorn of their horn handles was the last thing he had and that was replevined by the desksergeant.

McCarthy worked on *Suttree* for so many years that reading through the drafts and fragments feels like a kind of archaeological dig. At different strata, we find entirely different Gene Harrogates. Here he is a sensitive youth out of Thomas Wolfe, while at other levels he is an outsized grotesque out of George Washington Harris's Sut Lovingood tales.

Xenophanes (ca. 570–ca. 478 BCE)

SEE ALSO HERACLITUS IN *BLOOD MERIDIAN*

In his notes for *Suttree*, McCarthy wrote: "Xenophanes on the Thracians (in Heraclitus?)" (Box 19, Folder 13). Xenophanes's comments about the Thracians is not in Heraclitus, though scholars believe that Xenophanes's religious thought strongly influenced Heraclitus. The fragment from Xenophanes that McCarthy is referring to appears in a discussion of polytheism and anthropomorphism. Here is Felix M. Cleve's translation of the relevant fragments:

> But the mortals believe that the gods are born
> And have garment and voice and shape like themselves.
> (Fragment 14)

> But if oxen and horses and lions had hands
> And could draw with their hands and make statues as men do,
> Then horses would draw gods with figures like horses,
> And oxen, like oxen, and each (sort of) beast
> Would build up such bodies as they have themselves.
> (Fragment 15)

> Ethiops say their gods are flat-nosed and black,
> Thracians, theirs have blue eyes and red hair. (Fragment 16)

According to T. M. Robinson, Heraclitus's Fragment 5 echoes Xenophanes: "Furthermore, they *pray* to these statues!—(which is) as though one were to (try to) carry on a conversation with *houses*, without any recognition of who gods and heroes (really) are" (Heraclitus 13, emphasis in original). Robinson notes, "This fragment attacks certain features of current religious practice in the way that Xenophanes had earlier attacked religious anthropomorphism,... and the same *reductio ad absurdum* technique is used" (78).

McCarthy's association of Xenophanes with Heraclitus suggests that he was reading the latter at the time he was working on *Suttree*. The fact that almost all scholarly editions acknowledge Heraclitus's debt to Xenophanes explains his uncertainty about the source. Heraclitus was very much on McCarthy's mind when he was working on *Blood Meridian,* the composition of which overlapped with the composition of *Suttree* in its final stages. *Suttree's* quarrel with traditional and conventional religion may owe something to McCarthy's interest in the two pre-Socratic philosophers. *Suttree's* lecture to the priest who attempts to minister to him during his recovery from typhoid fever carries hints of Xenophanes's critique of anthropocentrism as well as Heraclitus's insistence on the transience of all things:

> God must have been watching over you. You very nearly died.
> You would not believe what watches.
> Oh?
> He is not a thing. Nothing ever stops moving. (461)

Heraclitus's comments about war, strife, and fire all work their way into *Blood Meridian,* but McCarthy's interest in the philosopher predates his philosophical western.

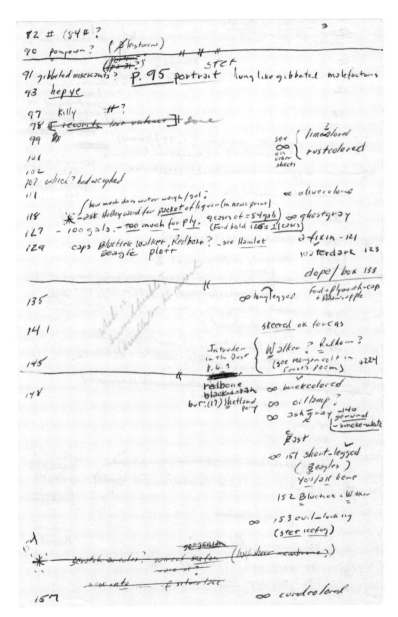

1. This page of copy-editing notes for The Orchard Keeper *contains references to William Faulkner's* The Hamlet *and Robert Frost's poem "The Runaway." McCarthy was trying to decide whether or not to capitalize the names of dog breeds and was consulting works by both authors for precedents. See entries for Faulkner and Frost in chapter 2 (Box 1, Folder 2).*

All of this has little to do with the fourcornered reality of
making a film, but a filmmaker without some esthetic stance is
like a businessman without an ethical stance and the end product
however well intended is ~~likely~~ liable to the sweet taint of
corruption. A classic work of art has no odor whatsoever.

It should be possible to make a film totally flexible in its
perceptions. That is, dependednt upon the gifts among the perceivers
The old man in tatters with untrimmed beard bearing a bag that read
in blue stencil Davis Travel Agency

The train wall: destruction of the natural world   Gryllos Capnbells
Gryllos grotesque faces set in the bellies of monsters   (Comanches)

Thing become so burdened with meaning that their forms are dimmed.
"Bird wings avid and disturbing as hands" Foucault
Dulle Griet
Pitiless
The madmen and the murderer are few among us and the saint as well.
But the seeds of their being lie dormant in all men.

2. *In notes for* Suttree *that overlap with notes for* Blood Meridian, *McCarthy
copied fragments from Foucault's* Madness and Civilization. *McCarthy's interest
in nonrational states of consciousness, one of the subjects of Foucault's book, finds
expression in Suttree's mountain vision quest and in the marauding Comanches
in* Blood Meridian. *See entry for Foucault in chapter 6 (Box 19, Folder 13).*

Miller "gnomic ɛoʀɪsт"
~ᴜtypᴏᴏ hᴜᴄ...

Carp came to U.S. in 1830's
Prepotency   It wasted him
Suttree: Beginning to find a way to smile at this anachronic noise.

Old Execrator, you was old fore I was born. I'm might near old as...
I am beside myself
Anile. Two smokehounds lay so drunk the flies had laid eggs in their

ears.

The execrator nodded with deep asseverance.

A dollar eighty six, said Suttree.

The storekeeper looked up with a cold look and went back to his

computations
                                    analogue   homologue

Paul and Silas bound in Jail

     All night long   It was good for P & S and its
                                         good enough for me
     Who shall deliver poor me

Dont that road look rough and rocky
Dont that sea look wide and deep   Friend, I'm goin to be talkin
Dont my baby look the sweetest   to Jesus some day just like
when she's in my arms asleep   I'm talkin to you

Faldstool an oratory in a church

CAVITATION   A knottyfingered keeper of the spoils   HunchinG
auterized salient   warp him in the head with something

Federated along one keel" Melville

Come to varve the shores of mata mara   sheehogue

Clitus   A few old homebent sots tilted and caromed along the walls

             like mechanical ducks amok   in a frozen carnival

epidemy   Jung   Salivaciously hostile

this gnostic, this shabby shape-show that masks the higher world of form

congeners   Pileated reticulated Roadstead redress trefoil adamantine

conventicle increate

fleering   sleavings, tailings   sponson wombat   peacoat (sp)

glabrous beatred member

3. This page of notes from Suttree contains references to Melville, Jung, and
Henry Miller. The fragment McCarthy copied from Moby-Dick, "federated along
one keel," comes from chapter 27 of Melville's novel and makes its way into Blood
Meridian as a description of the Glanton gang, who are "federated with invisible
wires of vigilance." See entries for Melville, Jung, and Henry Miller in chapter 6
(Box 19, Folder 13).

4. On this page of handwritten notes for Blood Meridian, *McCarthy refers to Eugen Herrigel's book about Zen Buddhism,* The Method of Zen. *The phrase "illustrated patent of their origins" comes from Herrigel's discussion of* satori, *a discussion that likely influenced McCarthy's thinking about the notion of "optical democracy." See entry for Herrigel in chapter 7 (Box 35, Folder 4).*

(after whitehead)

For the problem of the lost man is not his own whereabouts but rather the whereabouts of the others.

This is specious bullshit, Alfred North.

ME: For the whereabouts of a man lost is no different (in no wise varies) from his ordinary state nor is it only when where abouts of others that it is at odds

When the sun rose he was asleep with his feet to the smoldering skeleton of a blackened scrog. The storm had long passed off to the south and the new sky was raw blue and the spire of smoke from the burnt tree stood vertically in the dawn.~~like a gnomon.~~

made his way

⟨In the afternoon⟩ he wandered up the dry course of an arroyo

involves?

following in the sand the tracks of peccaries like little devilkins' hooflets. He surprised them drinking from a standing pool and they flushed snorting into the chaparral. He lay in the damp and trampled

He

sand and drank from the pool.~~xxx~~ rested and drank again.

(All the creatures with which he'd kept vigil in the night were

They cycof (our)

gone and he was alone. Seated tailorwise in that cratered waste he watched the world tend away at the edges to a shimmering surmise that ringed the distant desert round. Overhead in the eye of the vault two black hawks circled the sun slowly and perfectly opposed like paper birds upon a pole (tether?)

stylus?

burnt tree stood vertically in the dawn like a slender gnomon that marked the hour with its particular and faintly seething shadow upon the ~~faceless and timeless~~ face of a terrain without name or legend or cipher. All the creatures etc....

5. Here McCarthy takes a break from writing to conduct a philosophical argument. In the margin of an early draft of Blood Meridian, *McCarthy argues with the great philosopher Alfred North Whitehead, dismissing a passage from Whitehead's* Process and Reality *as "specious bullshit." See entry for Whitehead in chapter 7 (Box 35, Folder 9).*

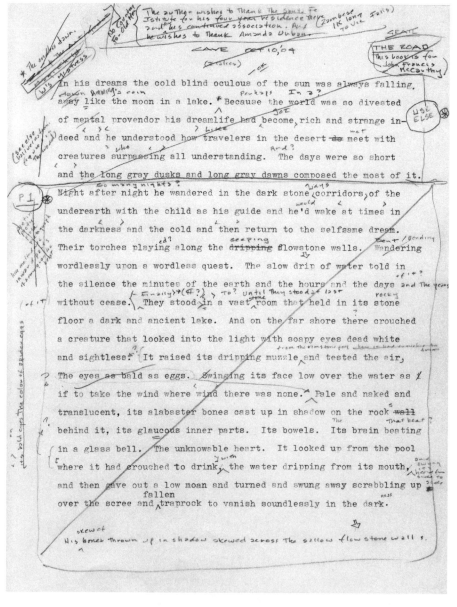

6. In the margin of this early draft of The Road, *McCarthy refers to Robert Pirsig's* Zen and the Art of Motorcycle Maintenance, *the story of a father and a son on the road, and to Samuel Beckett's* Waiting for Godot *and David Markson's* Wittgenstein's Mistress, *both works that explore apocalyptic themes dear to McCarthy's heart. See entries for Pirsig, Beckett, and Markson in chapter 11 (Box 87, Folder 6).*

CHAPTER 7

Blood Meridian: Or the Evening Redness in the West

*B*lood Meridian (1985), widely regarded as McCarthy's masterpiece, tells the story of "the kid" (early on "the child," and in the final chapter "the man") as he leaves his childhood home of Tennessee and becomes entangled with a group of vicious scalp-hunters. Most of the novel's action takes place when he is a young teenager. Though the kid is the protagonist of the novel, the center of interest is Judge Holden, usually just "the judge," who presides over the Glanton gang like a Western Mephistopheles. A struggle takes place between the kid, who harbors "clemency for the heathen," and the judge, the embodiment of a Satanic will-to-power who insists that war, with its ultimate stakes, is the only game worth playing, and that violence is what ultimately binds men together.

After running away from home and experiencing a brief encounter with the judge in Nacogdoches, the kid joins a group of filibusters, led by the appropriately named Captain White, on a doomed paramilitary assault into Mexico. Most of White's filibusters are slaughtered on the way by a fearsome band of Comanches who owe as much to Hieronymus Bosch as they do to the history of the West. The kid survives, gets arrested in Chihuahua, and is then released through the ministrations of John Glanton, the leader of a gang of killers contracted to hunt down Comanches on behalf of the Mexican towns suffering their violent raids. The kid joins the gang and sets off on a journey marked by carnage at every step. After setting up an extortion racket at a ford on the Colorado River, most of the gang comes to a violent end at the hands of a group of Yuma Indians. The kid survives the massacre and makes his way west with the other survivors.

After an encounter with the judge in the desert, where he has and loses the opportunity to kill him, the kid ends up in San Diego, where, while briefly jailed, he has yet another encounter with the judge, who places the blame for the gang's demise on him. The novel comes to its melancholy close years later when the kid, now the man, encounters the judge one last time, in Fort Griffin, Texas. Once again, the judge accuses the man of having failed to live up to the expectations of the gang, and, by extension, to having forfeited his place in the dance of death over which the judge presides. The judge attacks the man in an outhouse behind the bar, and so the man's life ends as it began, with fateful stars falling through the night sky.

Early drafts of the novel, which McCarthy began working on in 1974 (*Cambridge Companion* xix), indicate that McCarthy initially had a different sort of book in mind. In the drafts, the novel reads like a more raucous, and, despite the extreme violence and profanity, more traditional western. What seems to have turned the book into something new and strange is the emergence of the judge as the frightening center of a metaphysical work concerned with the nature of evil, and featuring a struggle between a tempter devil and a boy who, though bereft of moral guidance in his young and troubled life, resists the pull of the judge's call.

The archives point to several sources for this metamorphosis into a novel of ideas. Gustave Flaubert's *The Temptation of St. Anthony* was a major influence on the novel, and accordingly, it receives the longest entry in this chapter. The account of the saint's temptations in the desert inspired McCarthy to transform his western into a story of spiritual warfare in the deserts of Mexico and America. McCarthy's reading of Michel Foucault's *Madness and Civilization*, which features discussions of Renaissance paintings of the temptations of saints, also informs the narrative. Jacob Boehme's vision of the devil as a frightening but necessary component of the divine reality at the heart of things also had a significant impact. Indeed, along with McCarthy's papers for *Suttree*, the archival material related to *Blood Meridian* contains numerous cultural reference points that help to locate McCarthy's creative efforts within a dynamic intellectual network of books, writers, and ideas.

Beowulf *(ca. eighth century)*

SEE ALSO *SUTTREE*

McCarthy's notes for *Blood Meridian* contain two quotations from the Burton Raffel translation of *Beowulf*. Here is the first: "Rise from the darkness of war dripping with my enemies' blood (B/wulf)" (Box 35, Folder 7). And here is the second, typed on the line directly below the first: "God's dread loom was woven with defeat for the monster." The first line comes from the scene in which Beowulf introduces himself to Hrothgar and states, through the trope of epic boasting, his intention to slay Grendel:

> My people have said, the wisest, most knowing
> And best of them, that my duty was to go to the Danes'
> Great king. They have seen my strength for themselves,
> Have watched me *rise from the darkness of war,*
> *Dripping with my enemies' blood.* (lines 415–419, emphasis added)

The second line is part of the narrator's commentary on events, a commentary that often sounds a discordantly Christian note in the otherwise pagan epic. As Grendel makes his way to Herot, his end is foretold:

> *... But God's dread loom*
> *Was woven with defeat for the monster,* good fortune
> For the Geats; help against Grendel was with them,
> And through the might of a single man
> They would win. (lines 696–700, emphasis added)

The first quotation finds echoes throughout *Blood Meridian*. After murdering and scalping a defenseless old woman, Glanton "took the dripping trophy from McGill and turned it in the sun" (99). Glanton's men, slaughtering defenseless Indians in a small village, are described as "moving on foot among the huts with torches and dragging the victims out, slathered and dripping with blood" (156). The Yuma Indians who attack Glanton's camp at the ferry crossing emerge from the quarters of Dr. Lincoln holding "the doctor's dripping head by the hair" (274). Needless to say, much blood drips through the pages of the novel. McCarthy may have found an analogous martial code in *Beowulf*, but he also found a literary model for the depiction of gore.

The second quotation contains an image, "God's dread loom," that McCarthy has used to suggest fate, destiny, or doom. The italicized opening of *Suttree* contains the following line: "but lo the thing's inside and can you guess his shape? Where he's kept or what's the counter of his face? Is he a weaver, bloody shuttle shot through a timewarp, a carder of souls from the world's nap?" (4–5). Dianne Luce has argued that McCarthy borrowed Melville's weaver-god from *Moby-Dick* as an image for the Gnostic demiurge who rules the earth (*Reading the World* 178). The analogy with Gnosticism seems likely, but the connection with Melville is certain, as we can see by comparing Melville's description of the weaver-god with a similar description in *The Crossing*.

Here is Melville: "Nay—the shuttle flies—the figures float from forth the loom; the freshet-rushing carpet for ever slides away. The weaver-god, he weaves; and by that weaving is he deafened, that he hears no mortal voice" (344). And here is McCarthy: "In his dreams God was much occupied. Spoken to He did not answer. Called to did not hear. The man could see Him bent at his work. As if through a glass. Seated solely in the light of his own presence. Weaving the world. In his hands it flowed out of nothing and in his hand it vanished into nothing once again" (149). McCarthy takes an interest in images that he finds in multiple sources (see the discussion of statues' eyes in the entries for Lewis and Lampedusa in *Suttree*), and the image of the weaver-god provides one instance of this tendency. Luce was correct in noting the influence of Melville, but McCarthy's notes for *Blood Meridian* indicate that he found another striking instance of the image in *Beowulf*.

Boehme, Jacob (1575–1624)

SEE ALSO EUGEN HERRIGEL IN THIS CHAPTER

The seventeenth-century mystic Jacob Boehme, from whom McCarthy took one of the epigraphs for *Blood Meridian*, should be regarded as a major influence on McCarthy—not just on *Blood Meridian*, but on his entire western corpus, a body of work deeply invested in metaphysical questions of good and evil and about the spiritual foundations of human existence. McCarthy's archived papers contain references to Boehme that confirm the intuition of critics such as Edwin Arnold that his philosophical and theological speculations are deeply informed by the German mystic.

McCarthy's notes for *Blood Meridian* contain three references to Boehme. One appears as a holograph marginal note on a page of notes on language and vocabulary. It actually refers to the German scholar of Zen Buddhism Eugen Herrigel (see entry for Herrigel in this chapter), but this was a misattribution on McCarthy's part. The note reads, "The ground and the unground—see Herrigel Way of Zen 1st few pp)" (Box 35, Folder 4). Herrigel does not use these terms in the book to which McCarthy refers. They do appear in the first few pages of *Six Theosophic Points* by Boehme, however, which McCarthy was reading concurrently—it is the source of the epigraph—and apparently he confused their real source with Herrigel's work on Zen. The terms "ground" and "unground" are discussed at length in the introduction to Boehme's work written by the Russian philosopher Nicolas Berdyaev. So, to be very precise, McCarthy cited Herrigel while thinking of the first few pages of Berdyaev's introduction to Boehme.

The other two references to Boehme appear in Box 35, Folder 7, which contains typed notes for *Blood Meridian*. McCarthy typed out two quotations from Boehme's works. The first, "'When I see a right man there I see three worlds standing' Boehme," comes from *Six Theosophic Points*. The second quotation is from *The Confessions of Jacob Boehme*: "'This I write out of love as one who tells how it has gone with himself' Boehme." So we know that McCarthy was deeply interested in at least two works by Boehme and was likely reading others. We see the influence of Boehme most clearly in the judge and in the mystical concept of "the matrix," or *la matriz*, which is central to the metaphysics of *The Crossing*.

Edwin T. Arnold did the pioneering work on Boehme's influence on McCarthy in his essay "McCarthy and the Sacred," and the following brief summary of Boehme's ideas is indebted to Arnold's seminal piece. Arnold, whose focus is *The Crossing*, links that novel's concept of the matrix with a similar idea in Boehme. The following quotation, from *Mysterium Magnum*, crystallizes the notion: "Everything in the depths above the earth, upon the earth, and within the earth interacts reciprocally like a single thing . . . having various forces and effects, but only one matrix (*Mutter*), from which every thing originates and flows. And all creatures are made out of these qualities, and originate and live therein, as within their matrix" (qtd. in Arnold 222). Arnold cites McCarthy's lyrical description of Billy's mourning for the wolf as an example of his use of this concept:

> He took up her stiff head out of the leaves and held it or he reached to hold what cannot be held, what already ran among the mountains at once terrible and of a great beauty, like flowers that feed on flesh. What blood and bone are made of but can themselves not make on any altar nor by any wound of war. What we may well believe has power to cut and shape and hollow out the dark form of the world surely if wind can, if rain can. But which cannot be held never be held and is no flower but is swift and a huntress and the wind itself is in terror of it and the world cannot lose it. (127)

The novel alternates between "matrix" and the Spanish "*matriz*," which emphasizes the sense of a cosmic or primal womb from which all things originate, or a primordial chaos from which form emerges from formlessness. Boehme's notion of a primal matrix sounds much like the Dao of Chinese philosophy. Consider the following poem from the *Dao De Jing*, as translated by Roger T. Ames: "The life-force of the valley never dies— / This is called the dark female. / The gateway of the dark female— / This is called the root of the world. / Wispy and delicate, it only seems to be there, / Yet its productivity is bottomless" (85). Another likely source for McCarthy's thinking is Annie Dillard, who also uses the word "matrix" to describe a primordial spiritual foundation (see entry for Dillard in this chapter).

Boehme's concept of the "unground" sounds like a variant of the matrix/*Mutter* idea. Here is how Nicolas Berdyaev explains it in the introduction to *Six Theosophic Points*, which McCarthy erroneously attributed to Eugen Herrigel: "The Unground, thus, is nothingness, the unfathomable eye of eternity and at the same time a will, a will without bottom, abysmal, indeterminate. But it is a nothingness which is "the hunger for 'Something.' At the same time the Unground is 'Freedom.'

In the darkness of the Unground blaze the flames signifying freedom, meontic, potential freedom" (xix). According to *The Oxford English Dictionary*, the word "meontic" refers to "that aspect of artistic creativity which seeks to depict what has not been seen or experienced in reality." The word contrasts with "mimetic." The meontic freedom of the unground corresponds to the fecund formlessness of the cosmic womb that both Boehme and McCarthy posit as the primordial origin of all things. The meontic makes the mimetic possible. Like the Dao, it is the formless source of form. Dao, matrix, *la matriz*, *Mutter*, unground, Zen (a form of Buddhism heavily indebted to Daoist philosophy)—in whatever guise, McCarthy pursues this elusive idea through his fictional explorations of our spiritual state.

Arnold's assessment of Boehme's contribution to McCarthy's metaphysics tends to emphasize its positive influence. Arnold, rightly, sees the influence as evidence of McCarthy's fundamentally religious orientation. *The Crossing*, and, even more explicitly, *The Stonemason* and *The Sunset Limited* (which, granted, raises religious questions dialectically, but leaves the burden of synthesis on the reader), confirm this orientation. I would go further and say that all of McCarthy's works confirm it, but there is no question that it became more pronounced with his westward migration. Nevertheless, McCarthy's work, however much it affirms the potential for grace and spiritual enlightenment, hews closely to the night side of life. Carrying the light, as we learn in *The Road*, is difficult, because darkness seems to overwhelm it. Boehme's Christian Gnosticism is high-proof stuff, imminently suited to McCarthy's religiously oriented but darkly turned mind. Arnold draws attention to Boehme's heterodox reflections on the nature of evil, and to his apparent concession to the necessity of evil in the spiritual drama of life, but emphasizes, through his focus on the "deep ecology" of *The Crossing*, the role of goodness and light in Boehme. This is the right emphasis for that novel, but with *Blood Meridian* McCarthy seems to have been most interested in Boehme's reflections on evil.

One of the Boehme quotations in McCarthy's notes for *Blood Meridian* is directly related to Boehme's complex understanding of the relationship between good and evil, and of the positive reality of evil as a spiritual necessity—positive not in the sense of good or desirable, but in the sense of contrast with "privative" theories of evil, like St. Augustine's, which deny it positive being, insisting that evil is an absence of good. Boehme's theory denies this comforting (though logical, given certain premises) conclusion of orthodox theodicy. The quotation that McCarthy copied into his notes comes from *Six Theosophic Points*, which is also the origin of the novel's Boehme epigraph. Boehme writes, "Thus, if one see a right man, he may say: I see here three worlds standing, but not moving" (32). According to Arnold, "Boehme saw humankind existing in three states simultaneously: the external world composed of the natural elements; the world of darkness ... ; and the world of light" (223). Arnold quotes the Boehme scholar David Weeks's explanation of this metaphysical trinity: "The three worlds are not located and separated from one another by boundaries. They are three moments in a process of self-revelation of the divine will" (qtd. in Arnold 223). Evil is a necessary part of the divine mystery. This does not mean that evil should be embraced or endorsed—but it must be dealt with.

According to Berdyaev's reading of Boehme, both evil and good are preconditions of freedom, but that necessity ensures that existence is always marred by tragedy (xxxii). You must carry the light, but you must carry it in the darkness. According to Weeks, in words that Cormac McCarthy would surely grant his imprimatur, "because the three worlds are inextricably bound together, there is no redemption without terror and tragedy. Not only is grim death the root of life, there would be no joy if not for woe" (qtd. in Arnold 224). The term Boehme uses to describe the moment of enlightenment into this grim, but bracing reality is *Schrack*, "the sudden awareness and terror inspired in the one who suddenly comprehends both his corruption and divinity" (224). Perhaps McCarthy had this *Schrack* in mind when he had Don Arnulfo tell Billy that enlightenment was found in "such places [where] God sits and conspires in the destruction of that which he has been at such pains to create," places where "el fierro ya está en la tierra ... donde ha quemado el fuego [where the iron is already in the earth, where the fire has burned]" (47). McCarthy's religious views, if they are indeed indebted to Boehme, might drive some to the comforting arms of atheism. That they do not drive him there is a testimony to how seriously he takes them.

And that is why, in *Blood Meridian*, McCarthy gives the devil his due, as does Boehme—his due, but no more than that. The judge is a composite devil. Internal allusions to Milton (see entry for Spengler in *Suttree*), and McCarthy's papers, which contain references to Goethe's *Faust* and Flaubert's *Temptation of St. Anthony* (see entry for Goethe in this chapter and entry for Flaubert in *Suttree*), indicate that McCarthy gave much thought to how to create a fictional devil. McCarthy's friend Edward Abbey thought he may have consulted the devil himself while writing the novel—I hope not, but take Abbey's point. Boehme's Satan, as described in *Six Theosophic Points*, is another role model for the judge. He gets his due because, according to Boehme, "this world rests upon the foundation of the dark world. The dark world gives to this world essence, will and quality. And had not the good been introduced also at creation, there would be no other doing or will in this world than in the dark world" (94).

What does it mean for our world to rest on this dark foundation? It means that the world is pretty much as Arthur Schopenhauer describes it. Here is Boehme: "As is to be seen among men and beasts ... there is biting, hating and striking, and an arrogant self-will, each wishing to rule over the other, to kill and devour the other, and elevate itself alone" (94). And as above, so below: "What all wicked men in this world do in their malice and falsehood, that also the devils do in the dark world" (94). The judge, like Boehme's Satan, is the dancing-master at this gruesome scene.

The parallel between the judge, who wishes to be suzerain over all creation, and Boehme's devil is evident in the following passage from *Six Theosophic Points*, which follows immediately after the one from which McCarthy quoted in the novel's epigraph. "We cannot, then, say of the devil that he sits in dejection, as if he were faint-hearted. There is no faint-heartedness in him, but a constant will to kindle the poison-source more, that his fierceness may become greater. For this fierceness is his strength, wherein he draws his will to mount above the thrones and inflame them. He would be a mighty lord in the poison-source, for it is the strong and great life" (92). These words, along with the words of the epigraph, should be kept in mind when we read the—how else to describe it—exuberant finale of *Blood Meridian*: "Towering over them all is the judge.... His feet are light and nimble. He never sleeps. He says that he will never die. He dances in light and in shadow and he is a great favorite. He never sleeps, the judge. He is dancing, dancing. He says that he will never die" (335). Given the devil's propensity for lying, we might want to put the stress on *says* in that last line, but if the judge comes partly from the pages of Boehme, he just might be telling the truth.

But if he comes from the pages of Boehme, we might take comfort in this: "The light is his misery and dread; that checks his bravery" (92). Nothing seems to check the judge, but one of the most important questions raised in the novel is: Why his fixation on the kid? Boehme says that "gentleness is the enmity of the wrath-power" (94–95). The judge condemns the kid for his "clemency for the heathen." The only time we witness such clemency is when the kid extends his mercy and kindness to "the eldress in the rocks." His kindness, as he soon realizes, is too late—she is already dead—but the significance of this moment cannot be exaggerated, given the sharp contrast it presents to the rest of this abattoir of a novel: "He told her that he would convey her to a safe place, some party of her countrypeople who would welcome her and that she should join them for he could not leave her in this place or she would surely die" (315). The kid plays the part of the Good Samaritan, and it is this aspect of his character that causes the judge some alarm. Though McCarthy's devil's good spirits never flag, the kid is clearly a trouble to him. Gentleness is the enmity of the wrath-power. So says Jacob Boehme. So says Cormac McCarthy.

Céline, Louis-Ferdinand (1894–1961)

McCarthy refers to Louis-Ferdinand Céline on a page containing a fragment from an early draft of *Blood Meridian*. The fragment, a description of the Glanton gang traveling through the desert, is surrounded by a chaotic explosion of holograph notes. On the lower left side of the page, McCarthy wrote "Céline" right below "The Habit of Being" (Box 38, Folder 3), the title of Flannery O'Connor's collected correspondence. The purpose of these brief notations is unclear, though the influence of O'Connor on McCarthy is certain (see entry for O'Connor in this chapter), and the influence of Céline likely.

Author of *Journey to the End of Night* and *Death on the Installment Plan*, Céline's gritty accounts of life's underbelly seem like obvious sources for McCarthy's own explorations of grit, particularly in *Suttree*. Michael Dirda's description of Céline's work would serve as well as a description of McCarthy's novel: "Céline . . . celebrated the living language of the people, full of argot, profanity, and savage street rhetoric. To this he added a taste for gallows humor and a view of life as something far more nasty and brutish than anything ever imagined by Hobbes" (*Classics for Pleasure* 257). Dirda goes on to describe Céline's American descendants, among whom he lists Henry Miller, one of McCarthy's early literary heroes. Céline falls into a category of writers who made a large impact on McCarthy early in his writing career. In addition to Miller, J. P. Donleavy, Nelson Algren, and Norman Mailer would fall into the category. McCarthy seems to have gravitated to writers unafraid of inviting the profane and violent extremes of life into their work, writers willing to shock. *Suttree*, in all likelihood McCarthy's first artistic endeavor, bears the stamp of these early influences.

Chaucer, Geoffrey (1343–1400)

In his notes for *Blood Meridian* McCarthy recorded a colorful description of the moral plight of gamblers from Geoffrey Chaucer's "The Pardoner's Tale." In the preface to his tale, the Pardoner provides his fellow pilgrims with examples of his preaching, which, in its severe moral prescriptions, greases the consciences of those he is about to fleece by selling them relics and pardons. McCarthy, copying a phrase from the preface, typed, " 'two bitching bits of bone' Chaucer" (Box 35, Folder 7). The phrase occurs in the Pardoner's ironic cautionary rhetoric (McCarthy copied it from the Neville Coghill translation into contemporary English): "Overthrown / By two small dice, two bitching bits of bone / Their fruit is perjury, rage and homicide" (250). The original says, "This fruyt cometh of the bicched bones two" (282).

I can find no allusion to these lines in McCarthy's work, but the influence of Chaucer seems assured, given McCarthy's penchant for inserting interpolated tales into his main storylines. Some novels, most notably *The Crossing*, rely very heavily on the stories-within-stories motif. But we see it in *Blood Meridian* as well. For instance, the judge's story of the treacherous roadside harnessmaker is a tale told to travelers who are sometimes described, with pointed irony, as "pilgrims."

The Pardoner's tale is cautionary, and that, too, is a form that McCarthy favors. The digression about the kid's journey into town with two other members of the filibuster reads like an interpolated cautionary tale, and, like the Pardoner's tale, ends with violence. The old Mennonite's aperçu, "There is no such joy in the tavern as upon the road thereto" (40–41), highlights the cautionary function of the story. The violence that concludes the Pardoner's tale is engendered by the greed of three riotous young men who go searching for Death, only to find it in the form of bags of gold under a tree. *Greed is the root of evil* is the moral of the story, and this tale of greed and violence, which McCarthy's note suggests made a strong impression on him, finds an echo in the story of Llewellyn Moss and the savage consequences that follow from taking the money he finds at the site of a drug deal gone bad.

Collinson, Frank (1855–1943)

McCarthy used Frank Collinson's account of his experiences in the west, published posthumously as *Life in the Saddle* (1963), as a research source for the Fort Griffin section of the novel. In the upper left margin above an early draft of the scene featuring the "bonepickers," he wrote, "Ft Griffin: See Life in the Saddle" (Box 35, Folder 9). Collinson was an Englishman who immigrated to the United States in 1872. He worked as a cowboy during the trail-driving era, and later joined a group of buffalo-hunters in Fort Griffin, Texas. According to Garry L. Nall, who wrote the foreword to a 1997 reprint, "these accounts of Collinson's roles as a trail driver, a buffalo hunter, an Indian fighter, and a cattleman provide a firsthand insight to a life on the western frontier" (v).

Conrad, Joseph (1857–1924)

A fascinating, and perhaps illuminating, reference to Joseph Conrad's *Heart of Darkness* appears in McCarthy's notes for *Blood Meridian*. The reference follows a sentence, typed as a fragment within the notes and without the surrounding narrative context, that made its way into the published novel. McCarthy typed, "He spoke, the judge, of purging oneself of those things that lay claim to a man. (The horror, the horror? See H of Darkness)" (Box 35, Folder 7). In Conrad's novel, these are the notorious last words of Kurtz ("The horror! The horror!"), pronounced to Marlow as he lies on his deathbed. The judge's words appear in chapter 17: "Crouched under their hats they seemed fugitives on some grander scale, like beings for whom the sun hungered. Even the judge grew silent and speculative. He'd spoke of purging oneself of those things that lay claim to a man but that body receiving his remarks counted themselves well done with any claims at all" (248). As a figure of the Faustian will-to-power (see entry for Spengler in *Suttree*), the judge, in recommending a purge of outside claims, would seem to be affirming the savage, primitive will. Spengler, Schopenhauer, and Nietzsche all inform, in different ways, McCarthy's crafting of the judge as an apostle of the primal will and the violence that attends it. The reference to Conrad invites comparisons between the judge and Kurtz.

Though such a comparison, as McCarthy would have been aware, requires qualifications, broadly considered the two characters overlap at certain points. Both are exemplars of the will-to-power conceived in terms of a violently rapacious culture of colonial dominance, racist oppression, and exploitation of the natural world—the judge would have all the birds in zoos, buffalo hunters hounding to near-extinction an endangered animal, and the massive accumulation of ivory in the Belgian Congo. What makes them distinct is Kurtz's ambivalence about his enterprise, an ambivalence that the judge would not entertain. Kurtz learns the dance of death that the judge performs with sinister delight, but his journey into the heart of darkness is marked by contradictions within his character. He, unlike the diabolical judge, is terrified by what he sees when he looks into that heart. The kid also journeys into the heart of darkness, but, like Kurtz, experiences internal contradictions and moral ambivalence.

Nevertheless, there are striking parallels between Kurtz and the judge. The postscript that Kurtz appends to his report to the Society for the Suppression of Savage Customs—"Exterminate all the brutes!"—is the authentic voice of the judge, and Kurtz's handwritten addendum nullifies the treacly boilerplate altruism that forms the "official" report. Kurtz, like the judge, sees what lies behind the Faustian Western project of global expansion. The all-too-human Kurtz's final judgment on his actions and on human nature in general is contained in his final, frenzied expression of horror, but as a willing participant in that horror he is a Faustian suzerain, one who can lead others in a macabre dance of death. Both McCarthy and Conrad use the metaphor of the dance in connection with these two characters. Marlow notes that Kurtz participated in "certain midnight dances ending with unspeakable rites, which—as far as I reluctantly gathered from what I heard at various times—were offered up to him—do you understand—to Mr. Kurtz himself" (50). Unable to entirely repress his admiration for the man, Marlow acknowledges that "he had the power to charm or frighten rudimentary souls into an aggravated witch-dance in his honor" (50). Like the judge, he calls others into a unified enterprise sealed in blood.

Kurtz is also, like the judge, regarded as a prodigy or genius by those who come into contact with him, not least the ambivalent Marlow. In addition to great intelligence and eloquence, we are told that he is an exceptional musician (71), which is also one of the attributes of the judge. Like the judge in the life of the kid, he haunts Marlow as a permanent enigma, both frightening and enticing: "I had a vision of [Kurtz] . . . opening his mouth voraciously as if to devour all the earth with all its mankind. He lived then before me, he lived as much as he had ever lived—a shadow insatiable of splendid appearances, of frightful realities, a shadow darker than the shadow of the night, and draped nobly in the folds of a gorgeous eloquence" (73). McCarthy gave much thought to the judge, looking to several fictional models as guides to his creation—Milton's Satan, Goethe's Mephistopheles (see entry for Goethe in this chapter), Flaubert's devil in *The Temptation of St. Antony* (see entry for Flaubert in *Suttree*). To this list Conrad's Kurtz should be added.

Dillard, Annie (b. 1945)

A holograph reference to the medievalist and novelist Dorothy Dunnett that appears in McCarthy's notes for *Blood Meridian* is more likely a reference to a Dunnett quotation that appears in Annie Dillard's *Pilgrim at Tinker Creek*, first published in 1974. The note reads: "Dorothy Dunnet [*sic*] (no clear reply)" (Box 35, Folder 4). I have not been able to locate the quotation in Dunnett's work, most of which is historical fiction. However, two things suggest that McCarthy got it from Dillard rather than Dunnett: the nature writing genre, in which Annie Dillard is widely regarded one of the luminaries, is one to which McCarthy is strongly drawn (his notes and drafts contain references to Aldo Leopold, Henry Beston, Joseph Wood Krutch, Edward Abbey, and Barry Lopez), and the quotation appears in the context of a theological discussion that resonates with McCarthy's own interests in mysticism.

The Dillard passage in which the quotation appears begins with a humorous reflection on mountaintop mysticism: "I have never understood why so many mystics of all creeds experience the presence of God on mountaintops. Aren't they afraid of being blown away? ... For if God is in one sense the igniter, a fireball that spins over the ground of continents, God is also in another sense the destroyer, lightning, blind power, impartial as the atmosphere" (89). Dillard goes on to contemplate this dark vision of God, the fearful element in the fear of the Lord. I have highlighted the words that McCarthy quoted (with a slight inaccuracy): "In the open, anything might happen. Dorothy Dunnett, the great medievalist, states categorically: 'There is no reply, in clear terrain, to an archer in cover.' Any copperhead anywhere is an archer in cover; how much more so is God! Invisibility is the all-time great 'cover'; and that the one infinite power deals so extravagantly and unfathomably in death—death morning, noon, and night, all manner of death—makes that power an archer, there is no getting around it" (89–90, emphasis added).

This vision of the divine nature as ambiguously contained between the poles of life and death is in accord with McCarthy's own forays into theological speculation in his fiction. For instance, in *The Crossing*, the wisdom figure Don Arnulfo tells Billy that he should "find that place where acts of God and those of man are of a piece. Where they cannot be distinguished" (47). Arnulfo explains in Spanish that these are places where the iron is already in the earth, places where the fire has already burned (47). He concludes this lesson—*obscurum per obscurius*—with the following: "He said that it was at such places that God sits and conspires in the destruction of that which he has been at such pains to create" (47). This sentiment resonates with Dillard's vision of God as both creator and destroyer.

If Dillard, rather than Dunnett, was McCarthy's source, this would lend credence to my suspicions about another instance of Dillard's influence on McCarthy. In her 1982 book *Teaching a Stone to Talk*, Dillard offers the following reflection, one that also finds an echo in *The Crossing*: "In the deeps are the violence and terror of which psychology has warned us. But if you ride these monsters deeper down, if you drop with them farther over the world's rim, you find what our sciences cannot locate or name, the substrate, the ocean or matrix or ether which buoys the rest, which gives goodness its power for good, and evil its power for evil, the unified field: our complex and inexplicable caring for each other, and for our life together here. This is given. It is not learned" (19–20).

This passage may be a source for McCarthy's own speculations about a mystical mother field—the matrix—that is the ground of our being. McCarthy uses the word "matrix," as well as the Spanish word "*matriz*," dozens of times in *The Crossing*. Don Arnulfo, equivocating between two meanings of the word, one having to do with a formula used to bait wolf-traps, the other with the mystical field, tells Billy that "each hunter must have his own formula... that things were rightly named [the matrix's] attributes which could in no way be counted back into its substance" (45). This definition sounds tantalizingly close to a description of the judge in *Blood Meridian*: "Whatever his antecedents he was something wholly other than their sum, nor was there system by which to divide him back into his origins for he would not go" (309). The positive connotations of the word in *The Crossing* might make this resemblance troubling, but if Dillard is a source of inspiration behind McCarthy's forays into metaphysics and theology, we should recall that it is she who posits a vision of God as both creator and destroyer, a vision McCarthy recorded in his notes. Taken together with McCarthy's interest in Boehme (see entry for Boehme in this chapter), whose conception of the divine nature makes room for both love and wrath, the close approximation of the two sentences should, perhaps, be unsurprising, even if their yoking remains disturbing.

My sense is that McCarthy and Dillard are kindred spirits, and indeed she has expressed admiration for his work (see *The Annie Dillard Reader* 57). The fusion of hard-nosed, scientifically informed naturalism with metaphysical speculation and a Christian theological sensibility (unorthodox wing) is a hallmark of both writers. In *Teaching a Stone to Talk*, Dillard states that "we are here to witness.... If we were not here, material events like the passage of seasons would lack even the meager meanings we are able to muster for them. The show would play to an empty house, as do all those falling stars which fall in the daytime. That is why I take walks: to keep an eye on things" (90–91). And here, from *The Crossing*, is the ex-priest whom Billy encounters in Huisiachepic: "Acts have their being in the witness. Without him who can speak of it? In the end one could even say that the act is nothing, the witness all" (154). The ex-priest, though a troubling figure in some respects, is, like Don Arnulfo, one of the novel's wisdom figures. Perhaps Annie Dillard is such a figure for McCarthy.

Dobie, J. Frank (1888–1964)

J. Frank Dobie's books about Texas folklore, history, and natural history have earned him a special place among Texas regionalists, and his work, though largely neglected today, continues to find admirers among those who savor the local color palette of a gifted raconteur. Though Dobie was a professor at the University of Texas at Austin for many years, his explorations of the Southwest—he was a pioneer of southwestern studies—eschew academic formalities in favor of a front-porch storyteller's style and subjects with popular appeal. McCarthy is among his admirers, and when writing *The Crossing*, he drew heavily from a sketch Dobie wrote about William Randolph Hearst's Babicora Ranch in northern Mexico. McCarthy included details about daily ranching operations that Dobie had first described and based characters—most notably the Yaqui Indian Quijada—on Dobie's depictions of real-life figures. However, McCarthy first borrowed from Dobie when writing *Blood Meridian*, which is attested by a note typed during the composition of the novel.

Steven L. Davis, in his article "Mining Dobie: Cormac McCarthy's Debt to J. Frank Dobie in *The Crossing*," demonstrates McCarthy's reliance on Dobie for historical background on the Babicora Ranch. According to Davis, McCarthy sought out a copy of Dobie's article "Babicora," first published in the *American Hereford Journal* in 1954, from Special Collections at the University of Texas at El Paso (UTEP) (52). Davis identifies numerous correspondences between Dobie's article and McCarthy's fictionalized version of the ranch. He points out parallel phrasing and details in McCarthy's description of the Babicora *vaqueros* with similar descriptions in Dobie's piece (53). He notes McCarthy's reliance on Dobie's account of the ranch's paramilitary security force under Pedro Lopez, even identifying corrections made to the final draft that bring his description of Lopez's role at the ranch in line with Dobie's (54). And he highlights McCarthy's use of Dobie's descriptions of Lupe Quijada, an enigmatic wisdom figure for both Dobie and McCarthy.

According to Davis, Quijada "struck J. Frank Dobie as being nearly magical" (56), and much of his deferential regard finds its way into *The Crossing*. McCarthy's description of Quijada contemplating fire draws on Dobie's, for instance. Davis quotes Dobie's recollection of the ordinarily silent and taciturn Indian remarking that "the fire is the thinker, a silencer. It makes shadows; it reveals strange things" (qtd. in Davis 55). In *The Crossing*, McCarthy writes, "Quijada leaned back and sat with his boots crossed before him. The cup in his lap. Both watched the fire. As if some work were there annealing" (384). Davis's analysis reveals a significant debt to Dobie, a debt also noted by John Emil Sepich in an essay on historical sources for *Blood Meridian*.

Sepich identifies Dobie as the source for one of the most significant conversations in the novel. Tobin attempts to engage the kid in a theological discussion that turns on an apophatic account of God, suggesting that "the voice of the Almighty speaks most profoundly in such beings as lives in silence themselves" (124). He offers to the skeptical kid an analogical proof for this silent God:

> At night, said Tobin, when the horses are grazing and the company is asleep, who hears them grazing?
> Dont nobody hear them if they're asleep.
> Aye. And if they cease their grazing who is it that wakes?
> Every man.
> Aye, said the expriest. Every man. (124)

Sepich identifies the source for this conversation as Dobie's *Apache Gold and Yaqui Silver,* in which Dobie records the following words from a colorful treasure hunter:

> I had my hat over my face so as to shut out the fierce light and was dozing off when all at once something aroused me. I think it was the

sudden ceasing of the horses to graze. A grazing horse makes a kind of musical noise cropping grass and grinding it, and men out, with their lives depending on horses, often notice that music or the absence of it. Anyhow, when I raised up, I saw every animal with head up and ears pointed to the range of mountains we had last crossed. (qtd. in Sepich 136)

This passage, combined with what we know of McCarthy's mining of Dobie for *The Crossing*, suggests that Dobie should be regarded as a significant influence on McCarthy, and notes from *Blood Meridian* indicate that McCarthy read Dobie not only for historical details, but also for verbal color in his dialogue.

The note, contained in Box 35, Folder 7, records a quotation from a chapter in Dobie's 1955 collection *Out of the Old Rock*. This book also contains the Babicora essay that McCarthy sought at UTEP in 1987 (in this volume titled "Men of Babicora"). This means that McCarthy was already aware of the essay in the early 1980s, several years before his research for *The Crossing* began, and the reference to Dobie in his notes for *Blood Meridian* suggests that Dobie's work had a formative influence on his western turn. McCarthy's reading of Dobie planted seeds that flourished with *The Border Trilogy*. But as Sepich has shown, the influence is fully present in *Blood Meridian*. The note from the archives reads, "'I dont propose to be called a liar' Dobie." In the margin next to the quotation, McCarthy wrote, in pencil, "Used Tucson." The quotation comes from an essay titled "Beeville Talk," in which Dobie recounts his relationship with Jim Ballard, an old-timer whom Dobie visited in order to soak up his colorful talk and wisdom: "He likes old times and stories that have something of the mystery of life," Dobie wrote (13).

One of Ballard's stories features the recorded conversation in a barbershop between two patrons, one of whom is bragging about a fish he recently caught. When the other expresses incredulity, the braggart says, "I don't propose to be called a liar" (23). McCarthy liked the sound of this and planned to use it somewhere. His penciled marginal note is a reminder to himself that he had already done so. It appears in the scene in which the judge tells an army lieutenant, who is seeking the murderer of a restaurant owner who has been shot by one of Glanton's men, that he is Glanton's legal representative: "Kindly address your remarks to me, Lieutenant, said the judge. I represent Captain Glanton in all legal matters. I think you should know first of all that the captain does not propose to be called a liar and I would think twice before I involved myself with him in an affair of honor" (237). From Dobie's wry account of a fish story to McCarthy's tense but humorous encounter between the judge and the befuddled lieutenant is a long distance, but the passage provides further evidence of the delight McCarthy takes in borrowing from writers he admires.

Doughty, Charles Montagu (1843–1926)

McCarthy references Charles Montagu Doughty, the English author of *Travels in Arabia Deserta*, at least three times in his notes and marginalia. Doughty's two-volume account of his travels among nomadic Bedouins remains a classic work of travel literature and anthropology. It was the first in-depth exploration of that culture written in English—English noteworthy for its combination of archaic phrasing and vocabulary, biblical rhythms and diction, and a concretely descriptive pungency. That description might just as easily serve for McCarthy's prose in *Blood Meridian*, and, indeed, Doughty's book seems to have exerted a powerful influence over McCarthy. *Travels in Arabia Deserta* provided McCarthy with a model for the biblical, archaic narrative voice he adopted in *Blood Meridian*, and the sometimes violent world of desert wanderers Doughty depicts provided a model for McCarthy's own tale of desert wanderers. As an account of the austere purities of the nomadic life, *Arabia Deserta* became a primary source for one of McCarthy's favored motifs—the desert wanderer as seeker (see the entry for Bruce Chatwin in the chapter on correspondence for an extended discussion of McCarthy's interest in the nomadic ideal).

Doughty's book begins with his account of his travels with the annual hajj pilgrimage to Mecca, follows his increasingly dangerous travels to the towns and cities of the Arabian desert, and concludes with his efforts to get out of that same desert as he encounters growing hostility among local tribesmen (Bevis n.p.). Doughty, who assumes the name Khalil, becomes the protagonist of the narrative, playing the part of a "wandering anchorite in the fable of human life" (2:45). McCarthy attempts to incorporate a similar atmosphere into *Blood*

Meridian—desert wandering as spiritual wandering; wanderers as archetypes within a larger human drama. McCarthy, like Doughty, seems drawn to the ideal of austerity as central to spiritual elevation. Richard Bevis says of Doughty that "even after a year of tribulations, he praised the nomad existence as the best; its pain and hunger were essential to the spiritual life" (n.p.). McCarthy favors narratives of wandering, and he often locates wisdom, as in the gypsies of *The Crossing*, in men of the road.

Two of McCarthy's references to Doughty occur in Box 35, Folder 1, which contains notes, and a third occurs in a holograph marginal note included among early draft fragments in Box 38, Folder 3. The first, on a page of notes dated December 1983, reads, "Critical plain (Doughty)." I cannot find that phrase in *Arabia Deserta*. The second, from a page of notes dated 1 December 1983, reads, "They endured upon that plain (Doughty)." Again, I cannot find those exact words in the book. However, the third reference contains a quotation I have been able to locate. Above an excised fragment from an early draft, McCarthy handwrote, "a darling life indeed upon the savage plain," and next to that, "ck use (Doughty)." Those words, minus McCarthy's addition of "indeed," come from a passage in Doughty describing a horse: "Under the most ragged of these riders was a very perfect young and startling chestnut mare,—so shapely there are only few among them. Never combed by her rude master, but all shining beautiful and gentle of herself, she seemed *a darling life upon that savage soil* not worthy of her gracious pasterns" (30, emphasis added). McCarthy did not use the quotation, but the fragment above which McCarthy copied it is a description of the vastness of the desert. Doughty's account of desert wandering, like Gustave Flaubert's more phantasmagoric vision of the desert as a place of spiritual trial, served as inspiration for McCarthy's visionary deserts in *Blood Meridian*.

Durant, Will (1885–1981)

McCarthy's notes for *Blood Meridian* contain a reference to Will Durant's popular *The Story of Philosophy*, though his interest was in a passage quoted from Arthur Schopenhauer in the chapter on the German pessimist. The note, contained in Box 35, Folder 7, reads, "The

bulldog ant is given in Durant Story of Phil—Schop." The passage is
one in which Schopenhauer explains that, in the words of Durant, "life
is evil because life is war" (325). In it Schopenhauer uses examples
from nature to illustrate this fundamental principle, and it is worth
quoting at length because Schopenhauer's words are clearly a direct influence on the philosophy of violence and war that the judge endorses:
"But the bull-dog ant of Australia affords us the most extraordinary
example of this kind; for if it is cut in two, a battle begins between the
head and the tail. The head seizes the tail with its teeth, and the tail de-
fends itself bravely by stinging the head; the battle may last for half an
hour, until they die or are dragged away by the other ants. This contest
takes place every time the experiment is tried" (qtd. in Durant 325).

The passage Durant quotes ends with Schopenhauer's grim conclusion from the evidence of nature, articulated in words that could come
from the mighty suzerain of *Blood Meridian*: "Thus the will to live
everywhere preys upon itself, and in different forms is its own nour-
ishment, till finally the human race, because it subdues all the others,
regards nature as a manufactory for its own use. Yet even the human
race ... reveals in itself with most terrible distinctness this conflict,
this variance of the will with itself; and we find *homo homini lupus*"
(qtd. in Durant 325). The difference, of course, between the judge and
Schopenhauer is that the judge relishes this state of affairs, finding
in the violent sovereignty of the will the occasion for thrilling games
and diabolical dances. Schopenhauer laments the metaphysical su-
premacy of the primal will, looking to art and religious renunciation
for opportunities for people to distance themselves from its fevered
omnipotence.

Dwight Eddins, in an article linking McCarthy and Schopenhauer,
argues that the judge represents both the noumenal reality of the will
and its phenomenal representation in the world: "The judge, like the
other riders, wavers between phenomenon and noumenon, between
embodiment and the primal force field that is embodied. But he is,
in his cosmic dimension, more clearly identified with the will" (31).
Eddins notes, in support of his contention that the judge symbolizes
Schopenhauer's primal will, similarities between the final description
of the judge as one "who never sleeps" (335) and a passage from *The
World as Will and Idea*, which reads, "The will never tires, never grows
old ... and is in infancy what it is in old age, eternally one and the

same" (qtd. in Eddins 31). The brief note on the Schopenhauer quotation in Durant lends credence to Eddins's speculations.

Euan Gallivan also argues for the influence of Schopenhauer on McCarthy, finding evidence of Schopenhauer's ethics in *The Road*. He points out that the novel, by presenting humanity in the Hobbesian state of the war of all against all, crystallizes Schopenhauer's vision of the "conflict of egos" (99) reduced to its most barbaric level. Gallivan finds in the boy an exemplar of the kind of person Schopenhauer regards as truly ethical: "In *The Road* the son, in contrast to his father, is most able to see through the illusory principle of individuation, with the result that he reacts with compassion (*Mitleid*) towards others" (103). This compassion is born out of his ability to "perceive affinities among all those who walk the road," which enables him to "identify and empathize" with others' suffering (104).

While it is true that the boy's exemplary moral character provides a striking contrast to the destructive will-to-power that McCarthy discovers at the heart of human experience, we can see, in a dimmer light, to be sure, but clearly enough, that the kid in *Blood Meridian* also possesses the counterintuitive, and consequently rare, sense of compassion that Schopenhauer recognizes as cutting against the grain of the will. His "clemency for the heathen" (299), as the judge characterizes it, links the kid to the boy—both display empathy and compassion in violent settings in which doing so puts one at odds with the prevailing current. The kid's compassion for "the eldress in the rocks" (315) highlights, in an almost startling moment of contrast with the novel's relentless carnage and savagery, how far removed the kid is from the judge's philosophy of the will-to-power and its embodiment in the grotesque dance of death over which he is the master. McCarthy's pessimism owes much to Schopenhauer's, but so does his profound sense of sorrow for the suffering engendered by the ferocious movements of the primal will.

Fraser, Julius Thomas (1923–2010)

Julius Thomas Fraser was a philosopher who devoted his life to the study of time. He founded the International Society for the Study of Time in 1966 and wrote several books on the subject, including *Time, the Familiar Stranger*, and *Of Time, Passion, and Knowledge: Reflections on the Strategy of Existence* ("Fraser, Julius Thomas"). McCarthy read the latter with great interest when working on *Blood Meridian*; it is the source of the Paul Valéry epigraph, and Fraser's discussions of the philosophical significance of clocks likely influenced the epilogue to the novel.

Fraser worked as a machinist, technician, and draftsman both in Budapest, where he was born, and in the United States, where he became a citizen in 1953, and taught at several US universities, including the Massachusetts Institute of Technology and Fordham University ("Fraser, Julius Thomas"). McCarthy's reference to him appears on the back of a page of handwritten notes, where he wrote, in pencil, beneath a quotation from William James (see entry for James in this chapter): "See Paul Valery quote in Fraser Time Passion Knowledge" (Box 35, Folder 4). Here is the quotation, from Valéry's "The Yalu," as it appears in Fraser. The work records "an imaginary dialogue with a [Chinese] sage" who is "reflect[ing] on Western ways of doing things" (Fraser 139). I have highlighted the section that McCarthy used as an epigraph:

> You have neither the patience that weaves long lines nor a feeling for the irregular, nor a sense of the fittest place for a thing. . . . For you intelligence is not one thing among many. You . . . worship it as if it were an omnipotent beast. . . . A man intoxicated on it believes his own thoughts are legal decision, or facts themselves born of the crowd and time. He confuses his quick changes of heart with the imperceptible variation of real forms and enduring Beings. . . . You are in love with intelligence, until it frightens you. *For your ideas are terrifying and your hearts are faint. Your acts of pity and cruelty are absurd, committed with no calm, as if they were irresistible. Finally, you fear blood more and more. Blood and time.* (139, emphasis added)

The imaginary Chinese scholar offers a critique of the West that is in accord with Fraser's.

In *Of Time, Passion, and Knowledge*, Fraser explores the "profound spiritual malaise" (3) of modern humanity through his discussion of the disorientation generated by the conflict between "psychological time and time in modern physics" ("Fraser, Julius Thomas"). Fraser sees time as "a hierarchy of distinct temporalities corresponding to certain semiautonomous integrative levels of nature"; he believes that conflicts between these competing temporalities, which range across a spectrum that encompasses subatomic particles and the different parts of the human brain, are endemic to the experience of temporality (*Of Time* 435–444). The conflict that Fraser believes is at the root of modern humanity's spiritual condition is "between knowledge felt and knowledge understood, or, in ordinary terms, between passion and knowledge" (444). This is the condition of Western man, who, in the formulation of Valéry's imaginary Chinese scholar, has made an idol of intellect. The triumph of scientific knowledge—knowledge understood rather than felt—has led to this condition: "Though these methods and trends (analytical thought and experimental method) proved to be useful to the artisanry of science, they failed to inspire, illuminate, or unify the various ways man experiences reality in a world where the absence of inspiration, illumination, and a unity of vision are all too painfully evident" (3). McCarthy's work reveals an awareness of this distinctive problem of modern consciousness, namely, the inability to reconcile the undeniable fruitfulness of scientific methods and assumptions with a meaningful spiritual existence. We can go back to William Blake, with his worries about "single vision and Newton's sleep," to find expressions of this conflict of visions. For McCarthy, scientific rationality, in its totalizing, hegemonic form, is embodied in the Faustian figure of the judge.

The evocation of Faust is apposite. McCarthy's reading of Spengler (see entry for Spengler in *Suttree*), with his critique of the declining Faustian civilization of Europe, is one source of McCarthy's critique of the will-to-power implicit in the West's technological dominance of the natural world—a critique present at the beginnings of McCarthy's career in *The Orchard Keeper*. The government tank that symbolizes the malign encroachment of modernity into Arthur Ownby's wilderness is, like Judge Holden's ominous claim to suzerainty, an expression of that critique. McCarthy, given his long association with the Santa Fe Institute, is hardly hostile to science. But there is no question that his work shows a deep philosophical concern with the psychic and geographic dislocations created by the triumph of strictly rational techniques of ordering both the natural world and society (consider the social worker who visits Ownby, whom he regards as an "anomic type").

At a deeper level McCarthy is concerned with a triumphalist *scientism* that is both portrayed and parodied in the judge, whose research simultaneously records and obliterates the objects of his inquiry.

For Fraser, clocks are an important symbol of the human predicament in the age of science. He devotes a large portion of his book *Of Time, Passion, and Knowledge* to the development of different means of telling time and of the effects of various forms of timekeeping on the human perception of time. He suggests that the relationship between timekeeping and our ideas about the nature of reality are deeply interwoven, and that "the history of timekeepers demonstrates the reduction of successively more refined ideas about natural processes to working devices which confirm those ideas" (62). The modern mechanical clock represents the end of a continuum of development that, in the terminology of Fraser, takes humanity from Cronus to Faust (150–153).

Given McCarthy's interest in Fraser's book, it seems a likely source for the epilogue to *Blood Meridian*, where the mechanical clock also symbolizes the suzerainty of the scientistic will-to-power over nature and humanity. The internal parts of a clock are used as metaphors to describe "the man progressing over the plain" and those who follow him, "the gatherers of bones and those who do not gather" (337). These followers "move haltingly in the light like mechanisms whose movements are monitored with escapement and pallet so that they appear restrained by a prudence or reflectiveness which has no inner reality" (337). This is classical determinism in its purest form, and one answer to the question posed rhetorically at the beginning of the novel, when we are told that "not again in all the world's turning will there be terrains so wild and barbarous to try whether the stuff of creation may be shaped to man's will or whether his own heart is not another kind of clay" (4–5). To *appear* to be restrained by an intentional comportment (prudence or reflectiveness), when actually devoid of an inner reality, to be moved exclusively by mechanical clockworks, sounds like the more pessimistic interpretations of contemporary findings in genetics and neuroscience (my genes made me do it). This question is very much with us.[1]

McCarthy subtly suggests that the question of free will versus determinism is an oversimplification. In the section of chapter 7 with the heading "Tertium quid," he adumbrates an answer. When describing members of Glanton's gang watching the flames of a campfire blow about in the wind, he reports that they "watched how the ragged flames fled down the wind as if sucked by some maelstrom out there in the void, some vortex in that waste apposite to which man's transit and his reckonings alike lay abrogate. As if *beyond will or fate* he and his beasts and his trappings moved . . . under consignment to some *third and other destiny*" (96, emphasis added). The term *tertium quid,* according to *The Oxford English Dictionary,* refers to "something (indefinite or left undefined) related in some way to two (definite or known) things, but distinct from both." It was one of the key concepts in alchemy. Somewhere between the extremes that so often define our understanding of the world lies the truth that gives meaning to existence. That truth is, because indefinite, known obliquely through the defined, but would seem to transcend the dichotomies that structure thought. McCarthy dissolves these conflicts in a gesture toward what can only be called mysticism.

Gard, Wayne (1899–1986)

Wayne Gard, a historian of the old west, was one of McCarthy's sources for his research into buffalo hunting in Texas. Gard was a teacher, journalist, and historian who "helped rescue from distorted Hollywood images, and to show in their true light, such frontier figures as the cowboy, the buffalo hunter, the gunman, the vigilante, and the peace officer" ("Gard, Wayne"). In the margin of a draft of the Fort Griffin bar scene, McCarthy wrote, "The Great Buffalo Hunt," the title of Gard's 1959 study of the subject.

Goethe, Johann Wolfgang von (1749–1832)

Goethe's *Faust,* along with Milton's *Paradise Lost* and Flaubert's *The Temptation of St. Anthony* (see entry for Flaubert in *Suttree*), was one of the works McCarthy studied as a model for the fictional crafting of a devil. His notes contain two references to the same line from the "Prologue in Heaven" in Part 1 of *Faust.* One appears on a page of holograph notes that also includes references to Valéry, the Parsifal legend, and Leo Tolstoy's *War and Peace*, indicating that McCarthy was listing important literary and cultural sources for his novel. Here is the reference to Goethe: "Faust (you must sleep but I must dance Die sonne tont nicht alter weise)" (Box 35, Folder 1). The German line, which is the first line—spoken by Raphael—of the "Prologue," also appears on a separate page of notes and is followed by a parenthetical translation, "sound of sun" (Box 35, Folder 7). The words "you must sleep but I must dance," from the first reference, are from a translation of the poem "Hyacinth" by Theodore Storm.

The proximity of the quotations from Goethe and Storm, and the fact that the quotation from *Faust* appears in the "Prologue in Heaven," are clues to their importance for McCarthy. Here are Raphael's opening words in full (I have italicized the line that translates the German that McCarthy included in his notes—the translation is by Martin Greenberg):

The sun as always sounds his music
In contest with each brother sphere,
Marching round and around, with steps terrific,
His appointed circle, year after year.
To see him lends us angels strength,
But what he *is*, oh who can say?
The inconceivably great works are great
As on the first creating day. (lines 249–256, emphasis added)

The subject of Raphael's song resonates with the title of McCarthy's novel, and the placement of the line next to the one from Storm's poem suggests that McCarthy intended to use it as one of his chapter headings, as he did with the line from "Hyacinth." The chapter heading, included in the group for chapter 23, is in the original German: "Si mussen schlagen aber Ich muss tanzen" (316). The translation in McCarthy's notes—"you must sleep but I must dance"—makes clear the link between the poem and the scene featuring the judge's triumphant dance (John Sepich discusses the chapter heading on page 101 of *Notes*). But which chapter headings would have included the line from Goethe? McCarthy eventually chose not to use it.

The fact that the line comes from the "Prologue in Heaven" provides a clue as to how we should read the judge. In *Faust*, the "Prologue" mimics the opening of the Book of Job, in which God gives Satan permission to test Job's faithfulness by calling down repeated catastrophes upon him. In Goethe's version, Mephistopheles takes up the challenge of tempting Faust into his "broad ... primrose path" (line 322), claiming that "My way of working's the cat's way with a mouse" (line 330). Knowing that McCarthy had the "Prologue" in mind while writing *Blood Meridian* bolsters a reading of the judge as a tempter figure, and that reading is also supported by the importance of Flaubert's *The Temptation of St. Anthony* to McCarthy. This connection would suggest that the kid, however improbable the analogy in many respects, is McCarthy's Job/Faust. A correspondence between the judge and the urbane, wry, verbally adroit Mephistopheles is, of course, less improbable. The literary kinship would be unmistakable even without the clue from McCarthy's notes.

Heller, Joseph (1923–1999)

An excised passage from an early draft of *Blood Meridian* features a holograph quotation from Joseph Heller's *Catch-22* in the margin, where McCarthy wrote: "Catch 22 'Without the spirit man is garbage" (Box 35, Folder 6). The quotation comes from chapter 41 of *Catch-22*, when the protagonist, Yossarian, is recuperating in a military hospital from a knife wound. Yossarian recalls the gruesome death of his friend Snowden, which turned him against the war. In the passage, Yossarian recalls the epiphany he received while holding the dying Snowden in his arms:

> Yossarian was cold, too, and shivering uncontrollably. He felt goose pimples clacking all over him as he gazed down despondently at the grim secret Snowden had spilled all over the messy floor. It was easy to read the message in his entrails. Man was matter, that was Snowden's secret. Drop him out a window and he'll fall. Set fire to him and he'll burn. Bury him and he'll rot, like other kinds of garbage. *The spirit gone, man is garbage.* That was Snowden's secret. Ripeness was all. (440, emphasis added)

The Heller quotation appears in the margin of McCarthy's draft next to a fragment that is directly influenced by Heller's grim assessment of the human condition.

However, McCarthy's reflections on mortality expand into baroque excess, and he was right to cut them from the novel, though it is probably more accurate to describe the philosophical fragment as a standalone piece. In the margin below the Heller quotation, McCarthy wrote, "West?" This note suggests that he was trying to decide whether or not to place it in *Blood Meridian*—and, indeed, the morbid meditation on mortality could find a home in nearly any McCarthy novel. Here is the Heller-influenced fragment, happily appearing here rather than in the published pages of any McCarthy novel:

> That life that is in men is their soul and there is no soul other. It is the same with men as with men together in a community and when a soul is nurtured in a community and come [*sic*] out wrong, if that soul is put away to death by the community then the community has been poisoned. You see this man and how he is dead. The capillaries in the eyes drain and collapse, the light runs back through the pupils a billion years to nothingness where man never was. Something has flown. He is gone. What? The soul? The soul and life are one. What has animated this meat was the spirit of man and that spirit is single to him as is the spirit of any animal to its members. The spirit is gestalt. It is greater than the sum of its parts, of the cardiovascular system and brain and the kidneys. The labors of this mechanical abbatoir [*sic*] support the life that is thereby motivated but they are not that life, the spirit.

To my ear, the emphasis in McCarthy's riff on Heller's theme is on *spirit* rather than *matter*, but the upshot seems equally dispiriting in both forays into the mind/body problem. Though he did not use the passage, both the ideas and the images find expression throughout McCarthy's work. He likes to associate death with the capillaries in the eyes. In *Blood Meridian*, a dying Indian chief's death is marked by "the capillaries breaking up" (159), and Anton Chigurh, after shooting a man, watches "the capillaries break up in his eyes" (122). The fragment, in which we hear the voice that Georg Guillemin calls "the melancholy narrator" (9), expresses an existential horror at the thought of death, a horror born out of a Poe-like obsession with the body as corpse. For

Heller, absent the spirit man is garbage. McCarthy out-Hellers Heller in this passage from *Suttree* in which Suttree observes the suicide taken out of the river: "He was very stiff and he looked like a window-dummy save for his face. The face seemed soft and bloated and wore a grappling hook in the side of it and a crazed grin. They raised him so, gambreled up by the bones of his cheek. A pale incruent wound. He seemed to protest woodenly, his head awry" (9). That "seemed" in the last sentence is ghastly. Memento mori, indeed.

Heraclitus (ca. 535–ca. 475 BCE)

SEE ALSO XENOPHANES IN *SUTTREE*

McCarthy's notes for *Blood Meridian* give away the source of one of the judge's aphorisms as the pre-Socratic philosopher Heraclitus. McCarthy typed a quotation from Heraclitus and then made a note-to-self about how he intended to use it: "War is the father of us all and out [*sic*] king. War discloses who is godlike and who is but a man, who is a slave and who is a free man. —Heraclitus" (Box 35, Folder 1). Below the quotation McCarthy wrote, "See *other* translation Let the judge quote this in part and without crediting source." Here is the judge quoting (with his typical baroque flourishes) Heraclitus: "War is the truest form of divination. It is the testing of one's will and the will of another within that larger will which because it binds them is therefore forced to select. War is the ultimate game because war is at last a forcing of the unity of existence. War is god" (249). Since, as this study reveals, McCarthy often interpolates the work of other writers into his own, this direct admission of his adherence to T. S. Eliot's views on literary theft (good artists steal rather than borrow) stands out as a rare example of McCarthy admitting to the crime.

Very little has been made of McCarthy's interest in Heraclitus, though Steven Frye, commenting on this same note, recognizes its significance as a clue to McCarthy's reflections on violence in *Blood Meridian* as well as a clue to the intellectual provenance from which the judge emerged. Frye astutely points out that "although McCarthy's interest in violence may be in part political, it is in a deeper sense onto-logical, as the Heraclitus reference suggests" (*"Blood Meridian"* 109).

McCarthy's work explores the metaphysics of violence. Frye's previous work on McCarthy had already divined the influence of Heraclitus, and the note from the archives confirms his earlier intuition. In particular, Frye believes that the philosophy of Heraclitus is relevant to an understanding of McCarthy's cosmological speculations:

> The Heraclitus reference is a significant discovery, revealing perhaps a central, though by no means the only, conception that undergirds Judge Holden's worldview. In my own *Understanding Cormac McCarthy*, in a discussion of *Suttree*, I note the influence of Heraclitus in what became known in the twentieth century as "panentheist," theology. Panentheism conceives God as a being that both comprises the universe itself and in equal measure transcends the physical realm. Given McCarthy's citation of Heraclitus, it now appears that this penentheist cosmology may have greater implications in McCarthy's works than previously understood. (119)

I think that Frye is right. Despite the unfortunate ugliness of the word, panentheism seems an apt label for McCarthy's cosmology. *The Crossing*, in particular, with its focus on a matrix of being that is somehow both immanent and transcendent, confirms Frye's helpful assessment of McCarthy's metaphysics.

Vereen Bell also grasped the importance of Heraclitus to McCarthy long before the archives confirmed it. However, his reading of McCarthy entails a very different take on this influence. According to Bell, the revelation granted to Suttree after his bout with typhoid fever—"God is not a thing. Nothing ever stops moving" (461)—echoes the famous claim of Heraclitus about the fleeting transiency of all things, now proverbially rendered as, "You can never step into the same river twice." But Bell, unlike Frye, thinks McCarthy gives us "Heraclitus without the Logos" (9). Later in the same study, Bell grudgingly allows that McCarthy's understanding is "not so much Heraclitus without Logos as it is Heraclitus with Logos rudely de-sanctified" (108). Crumbs from the table, that, but with such meager qualifications readers must be satisfied when reading Bell. Regardless of the precise state of the Logos in McCarthy's fiction, Bell's essential point is well taken. *Suttree* is a river novel, and in light of McCarthy's acknowledged interest in the ancient

Greek philosopher, it seems clear that the Tennessee River represents the ceaseless flux characterizing the world as conceived by Heraclitus.

Herrigel, Eugen (1884–1955)

SEE ALSO JACOB BOEHME IN THIS CHAPTER

McCarthy's notes for *Blood Meridian* contain two references to Eugen Herrigel's *The Method of Zen*, one of them correct, the other a misattribution, as the note actually refers to Jacob Boehme's *Six Theosophic Points* (see entry for Boehme in this chapter). Both books explore a kind of apophatic mysticism that informs much of McCarthy's treatment of religious and theological themes. Herrigel was a German philosopher who studied Buddhism while teaching in Japan. His books, especially *Zen and the Art of Archery*, helped to popularize Buddhist ideas in the West, though his associations with Nazism have clouded his reputation. According to the scholar of Jewish mysticism Gershom Scholem, Herrigel was a "convinced Nazi" whose widow attempted to obfuscate that fact after his death (96). Nevertheless, Herrigel's works on Buddhism continue to find an audience. McCarthy seems to have had Herrigel's explanation of the Zen concept *satori* in mind in the significant passage on "optical democracy" that serves as an anchor to the novel's metaphysical speculations.

The two notes appear in Box 35, Folder 4, which contains holograph checklists and notes keyed to manuscript pages. The notes appear in the margins of two separate pages and do not appear to be keyed to the paginated checklists. The first reads, "THE GROUND AND THE UNGROUND—see Herrigel Way of Zen 1st few pp." McCarthy's memory is off here, as the book is titled *The Method of Zen*, and the reference is to Boehme's *Six Theosophic Points*, which heavily influenced McCarthy's philosophical flights in the novel. In fact, McCarthy is probably referring to the introduction to Boehme's book by the Russian philosopher Nicolas Berdyaev, in which the concepts of the ground and the unground are discussed at length. It is easy to see how McCarthy could have confused the two books, as both posit nonbeing (the unground of Boehme) as the ground of being. Herrigel

says that the experience of *satori*, a kind of sudden, nonrational illumination, brings with it an awareness that "things *are* by virtue of what
they are *not*, and that they owe their being to this not-being which is
their ground and origin" (*The Method of Zen* 47, emphasis in original). How much of this explanation accurately reflects Buddhism and
how much of it derives from the murky fog of German metaphysics is
a question beyond my unenlightened capacity, but it is clear from the
two notes on Herrigel/Boehme that, whatever its province, McCarthy
takes the notion of the *via negativa* quite seriously.

Christopher Metress, in an insightful reading of *Outer Dark*, calls
attention to McCarthy's interest in apophatic mysticism as a partial
rebuttal to Vereen Bell's claim that McCarthy's philosophy is nihilistic—partial because Bell fails to acknowledge the role of "nothingness"
in certain forms of Christian mysticism. Metress argues that "the darkness and nothingness that pervade [*Outer Dark*] . . . can take us in a
different direction, down a path of 'unknowing' that will reveal to us
the incomprehensibility, rather than the emptiness, of the divine mystery. Seen this way, nothingness and darkness are not antithetical to
the novel's metaphysical vision; nor are they to be rejected or overcome
in order for the novel to be theologically satisfying" (149). Whether or
not McCarthy's interest in the *via negativa* provides readers with theological satisfaction, Metress is right to emphasize its presence and significance, and is surely right that McCarthy's awareness and appreciation of mystical traditions bely the charge of nihilism that some have
found persuasive.

The second reference to Herrigel reads, "Herrigel *Zen* opening
pages illustrious patent of their origins ?" (Box 35, Folder 4). Though
it is not located in the opening pages of Herrigel's book (McCarthy may
have still been confusing Boehme and Herrigel), this note does refer to
The Method of Zen. McCarthy is quoting from a passage that appears
to be a direct influence on his notion of "optical democracy," a kind of
Daoist or Buddhist understanding of the ultimate parity of all things.
In the passage, Herrigel is describing the kind of altered vision that
accompanies *satori*. According to Herrigel, "the first characteristic, it
seems to me, of the new way of seeing is that all things are of equal importance in its sight, the most trivial as well as the most significant by
ordinary human standards" (46). He elaborates this notion: "Things

are thus seen, and at the same time understood, from the origin, out of the 'being' which manifests itself in them. To that extent they are all of equal rank, all possessing the illustrious patents of their origin. They are not objects isolated in themselves; they point beyond themselves, to the common ground of their being, and yet this ground can be perceived only through them, through what exists, although it is the origin of all existence" (46–47).

When compared with the following passage from McCarthy, the debt to Herrigel seems clear: "In the neuter austerity of that terrain all phenomena were bequeathed a strange equality and no one thing nor spider nor stone nor blade of grass could put forth claim to precedence. The very clarity of these articles belied their familiarity, for the eye predicates the whole on some feature or part and here was nothing more luminous than another and nothing more enshadowed and in the optical democracy of such landscapes all preference is made whimsical and a man and a rock become endowed with unguessed kinships" (247).

Though one need not travel to the Far East to find a philosophy of metaphysical parity—Walt Whitman comes to mind as an American proponent of such a view—it is clear that McCarthy found in Herrigel's exposition of Zen Buddhism a congenial ontological vision, one that underpins the metaphysics and ethics of *Blood Meridian*.

James, William (1842–1910)

On the back of a page of notes on language and vocabulary in *Blood Meridian*, and keyed to manuscript page numbers, McCarthy made a holograph copy of a passage from an address on the subject of determinism that William James made to Harvard Divinity students in 1884. Interestingly, he misattributes the quotation to Henry James, a writer McCarthy dislikes, though a question mark above the name indicates that he was unsure about the attribution. The mistake is odd because McCarthy clearly admires Henry's brother William. Why would he have made such a mistake, or been unsure of the source of the quotation? Whatever the cause of the confusion, the quoted passage is one in which James questions the nineteenth-century notion of progress. McCarthy's view, expressed both in fiction and in interviews, is that the West is in steep decline, so it is easy to see why James's flirtation with pessimism would appeal to him.

The address, later published as "The Dilemma of Determinism," contains James's optimistic views about free will. In the age of Marx, Darwin, and Freud, many intellectuals were adopting a more pessimistic stance in relation to the question of the freedom of the will. In the spirit of the age, Mark Twain once gave a speech to the Monday Evening Club in Hartford in which he argued against affirmations of free will. The scandalized response was that he was robbing man of his dignity. Twain's rejoinder was that "it would not be possible to strip him of a quality which he did not possess" (*Mark Twain in Eruption* 240–241). Twain gives pessimism a good name. William James, in "The Dilemma of Determinism," attempts to sully it, and to restore to man that dignity that Twain (Twain and James were mutual admirers) denies.

McCarthy was deeply interested in the question of the freedom of the will when working on *Blood Meridian*. His notes refer to Tolstoy's pessimistic pronouncements on the subject at the conclusion of *War and Peace* (see entry for Tolstoy in this chapter), and he raised the question very pointedly in the early pages of *Blood Meridian*: "Only now is the child finally divested of all that he has been. His origins are become remote as is his destiny and not again in all the world's turning will there be terrains so wild and barbarous to try whether the stuff of creation may be shaped to man's will or whether his own heart is not another kind of clay" (4–5). Though McCarthy is reliably pessimistic on most matters, later in the novel he subtly insinuates a positive answer to his own question—but he does so by sneakily disposing of the ancient terms of the debate.

In chapter 7, at the conclusion of the tarot reading scene, and corresponding to the chapter heading "Tertium quid," the following passage—and if you blink you could miss it—seems to answer, however obliquely, the narrator's challenge: "[The gypsies] watched how the ragged flames fled down the wind as if sucked by some maelstrom out there in the void, some vortex in that waste apposite to which man's transit and his reckonings alike lay abrogate. As if beyond will or fate he and his beasts and his trappings moved both in card and in substance under consignment to some third and other destiny" (96). The word "destiny" might seem to bring us round to where we started, but McCarthy clearly implies that this third thing—this *tertium quid*, which by definition encompasses will and fate while also transcending them—makes the narrator's framing question nugatory. James attempts something similar in "The Dilemma of Determinism." Both James and McCarthy affirm a spiritual dimension to human nature that transcends the limitations of debates locked within the static logic of binary oppositions. Each term creates its own dilemmas, and we are left impaled upon one or another of two horns. McCarthy, like James, is a both/and, rather than an either/or, kind of thinker.

However, McCarthy and James display very different temperaments—James tends to adopt a sunny disposition, while McCarthy is a pessimist's pessimist. James studiously avoids Pollyannaism, qualifying, whenever possible, his flights of Emersonian confidence. The passage McCarthy copied onto the back of his notes is an example of such a qualification, though it is also a bracing affirmation of moral struggle. It is both a rejection of the idea of inevitable historical progress and an affirmation of the good fight, of being "the good guys," as McCarthy puts it in *The Road*. I have italicized the portion from James that McCarthy copied into his notes. Without the sentences I have included, James's pronouncement sounds darker than it really is:

> Not the absence of vice, but vice there, and virtue holding her by the throat, seems the ideal human state. And there seems no reason to suppose it not a permanent human state. *There is a deep truth in what the school of Schopenhauer insists on,—the illusoriness of the notion of moral progress. The more brutal forms of evil that go are replaced by others more subtle and more poisonous.* Our moral horizon moves with us as we move, and never do we draw nearer to the far-off line where the black waves and the azure meet. (169, emphasis added)

This passage sounds similar to a blunt statement about the human condition that McCarthy made in his first major interview, with Richard B. Woodward, in 1992: "I think the notion that the species can be improved in some way, that everyone could live in harmony, is a really dangerous idea. Those who are afflicted with this notion are the first ones to give up their souls, their freedom. Your desire that it be that way will enslave you and make your life vacuous." McCarthy's statement is grimmer in tone than James's, but the thrust of the two comments is the same.

Despite the different tonalities, we know that McCarthy's thoughts about human spirituality are indebted, to some degree, to William James, thanks to Garry Wallace's fascinating record of a conversation he had with McCarthy. Wallace, in his short piece "Meeting McCarthy," recalls a discussion of religion in which McCarthy clearly indicated his sympathy with affirmations of the spiritual life:

> He said that the religious experience is always described through the symbols of a particular culture and thus is somewhat misrepresented by them. He indicated that even the religious person is often uncomfortable with such experiences and accounts of them, and that those who have not had a religious experience cannot comprehend it through second-hand accounts, even good ones like James's *Varieties of Religious Experience*. He went on to say that he thinks the mystical experience is a direct apprehension of reality, unmediated by symbol, and he ended with the thought that our inability to see spiritual truth is the greater mystery. (138)

Despite the qualified praise of James in this quotation, Wallace, in a preceding paragraph, attests to McCarthy's great admiration for James's classic work on the psychology of religion. James should be regarded as one of McCarthy's major influences.

As a final note on McCarthy's pessimism, he owns up to it in interviews, but also qualifies its bleakness. In a roundtable discussion for National Public Radio on the relationship between science and art in 2011 featuring McCarthy, Werner Herzog, and physicist Lawrence Krauss, McCarthy said, "I'm pessimistic about a lot of things, but as Lawrence has quoted me as saying, there's no reason to be miserable about it" ("Connecting Science and Art"). Perhaps, as a philosopher of the *tertium quid*, McCarthy is only a pessimist *manqué*.

Kierkegaard, Søren (1813–1855)

McCarthy refers to Søren Kierkegaard in holograph marginalia in an early draft of *Blood Meridian*. The references to Kierkegaard in the manuscript appear on a page of the Fort Griffin scene, when the kid, now the man, encounters the judge for the last, fatal time. It is right after the dancing bear has been shot, where the judge first addresses the man, who is referred to as "the stranger" in this draft. These references identify an important source of inspiration for McCarthy's depiction of the relationship between the kid and the judge.

The first reference to Kierkegaard follows a quotation from Luke 12:20: "This night thy soul shall be required of thee (Bible—quoted by SK)" (Box 35, Folder 9). Farther down on the same page McCarthy wrote: "SK 'imagine a young officer—there is a battle.'" The source of these references is a collection of documents that Kierkegaard's biographer Walter Lowrie describes as "scattered papers dating probably from the last year of S. K.'s life" (520). Among these Kierkegaard papers is the document McCarthy had in mind, entitled "My feelings at the time when I was contemporary with Bishop Mynster." Lowrie includes this short piece in his biography, which may have been McCarthy's source. It contains three parables that Kierkegaard used to illustrate his relationship with Bishop Jakob Peter Mynster, Bishop Primate of the Danish Church, about whom Kierkegaard harbored very mixed feelings. The relationship appears to have been something of a double-bind, given Kierkegaard's ambiguous wavering between admiration for Mynster's piety and disappointment over his coziness with the Established Church, which was a frequent target, given what he perceived to be its tepid brand of Christianity, of Kierkegaard's attacks on complacent Danish religiosity (Lowrie 517–520).

What is significant about McCarthy's interest in Kierkegaard's parables is that it suggests a reading of the relationship between the kid and the judge that parallels, in a purely formal analogy, the relationship between Kierkegaard and Bishop Mynster. The parables suggest that Kierkegaard's feelings about Mynster were those of a disappointed admirer who has come to view a potential mentor and guide as a threat to a more genuine New Testament Christianity. The specific nature of the conflict between Kierkegaard and the minister prompts my characterization of the analogy as purely formal, but when we look at the parables through the lens of critical formalism, we can see how they became something like archetypes for McCarthy's thinking about the relationship between his two main characters in the novel.

The first parable describes a ship at sea and focuses on the captain

and his second-in-command. The ship is a luxurious passenger car-
rier and a celebration is taking place in the cabin as the captain and
his lieutenant observe a storm on the horizon, "a little white speck"
(qtd. in Lowrie 520). The captain returns to his cabin and, in order
to fortify himself for the "dreadful night," opens his Bible to the quotation from Luke that McCarthy copied in his manuscript. After his
portentous devotional, the captain returns to duty, "but in the cabin
the merriment goes on; song is heard there and music and noise, the
clatter of dishes and flagons, champagne sparkles, and the captain's
health is drunk, etc., etc.—'It will be a dreadful night,' and perhaps
this night thy soul shall be required of thee" (521). Here the captain, an
allegorical Bishop Mynster, holds bravely to his duty while the heedless partiers carry on below deck, and while the ship sails ever closer
to catastrophe.

This parable suggests that Kierkegaard saw Danish Christianity as
moving toward a catastrophe, and the bishop as doomed but heroic.
For McCarthy, the heedless partiers in the parable find their formal
complement in the dancers at the Fort Griffin whorehouse where the
stranger encounters the judge. The drunken revelry, sexual license,
and decadent theatricality of the dancing bear correspond to the pas-
sengers on Kierkegaard's party boat. McCarthy takes another element
from this parable as well: the quotation from scripture, which he puts
into the mouth of the judge as he addresses the stranger (327). The
quotation appears in the published version of the scene when the judge
tells the kid, "Drink up. This night thy soul may be required of thee"
(327).

Kierkegaard, however, then rejects this first parable as an inade-
quate characterization of the peril facing "the ship" of the Established
Church: "Is not this dreadful? And yet I know of a still more dreadful
thing" (qtd. in Lowrie 521). The "more dreadful" parable features the
same ship sailing toward the same "white speck," but now the captain is below deck, partying with the revelers. A passenger divines the
imminent danger and tells the captain, who chooses to ignore it, returning to the celebration. Here the passenger is Kierkegaard, who believed that his warnings about the spiritual dangers facing the church,
expressed in his book *Training in Christianity*, had been ignored. That
book was perceived by many at the time as critical of Bishop Mynster
(518). Here the formal similarity between the parable and McCarthy's

Fort Griffin scene lies in how the captain and the judge both join in with the revelers. The final paragraph of *Blood Meridian* features the notorious image of the dancing judge, who is "a great favorite" (335). In Kierkegaard's parable, the captain "hastens down again to the noise and the reckless joy of the society in the cabin, where the captain's health is drunk and he responds complacently" (521). The captain, like the judge, is also a great favorite, master of ceremonies on a doomed voyage.

The final parable switches the scene to a battlefield. The characters in it represent the bishop and the philosopher, and once again we can see how McCarthy has borrowed formal elements from the parable for his own narrative purposes. Kierkegaard's third parable begins with the words that McCarthy directly quotes on the manuscript page: "*Imagine a young officer*, we can imagine him a competent young officer. *There is a battle.* Our young officer commands half a battery" (522, emphasis added). The scene that follows appears to be the inspiration for the judge's claim in *Blood Meridian* that the kid once had him in his sights but refused to fire. The young officer in the parable has his cannons trained upon a spot that if fired upon will win the battle. That spot corresponds to the white speck in the first two parables, but here the young officer, or second-in-command (or passenger or kid), can take action to avert the catastrophe that looms as a point on the horizon. However, "just at that spot (or if not exactly at that spot, yet in such a position that it is impossible to train the cannon upon that spot), just there stands his own general, the old Fieldmarshal Friedland, with his staff" (522). In the parable, the young officer does not fire at the general (judge), and he laments his inability to act: "The instant passes. 'A fig for myself,' says the young officer, 'but the battle could be decided if only I might employ my cannon. Oh, this is indeed dreadful that it is my own general who stands there so that I cannot succeed in employing my cannon" (522). As in the case of the first two parables, McCarthy again uses the structure of the narrative in his own work.

We can see the same structure in McCarthy's account of the judge's pursuit of the kid and Tobin in the desert. Though McCarthy never shows the reader the precise moment when the kid has a shot at the judge, the judge claims that the kid had the opportunity to shoot him and refused: "I've passed before your gunsights twice this hour and will pass a third time. Why not show yourself? No assassin, called the judge. And no partisan either. There's a flawed place in the fabric of your heart. Do you think I could not know? You alone were mutinous. You alone reserved in your soul some corner of clemency for the heathen" (299). The appearance of McCarthy's references to Kierkegaard's parables on a manuscript page containing the encounter between the kid and the judge in Fort Griffin, and the structural parallels between the parables and *Blood Meridian*, make a linking of the two inescapable.

The formal parallels tell us something important about the content of McCarthy's novel. What is constant in all three parables is that a younger man stands in a relationship to an older man who occupies a position of authority. Cumulatively, the three successive tales suggest deep ambiguity about that authority, and at times dismay over the fact that the authoritative figure blocks the younger man's hope to avoid an impending catastrophe. McCarthy's appropriation of the parables suggests that the relationship between the kid and the judge should be read in a particular way. However different that relationship is from that of the characters in Kierkegaard's parables, let alone from Kierkegaard and Mynster, it should be understood as a moral struggle, one in which the fate of an allegorical group (ship/army) depends upon the ability of the younger figure in the allegory to act effectively. Kierkegaard's fatalistic parables suggest that he believed his own efforts to steer the ship of Danish Christianity away from danger had failed. The kid's struggle, one that is admittedly often difficult to locate in the text, is equally doomed.

On the page following the one where the Kierkegaard references appear, McCarthy wrote a note at the top of the typed page in which he offers a rare insight into his creative thinking as well as a comment about the doomed nature of the kid's struggle: "There must be a fatal weakness that gives the judge the edge. Something perhaps hinted in N.O. that he cannot do that seals his fate" (Box 35, Folder 9). Although it is unclear what that New Orleans hint might be, what is certain is that the kid has a fatal weakness: the thing he cannot do is to give himself over to the judge's apocalyptic violence, the movement toward "the evening redness in the west" (the speck, the spot on Kierkegaard's parabolic horizon). His "mutiny," as the judge calls it, is precisely his "clemency for the heathen," but the parables McCarthy is riffing on in creating the final scenes of the novel hint that the kid's inability to kill the judge has less to do with mercy than with his own awareness of an inextricable (if inexplicable) bond between them.

Kinnell, Galway (1927–2014)

The following reference appears in McCarthy's notes for *Blood Meridian*: "The Wolves—poem by Galway Kinnell" (Box 35, Folder 7). McCarthy had wolves on his mind. Below the Kinnell note he typed, "As salt as wolves in pride—Shaks (as horny as wolves in heat)." This phrase, from *Othello* (Act 3, Scene 3, line 404), is spoken by the villain Iago in his effort to stir up Othello's jealousy. Both Kinnell's poem and the Shakespeare quotation have less to do with the nature of wolves than with the nature of human beings, and, not to put too fine a point on it, wolves come out much better.

Galway Kinnell was an American poet and teacher whose thematic concerns align closely with many of McCarthy's. Charles Frazier's description of his work could easily be taken for a description of McCarthy's novels:

> The subjects and themes to which he has returned again and again are the relation of the self to violence, transience, and death; the power of wilderness and wildness; and the primitive underpinnings of existence that are disguised by the superstructure of civilization. Kinnell's approach to these topics is by way of an intense concentration on physical objects, on the constant impingement of the other-than-human on our lives. As he indicates in one of his many interviews, for him the non-human is a realm charged with meanings we hardly understand. (n.p.)

Take out the bit about frequent interviews, and Frazier is clearly describing kindred spirits.

The poem "Wolves" describes a group of savage buffalo hunters whose wanton slaughter of their prey is matched in ferocity by their violence against each other. The speaker in the poem, one of the hunters, after describing the senseless killing of huge numbers of buffalo, says, "All day wolves / Would splash blood from those great sides" (lines 35–36). This is the only mention of wolves in the poem, leaving the reader with the clear impression that the title refers not to animal predators, but to the far more vicious human predators.

Though it is easy to see why McCarthy would be drawn to Kinnell's poetry, he may have heard about this poem in Barry Lopez's book *Of Wolves and Men*, which made an impact on McCarthy. The title of his unpublished screenplay *Whales and Men* is obviously indebted to Lopez, who is mentioned by characters in the screenplay (see Lopez in *Whales and Men*). Of Kinnell's poem, Lopez observes that he "speaks of buffalo hunters and wolves in such a way as to leave the hunters saddled with the bestial imagery usually put to the wolf" (268).

The poem appears to find a clear echo in the scene in which the kid (now the man) encounters an old buffalo hunter on the north Texas plains. He describes the wholesale slaughter of buffalo that he has witnessed in his years as a hunter, "the animals by the thousands and tens of thousands and the hides pegged out over actual square miles of ground" (316). But Kinnell's poem is under the surface of the hunter's description of wolves following in the wake of the hunters. He tells the kid about "the meat rotting on the ground and the air whining with flies and the buzzards and ravens and the night a horror of snarling and feeding with the wolves half crazed and wallowing in the carrion" (317). Both the poem and the novel focus on the savagery of predation. Both occasionally make mention of wolves.

Krutch, Joseph Wood (1893–1970)

McCarthy's *Suttree* notes contain a reference to Joseph Wood Krutch on a page labeled "Dexter-Sinister-Coriolis" (Box 19, Folder 14). Krutch was a literary critic and nature writer. As a practitioner of the nature-writing genre, he was a staunch critic of "the increasing materialism and spiritual vacuity of mid-century America" ("Krutch, Joseph Wood"), which he believed resulted from modern man's alienation from the natural world. He coined the term "thanatology" as a more accurate replacement for the word "biology," because he regarded the modern scientific study of nature as a cause of our alienated condition (Krutch 109). Whether McCarthy had it in mind or not, thanatology would be a good name for Judge Holden's "point of view as a scientist," given his desire to reduce the complex organic world to entries in his sketchbook, or to inmates in his suzerain's zoological garden.

The note reads, "See The Desert Year Krutch—Carlsbad bats." McCarthy's reference is to a section of *The Desert Year* in which Krutch discusses the flight pattern of bats as they emerge from Carlsbad Caverns in the afternoon for their nightly assault on the bug population of New Mexico. Krutch wonders if bats spiral out of the cave in a counterclockwise direction because of the Coriolis effect (in physics, an effect arising from the forces that affect rotating masses), and if bats in the Southern Hemisphere might adopt a clockwise trajectory (145–146). His speculations relate to his general interest in how things in the natural world tend to organize themselves into regular patterns—an interest related to his unease with mechanistic theories: "On the other hand, since I am rather prone to hope that there is not a mechanical explanation for practically everything, it would also be gratifying to learn that there was positively nothing at all in my Coriolis Effect theory," he wrote. "One would then be left to wonder just how the Carlsbad community came to agree upon its traffic laws" (264).

McCarthy's interest in Krutch's reflections finds expression in his use of symmetry as a recurring motif in *Suttree*. In the italicized opening section, the narrator observes that "gray vines coiled leftward in this northern hemisphere, what winds them shapes the dogwhelk's shell" (3). The notes that appear on the page with the heading "Dexter—Sinister—Coriolis" almost all relate to this natural phenomenon. For instance, we find the following observations: "Plaice flounder sole in the tropics are lefteyed ... while those in the north are dextral. But the halibut is sinistral in both hemispheres—perhaps just for the halibut," or, "Hottentots and bushmen 70% sinistral. Their austral natures." The word "austral" shows up in Suttree's reflections on his Uncle Milo, who is lost at sea off the coast of Chile: "Foreign stars in the nights down there. A whole new astronomy. Mensa, Musca, the Chameleon. Austral constellations nigh unknown to northern folk" (128).

McCarthy often uses geographical and spatial symmetries—north/south, left/right—as metaphors for Suttree's own sense of himself as *sinister*. These metaphors occur in scenes in which Suttree reflects on his stillborn twin, or when he encounters his own sinister double in mirrors or hallucinations. After one of Suttree's drunken binges, he imagines his twin as a "Sinister abscission," and recalls seeing the child in dreams, "mansized at times and how so? Do shades nurture? As I have seen my image twinned and blown in the smoked glass of a blind man's spectacles I am, I am" (80). Twins and doubles haunt Suttree's imagination. During his vision quest in the mountains, he has visions of "Some doublegoer, some othersuttree," and imagines that if he encounters this double he will be "set mindless to dodder drooling with his ghostly clone from sun to sun across a hostile hemisphere forever" (287). The word "hemisphere" also occurs in a passage describing a dream of his twin. The drunken phantasmagoria he experiences emerges out of the "dark of the hemisphere" (80).

From McCarthy's reading come seeds that grow into the lush imaginative worlds of the novels. Krutch's reflections on Carlsbad bats and the Coriolis effect entered into McCarthy's efforts to depict, through geographical and spatial conceits, the moral and spiritual disillusionment and struggles of his protagonist.

McGinniss, Joe (1942–2014)

Joe McGinniss was an American journalist most famous for his expose on the subject of Richard Nixon's 1968 presidential campaign, *The Selling of the President 1968*. McCarthy makes two references to McGinniss's *Going to Extremes*, a 1980 travelogue recounting McGinniss's experiences in Alaska. The first, in Box 35, Folder 7, which contains notes for *Blood Meridian*, is a short quotation describing a landscape. The second occurs in Box 35, Folder 9, which contains an early draft of the novel. There McCarthy references the same quoted passage in connection with his own description of a landscape when the kid is wandering alone in the mountains.

McCarthy's interest in McGinniss's book is unsurprising, given that he spent part of his Air Force career stationed in Alaska. But whatever his interest in the book as a reader, as a writer he was taken by a single paragraph describing the sun setting behind mountains. McCarthy often seizes on small descriptive touches in books he admires, and then translates his readerly enthusiasm for another's prose into writerly crafting of his own work (see, for instance, the entries for Tom Wolfe and Tim O'Brien in this chapter).

The paragraph that inspired McCarthy is one in which McGinniss, visiting a pump station on an oil pipeline, watches the sunset from the top of an oil-storage tank. Here is the paragraph, with the portion that McCarthy typed into his notes italicized:

> After lunch, I climbed some winding metal stairs to the top of an oil-storage tank. It was the highest point for miles around. Thirty-five below, a slight wind starting to rise, and, from the top of the tank, I could see *the distant, flat sun setting over the faraway mountains. There was a bright orange glare, then the onset of twilight, and a quick blue darkening of the pine trees and the snow. Then snow and stillness everywhere.* Except for the machinery in the foreground. Except for the pipeline. (46, emphasis added)

Beneath the quotation, McCarthy typed, "See kid in mountains of Sonora," indicating precisely where in his own work he wished to convey something of the prose artistry he admired in McGinniss's description.

In the early draft, the scene in the mountains of Sonora is the one in which the kid looks down on "the collision of armies remote and silent upon the plain below" (213). In the draft, McCarthy prefaces the description of the battle below with a description of the sunset. We know this sunset was inspired by McGinniss because at the end of the scene McCarthy typed, in parentheses, "see McGinniss." He really liked Joe's sunset. However, in the early draft, the elegantly muted tone of McGinniss's prose prompts, oddly, an almost hysterically bombastic description of a "ferric holocaust" (see entry for Tim O'Brien in this chapter for the source of McCarthy's delight in the word "ferric"): "In the long light of evening from the edge of the rim he could see far out over the plain and to the paling shapes of the mountains beyond where their [in pencil McCarthy wrote "the earth's"] colors grew remote and the planewise clouds burned in a ferric [in pencil he wrote "used"—see Tim O'Brien entry for how he used it] holocaust that sucked up the silent dreaming desert in a problematic otherscape neither earth nor air." Following this description, McCarthy wrote, "On that mute landscape he saw the collision." The account of the distantly viewed battle then proceeds.

An interesting holograph note-to-self appears above this passage.

McCarthy wrote, "<u>You can</u> use this but you must rewrite and have another <u>day in mtns</u>." Happily, he followed his own advice, and the passage as it appears in the published novel features a description of the sunset that, like McGinniss's, is elegantly restrained. In fact, the final version is stately, lyrical, and lovely, in sharp contrast to the bathetic mess of the early version. In the final draft, the sunset, rather than prefacing the battle on the plain, is interwoven into it, and the contrast between the splendor of sunset and nightfall and the clashing armies is one of the moments of true sublimity in the novel. Here is the passage in which we see McCarthy's nod to McGinniss: "He watched all this pass below him mute and ordered and senseless until the warring horsemen were gone in the sudden rush of dark that fell over the desert. All that land lay cold and blue and without definition and the sun shone solely on the high rocks where he stood" (213).

Compare McCarthy's "sudden rush of dark" and the land as "cold and blue" with McGinniss's "quick blue darkening of the pine trees and the snow." Again, compare McGinniss—"Then cold and stillness everywhere"—and McCarthy—"All that land lay cold and blue." The resemblances are subtle, but they are unmistakable, particularly in light of McCarthy's acknowledgment, in his notes and in the draft itself, of the source. What makes this so interesting is the knowledge that McCarthy was so impressed by one short paragraph in a journalist's Alaska travelogue that he made a deliberate point of trying to create a similar descriptive atmosphere in his own work.

Nietzsche, Friedrich (1844–1900)

Critics have long suspected that Friedrich Nietzsche's doctrine of the will-to-power and his celebration of the *Übermensch*, or Overman (popularly known as the Superman), served as influences on McCarthy's development of Judge Holden's character and philosophy. Internal evidence within the novel invites this conclusion, but the archives confirm that McCarthy was reading Nietzsche during the composition of *Blood Meridian*. In the margin of a page of handwritten editorial notes, McCarthy wrote "Twilight of the Idols (Orig)" (Box 35, Folder 1).

Robert L. Jarrett, in his study of McCarthy, foregrounds the relationship to Nietzsche in his exposition of the judge: "Appealing like Hegel to history, the judge replaces the spirit driving history by a unitary will. But his philosophy is more Nietzschean than Hegelian, amounting to a précis of Nietzsche's *Towards a Genealogy of Morals* (1887), especially its devastating critique of Western ethics through an analysis of the relations between master and slave" (82). Steven Frye, in his "Histories, Novels, Ideas," also makes this connection explicit in his reading of the judge, noting that McCarthy deliberately evokes the concept of the *Ubermensch*: "The Nietzschean *Ubermensch* rejects external notions of value and through a process of self-discovery defines morality through the force of will. Judge Holden is in many ways a superman figure" (7). Much of the judge's rhetoric, with its often striking similarities to Nietzsche, confirms Jarrett's and Frye's judgments. For instance, the judge's rejection of moral law in favor of the will-to-power could have come straight out of one of the German philosopher's works: "Moral law is an invention of mankind for the disenfranchisement of the powerful in favor of the weak. Historical law subverts it at every turn" (250). His charge against Tobin—"The priest also would be no godserver but a god himself" (250)—is a purely Nietzschean notion.

Morality, according to Nietzsche, is the form that the universal will-to-power takes among the weak, and his sneering contempt for this "herd morality" is undisguised. Like the judge, who is an advocate for "culling" weakness, Nietzsche, in *The Gay Science*, excoriates "moral man": "Now consider the way 'moral man' is dressed up, how he is veiled behind moral formulas and concepts of decency—the way our actions are benevolently concealed by the concepts of duty, virtue, sense of community, honorableness, self denial" (295). And in a chilling follow-up to this, Nietzsche explains why he believes "moral man" must veil himself: "The European disguises himself *with morality* because he has become a sick, sickly, crippled animal that has good reasons for being 'tame'; for he is almost an abortion, scarce half made up, weak, awkward" (295, emphasis in original). The noxious bouquet of Fascism can be detected in Nietzsche's rhetoric, as it can in the judge's. Consider the analogy with animal predation at the heart of both Nietzsche's and Holden's words. Here is Nietzsche following up on his comments about the "sickly" Europeans he so despises: "It is not the ferocity of the beast of prey that requires a moral disguise but the herd animal with its profound mediocrity, timidity, and boredom with itself" (295). And here is the judge on—Lord help us—"the way of raising a child": "If God meant to interfere in the degeneracy of mankind would he not have done so by now? Wolves cull themselves, man. What other creature could? And is the race of man not more predacious yet? The way of the world is to bloom and to flower and die but in the affairs of men there is no waning and the noon of his expression signals the onset of night. His spirit is exhausted at the peak of its achievement" (146).

These statements elaborate on Holden's suggestion that one way to bring up a child would be to put the child into a pit of wild dogs (146), which John Vanderheide suggests might be "a slyly humorous reference to a passage from *Zarathustra*: 'Once you had fierce dogs in your cellar: but they changed at last into birds and sweet singers'" (qtd. in Vanderheide 182). Regardless of whether McCarthy had this specific quotation in mind, Holden's words are thoroughly Nietzschean. The toxic notion of degeneracy that we can see in these two quotations lies at the heart of the racist, eugenics, and Fascist movements of the twentieth century. That McCarthy is critiquing this rancid stuff is surely the correct way to read him.

And yet, critics seem reticent to say so without qualifying their words. Frye, for instance, writes, "Given that the judge is destructive and malevolent, it may appear that McCarthy is critical of Nietzschean ideas, but he allows the judge to speak at length in a distinct blend of philosophical argument and poetic expression" (7). If the judge is "destructive and malevolent," we may well hope that McCarthy is, indeed, critical of Nietzschean ideas insofar as the judge seems to embody and espouse them. After pointing out that "aspects of Nietzschean philosophy appear most often through unsympathetic characters," Frye goes on to suggest that "they are presented in his fiction as potentially accurate descriptions of the world" (8). They are certainly accurate descriptions of a certain view of the world, but I think we can take the hints that Frye himself notes—all those unsympathetic characters—and propose that McCarthy's work can be read as a critique of evil. That "blend of philosophical argument and poetic expression" that Frye sees in the judge's rhetoric should surprise no one. The devil always gets the good lines. See *Paradise Lost* for the classic instance. Milton's Satan, one of the models for the judge, has seduced many readers, but, *pace* Blake, Milton was not of the devil's party. Holden's rhetoric is very seductive, and his speeches may at times provide "accurate descriptions of the world"—though their accuracy is refracted by the lens of his rhetoric. Nevertheless, all that destruction and malevolence might incline the reader, like the kid, to resist seduction.

Perhaps McCarthy has provided an explicit direction to treat the judge's words (and Nietzsche's) with caution in the kid's dream of the "coldforger": "It is this false moneyer with his gravers and burins who seeks favor with the judge and he is at contriving from cold slag brute in the crucible a face that will pass, an image that will render this residual specie current in the markets where men barter. Of this is the judge judge and the night does not end" (310). However one wishes to interpret this enigmatic passage, the upshot seems clear enough: the judge is head of a counterfeiting operation. The devil, after all, is the father of lies.

O'Brien, Tim (b. 1946)

McCarthy refers to Tim O'Brien's 1978 novel *Going After Cacciato* in typed notes for *Blood Meridian*. The note reads, "'pink coral and ferric reds' Cacciato (see mtns)" (Box 35, Folder 7). McCarthy's interest in O'Brien's work during the composition of *Blood Meridian* is unsurprising, given O'Brien's focus on men caught up in violent conflict. However, McCarthy's proximate interest in the quoted phrase seems to have been in the word "ferric," which refers to materials containing iron. The word makes its way into McCarthy's novel, providing an example of how McCarthy's debt to other writers often works: in many instances, he appropriates minutiae far removed from the larger thematic concerns that draw the attention of most readers.

O'Brien's novel follows the sometimes surreal journey of a squad of soldiers during the Vietnam War as they attempt to track down a deserter, Cacciato, who attempts to make his way to Paris by foot. The phrase McCarthy quotes comes from a passage describing the landscape the squad travels through in its pursuit of the deserter: "The land was luminous. Pink corral and ferric reds, great landfalls of wilderness, and they moved through it for twelve days at a buffalo's pace" (60). As McCarthy's note indicates, he borrows the word for his own descriptions of the Glanton gang's travels through mountainous terrain:

"They crossed the blackened wood of a burn and they rode through a region of cloven rock where great boulders lay halved with smooth uncentered faces and on the slopes of those *ferric* grounds old paths of fire and the blackened bones of trees assassinated in the mountain storms" (187–188, emphasis added). Though it would be interesting to know McCarthy's thoughts about O'Brien's Vietnam novel, what we actually know is that he really liked the word "ferric."

O'Connor, Mary Flannery (1925–1964)

McCarthy is on record as an admirer of Flannery O'Connor, and readers have noted similarities between the two writers—notably, their liberal reliance on the grotesque, narratives punctuated by shocking moments of violence, characters drawn from the shabbier purlieus and lower classes of society, and an unflinching commitment to exploring the conflict between good and evil. At a deeper level, both writers conceive of grace as an unsought cleansing ordeal, something like St. Paul's "salvation, yet as through fire." McCarthy has mentioned O'Connor in interviews and correspondence as well as in a marginal note in an early draft of *Blood Meridian*.

The first time McCarthy mentioned O'Connor in an interview was in a short 1969 piece in the *UT Daily Beacon*, the student newspaper at the University of Tennessee, which McCarthy attended, without taking a degree, in 1951–1952 and 1957–1959. Asked for advice for aspiring writers, he responded: "Practical advice, I believe, would be to read. You have to know what's been done. And you have to understand it. I like the gutsy writers—Dostoyevski, Tolstoy, Joyce, Faulkner. I like Melville, particularly, and, more recently, Flannery O'Connor. She has a wonderful sense of the macabre" (Jordan 6). He also mentions O'Connor in a 2009 interview for the *Wall Street Journal*. Asked about his writing productivity, he said, "Someone asked Flannery O'Connor why she wrote, and she said, 'Because I was good at it.' And I think that's the right answer. If you're good at something it's very hard not to do it" (Jurgensen, "Hollywood's Favorite Cowboy" n.p.). McCarthy's correspondence with J. Howard Woolmer also contains a reference to O'Connor. In a letter to Woolmer dated 1 April 1980, McCarthy mentions his interest in John Huston's film adaptation of *Wise Blood*:

Wise Blood has not appeared here yet.... A number of people have told me that the film is just first rate. The lead, Brad Dourif, is the actor who played Bob McEvoy in *The Gardener's Son*, and Ned Beatty was also in both films. I'll keep my eye out for any sign of it appearing in these parts. I think the film has a peculiar history. Some friends of Flannery's getting together and deciding to do it and asking Huston if he would direct. He agreed, never thinking that they would get the money, and they turned up with it not too long afterwards, money from Germany, if I'm not mistaken. (Box 1, Folder 4)

McCarthy's familiarity with the history behind the production—and his familiar use of "Flannery" to refer to O'Connor—suggest a deep appreciation for the author. This is the enthusiasm of a fan.

The note from the archives appears in Box 38, Folder 3, which contains fragments from early drafts of *Blood Meridian*. McCarthy wrote, in pencil, "Habit of Being," the title of O'Connor's published correspondence. This appears on a page containing dozens of hastily scrawled holograph notes surrounding a typed paragraph describing the Glanton gang (an early draft of the description that appears on page 172 of the published book). There is no context that would link the note with anything in *Blood Meridian*. McCarthy wrote "Céline," the name of the French novelist who wrote *Journey to the End of the Night* (1932), right under "Habit of Being," so there may have been some connection in his mind between these two writers—but again, there is no context to elucidate their appearance on the page (see entry for Céline in this chapter).

O'Connor mentions Louis-Ferdinand Céline in three letters in *The Habit of Being*, all written to the correspondent designated as "A," and all focused on a comparison between Céline and Nelson Algren. In a letter dated 21 August 1955, O'Connor writes, "I don't have much to compare Nelson Algren with in this country as I have never read J. T. Farrell or Steinbeck [references or quotations to all three writers appear in McCarthy's archives—see the entries for each] or any of the people who deal with the afflicted.... I have read Céline though (*Journey to the End of the Night*) and there is no comparison. Nelson Algren doesn't look like a serious writer beside Céline" (95). In another letter, dated 16 December 1955, she elaborates on her criticism of Algren by saying that "his moral sense sticks out, is not one with his dramatic sense" (124). In the same letter she says, "the devil's moral sense co-incides at all points with his dramatic sense," which makes clear that O'Connor, while taking the moral dimension of art seriously, is primarily criticizing Algren on aesthetic grounds.

Pirsig, Robert M. (1928–2017)

SEE ALSO *THE ROAD*

In McCarthy's handwritten editorial notes for *Blood Meridian*, he wrote, "See Zen and Motorcycle." Underneath that he wrote "little animals" (Box 35, Folder 4). I cannot make a connection between either of these notes and the novel, or with little animals and Robert M. Pirsig's novel (*Zen and the Art of Motorcycle Maintenance*). See the entry for Pirsig under *The Road* for a discussion of his influence on McCarthy.

Salinger, J. D. (Jerome David) (1919–2010)

J. D. Salinger's name appears in McCarthy's notes for *Blood Meridian*, though *Suttree* would seem to share a deeper kinship with Salinger's masterpiece, *The Catcher in the Rye*. Cornelius Suttree is a literary descendant of the highly intelligent, but deeply disaffected, Holden Caulfield, whose disavowal of "phoniness" resembles a more adolescent version of Suttree's rejection of his father's ideals of respectability. Suttree is an adult version of Caulfield, a lonely, alienated consciousness exacerbated by an unyielding commitment to authenticity and truth and a sorrowful sense of responsibility for the lost, forlorn, and vulnerable.

The note does not refer to any of Salinger's works, but rather to an awkward account of meeting Salinger, "Catching the 'Catcher in the Rye' J. D. Salinger," first published by Michael Clarkson in 1979. McCarthy's note indicates that he came across the piece in a newspaper, but it has since been published in a collection of articles and essays about Salinger, many of which chronicle sometimes embarrassed efforts on the part of Salinger fans to meet the reclusive author. The collection's title, *If You Really Want to Hear About It: Writers on*

J. D. Salinger and His Work, hints at these embarrassing efforts. Clarkson's piece is a literary groupie's pained confession of a strained encounter between devotee and idol. What caught McCarthy's attention was Clarkson's description of Salinger's eyes. After detailing Salinger's exasperated expression of fatigue with the efforts of admirers to meet him, Clarkson writes that "his eyes were a day's work to look into" (53). McCarthy typed out that quotation, and in parentheses added, "newspaper story on Salinger" (Box 35, Folder 7).

We know of McCarthy's admiration for Salinger from Garry Wallace's article "Meeting McCarthy." Wallace records a conversation between McCarthy and the professional poker player Betty Carey in which the two discuss their aversion to interviews: "He told Betty that J. D. Salinger had given only one interview throughout his career as a novelist, to elementary children" (135). McCarthy's approval of Salinger's reclusiveness suggests that his own efforts to eschew the limelight may be modeled to some extent on Salinger's Caulfield-like avoidance of the "phony" world of literary journalism. This, in turn, suggests that the significance of Salinger as an influence on McCarthy should be taken more seriously. When Salinger is mentioned in connection with McCarthy, it is usually by way of comparing their shyness about publicity. But the mention of Salinger in the Wallace piece, and McCarthy's interest in the Clarkson article, make the case for a strong influence. As indicated above, there are similarities between Suttree and Holden Caulfield that invite further exploration. Add to all this a shared interest in Eastern religion and spirituality, particularly Buddhism (see entry for Herrigel in this chapter), and the case seems even stronger.

McCarthy's notice of Clarkson's arresting description of Salinger's eyes is interesting, because the motif of the eyes as windows to the soul is one McCarthy favors. It appears twice in *Blood Meridian*. McCarthy's first use of the device is in a description of Black Jackson shortly before White Jackson murders him at the gang's campfire: "About that fire were men whose eyes gave back the light like coals socketed hot in their skulls and men whose eyes did not, but the black man's eyes stood as corridors for the ferrying through of naked and unrectified night from what of it lay behind to what was yet to come" (106). The second occurrence is during the kid's dream of the judge while in jail in San Diego, when he sees the judge's "pig's eyes wherein this child just sixteen years on earth could read whole bodies of decisions not accountable to the courts of men" (310). In *The Crossing*, the Native American whom Billy and Boyd encounter early in the novel also has eyes that are a day's work to look into. Billy "had not known that you could see yourself in others' eyes nor see therein such things as suns" (6). We again see the motif in *No Country for Old Men*, where it is explicitly invoked by Sheriff Bell in his reflections on the young man he sent to the gas chamber: "*They say the eyes are the windows to the soul. I dont know what them eyes was the windows to and I guess I'd as soon not know*" (4, italics in original). It is intriguing to think that the inspiration for this fascination with eyes may have come from an obscure newspaper piece about J. D. Salinger.

Shakespeare, William (1564–1616)

SEE ALSO *SUTTREE* AND *THE ROAD*

McCarthy's notes for *Blood Meridian* contain a reference to Shakespeare's *Othello*. McCarthy typed, "As salt as wolves in pride—Shaks (as horny as wolves in heat)" (Act 3, Scene 3, line 404). Iago uses these words to describe Cassio and Desdemona in his attempt to stir up Othello's jealousy. I cannot locate any passage in McCarthy's work where he used the quotation, but it appears in his notes beneath a reference to Galway Kinnell's poem "The Wolves," which suggests that wolves, not Shakespeare, were on McCarthy's mind when he typed the quotation (see the entry for Galway Kinnell in this chapter).

Sri Aurobindo (1872–1950)

McCarthy's notes for *Blood Meridian* contain a reference to the Indian philosopher Sri Aurobindo Ghose. McCarthy typed the words "A mere and . . . Sri Aurobindo" (Box 35, Folder 7). Sri Aurobindo is considered one of India's greatest modern philosophers and was a prolific writer. He wrote mostly in English on a broad range of topics, including, according to Richard Chapman, "politics, political theory, history, art, literature, philosophy, metaphysics, sociology and yoga"

("Ghose, Aurobindo"). His work became known in the West as a result of the publication of thirty volumes in the 1970s. Chapman judges his main theme to be "the unity of all things—material, intellectual, and spiritual," further explaining that "the central theme in his writings is the divinization of life on earth." Presumably "A mere and" appears somewhere in those thirty volumes, but I have saved the project of finding it for another day.

Tolstoy, Leo (1828–1910)

A major motif in *Blood Meridian* is announced early in the novel: "Only now is the child finally divested of all that he has been. His origins are become remote as is his destiny and not again in all the world's turning will there be terrains so wild and barbarous to try whether the stuff of creation may be shaped to man's will or whether his own heart is not another kind of clay" (4–5). This question—Are we free or determined?—is at the center of Leo Tolstoy's speculations about history in the epilogue of *War and Peace*, which McCarthy references in his notes for *Blood Meridian*.

Box 35, Folder 7, contains several pages of handwritten notes keyed to manuscript page numbers. On two pages from these notes—written in the margins, and therefore not corresponding to page numbers—McCarthy wrote, "War and Peace." The second reference adds, "Last pp War and Peace," which specifies the philosophical epilogue as the subject of McCarthy's interest. This attraction makes sense in light of the passage about free will quoted above. In fact, the question of free will recurs throughout McCarthy's "western" corpus, where it finds its most chilling expression in Anton Chigurh's eerie coin-tossing. Tolstoy's concern in the epilogue of *War and Peace* is with the paradoxical awareness within individuals of being both bound by natural laws *and* motivated by free will, the paradox inherent in being both a subject and an object.

In the eighth section of the epilogue, Tolstoy puts it this way: "Looking at man as a subject of observation from any point of view—theological, historical, ethical, philosophical—we find a general law of necessity to which he is subject like everything existing. Looking at him from within ourselves, as what we are conscious of, we feel ourselves

free" (1370). Tolstoy's grim conclusion is that the drift of human knowledge is toward an inexorable loss of sovereignty for human beings.
Just as Copernicus's theories eventually overcame the commonsense
feeling that the earth is stationary in space, so our understanding of
history as the undirected "summing up [of] unknown infinitesimals"
(1384), rather than a process directed by human wills, makes it "essential to surmount a consciousness of an unreal freedom and to recognize
a dependence not perceived by our senses" (1386).

It is fascinating to consider that McCarthy's own reflections on
this intractable philosophical question were shaped in part by those
of Tolstoy, whom McCarthy identified early in his career as one of the
"gutsy writers" (Jordan 6) that he most admired. What is gutsy about
Tolstoy's conclusion at the end of the epilogue is that he admits the
near impossibility of denying the *sense* we have that we are free, while
insisting that we deny the *reality* of free will. We cannot think without
it, but our thinking, like a universal acid, corrodes the foundations of
that very belief. According to Tolstoy, we *feel* free, but we *know* that
we are not.

McCarthy does not attempt to resolve the question either, but, in
a key passage from *Blood Meridian*, he does suggest that it may be
more complicated than Tolstoy's conclusion suggests. In the section
of chapter 7 given the chapter heading "Tertium quid," the narrator
introduces a wrinkle into the classic formulation of the free will/de-
terminism dilemma. Describing the windstorm in the desert that follows the gypsy tarot reading, the narrator offers a cryptic aside that is
germane to the question posed in the first chapter and quoted above:
"These four [the gypsies] crouched at the edge of the firelight among
their strange chattels and watched how the ragged flames fled down
the wind as if sucked by some maelstrom out there in the void, some
vortex in that waste apposite to which man's transit and his reckonings alike lay abrogate. As if *beyond will or fate* he and his beasts and
his trappings moved both in card and in substance under consignment to some third and other destiny" (96, emphasis added). According to *The Oxford English Dictionary*, *tertium quid* means "something
(indefinite or left undefined) related in some way to two (definite or
known) things, but distinct from both." McCarthy certainly does leave
the something under consideration here very much undefined, but the
reticence seems akin to the notorious ineffability often associated with

mystical experience. Words cannot do it justice, but in it the most profound meanings inhere.

Of related interest is the chapter heading preceding "Tertium quid," which is "The felon wind." This is likely an allusion to Milton's "Lycidas," in which the speaker wonders about fate when mourning the loss of his friend: "He asked the waves, and asked the *felon winds*, / What hard mishap hath doomed this gentle swain?" (lines 91–92, emphasis added). This is typical of McCarthy's almost sneaky approach to weaving literary allusions into his own work.

Valéry, Paul (1871–1945)

Two folders from Box 35 contain references to the French writer Paul Valéry, from whom McCarthy got one of *Blood Meridian*'s striking epigraphs. The first, from Folder 1, appears on a page of holograph editorial notes, and it reads, "Paul Valery—The Yalu (in French)." The note refers to a short 1895 sketch—the source of McCarthy's epigraph—featuring a conversation between a Western intellectual and a Chinese scholar, a wise mandarin who critiques the West's worship of intellect. The second reference appears on the back of a page of holograph notes on language and vocabulary contained in Folder 4. Underneath a passage copied from William James's essay "The Will to Believe" (and misattributed to Henry James—see entry for William James in this chapter), McCarthy wrote, "See Paul Valery quote in Fraser Time Passion Knowledge." Fraser's book, *Of Time, Passion, and Knowledge*, seems to be where McCarthy learned about "The Yalu" (see entry for Fraser in this chapter).

Though Valéry's short piece came to McCarthy's notice through the Fraser book, McCarthy appears to have taken a keen interest in the work in its own right, so much so that he made of point of reading it in the original French, as indicated by the note in Box 35, Folder 1. In the imagined conversation between the westerner and the Chinese scholar, the latter critiques the West's worship of "intelligence," its tendency to equate, in Francis Bacon's formula, knowledge and power. The scholar tells the westerner: "For you, intelligence is not one thing among many. You neither prepare nor provide for it, nor protect nor repress nor direct it; you worship it as if it were an omnipotent beast.

Every day it devours everything. It would like to put an end to a new state of society every evening. A man intoxicated on it believes his own thoughts are legal decisions, or facts themselves born of the crowd and time" (Valéry 373).

This description of a devouring intelligence sounds similar to Oswald Spengler's description of the "Faustian" civilization of modern Europe (see entry for Spengler in *Suttree*), and of Judge Holden's "point of view as a scientist," one who would erase the past and put all the birds in zoos. The scholar is describing the philosophy of the suzerain, one who believes that "the smallest crumb can devour us. Any smallest thing beneath yon rock out of men's knowing. Only nature can enslave man and only when the existence of each last entity is routed out and made to stand naked before him will he be properly suzerain of the earth" (*Blood Meridian* 198). The judge links knowledge and power and fear into a witch's brew that makes the knowledge of the natural world coterminous with—the political metaphor makes this inescapable—tyranny over the natural world.

The judge, in his scientific sermons, appeals rather nakedly to fear: "The man who believes that the secrets of the world are forever hidden lives in mystery and fear. Superstition will drag him down. The rain will erode the deeds of his life. But that man who sets himself the task of singling out the thread of order from the tapestry will by the decision alone have taken charge of the world" (199). The scholar says of this overweening intellectual hubris: "This is the law by which the intelligence despises law ... and you encourage its violence!" (Valéry 373). Not only does he recognize the equation of knowledge and power in what he calls the West's "raging science" (375), but he recognizes both the fear that underlies it and the violence it entails. However, born of fear, heartless intelligence generates new fears (I have italicized the words McCarthy included in his epigraph): "You are in love with intelligence, until it frightens you. *For your ideas are terrifying and your hearts are faint. Your acts of pity and cruelty are absurd, committed with no calm, as if they were irresistible. Finally, you fear blood more and more. Blood and time*" (373, emphasis added).

This epigraph used to puzzle me, because the members of the Glanton gang do not seem to fear blood; instead they glory in spilling it. However, the Valéry quotation provides an important clue to the novel. The bloodshed in *Blood Meridian*, McCarthy is telling us, is not prompted by courage, but rather by fear. The judge calls men not to noble exploits, but to a sordid fraternity that binds itself together through slaughter: "What joins men together, he said, is not the sharing of bread but the sharing of enemies" (*Blood Meridian* 307). Fear and violence are closely knit, and the judge's awareness of this tawdry fact of human nature reveals the cynicism at the heart of his Mephistophelean wooing of the kid.

The scholar offers a contrast to the "crazy disorder of Europe" (Valéry 372) in his idealized portrait of "the land of Tsin, near the Blue Sea" (374). He tells his interlocutor, "Our empire is woven of the living, the dead, and Nature" (374), contrasting this continuum with the West, or "you who cut your roots and dry your flowers" (374). Unlike Faustian Europe, he says, "we do not wish to know too much" (375). He describes a way of joining men together that is also a bond of blood, but in a very different sense: "Yes, we men of these parts feed by continual millions in the most favorable valleys of the earth; and the depth of this immense sea of individuals has kept the form of a family, in an unbroken line from the earliest days. Every man here feels that he is both son and father, among thousands and tens of thousands, and is aware of being held fast by the people around him and the dead below him and the people to come, like a brick in a brick wall" (374).

This is a view that McCarthy's works tacitly, and often explicitly, endorse. Consider, for instance, the following reflections on the stonemason's trade (McCarthy is, by some accounts, a "passable mason," and would have appreciated the scholar's simile about the brick wall), voiced by Ben in *The Stonemason*, a work that, through the metaphor of masonry, expresses a similarly conservative vision of continuity between human communities (both the dead and the living) and the natural world:

And if it is true that laying stone can teach you reverence of God and tolerance of your neighbor and love for your family it is also true that this knowledge is instilled in you through the work and not through any contemplation of the work. (64–65)

The reason the stonemason's trade remains esoteric above all others is that the foundation and the hearth are the soul of human society and it is that soul that the false mason threatens. (66)

The calculations necessary to the right placement of stone are not performed in the mind but in the blood. Or they are like those vestibular
reckonings performed in the inner ear for standing upright. I see him
standing there over his plumb bob which never lies and never lies and
the plumb bob is pointing motionless to the unimaginable center of
the earth four thousand miles beneath his feet. Pointing to a blackness
unknown and unknowable both in truth and in principle where God
and matter are locked in a collaboration that is silent nowhere in the
universe and it is this that guides him as he places his stone one over
two and two over one as did his fathers before him and his sons to follow and let the rain carve them if it can. (66–67)

These words are spoken by a character in a play, but McCarthy's corpus,
taken as a whole, suggests that we might read them as "The Analects
of Cormac McCarthy" (the final pages of *The Stonemason* are actually
composed of apothegms that read like "wisdom sayings"). They limn
a metaphysics and an ethics that are present as early as *The Orchard
Keeper*, but that come increasingly to dominate McCarthy's western
novels. The philosophy that McCarthy's works embody is strikingly
close to the kind of organic vision of cosmic, natural, human, and
divine interrelation (the scholar: "At the point where our forefathers
fade, begin the crowds of Gods" [Valéry 374]) that Valéry's Confucian
philosopher proposes.

As a final note, it is worth recalling, in connection with the scholar's
comparison of human generations with bricks in a wall, that one of
McCarthy's personal forays into stonemasonry involved using bricks
salvaged from James Agee's home. As I have suggested in this work,
McCarthy's habit of occasionally weaving the words of writers he admires into his own novels fulfills a similar aim in prose rather than
stone. Such bricolage serves as homage to and acknowledgment of
continuities that bind human lives and enterprises together.

Whitehead, Alfred North (1861–1947)

An amusing holograph marginal note in an early draft of *Blood
Meridian* finds McCarthy engaged in a philosophical dialogue with
Alfred North Whitehead, who was a British mathematician and expo-

nent of process metaphysics. The note appears in the margin above the scene in which the kid, separated from his companions and wandering in the desert, wakes up after spending the night by a zoologically inviting "burning bush." McCarthy wrote the following: "(after Whitehead) For the problem of the lost man is not his own whereabouts but rather the whereabouts of the others" (Box 35, Folder 9). He followed this with a reply, but between the paraphrase of Whitehead and his reply, McCarthy wrote, "This is specious bullshit, Alfred North." Here is McCarthy's reply: "ME: For the whereabouts of a man lost is no different (in no wise varies) from his ordinary state and it is only the whereabouts of others that is at odds."

Apart from McCarthy's amusing twist on the Platonic dialogue (Socrates: "That is specious bullshit, Alcibiades"), this bit of scribbled marginalia not only testifies to his deep interest in philosophy, but also serves as a reminder that McCarthy reads as a writer. Both McCarthy's paraphrase of Whitehead and his response sound like the anguished musings of a lonely existentialist, lost in a cosmos where man must find his way, without a map, across a psychic terrain marked by alienation and disorientation. Somehow McCarthy finds these themes in Whitehead, but, granting my own inability to penetrate the opaque depths of Whitehead's prose, the passage McCarthy paraphrases is written in a less histrionic register. The paraphrase comes from the notoriously difficult *Process and Reality*. The passage is about the relationship between different levels or modes of experience, ranging from purely physical experiences to experiences characterized by symbolic understanding. Here is Whitehead: "Every statement about the geometrical relationships of physical bodies in the world is ultimately referable to certain definite human bodies as origins of reference. A traveler, who has lost his way, should not ask, Where am I? What he really wants to know is, Where are the other places? He has got his own body, but he has lost them" (170).

McCarthy is reading as a writer, and he has found, in poor Whitehead's innocent musings about the relationship between spatial orders, perception, and higher levels of cognition, an insufficiently anguished appreciation of the human predicament. Given the location of this philosophical aside—in the margins above a passage from the scenes in which the kid's lonely wanderings through the desert are most explicitly characterized as the wanderings of a lost spiritual pilgrim (McCarthy uses the word "pilgrim" to describe him, and the mysterious burning bush is an almost heavy-handed biblical allusion), we can assume that McCarthy was reading Alfred North Whitehead, but he was thinking about the kid. In much the same way, Kierkegaard's parables about Bishop Mynster became, in McCarthy's mind, analogues for the relationship between the kid and the judge (see the entry for Kierkegaard in this chapter). McCarthy is reading Whitehead as a writer on the lookout for material.

Wolfe, Tom (b. 1931)

McCarthy references Tom Wolfe in a holograph marginal note contained in Box 38, Folder 3, which is labeled "Early Draft Fragments" (for *Blood Meridian*). The note is written in the upper right corner above the scene in which the kid and Tobin flee from the judge across the desert. The note reads, "Wolfe arthritic trees see Right Stuff early." Wolfe describes Joshua trees as "arthritic" four times in *The Right Stuff*. The early reference McCarthy notes is found in the chapter entitled "Yeager," and is part of a description of the desert locale of Muroc Field in California, where the famous test pilot did some of his training.

McCarthy borrowed nothing directly from Wolfe's description of the Mojave, but that description does exhibit some of the unearthliness that we find in McCarthy's descriptions in *Blood Meridian*. Here is the description from Wolfe's novel: "Muroc was up in the high elevations of the Mojave Desert. It looked like some fossil landscape that had long since been left behind by the rest of terrestrial evolution.... At dusk the Joshua trees stood out in silhouette on the fossil wasteland like some *arthritic* nightmare" (38, emphasis added). The paragraph below McCarthy's note reads, "The following day [the kid] crossed through a high forest of Joshua trees ranged upon a tableland beset with granite peaks, pale naked rock and snow and dark eagles that circled the sun." In the published version, the text reads, "All that day they climbed through a highland park forested with Joshua trees and rimmed about by bald granite peaks" (302). This version also mentions the circling eagles, and adds bears to the desolate scene. There are no eagles in Wolfe's description, but he does mention "flocks of sea gulls wheeling around in the air out in the middle of the high desert in the dead of winter and grazing on antediluvian crustaceans in the primordial ooze" (39).

The relationship between these two works is thin, but the note provides another example of how McCarthy takes inspiration from other writers. An image or idea inspires his own imagination, which then transforms the source into his own material. Without the marginal note, there would be no way to find Tom Wolfe in the creative strata of *Blood Meridian*; nevertheless, something in that scene, and in those arthritic trees, sparked McCarthy's own creativity.

CHAPTER 8

The Stonemason

McCarthy's first venture into theater, *The Stonemason*, follows the troubles of a middle-class African American family in Louisville, Kentucky, in the early 1970s. He wrote the play in 1986 for a dramatic series sponsored by the National Theatre in Washington, DC. Although it was not ultimately performed in that venue, it has been staged several times since then, beginning with a 2001 production at the Arts Alliance Center at Clear Lake in Houston, Texas. The play is not entirely successful as a work of drama but is still of interest, particularly because of the extended philosophical monologues of the main character, Ben Telfair. Like McCarthy's unpublished screenplay *Whales and Men* and his second published play, *The Sunset Limited*, *The Stonemason* gives McCarthy an outlet for exploring philosophical and theological ideas. Indeed, in *The Stonemason*, we have something like a McCarthy *summa theologica*. Through Ben, McCarthy articulates a *Weltanschauung*: here is McCarthy's philosophy, theology, ethics, and aesthetics. They are sketched out more in the style of epigrammatic wisdom literature—the *Analects* of Confucius, or the *Meditations* of Marcus Aurelius—than in a discursive style. And, it should be noted, the *Analects of Papaw* are complicated by the fact that we receive them through the troubled consciousness of his grandson Ben. Nevertheless, it is hard to evade the conclusion that Ben is an authorial mouthpiece, and that in this play McCarthy has attempted to put some of his convictions about life down on paper.

The Telfairs are a family of stonemasons, though only Papaw and Ben maintain continuity with the deep traditions of masonry. Ben's father, Big Ben, has abandoned the quasi-religious devotion to "the craft" that Papaw and Ben uphold. Burdened by the pressure of financial difficulties, he commits suicide late in the play. Ben's sister Carlotta has a son, Soldier, who brings further grief to the family when he dies of a heroin overdose; he had also been involved in crime. Ben struggles with his messy commitments to his family and his devotion to the craft, insofar as masonry seems to be both his guide to life and his excuse for aloofness in the face of his family's troubles. He finds truth and peace in masonry, but may be guilty of using it as a means of escape from the troubles of his loved ones. He comes to realize that a philosophy, however noble, that atrophies the difficult and complicated ties of love and responsibility is incomplete.

In addition to the well-known writers included in this chapter, McCarthy referred to several lesser-known writers and books related to his research for the play. Three areas of research occupied his attention as he worked on the project: architecture, Freemasonry, and African American life in the South. On the subject of architecture, McCarthy consulted Paul Frankl's *The Gothic*, the works of Batty Langley, and Joseph Rykwert's *The First Moderns*. His research into freemasonry took him to Robert Gould's *History of Freemasonry* as well as *Old Charges of Freemasonry*. There are many versions of the Masonic Charges, documents that describe the duties of members. It is not clear which one McCarthy consulted. McCarthy's research into African American life in the South led him to John Langston Gwaltney's *Drylongso*, Michael Lesy's collection of photographs *Real Life: Louisville in the 20s*, and Theodore Rosengarten's *All God's Dangers: The Life of Nate Shaw*.

Cicero, Marcus Tullius (106–43 BCE)

McCarthy's notes for *The Stonemason* contain a reference to the great Roman orator and statesman's "The Dream of Scipio." The note reads, "Pythagorean harmony—plucked string—see Cicero's *Dream of Scipio*" (Box 66, Folder 4). It appears on a page of research notes on Freemasonry that functions as a shorthand for the spiritual vision that the play articulates, which focuses on harmony between God, humanity, and nature. Cicero's dream-vision also explores the theme of spiritual harmony. In the dream, Scipio Africanus the Younger, a great Roman soldier and statesman, is visited by his grandfather, a hero of the Second Punic War, who takes his grandson into the heavens in order to explain the structure of the universe; the explanation relies heavily on the mystical cosmology of the ancient world, which was rooted in the vision of the nine heavenly spheres, and on the Pythagorean belief in the musical harmony produced by the movement of those spheres. As Africanus the Elder explains, the spheres "create [the harmony] by their own motion as they rush upon their way. The intervals between them, although differing in length, are all measured according to a fixed scheme of proportions; and this arrangement produces a melodious blend of high and low notes, from which emerges a varied harmony" (348). McCarthy's interest in Cicero's imagined dream finds expression in Ben Telfair's philosophical vision of cosmic harmony as it is embodied in his work as a mason, where creative efforts are in accord with God's created order.

McCarthy's note contains the phrase "plucked string," which probably alludes to Africanus the Elder's analogy between human artistic productions and the music of the spheres. As he explains, "clever men, by imitating these musical effects with their stringed instruments and voices, have given themselves the possibility of eventually returning to this place; and the same chance exists for others too, who during their earthly lives have devoted their outstanding talents to heavenly activities" (348). Here we see an aesthetic theory that seems in line with McCarthy's own understanding of creativity as expressed in *The Stonemason*. Here is how Ben articulates what he takes to be his grandfather's view:

> The calculations necessary to the right placement of stone are not performed in the mind but in the blood. Or they are like those vestibular reckonings performed in the inner ear for standing upright. I see him standing there over his plumb bob which never lies and never lies and the plumb bob is pointing motionless to the unimaginable center of the earth four thousand miles beneath his feet. Pointing to a blackness unknown and unknowable both in truth and in principle where God and matter are locked in a collaboration that is silent nowhere in the universe and it is this that guides him as he places his stone one over two and two over one as did his fathers before him and his sons to follow and let the rain carve them if it can. (66–67)

McCarthy's cosmological vision is sparse by comparison with Cicero's grand universal architecture, and yet the core idea is the same. Authentic creative work—and masonry functions as a symbol of all creative work—must, if it is to have genuine spiritual value, harmonize with the total cosmic ambience.

An additional similarity between Cicero's work and McCarthy's play is in the way each endorses deference for ancestors that approaches ancestor worship. McCarthy concludes the play with Ben's own dream-vision of his grandfather, reiterating the theme of creative harmony between humanity and God's created order:

> He came out of the darkness and at that moment everything seemed revealed to me.... He was just a man, naked and alone in the universe, and he was not afraid and I wept with a joy and a sadness I'd never known and I stood there with the tears pouring down my face and he smiled at me and he held out both his hands. Hands from which all those blessings had flowed. Hands I never tired to look at. Shaped in the image of God. To make the world. To make it again and again.
> (132–133)

Ben concludes this reverential reflection by confessing that the vision of his grandfather moved him to prayer, "and I knew that he would guide me all my days and that he would not fail me" (133). Again, McCarthy's spiritual vision is sparse by comparison with Cicero's, but both are rooted in a closely aligned set of premises about the world and humanity's place in it.

Faulkner, William (1897–1962)

SEE ALSO *THE ORCHARD KEEPER*

One reference to William Faulkner appears in McCarthy's notes for *The Stonemason*. McCarthy typed, "Hit me you got to hit to somebody (Dilsey?)" (Box 66, Folder 5). McCarthy appears to be exploring dialogue options for one of the characters. This line does not appear in the published work, but the parenthetical question indicates that McCarthy was concerned that he was "lifting" a line from Dilsey in

The Sound and the Fury. Though McCarthy's line is not an exact copy, he was thinking about the scene in Jason's section of Faulkner's novel when Jason threatens to whip Caddy's daughter Quentin with his belt. Dilsey steps between them: "'Hit me, den,' she says, 'ef nothing else but hittin somebody wont do you. Hit me,' she says" (185). Faulkner's work continued to echo in McCarthy's imagination into his third decade as a writer. McCarthy has not always been successful in filtering that echo out of his own narrative voice, but this note indicates his awareness of the need for such filtering.

Frankl, Paul (1878–1962)

In McCarthy's notes on the history of architecture and masonry, he lists as one of his references a work by Paul Frankl on medieval architecture: "*The Gothic*—P Frankl—1960 (on masons)" (Box 66, Folder 4). Frankl, who was born in Prague, taught at Princeton University's Institute of Advanced Studies. He belonged to a school associated with a highly theoretical approach to art history known as *Kunstwissenschaft*. Frankl's work focused on "principles and categories—visual and intellectual—that control the viewer, the work of art and the conditions of its construction" ("Frankl, Paul").

Gaines, Ernest J. (b. 1933)

McCarthy's notes for *The Stonemason* indicate an interest in Ernest J. Gaines's novel *The Autobiography of Miss Jane Pittman*, an account of an African American woman's journey through America's fraught racial history, including slavery and the burgeoning civil rights movement. She tells her story at the prompting of a young schoolteacher, whose awe at her vast experience may have served as a model for Ben Telfair's reverential comportment toward his grandfather's history. Gaines's novel is one among a number of mostly nonfiction works that McCarthy used as models for depicting the African American experience. The first reference is found in notes contained in Box 66, Folder 5, where McCarthy typed "Jane Pittman" right below another title, *Roll Jordan Roll*, another work McCarthy used to research African American history and experience. The second reference is found in Box 66, Folder 7, where McCarthy wrote "Jane Pittman" in the margin of a draft.

Galsworthy, John (1867–1933)

John Galsworthy is now best known for his Forsyte Chronicles, a series of novels and stories that satirize the Edwardian-era British upper class. Interest in his dramatic works has waned, but at one time he was almost as esteemed as George Bernard Shaw (Sternlicht n.p.). McCarthy's notes for *The Stonemason* contain a reference to a short narrative essay about a master boot-maker who is clearly an inspiration for the master stonemason Papaw. McCarthy typed, "Short story Quality" (Box 66, Folder 5). Though he does not name Galsworthy, and the short sketch is not, strictly speaking, a short story—it appears in a volume entitled *Studies and Essays: "Quality" and Others*—a reading of the work confirms that McCarthy must be referring to the Galsworthy piece. In fact, "Quality" bears such a striking similarity to *The Stonemason* that it is tempting to describe it as a direct influence on McCarthy's play.

"Quality" records the interactions between an unnamed narrator and a Mr. Gessler, a German immigrant who, along with his older brother, runs a boot-making shop in London. The narrator, a customer over the course of many years, ruminates on Mr. Gessler's mastery of his craft and bemoans the decline of the business as larger companies, through mass production and the use of advertising, put the squeeze on Mr. Gessler's smaller operation. The narrative concludes with Gessler's death, which seems to be brought on by the elimination of a place for the master craftsman in the modern economy.

The narrator sounds very much like McCarthy's Ben Telfair. Both are younger men who revere an older man whose mastery of an old trade seems akin to the mastery of a religious adept. Both find spiritual significance in the work of the older men. Both lament the loss of such men and their work in the modern economy. The following example from "Quality" illustrates the similarities in tone and theme between the two works: "Those pairs could only have been made by one who saw before him the Soul of Boot—so truly were they prototypes incarnating the very spirit of all foot-gear. These thoughts, of course, came to me later. . . . For to make boots—such boots as he made—seemed to me then, and still seems to me, mysterious and wonderful" (4). Later he says that Gessler's eyes "had in them the simple gravity of one secretly possessed by the Ideal" (4). Such Platonic boot-making ensures boots that hold up over time: "For it was not possible to go to him very often—his boots lasted terribly, having something beyond the temporary—some, as it were, essence of boot stitched into them" (5). And Platonic boot-making is no respecter of modern mass-production: "Dose big virms 'ave no self-respect. Drash!" (6). In these passages, we find parallels with Ben Telfair's reflections on his grandfather—reverence for a master craftsman, a quasi-religious view of an exalted trade, esteem for work that stands out from that of others and that lasts over time, and a critique of less organic modern methods of production.

The following quotations from Ben's ruminations on his grandfather in *The Stonemason* illustrate the parallels. Ben reveres the distinctiveness of Papaw's work: "I can look at a wall or the foundation of a barn and tell his work from the work of other masons even in the same structure" (8). He dislikes modern methods. About a house that his grandfather built, he says, "It was built long before the introduction of portland cement made it possible to build with stone and yet know nothing of masonry" (9). Like the narrator of "Quality," he finds that the mastery of the trade corresponds to a spiritual knowledge of reality: "For true masonry is not held together by cement but by gravity. That is to say, by the warp of the world. By the stuff of creation itself. The keystone that locks the arch is pressed in place by the thumb of God" (9–10).

McCarthy often builds large structures out of small cornerstones borrowed from the work of others. From a forgettable poem by Nelson Algren he fashioned the baroque extravagancies of the first pages of *Suttree* (see entry for Algren in *Suttree*). From an obscure parable by Kierkegaard he seems to have derived some sense of what the relationship between Judge Holden and the kid should be (see entry for Kierkegaard in *Blood Meridian*). From "Quality," a very minor sketch by a minor writer (now major—he won the Nobel Prize in 1932), McCarthy seems to have taken much of the inspiration for a play that is probably the most complete statement of "The Philosophy of Cormac McCarthy" that we have.

Genovese, Eugene (1930–2012)

McCarthy typed the title of Eugene Genovese's classic history of American slavery, *Roll, Jordan, Roll*, into his notes for *The Stonemason*. The title appears above another, Earnest J. Gaines's *The Autobiography of Miss Jane Pittman* (Box 66, Folder 5). These two works, along with several others logged into his notes, are part of McCarthy's research into African American history, culture, and experience. A consummate researcher and stickler for detailed accuracy, McCarthy consulted the work of several writers in his effort to create a convincing portrait of a black family living in the American South in the 1970s with a history going back to slavery. David Brion Davis, writing in *The New York Review of Books*, called Genovese's acclaimed history "the most vivid, imaginative, and comprehensive picture we have of slave life in the South" (n.p.). Written from a Marxist perspective, Genovese's history paints a portrait of systematic oppression that undermines more benign accounts of the relationship between slave owners and slaves. Such a perspective would have been of interest to McCarthy, as the play contains discussions of Hegel, Marx, and the master-slave dynamic.

Gould, Robert Freke (1836–1915)

In McCarthy's notes for *The Stonemason* he cites Robert Freke Gould among his research sources on Freemasonry (Box 66, Folder 5). The work listed in McCarthy's notes is the one for which Gould is best known, a three-volume set entitled *The History of Freemasonry* that he wrote between 1882 and 1887.

Herbert, Edward (1583–1648)

In his research notes for *The Stonemason*, McCarthy listed a work by the now little-read philosopher Edward Herbert: "De Veritate— minimalists religious tract. Foundation of Deism. Lord Herbert" (Box 66, Folder 4). Herbert's book *De Veritate*, as McCarthy indicates, is widely regarded as one of the foundational texts in the formation of Deism (which distinguishes him from his more famous brother, George Herbert, the poet and thoroughly orthodox Christian believer). In it Edward Herbert strips religious belief down to what he sees as its essentials, describing a pristine "religion of reason" that he said predated the "covetous and crafty sacerdotal order" of institutional religion ("Herbert, Edward of Cherbury"). Herbert's tract may have served as a model for the religious musings of McCarthy's Ben (which Ben believes derive from Papaw). Ben, like Herbert, exhibits a preference for a simple piety that finds God to be revealed primarily in his created order.

Langley, Batty (1696–1751)

McCarthy refers to Batty Langley, an eighteenth-century professional gardener and writer on architecture, in this comment contained in his research notes for *The Stonemason*: "*Ancient Masonry*—Betty [*sic*] Langley—Largest Eng Architecture book" (Box 66, Folder 4). McCarthy has the title wrong as well as Langley's first name. Published in 1742, the book McCarthy has in mind is *Ancient Architecture Restored*, which was reissued in 1747 as *Gothic Architecture, Improved by Rules and Proportions*, the title by which it has been known since ("Langley, Batty").

A derisive quotation by Horace Walpole suggests that Langley's understanding of Gothic architecture was defective: "All that his books achieved, has been to teach carpenters to massacre that venerable species, and to give occasion to those who know nothing of the matter, and who mistake his clumsy efforts for real imitations, to censure the productions of our ancestors, whose bold and beautiful fabrics Sir Charles Wren viewed or reviewed with astonishment and never mentioned without esteem" ("Langley, Batty"). Walpole's judgment accords with the assessment of the curators of the Twickenham Museum, who, with greater diplomacy than Walpole, claim that he was "educated beyond his natural talents" ("Langley, Batty"). Perhaps McCarthy had this eighteenth-century adept at self-promotion in mind as an example of the false mason.

Lesy, Michael (b. 1945)

In his notes for *The Stonemason*, McCarthy cites Michael Lesy's book *Real Life: Louisville in the Twenties* among his research sources (Box 66, Folder 5). Lesy has published numerous collections of historical photographs, the most famous being *Wisconsin Death Trip*. *Real Life* is almost entirely photographs, so McCarthy must have used it as a source for images of Louisville's past.

Melville, Herman (1819–1891)

SEE ALSO *SUTTREE* AND *WHALES AND MEN*

In McCarthy's notes for *The Stonemason* he refers to Herman Melville in connection with bricklaying. The typed note reads, "Headers and stretchers (Mville—like cautionary fables)" (Box 66, Folder 5). I cannot identify the "cautionary fables" in Melville, but the reference to "headers and stretchers" is congruent with the other notes on the same page, which are proposed lines for Ben to speak during his sermons on the gospel of stonemasonry. These two terms refer to the placement of bricks in masonry—a header is a brick placed so that its short end faces out (displaying the width), a stretcher so that its longer side faces out (displaying the length).

Throughout the play McCarthy employs masonry as a key metaphor for a life of spiritual uprightness. That he was thinking about headers and stretchers in metaphorical terms is borne out by the other passages that appear on the page: "That God made the stones flat so that they could be placed so to make houses for his bodies and temples for his soul. Or he made beings with just such bodies and just such souls to require just such stones." Or: "The gravity is in the stone and it makes you strong. Flesh needs stone. Something to come to grips with. Something that in resisting so firmly being shaped does shape the shaper. For all true masons are formed by their calling. They assume such shapes as suit life." These passages do not appear in the published play, but the play contains musings of a similar character.

Northrop, Filmer Stuart Cuckow (1893–1992)

McCarthy's notes for *The Stonemason* contain a reference to the last work by the American philosopher F. S. C. Northrop, the formidable sounding *The Prolegomena to a 1985 Philosophiae Naturalis Principia Mathematica Which Will Be Able to Present Itself as a Science of the True*. McCarthy's note reads, "F S C Northrop: *Prolegomena*" (Box 66, Folder 4). More a prospectus than a fully formed work, *The Prolegomena* is reportedly as dense and difficult as the title implies. Nevertheless, McCarthy tackled it, or meant to tackle it, while working on his play. I have no intention of tackling it, and cannot report on its significance for McCarthy. Northrop is probably most famous for his book *The Meeting of East and West*, in which he argues that Eastern cultures base their systems of thought on "concepts by intuition," whereas Western cultures base them on "concepts by postulation" (Hall 183). The latter derive their meaning from their place within a deductive scheme of reasoning, whereas the former derive their meaning from immediate apprehension (183). Northrop's distinction bears on other thorny dichotomies, such as the fact/value problem and the divide between science and more intuitive modes of perception, such as art and mysticism.

Rilke, Rainer Maria (1875–1926)

McCarthy's notes for *The Stonemason* contain a reference to Rainer Maria Rilke's novel *The Notebooks of Malte Laurids Brigge*. A single line of type includes the words "Malte Brigge" (Box 66, Folder 5). The reference seems out of place in the midst of notes for the play, but the published edition does contain a clear allusion to Rilke's "Second Duino Elegy." However surprising the note may be in this group of papers, Rilke's novel seems a likely influence on *Suttree*. The *Suttree* connection, the Rilke allusion in *The Stonemason*, and the "Malte Brigge" comment all suggest that the poet is a favorite of McCarthy's as well as a significant influence.

Rilke's *Notebooks* feature the fictional journal entries of a young Danish poet adrift in Paris, an observant, melancholy flaneur who explores the darker strata of Parisian life. Poverty, madness, decay, and death, along with his relationship to his aristocratic family, are all frequent subjects of contemplation. Though Cornelius Suttree is not described as a poet in the published edition of *Suttree*, early drafts of the novel suggest that McCarthy's original vision for his protagonist was of a character very much like Malte Brigge (early fragments refer to him as The Poet), and even when we set aside the absence of a poetic vocation for Suttree in the published version, the similarities remain significant. Rilke's novel was likely one of the seeds from which *Suttree* grew.

The allusion to the "Second Duino Elegy" appears in Act 5, Scene 1 of *The Stonemason*, in which Ben, mourning the death of his beloved grandfather, reflects on the transience of things. The last sentence in the following quotation contains the allusion. Ben is speaking: "The big elm tree died. The old dog died. Things that you can touch go away forever. I dont know what that means. I dont know what it means that things exist and then exist no more. Trees. Dogs. People. *Will* that namelessness into which we vanish then taste of us?" (104, emphasis in original). Here is the source in Rilke's poem, in which the speaker also reflects on life's transience (from Stephen Mitchell's translation): "Like dew from the morning grass, / what is ours floats into the air, like steam from a dish / of hot food. O smile, where are you going? O upturned glance: / new warm receding wave on the sea of the heart ... / alas, but that is what we *are*. Does the infinite space / we dissolve into, taste of us then?" (157, lines 25–30, emphasis in original). Georg Guillemin, in his *Pastoral Vision of Cormac McCarthy*, usefully describes the point of view of Suttree as that of a "melancholy narrator" (9). Some part of that mournful voice derives from Rainer Maria Rilke.

Rosengarten, Theodore (b. 1944)

McCarthy lists Theodore Rosengarten's *All God's Dangers: The Life of Nate Shaw* as a source for his research into African American life in the South (Box 66, Folder 5). The book is an oral history of an eighty-four-year-old illiterate black sharecropper—his real name was Ned Cobb (1885–1973)—based on Rosengarten's extensive interviews with him. It won the National Book Award for nonfiction in 1974. Dwight Garner, writing about the book for the *New York Times* in 2014, quotes Rosengarten's account of how the relationship with Cobb began. Rosengarten sought him out after hearing that Cobb was a surviving member of a radical organization of the 1930s, the Alabama Sharecropper Union. Here is how Rosengarten recalls that first meeting: "We asked him right off why he joined the union. He didn't respond directly; rather, he 'interpreted' the question and began, 'I was haulin' a load of hay out of Apafalya one day . . .' and continued uninterrupted for eight hours. He recounted dealings with landlords, bankers, fertilizer agents, mule traders, gin operators, sheriffs and judges—stories of the social relations of the cotton system. By evening, the fire had risen and died and risen again, and our question was answered" (qtd. in Garner).

Rosengarten took full advantage of Cobb's generous loquacity and compiled a book rich enough for H. Jack Geiger, writing a review for *The New York Times Book Review*, to proclaim that he "had found a black Homer, bursting with his black Odyssey" (qtd. on the back cover of Rosengarten's book). Though Rosengarten's name appears on the cover, it is really Cobb's book, a tale told in his own words. Geiger's enthusiasm does not overstate the wonders of this marvelous book, which deserves to be better known. Garner, in his effort to make it better known, said that the book is "Faulknerian in its weave"; Robert Coles, reviewing the book for the *Washington Post's Book World*, also associated it with Faulkner's work—which explains its appeal to McCarthy, who was so taken with the book that he filled up a single typed page of his notes with short quotations from it, arresting turns of phrase that caught his attention.

Rykwert, Joseph (b. 1926)

McCarthy cites Joseph Rykwert's 1980 book *The First Moderns: The Architects of the Eighteenth Century* as one of the sources for his research into the history of architecture (Box 66, Folder 4). Rykwert is currently a professor emeritus in architecture at the University of Pennsylvania, and *The First Moderns* is a work of cultural and architectural history. According to the description on the back of the book, "Rykwert's study goes well beyond the tradition of the architectural history, which has largely been concerned with the outward, stylistic evolution from the classic to the Baroque and Rococo. It examines buildings as embodiments of the whole culture, founded on basic philosophical concepts and shaped by ongoing political and religious upheavals." This description accounts for McCarthy's interest in the book, as *The Stonemason* is, to a great extent, about the relationship between ideas and their expression in stone. McCarthy's interest in architecture, like Rykwert's, is as much philosophical—and in McCarthy's case, perhaps theological—as it is an interest in outward form.

CHAPTER 9

The Crossing

The second installment of *The Border Trilogy*, 1994's *The Crossing*, is McCarthy's most philosophical novel, blending western-style action with long sections given to the metaphysical and theological speculations of the wisdom figures whom Billy encounters over the course of his three journeys to Mexico. These wisdom figures often tell Billy stories, and the interpolated tales create a stories-within-stories motif that, as Dianne Luce points out in "The Road and the Matrix," also serves as a metaphor for the mystical concept of "the matrix," a kind of mother-field or cosmic womb from which all things arise, which binds them together into a larger whole.

The main character is Billy Parham, who is from a ranching family in New Mexico. Set in the period right before and during World War II, the novel follows Billy through his three journeys, all of which end in tragedy. Billy crosses into Mexico the first time in order to return a wolf that has been killing cattle on his father's ranch back to its homeland. After capturing the wolf, he finds it is an arduous task to take a wild animal across hundreds of miles of territory. Billy is fascinated by the animal's wild otherness, and he attempts to protect her from the dangers they encounter on the road. However, the Mexican authorities take the wolf from him and she ends up caged in a sideshow. Later she is forced into a wolf-baiting spectacle. Billy shoots her rather than see her savaged by the attack-dogs set loose upon her. He then bargains for her bones and, in great sorrow, buries them in Mexico.

Billy returns to New Mexico to find that his mother and father have been murdered by thieves, who have taken the family's horses to Mexico. Billy finds his brother, Boyd, who is staying with another family, and the two set off for Mexico to retrieve the horses. Boyd falls in love with a young girl whom the boys save from being raped, and a rift begins to open between the brothers. Boyd is wounded in an attempt to retrieve the horses, and after his recuperation leaves with the girl. His exploits in attempting to retrieve the horses become exaggerated and Boyd becomes a hero of the people, lionized in folksongs called *corridos*. Billy returns to the United States and attempts to enlist in the army, but he is denied for medical reasons. He makes a third trip to Mexico to seek Boyd, who has now been killed. He retrieves Boyd's bones, and after barely escaping a robbery attempt, returns them to the United States. The novel ends with Billy weeping over his own cruelty to a crippled dog after being awakened from sleep by the "false sun" of the Trinity nuclear test in the New Mexico desert.

McCarthy's papers for *The Crossing* contain only two references to writers. In a holograph marginal note, he cites a novel entitled *La Charca*, or *The Pond*, by the Puerto Rican novelist Manuel Zeno Gandía. The novel depicts the injustices committed by wealthy landowners against the poor farmers in Puerto Rico's coffee-growing regions. The connection between this novel and *The Crossing* is not clear, but the reference is evidence of how well and widely McCarthy has read. The other reference is to Aldo Leopold's *A Sand County Almanac*, which influenced McCarthy's handling of the depiction of the wolf in the first section of *The Crossing*. Some readers find *The Crossing*, with its long philosophical digressions, to be a falling off after the triumph of *All the Pretty Horses*. It is certainly more demanding, and, no doubt, it contains longueurs, but it is a powerful and beautiful novel that repays the demands it makes on patience. And the first section—Billy's attempt to return the wolf to Mexico—is a small masterpiece of its own.

In early drafts of the novel, McCarthy attempted to depict the world from the wolf's perspective. These excised sections make for fascinating reading. While cutting them seems like the right move—McCarthy needed to stress the wolf's strangeness, her otherness—they possess their own artistic power.

Gandía, Manuel Zeno (1855–1930)

Manuel Zeno Gandía's *La Charca*, or *The Pond*, is widely regarded as the most important literary work to come out of Puerto Rico. Gan-

día's novel, which adopts both the style and the philosophical substance of late nineteenth-century naturalism, explores the conflicts between rich coffee plantation owners and the workers whose labor they
exploit (Nalbone 23). At the top of a page from an early draft of *The
Crossing*, a handwritten marginal note reads, "La Charca ? ice ponds
on the high meadows" (Box 57, Folder 2). McCarthy's interest appears
to be in Gandía's landscape descriptions rather than in his thematic
concerns. *La Charca*, though highly regarded by those who are familiar
with it, is not well-known in the United States. McCarthy's familiarity
with the novel is a further indication of the breadth of his reading.

Leopold, Aldo (1887–1948)

McCarthy refers to Aldo Leopold in a holograph marginal note in
an early draft of *The Crossing* (Box 55, Folder 6). The note appears on
a page numbered 51H, which features the scene in which Billy encounters the mysterious wolf trapper and mystic Don Arnulfo. Billy visits
the old and ailing Don Arnulfo to seek advice on how to capture the
wolf, as it is killing cattle on the Parham ranch. Don Arnulfo instead
provides religious instruction. He equates the wolf with a kind of mystical knowledge of the divine matrix, or *la matriz*, the mother womb of
creation. McCarthy's marginalia reads, "see A. Leopold," and is located
next to a passage in which Don Arnulfo compares wolves to snow-
flakes: "If you could breathe a breath so strong you could blow out the
wolf. Like you blow out the cope [snowflake]. Like you blow out the fire
of the candela. The wolf is made the way the world is made. You cant
touch the world. You cant see the world. It is made of breath only." Aldo
Leopold equates wolves with a more spiritual awareness of the world
in *A Sand County Almanac*.

In a section entitled "Thinking Like a Mountain," Leopold recalls a
youthful hunting expedition in which he and his party opened fire on a
wolf pack. His description of a dying wolf echoes one of the key scenes
in *The Crossing*. Here is Leopold:

> We reached the old wolf in time to watch a fierce green fire dying in her
> eyes. I realized then, and have known ever since, that there was some-
> thing new to me in those eyes—something known only to her and to

the mountain. I was young then, and full of trigger-itch; I thought that because fewer wolves meant more deer, that no wolves would mean hunters' paradise. But after seeing the green fire die, I sensed that neither the wolf nor the mountain agreed with such a view." (138–139)

The passage from *The Crossing* that resonates with Leopold's description of the dying wolf appears in a scene following Billy's capture of the wolf that has been killing his father's cattle. Rather than killing her, Billy attempts to return the wolf to Mexico. During the journey he comes to see the wolf in the same light as Don Arnulfo did, and, like Leopold, he sees spiritual depths within the wolf's eyes. Here is the passage from *The Crossing*:

When the flames came up her eyes burned out there like gatelamps to another world. A world burning on the shore of an unknowable void. A world construed out of blood and blood's alkahest and blood in its core and in its integument because it was that nothing save blood had power to resonate against that void which threatened hourly to devour it.... When those eyes and the nation to which they stood witness were gone at last with their dignity back into their origins there would perhaps be other fires and other witnesses and other worlds otherwise beheld. But they would not be this one. (73–74)

Though McCarthy's mystical vision of the wolf is more elaborate than Leopold's, the marginal note suggests that Leopold is the source for the image of the wolf's eyes. And when the wolf dies at the end of the first section of *The Crossing*, Billy, like Leopold, notices the absence of light in her eyes (127).

CHAPTER 10

Cities of the Plain

T he final installment in *The Border Trilogy*, *Cities of the Plain*, brings together John Grady Cole and Billy Parham, who work together on a ranch near El Paso, Texas, in 1952. The 1998 novel ends with John Grady's tragic death following his quixotic attempt to rescue a Mexican prostitute, Magdalena, who also dies.

The novel opens in the Juárez brothel where John Grady first sees Magdalena. It is love at first sight, and he begins "courting" her by visiting the brothel, where she works for the pimp Eduardo. The pimp, who is also in love with the girl, refuses to sell her to John Grady, and the young man begins planning her escape, despite the warnings of a blind pianist, called "the maestro," who recognizes star-crossed lovers when he hears them. The love story is punctuated by an exhilarating account of a hunt for wild dogs that are harassing cattle on the ranch. John Grady's sympathy for the weak and the vulnerable is symbolized by his rescue, at the end of the hunt, of a puppy. Shortly thereafter he executes his plan to rescue Magdalena, who is also weak and vulnerable (she is epileptic). However, the plan fails when Eduardo has Magdalena murdered. Seeking revenge, John Grady confronts him at the brothel, and after a savage knife fight, Eduardo fatally wounds him. He dies in the arms of Billy Parham, whose effort to save him is too late. The novel ends with a strange epilogue featuring a seventy-eight-year-old Billy, now homeless and wandering through Arizona. Under an overpass, he encounters a mysterious stranger, and the two discuss dreams and reality in a long philosophical denouement.

The papers for *Cities of the Plain* contain very few references to other writers, but a marginal note on the physicist John Stewart Bell offers an illuminating insight into portions of the epilogue.

Artemidorus (second century CE)

As Edwin T. Arnold notes in a study of dreams in *The Border Trilogy*, "one of the many possible manifestations of 'borders' in the trilogy is that between this world and that of sleep, between our waking awareness and the mysterious knowing of the dream" ("Go to Sleep" 49). Arnold's essay focuses on modern theories of dreams, but, unsurprisingly, McCarthy, in his own research into the meaning and significance of dreams, turned to the ancient Greek writer Artemidorus, whose five-volume study, *Oneirokritikon*, or *The Interpretation of Dreams*, McCarthy references in his notes for *Cities of the Plain*. The reference appears on a page containing research notes pertaining to beliefs about divination and magic. Since many of the references are to views of epilepsy as expressed in folklore, McCarthy's research was likely pertinent to his development of John Grady's love interest, Magdalena. The note reads, "Artemidorus on dreams" (Box 71, Folder 3).

According to Janet Downie, in an article that links ancient dream theory to modern hermeneutics, Artemidorus was attempting to put the practice of dream divination on something like a professional footing (99). Downie argues that his goal was "to rehabilitate dream divination in the eyes of contemporaries ... inclined to discredit the practice, as well as to offer a reliable source of information to those who seek the kind of help that divination offers" (98). McCarthy's interest in Artemidorus is a reminder of how deep McCarthy's research often goes, as well as how far off the beaten track he is willing to travel in his efforts at understanding.

Bell, John Stewart (1928–1990)

In the margin of an early draft of *Cities of the Plain*, McCarthy refers to the Irish physicist John Stewart Bell's work on the quantum phenomenon of *nonlocality*, or, as it is sometimes described, "spooky action at a distance." The holograph marginalia appears next to a passage in the epilogue in which Billy encounters a stranger who seems to promote a theory of radical determinism. McCarthy wrote, in pencil, "See Bell's Theorem" (Box 76, Folder 3).

Bell was interested in one of the more bizarre discoveries of quantum mechanics of the twentieth century. As Timothy Ferris puts it, "Bell's proposed experiment was a variation on the EPR apparatus — a setup in which two particles that start out together are dispatched across a macroscopic distance before one is observed in a fashion that instantly defines the state of the other" (284). The phenomenon challenges the deterministic assumptions of classical physics, which insist on *local* causal interactions that proceed according to the mechanical laws of dynamics. To substitute the components of a game of pool for the particles that exist at the atomic level, for purposes of illustration: Classical physics says that when the pool cue hits a ball, the ball will move across the table to hit another ball, which will collide with another, and so on. Quantum mechanics describes a counterintuitive situation in which, when the cue hits one ball, it causes another ball, on the other side of the table with no perceptible connection to the first, to also move — spooky action at a distance, i.e. *nonlocality*. According to Ferris, the results of Bell's experiment revealed that "the classical assumption is wrong — that nature is in some sense *nonlocal* (284). This is one of the aspects of quantum mechanics that troubled Einstein. Bell's theorem says, in effect, too bad for Einstein. The appeal of the theory is that it suggests that, in Ferris's words, "the universe is interconnected in some deep and as yet only dimly perceived way, on a level where time and space don't count" (285).

On first glance, the passage from *Cities of the Plain* next to which McCarthy refers to Bell is one in which Billy's enigmatic interlocutor argues for a rather extreme version of determinism. Bell's theorem welcomes the fuzzy indeterminacy of quantum mechanics; however, Bell himself has argued that one way to restore the classical assumptions about the universe is through a theory of "super-determinism," which sounds very much like what the stranger proposes to Billy. Bell discussed the idea in an interview published in *The Ghost in the Atom* in 1986 by P. C. W. Davies and J. R. Brown. Asked "whether it is still possible to maintain, in the light of experimental experience, the idea of a deterministic universe, Bell responds, "You know, one of the ways of understanding this business is to say that the world is super-deterministic. That not only is inanimate nature deterministic, but we, the experimenters who imagine we can choose to do one experiment rather than another, are also determined. If so, the difficulty which this experimental result creates disappears" (47). A follow-up question is posed: "Free will is an illusion—that gets us out of the crisis, does it?" Bell's response: "That's correct" (47). Quantum indeterminacy presupposes a degree of free will in the observer. According to Bell, if you must have determinism, you are stuck with super-determinism.

And here, from *Cities of the Plain*, is a theory of super-determinism, courtesy of the epilogue's mysterious stranger (I am quoting the published version of the speech—the draft contains variants, but the gist of the stranger's words is the same):

> You call forth the world which God has formed and that world only. Nor is this life of yours by which you set such store your doing, however you may choose to tell it. Its shape was forced in the void at the onset and all talk of what might otherwise have been is senseless for there is no otherwise. Of what could it be made? Where be hid? Or how make its appearance? The probability of the actual is absolute. That we have no power to guess it out beforehand makes it no less certain. That we may imagine alternate histories means nothing at all. (285)

If you prefer your determinism strong, that is 100-proof (though perhaps you do get to choose the false story you tell yourself). McCarthy may not have meant to invoke Bell's own speculative antithesis to his theorem, but the antithesis sounds more in line with the stranger's proposal.

McCarthy's interest in the free will vs. determinism conundrum goes back to *Blood Meridian*, where the narrator early on throws down a philosophical gauntlet: "Only now is the child finally divested of all that he has been. His origins are become remote as is his destiny and not again in all the world's turning will there be terrains so wild and barbarous to try whether the stuff of creation may be shaped to man's will or whether his own heart is not another kind of clay" (5). The narrator leaves the question open. The peripatetic philosopher of the epilogue, however, does not (at least in that paragraph—his twists and turns are hard to follow); nor does Anton Chigurh in *No Country for Old Men*.

The question of determinism is one that obviously nags at McCarthy, as it appears in all of his Western novels. The more optimistic notion of free will gets rough treatment in these works, but I do not find McCarthy making anything like a pronouncement on the matter. I think it is simply his way, when pursuing an idea, to pursue it down the darkest alleyways rather than down the well-lighted roads that most of us would prefer to travel. A clue to his own approach to the question can be found in the *Tertium quid* passage in *Blood Meridian*, in which the narrator hints at a third way, one that is "beyond will or fate" (96).

Kanner, Leo (1894–1981)

McCarthy cites an article by the famous child psychiatrist Leo Kanner as a source for his research into Magdalena's epilepsy. The citation in McCarthy's notes reads: "'The Folklore and Cultural History of Epilepsy'—Leo Kanner" (Box 71, Folder 3). McCarthy identifies the source as the periodical *Medical Life*, from a 1930 issue. According to David Bird's obituary of Kanner for the *New York Times*, he was "known in psychiatric circles as the father of child psychology" and was the first to describe infantile autism, known then as "Kanner syndrome."

Thorndike, Lynn (1882–1965)

McCarthy cites the entry for epilepsy in Lynn Thorndike's eight-volume *Magic and Experimental Science* as a source for his research into Magdalena's epilepsy, and in particular into understandings of epilepsy in folklore (Box 71, Folder 3). Thorndike was a historian who taught at Columbia University, where he specialized in medieval history and science. *Magic and Experimental Science*, which he published between 1923 and 1958, was his major achievement ("Thorndike, Lynn").

Williams, James Robert (1888–1957)

James Robert Williams, who signed his works as J. R. Williams, was a popular cartoonist whose single-panel depictions of working-class and cowboy life ran in hundreds of newspapers from the early 1920s through the 1940s. McCarthy refers to Williams on a page of holograph notes written in a small spiral notebook. Although the items he cites are not dated, McCarthy notes that they are from 1953, and it seems that McCarthy was using a specific publication as his source rather than a variety of newspapers and other periodicals. The page begins with the date Thursday, 1 January 1953, and records that the Sun Carnival Queen was Jean McGregor, that Truman was the president, and that Eisenhower was president elect. The note about the Sun Carnival Queen suggests that McCarthy was looking at an El Paso newspaper—the reference is to an annual parade held in that city. In addition, McCarthy refers to the film *Battle Zone*, which was in theaters at that time, and to *Out Our Way*, Williams's famous cartoon series.

The notes reveal McCarthy's desire to get a sense of the time he was writing about, and yet his interest in Williams's work likely went beyond that level. *Out Our Way* is a fascinating portrait of how cowboys lived and worked in the mid-twentieth century, which explains why it was of particular interest to McCarthy, who was concerned with accurately portraying the texture of cowboy life. In his introduction to a collection of Williams's cartoons, J. Frank Dobie points out the authenticity of the cartoonist's vision by citing features of a panel entitled "The Rusty King":

> In the first place, he's smoking a pipe, which all authorities on cowboy life as depicted by cigarette and mail order advertisements say is never done on the range. His bridle reins are made of an old rope. His hat, if it did not leak, would hold about nine gallons and three quarts less than the orthodox Stetson. Instead of wearing boots, he's wearing shoes. The ignominious mare he straddles has cholla joints in her tail and is asleep on one hip while he sits sizing up a bunch of cattle that only the cow people can see. (4–5)

McCarthy, who is devoted to realistic detail, would have prized these cartoons.

Another reason for thinking that Williams's work was important to McCarthy is that we know he values the work of skilled cartoonists. He mentions his enthusiasm for Fernando Krahn in a letter to Albert Erskine included in the archived papers for *The Orchard Keeper* (Box 1, Folder 1). Wesley Morgan has documented that McCarthy was listed as the staff artist for his high school newspaper during his senior year, though he was unable to locate a cartoon signed by McCarthy (7). However, one signed cartoon by McCarthy has been published. It appeared in a collection of single-panel self-portraits by well-known authors entitled *Self-Portrait: Book People Picture Themselves* (McCarthy's self-portrait is on page 33). McCarthy's contribution to the book depicts him at his typewriter with an electrical cord plugged in to the top of his head—no doubt channeling a current straight from the Muses' dynamo. Moreover, the only known blurb by McCarthy appears on the back of the novelist Alexander Theroux's biography of the cartoonist Edward Gorey: "Just read a few weeks ago your book on Gorey and enjoyed it very much—Cormac McCarthy, April, 2010." Finally, McCarthy's notes for *Suttree* contain a reference to the famous Chuck Jones animated cartoon *Duck Amuck*, which features a malicious animator, Bugs Bunny, tormenting his creation, Daffy Duck, who resists the machinations of this Gnostic demiurge. Though it's not used in the published novel, the line clearly refers to the Daffy Duck cartoon: "A few old homebent sots tilted and caromed along the walls like mechanical ducks amuck" (Box 19, Folder 13). Given the evidence for what appears to be more than a passing enthusiasm for cartooning, the reference to J. R. Williams likely signals a genuine interest in the popular cartoonist.

CHAPTER 11

The Road

Winner of the 2007 Pulitzer Prize for Fiction, *The Road* is one of McCarthy's most emotionally affecting novels. Set in a post-apocalypse wasteland of snow, ash, and sunless skies, it follows the fortunes of a boy and his father as they travel south to warmer lands along the coast. The prose is as sparse as the landscape, and McCarthy provides few clues about the cause of the apocalypse.

Pushing a shopping cart full of their meager possessions, the father and son travel a literal and figurative road that is fraught with danger. McCarthy imagines that in the wake of such an event, humanity would revert to savagery, and the travelers must avoid the cannibals that roam about. Over and over the father insists that he and the boy are "good guys," and that they "carry the light" about with them. As the novel progresses, it becomes increasingly clear that the light shines very bright in the boy, who continuously urges his father to compassionate actions, even when those actions place them in danger.

The boy's capacity for love and empathy, his attunement to the suffering of others, even to the suffering of a thief who attempts to steal their things, makes him the moral center of the novel. He becomes an exemplar for his father, whose death at the end of the novel leaves the boy an orphan, though in the final scene we see him taken in by other "good guys." Despite the novel's bleakness, it is deeply life-affirming, and the final words offer a lyrical celebration of the beauty and goodness of existence.

Beckett, Samuel (1906–1989)

McCarthy refers to Samuel Beckett's *Waiting for Godot* in a hand-written marginal note at the upper left corner of a page from an early draft of *The Road*. It appears in connection with references to Robert Pirsig's *Zen and the Art of Motorcycle Maintenance* and David Markson's *Wittgenstein's Mistress* (see separate entries for Pirsig and Markson in this chapter). Three lines read, "Zen and the Art / Godot—Man and Child—W's Mistress" (Box 87, Folder 6). That Beckett would be an influence on *The Road* is unsurprising. The sparseness of both the prose style and the landscape it evokes invite comparisons with Beckett's linguistic parsimony and stark stage settings. The father's anxieties about the apparent absence of God or stable meaning in a denuded world mirror the anxieties of Vladimir and Estragon in Beckett's play. The affinities with Beckett were recognized early on by Ron Charles in his review of the novel for the *Washington Post*, where he wrote that "with this apocalyptic tale, McCarthy has moved into the allegorical realm of Samuel Beckett and Jose Saramango—and, weirdly, George Romero."

There are obvious limitations to this comparison with Beckett. McCarthy, even in this grim novel, holds on to the possibility of some kind of spiritual transcendence, a possibility embodied by the almost saintly boy. That is not the case for Beckett. Moreover, *Waiting for Godot* is funny, full of black comedy of the "tis so I may not weep" school. McCarthy, undervalued as a comic writer, does invite us to weep in this most humorless among his works. These differences alone open a fairly wide gulf between *The Road* and *Waiting for Godot* (though in this regard McCarthy and Romero sort rather well with each other—cannibalism really is not a laughing matter).

Jay Ellis, in his *No Place for Home*, discusses McCarthy's sense of humor (or lack thereof) in connection with Beckett: "In Beckett, a sense of humor outruns even those bleakest moments that cannot be endured by the most heroic existentialism" (266). Ellis sees McCarthy using humor in similar fashion, but notes its absence in his later work, which he attributes to a growing eschatological seriousness in *The Border Trilogy* and *No Country for Old Men* (Ellis's study predates the publication of *The Road*, but his thesis is abundantly confirmed by the overtly apocalyptic novel):

> I see an arc toward eschatology that has conterminously extinguished the light of humor. Humor, too, has risen through the early novels before its recent death. We first laughed at Sylder's sarcasm, a little. We laughed a little more at a stampede of hogs, but only a little more (*OD* 217–218). For all his horrors, we laughed more at Ballard's "Do what?" and at the dumpkeeper's daughters, "Urethra," "Cerebella," and "Hernia Sue" (*COG* 74, 26). We laughed uncontrollably at Harrogate and his melons, pigeons, someone else's shoat, his boat and bats, and his aborted Stygian bank heist as he becomes a living turd of humanity in a river of literal shit (*S* 31–35, 117, 168–142, 207–219, 269–270). The darkness of humor seemed only to enrich the laughter rising up to its zenith in *Suttree*. (290)

Though Ellis does not say it outright, his suggestion here is that McCarthy was closer to Beckett in his southern novels than in his later work. Despite the often lush, baroque, Faulknerian stylings of those novels, so different from the stark prose of Beckett, the comic sensibility is remarkably similar. Of course, McCarthy's deepest affinity is with the tradition of southwestern humor found in Twain and, given a modernist turn, Faulkner. The point is that absent that sense of compassionate black comedy, McCarthy's late work resembles Beckett's less than his earlier novels do.

Nevertheless, there are resemblances at the levels of atmosphere and theme, and Lydia Cooper makes a compelling case for reading McCarthy's late theatrical work *The Sunset Limited* in light of Beckett. In her essay "'A Howling Void': Beckett's Influence in Cormac McCarthy's *The Sunset Limited*," Cooper notes numerous similarities: "McCarthy's (literal) kitchen drama about the core questions of existence and meaning evokes Samuel Beckett's similarly underpopulated stage worlds in which characters trapped in physical stasis argue philosophically through dialogue that plays on the meaninglessness of disconnected, unproductive language" (1). Although I agree with this assessment, I think the differences are stark. For instance, the following words of White, one of the characters in *Sunset* (the other being Black), echo the thematic content of Beckett's plays, and yet it is difficult to imagine a character in Beckett expressing the thought in quite this way: "The truth is that the forms I see have been slowly emptied out. They no longer have any content. They are shapes only. A train, a wall, a world. Or a man. A thing dangling in senseless articulation in a howling void. No meaning to its life. Its words. Why would I seek the company of such a thing?" (139). These words sound more like a college professor expounding on Beckett (which, in a sense, is what McCarthy was going for) than an actual character in Beckett's work. The nihilist professor is given to orotund musings about meaninglessness that fall just short of bathos.

Readers would be hard pressed to find anything like White's histrionic pessimism in Beckett, whose pessimism often comes through the punchline of a joke, like the one about the tailor in *Endgame*. An Englishman needs a pair of trousers for the New Year festivities, and goes to a tailor who takes an excessively long time to finish the work. The exasperated Englishman exclaims, "God damn you to hell, Sir, no, it's indecent, there are limits! In six days, do you hear me, six days, God made the world. Yes Sir, no less Sir, the WORLD! And you are not bloody well capable of making me a pair of trousers in three months!" (22). The scandalized tailor replies, "But my dear Sir, my dear Sir, look—(*disdainful gesture, disgustedly*)—at the world—(*pause*) and look—(*loving gesture, proudly*)—at my TROUSERS!" (22–23). McCarthy has mined this vein of humor, but Ellis is right that he eschews it in his later work.[1] Though McCarthy's marginalia verify the interest in Beckett suspected by many critics, the differences between the two writers showcase a turn away from the sometimes ribald comedy that marked McCarthy's early work.

Defoe, Daniel (1660–1731)

A holograph marginal note written above an early draft of the scene in which the father boards the foundered boat reads, "Defoe Plague Years" (Box 87, Box 6). Daniel Defoe's novel presents a fictional account of the devastating outbreak of bubonic plague that afflicted London in 1665. I cannot find a direct connection between Defoe's novel and *The Road*, though its interest to McCarthy as a model for how to write about human beings suffering the effects of a devastating catastrophe appears obvious enough.

Eliot, T. S. (Thomas Stearns) (1888–1965)

SEE ALSO *SUTTREE*

An early draft of the scene in *The Road* in which the father remembers standing in "the charred ruins of a library" (187) contains an allusion to T. S. Eliot's *The Waste Land*. The line reads, "So many. He could not have thought there were so many" (Box 87, Folder 6). The allusion is to the "Unreal City" section of Part One of Eliot's poem, in which the speaker, gazing upon the crowds crossing London Bridge, alludes to Dante's *Inferno*, which makes London a metaphorical underworld. So McCarthy alludes to an allusion. Here is Eliot: "Unreal City, / Under the brown fog of a winter dawn, / A crowd flowed over London Bridge, so many, / I had not thought death had undone so many" (lines 60–63). McCarthy did not use the Eliot allusion in the published novel, but one can see how Eliot's wasteland motif would be on his mind during the composition of *The Road*.

Frost, Robert (1874–1963)

SEE ALSO *THE ORCHARD KEEPER*

In an excised literary allusion from an early draft of *The Road*, McCarthy outdoes Robert Frost's congenial Yankee apocalypse, "Fire and Ice," by presenting a grim empirical case for the hot version of the end of time. According to McCarthy, "The library at Alexandria perished twice, both by fire. No ice" (Box 87, Folder 6). Frost associates fire with desire and ice with hate. It would be unsurprising to discover that McCarthy believes that our species has most to fear from the flames of desire, given his interest in Schopenhauer (see entry on Will Durant in *Blood Meridian*) and his attachment to T. S. Eliot's *The Waste Land* (see entries in *Suttree* and this chapter), which, in the section entitled "The Fire Sermon," evokes the Buddha's diagnosis of the human predicament as a problem of desire (a diagnosis Schopenhauer regarded as accurate).

Because McCarthy rarely reveals, at least in an explicit way, the inner emotions of his characters, evidence of McCarthy's views on the problem of desire might seem hard to come by. McCarthy is as concerned about human emotion as any other novelist, but he prefers to reveal emotions from the outside rather than describe them, à la Henry James or Marcel Proust, from the inside. Here is an example of McCarthy showing desire, and, by implication, linking it to humanity's penchant for violence: In *Blood Meridian*, when the kid encounters the recruiter for Captain White's paramilitaries, he seems both ignorant about and uninterested in the ideological mission of the filibusters. However, McCarthy subtly alerts the reader to something the kid is interested in: "The kid squatted in the grass. He looked at the man's horse. The horse was fitted out in tooled leather with worked silver trim. It had a white blaze on its face and four white stockings and it was cropping up great teethfuls of the rich grass" (30). The recruiter then tells his come-to-Jesus tale of how Captain White "set my feet in the path of righteousness" (30). Here is how McCarthy describes the boy's response: "The boy pulled at the halms of grass. *He looked at the horse again*. Well, he said. Dont reckon it'd hurt nothin" (30, emphasis added). We are then told that "they rode through the town with the recruiter splendid on the stockingfooted horse and the kid behind him on the mule like something he'd captured" (30). The implication is that the kid's journey into organized paramilitary violence is motivated by a desire to have what another has, and, more profoundly, to attain the status that the tooled leather and splendid horse bestow.

Of related interest, Glanton is later described as riding in "a new Ringgold saddle" (241). Again, the saddle is associated with status, and, in what I take to be a deliberate confluence of research (Ringgold was a real type of saddle) and symbolism, McCarthy alludes to Wagner's Ring Cycle of operas. Numerous references to Wagner appear in McCarthy's notes, and Mark Morrow confirms McCarthy's love of Wagner in his book *Images of the Southern Writer*. Wagner's opera also explores the dangerous fires of desire. And, it should be noted, Schopenhauer was an influence on Wagner, and the Ring operas were an influence on T. S. Eliot—he alludes to them in *The Waste Land*. McCarthy is working this same metaphysical terrain.

Kierkegaard, Søren (1813–1855)

SEE ALSO *BLOOD MERIDIAN*

McCarthy refers to Søren Kierkegaard in his papers for both *Blood Meridian* and *The Road*. The latter reference appears on a page of fragments from an early draft of the novel. The fragments are from the work-in-progress; the Kierkegaard reference is a parenthetical note. It reads, "(Kierkegaard: Abraham and Isaac)" (Box 87, Folder 6). McCarthy is thinking about Kierkegaard's well-known reflections on the account in Genesis of the almost-sacrifice of Isaac by his father Abraham (Gen. 22:1–14). In *Fear and Trembling*, Kierkegaard contemplates the disturbing story of God's command to Abraham to kill the miraculous son of his old age. In Genesis, God calls off what is ultimately a test of Abraham's faith by providing a ram for the sacrifice at the last minute. Kierkegaard calls Abraham's willingness to obey God a "teleological suspension of the ethical" in favor of a higher religious calling to disregard the ordinary claims of morality. Abraham must act, in fear and trembling, on faith that God's unknown purposes justify an abhorrent action. Abraham's leap into an act of faith that looks like a leap into the abyss serves, for Kierkegaard, as a model of the dizzying existential freedom of human beings.

It seems likely that McCarthy was thinking of Kierkegaard in relation to the father's anxieties in *The Road* about being faced with the choice of killing his son or seeing the boy fall into the hands of the cannibal hordes. However, McCarthy's notes suggest another angle as well. Below the reference to Kierkegaard, McCarthy wrote, "Ancient bloodcults." In McCarthy's imagined apocalypse, the fall of civilization led to a revival of bloodcults (16). The linking of Abraham and Isaac with ancient bloodcults is interesting because the Genesis story is often read as a kind of etiological account of God's renunciation of human sacrifice, a practice with a disturbingly widespread pedigree among ancient human communities across the globe. For writers such as René Girard, the story marks the moment of transition from human sacrifice to the substitution of an animal scapegoat.

McCarthy, no doubt aware of both the theological and anthropological dimensions of the Genesis story, suggests that the end of civilization, which rejects human sacrifice, will be followed by a regression to the bloodcults that preceded it. The father in *The Road* thinks that "the bloodcults must have all consumed one another" (16). So the novel records a descent into even lower stages of primitivism than what the horrible but still organized and purposeful sacrificial cults represent. As René Girard argues throughout his works on this subject, sacred violence is the foundation for the order that leads to civilized existence (see *Violence and the Sacred, Things Hidden Since the Foundation of the World*, or, for that matter, anything by Girard). McCarthy's novel envisages a movement into an apocalyptic future that parallels in reverse humanity's rise from the Hobbesian war of "all against all."

London, Jack (1876–1916)

An early draft of *The Road* features a holograph reference to Jack London's short story "To Build a Fire" in the margin. Next to the title, McCarthy wrote, in parentheses, "dog," and underlined the word twice (Box 87, Folder 6). London's story is about a miner in the Yukon Territory attempting to get to a mining camp in freezing temperatures. Ignoring the advice of an "old-timer on Sulphur Creek," he sets out, in a tragic display of hubris, on a journey that ends in his death by freezing. He travels with a dog, who, like the old-timer, has better sense than the miner. The man attempts to kill the dog in order to use its carcass for warmth, but the dog survives and leaves the owner's frozen carcass behind as it heads off for the mining camp.

Despite McCarthy's emphasis on the dog in his marginal note, the dog in London's story bears little resemblance to the dog in *The Road*—though the issue of whether or not to kill a domesticated animal in order to survive punishing conditions is present in both works. Whereas London's doomed protagonist has no qualms about killing the dog that is accompanying him, the father in *The Road* assures his son that they will not kill a skeletal dog that has been following them for two days. Because of how this reassurance comes about, however, it seems to be another instance of the son's more profound goodness. The father recounts, "She walked away down the road. The boy looked after her and then he looked at me and then he looked at the dog and he began to cry and to beg for the dog's life and I promised I would not hurt the dog" (87).

Dogs aside, there is a striking similarity of atmosphere between the two stories. Both are about the effort to survive in harsh and bitter-cold conditions. Both are about the elemental need for warmth. And both are suffused with a sense of existential anxiety about man's place in the world. The man in London's story is a naïf, sturdy but stupid, and it is the narrator, rather than the man himself, who creates that mood of existential dread: "[The cold] did not lead him to meditate upon his frailty as a creature of temperature, and upon man's frailty in general, able only to live within certain narrow limits of heat and cold; and from there on it did not lead him to the conjectural field of immortality and man's place in the universe" (137). London's story seems a clear precursor to *The Road*.

Markson, David (1927–2010)

A handwritten marginal note at the upper left corner of a page from an early draft of *The Road* refers to David Markson's 1988 novel *Wittgenstein's Mistress*. It appears in conjunction with references to Robert Pirsig's *Zen and the Art of Motorcycle Maintenance* and Samuel Beckett's *Waiting for Godot*. Three separate lines read, "Zen and the Art / Godot—Man and Child—W's Mistress" (Box 87, Folder 6).

Markson's novel, not widely known but often highly praised by zealous admirers—David Foster Wallace called it "pretty much the high point of experimental fiction in this country" (qtd. in Dempsey)—is about a painter, Kate Winter, who believes she is the last person on earth. From her Long Island beach house she records her fragmented but intellectually rich thoughts about life and Western culture. Her belief that she is the last person on earth may be the result of a mental collapse, but the first-person perspective does not allow the reader the necessary context to determine this with certainty. In an essay about the novel written for the *Review of Contemporary Fiction*, Wallace argues that the novel poses the question, "What if somebody really had to live in a *Tractatus*ized world?" (219). The term refers to Ludwig Wittgenstein's work *Tractatus Logico-Philosophicus*, and Wallace uses it to denote Kate's solipsistic perspective, which Wallace sees as one of the "dire emotional implications of [Wittgenstein's] early metaphysics" (219).

Markson's novel bears little resemblance to *The Road*—it is very much in the postmodern vein of art about art—but Kate's personal apocalypse, her belief that she is alone in the world, accounts for McCarthy's interest in it. And though I am ill-equipped to comment on Wittgenstein, the question Wallace suggests is at the heart of the book sounds applicable to *The Road*. Was McCarthy imagining a *Tractatus*ized world when he composed it?

Martin, Paul (b. 1958)

In the upper left margin of an early draft of *The Road* McCarthy wrote, "The Healing Mind—Martin" (Box 87, Folder 5). Written by a behavioral biologist, Dr. Paul Martin, *The Healing Mind* explores links between the brain and the immune system. The page on which the note appears is a draft version of the scene in which the father and son stop at a waterfall. I cannot determine a connection between Martin's book and *The Road*.

Ovsyanikov, Nikita

In a handwritten marginal note at the top left corner of an early draft of *The Road*, McCarthy wrote "Nikita Oseanikof on Polar Bears" (Box 87, Folder 6). Dr. Ovsyanikov is the senior researcher at the Pacific Institute of Geography, a Russian science institute, and the author of *Polar Bears: Living with the White Bear* (1996). The note is in keeping with McCarthy's interest in animals (predators, in particular), but I can find no connection to the novel.

Pagels, Heinz (1939–1988)

In the upper margin of an early draft of *The Road* McCarthy wrote "Phil ? and Heinz Pagels" (Box 87, Folder 3). I do not know the identity of Phil, but Pagels was a well-known physicist and the author of several works of popular science. He died at the tragically young age of forty-nine in a mountaineering accident. In his last years he began writing about the science of complexity, the focus of the Santa Fe Institute, of which McCarthy is a Fellow. His last book was *The Dreams of Reason: The Computer and the Rise of the Science of Complexity* (1988), with which McCarthy may have been familiar. In his 1992 interview with Richard B. Woodward for the *New York Times*, McCarthy lists, as one of the subjects he would rather talk about than writing, molecular computers, one of the subjects addressed in Pagels's book.

Pirsig, Robert M. (1928–2017)

SEE ALSO *BLOOD MERIDIAN*

McCarthy refers to Robert M. Pirsig's *Zen and the Art of Motorcycle Maintenance* in a handwritten marginal note appearing in the upper left corner of a page from an early draft of *The Road*. It appears in conjunction with references to Samuel Beckett and the novelist David Markson. In three separate lines, McCarthy wrote, "Zen and the Art / Godot—Man and Child—W's Mistress" (Box 87, Folder 6; see entries for Beckett and Markson in this chapter).

McCarthy's interest in Pirsig goes back to the period when he was writing *Blood Meridian*, and he refers to *Zen* in his notes for that novel. Pirsig's influence on *The Road* is evident. *Zen*, like *The Road*, is about a road trip made by a father and a son (the second line in the marginal note makes the connection between *The Road* and *Zen* plain); in both journeys, the goal is to make it to the ocean, though in the case of Pirsig's book it is to the Pacific, whereas in McCarthy's it is to the Atlantic. In both novels the destination is associated with salvation and hope, and in both a vulnerable boy must come to terms with his father's demons. Both are tales of father-and-son bonding, and both are imbued with a plangent sense of the human frailties that underlie such bonds, as well as a strong sense of the fierce protective impulses that are so much a part of parental love. Given these similarities, it seems clear that *Zen* should be regarded as a source of inspiration for *The Road*—a book that stayed with McCarthy for years.

Though the references to *Zen* in the *Blood Meridian* notes provide no clue as to the novel's significance for that work, McCarthy's philosophical interests at the time of its composition would suggest that his earlier interest was likely in the novel's philosophical *chautauquas* (significantly, the name that Ben Telfair gives to his disquisitions on the craft of masonry in *The Stonemason*), which, taken together, form something like a history of Western philosophy, as well as an extended meditation on the traditional divide between classical and Romantic sensibilities. Other works McCarthy was reading when working on *Blood Meridian* strongly suggest that he was attempting to think through these aesthetic categories (see entries for Michel Foucault and Wyndham Lewis in *Suttree* and F. S. C. Northrup in *The Stonemason*). However, during the writing of *The Road*, the focus of his interest appears to have shifted to the story itself, the story of the father and son that frames the philosophical subtext and that provides the dramatic heart of the book. Perhaps, given McCarthy's admission that his own son John Francis McCarthy inspired the character of the boy in *The Road*, *Zen*'s main storyline became more poignant. The second line of McCarthy's note reads "Man and Child." The first line seems to link Pirsig and Beckett, and, indeed, *The Road* might be read as the story of a father and a son on a spiritual journey through a terrifying wasteland that bears not a little resemblance to the one inhabited by Vladimir and Estragon in *Waiting for Godot*.

The third line refers to David Markson's novel *Wittgenstein's Mistress*, in which a brilliant but troubled artist believes she is the last person on earth. *Wittgenstein's Mistress* is often compared to Beckett's fiction. It would, then, appear that this little cluster of references to three literary works provides a great deal of insight into some of the sources for McCarthy's foray into the post-apocalypse genre. Though neither *Zen and the Art of Motorcycle Maintenance*, nor *Waiting for Godot*, nor *Wittgenstein's Mistress* bears any marked similarities to *The Road*, all three provide examples of character dynamics, moods, themes, and stylistic expressions that informed McCarthy's tale of a denuded world.

Shakespeare, William (1564–1616)

SEE ALSO *SUTTREE* AND *BLOOD MERIDIAN*

McCarthy's papers for *The Road* contain one reference to Shakespeare. In Box 88, Folder 1, in the margin of an early draft, McCarthy wrote, "'questionable shape'—Hamlet." The phrase comes from Hamlet's first encounter with the ghost of his father:

> Angels and ministers of grace defend us!
> Be thou spirit of health or goblin damn'd,
> Bring with thee airs from heaven or blasts from hell,
> Be thy intents wicked or charitable,
> Thou com'st in such a questionable shape
> That I will speak to thee. I'll call thee Hamlet,...
>   (Act 1, Scene 4, lines 39–44).

The quotation appears next to a draft of the scene in which the boy and his father encounter the old man Ely.

Twain, Mark (Samuel Langhorne Clemens —1835–1910)

Though many readers sense the strong influence of Mark Twain on *Suttree*, not least in McCarthy's use of the kind of southwestern humor Twain perfected, the lone reference to him in McCarthy's papers is in connection with *The Road*. On a page of excised fragments, McCarthy wrote, "Bit [*sic*] the night is filled with dying stars and he knows his days are run. (see Twain and Halley's comet)" (Box 87, Folder 3). Neither this sentence nor anything resembling Twain's comments finds its way into the published novel; nevertheless, the reference does verify McCarthy's interest in Twain (for a book-length treatment of Twain's influence, see *Cormac McCarthy and the Ghost of Huck Finn*, by Leslie Harper Worthington).

Mark Twain is one of the most frequently quoted of American writers, and the quotation to which McCarthy alludes here is one of his most famous sayings. It comes from Albert Bigelow Paine's 1912 four-volume biography of Twain. In it he records some of Twain's comments about his own death. The famous quotation is prefaced by an observation Paine made about Twain's fascination with the vastness of space: "He was always thrown into a sort of ecstasy by the unthinkable distances of space" (3:1509). Thoughts about space prompted Twain's wry remarks on the comet: "I came in with Halley's comet in 1835. It is coming again next year, and I expect to go out with it. It will be the greatest disappointment of my life if I don't go out with Halley's comet. The Almighty has said, no doubt: 'Now here are these two un-accountable freaks; they came in together, they must go out together.' Oh! I am looking forward to that" (3:1511).

Whatever McCarthy had in mind when he typed this quotation, it is possible that he had the same quotation in mind when writing *Blood Meridian*. The kid is born in 1833, when the Leonids were visible. His death appears to be marked by meteor showers, likely the Leonids: "Stars were falling across the sky myriad and random, speeding along brief vectors from their origins in night to their destinies in dust and nothingness" (333). Ideas, words, and images often follow McCarthy through the composition of several novels. McCarthy shares Twain's sense of cosmic awe, as well as his sense that things hang together in unsuspected ways, so it is not surprising that Twain's musings on sidereal patterns lodged in his imagination.

CHAPTER 12

Whales and Men

T he unpublished screenplay *Whales and Men* features unusually talkative and educated characters for a work by Cormac McCarthy, but it fits into what has come to be a pattern
within his corpus. McCarthy uses his dramatic works as a stage for the
rehearsal of philosophical ideas. *The Stonemason* and *The Sunset Limited* are noteworthy examples. *Whales and Men* is an abject failure as
a screenplay, though it might merit consideration as Socratic dialogue,
which it essentially is. That is true of *The Sunset Limited* as well. Consequently, dialectic, rather than dramatic action, drives these works.

In *The Stonemason*, the dialectic is internal to Ben Telfair, but the
effect is similar. McCarthy uses these works to think through ideas,
and *Whales and Men* is heady stuff. The characters discuss God, evolution, ecology, physics, biology, math, art, the nature of evil, and, of
course, whales (wolves get some time as well). They discuss whales
at length, in fact, and, depending on your point of view, possibly ad
nauseum. These discussions can be fascinating, and nothing else by
McCarthy provides so transparent a view into his intellectual interests.
However, it is all so high-minded, so po-faced and earnest, that one
begins to yearn for just the faintest leavening of irony or humor. That
yearning goes unanswered.

The dramatis personae are Guy Schuler, a whale biologist who may
be based on McCarthy's friend Roger Payne; John Western, a nonprac-
ticing doctor who leads an adventurous playboy life, though he is also
given to deep thinking; Kelly McAmon, John's girlfriend, who is kind
and good; and Peter Gregory, an Irish aristocratic, who, like his close
friend John, leads something of a playboy life himself—and who is also
given to deep thinking. The story begins at Le Club International in Ft.

Lauderdale, where John, Kelly, and Peter meet Guy. At the end of the club episode, they agree to accompany Guy on one of his scientific boating expeditions. The characters gather for an "Irish Idyll" before Christmas at Peter's estate, where they read poetry, discuss God and evil, among other things, and part as dear friends. The rest of the screenplay takes place on Guy's boat. On board, the characters study and discuss whales, among other things, and attempt to save a whale from hunters. The experience changes each one of them. John, no longer a playboy, travels to a war-torn Latin American nation to provide medical care for the poor and the wounded. Peter also gives up the playboy lifestyle; he marries Kelly, John's former girlfriend, and becomes a member of the Irish parliament and a save-the-whales crusader.

There are numerous references to writers, artists, scientists, and thinkers in the screenplay. Though most, but not all, of the references come from the characters, and not from McCarthy's notes and marginalia, it is safe to assume that their interests are his interests, so I have included them here.

The screenplay exists in three drafts, and McCarthy's marginal scribblings and revisions testify to how seriously he took this work. All of the references in this section are to Box 97, Folder 1, which contains the earliest draft; it is also the one with the most references.

Arendt, Hannah (1906–1975)

Peter, during a long conversation with Guy about the nature of evil, invokes Hannah Arendt's famous notion of "the banality of evil." He tells Guy that "all evil acts were identical while no two acts of love were the same." His reflections on evil following a childhood case of the measles have led him to the conclusion that love and courage together constitute the antithesis of evil, which is rooted primarily in fear. For Peter, its banality is linked to its provenance in fear.

Augustine of Hippo (354–430)

Peter refers to St. Augustine during a long discussion with Guy about the nature of evil. His theory is that evil is a manmade inven-

WHALES AND MEN 259

tion, "and that was why Augustine couldn't find it. Not only was mankind the source of all evil but he was the agent as well." He lets the serpent and the devil off the hook, placing the blame squarely on humanity. Presumably, Peter is arguing against Augustine's privative theory, which says that evil is an absence of good, that it lacks *being*. Augustine's theory is designed to refute Gnostic, and specifically Manichaean, views that see evil as an ontological category. The Manichaean view puts God, if he is the creator of all things, in a bind, and Augustine's valiant theodicy attempts to resolve that thorny conundrum. The nature of evil is an important question for McCarthy, who seems to be doing his own thinking through Peter Gregory in this scene, which he obsessively rewrote dozens of times.

Since *Blood Meridian*, evil has been one of McCarthy's major themes. It would be hard to pin him down to a theory—what we find in his fiction is something like a troubled dialectic that never arrives at any kind of synthesis. The early draft of the screenplay features copious marginalia, variants within variants—evidence of the dialectic—and McCarthy continued to wrestle with the issue throughout the later revisions of the scene. Other perspectives find their way into his western novels. Perez, in the prison scene in *All the Pretty Horses*, has a very different take on the subject from Peter Gregory's. He tells John Grady that "there can be in a man some evil. But we dont think it is his own evil. Where did he get it? How did he come to claim it? No. Evil is a true thing in Mexico. It goes about on its own legs" (194–195). Peter puts the onus squarely on man; Perez lets man off the hook, taking a darkly Manichaean turn. The scene with Peter fails, as almost everything fails in the screenplay, because it lacks dramatic interest. However, it possesses philosophical interest, and therefore should be of interest to McCarthy scholars. In it we see a soul (Peter's or Cormac McCarthy's—what you will) "at the white heat," to quote Emily Dickinson. This scene was of vital importance to Cormac McCarthy.

Beston, Henry (1888–1968)

The naturalist Henry Beston, whose book *The Outermost House*—direct kin to Thoreau's *Walden*—recounts Beston's experiences with the natural world while living for a year in a cottage on Cape Cod, was a major influence on McCarthy during the years he worked on the screenplay *Whales and Men* as well as *The Border Trilogy*. At the end of *Whales and Men*, Peter Gregory, now a member of the Irish parliament, gives a speech to that body in defense of the whale's right to exist without human harassment. In it he clearly alludes to Beston by describing whales as another "nation." The passage from Beston to which Gregory alludes could serve as a thematic summary of the ecological concerns of the screenplay: "For the animal shall not be measured by man. In a world older and more complete than ours they move finished and complete, gifted with extensions of the senses we have lost or never attained, living by voices we shall never hear. They are not brethren, they are not underlings; they are other nations, caught with ourselves in the net of life and time, fellow prisoners of the splendor and travail of the earth" (20). In addition to the allusion to Beston in the whale saga, McCarthy uses Beston's nations metaphor in his description of the wolf in *The Crossing*, as Dianne Luce notes ("Vanishing World" 188). From John Grady's attunement to the lives of horses to Billy's tragic encounter with the wolf, in *The Border Trilogy* McCarthy explores the borders between human and nonhuman nations with real heart.

However, McCarthy's interest in those borders goes back to his earliest works. In *The Orchard Keeper*, he actually shifts the point of view to that of a cat. He tried something similar in early drafts of *The Crossing*, devoting large portions of the wolf narrative to the animal's point of view. The decision to leave these scenes out seems aesthetically warranted—the pathos of Billy's relationship to the wolf is heightened by her otherness. However, the scenes featuring the wolf's point of view are hardly aesthetic failures and are intriguing in their own right. They testify to the seriousness of McCarthy's spiritual commitment to a mystical understanding of the natural world that includes other creatures.

Borges, Jorge Luis (1899–1986)

Guy Schuler mentions a Jorge Luis Borges story, "The Secret Miracle," during a long disquisition on the imminent demise of the human race. After an outpouring of distilled pessimism, he offers what amounts, in context, to a hopeful qualification: "Knowing how poor our prognostic powers are, perhaps predicting the holocaust will avert it in some way. Borges has a story in which a man condemned to be shot consoles himself with the thought that most of the things that you worry about never come to pass anyway."

In the story, a Jewish writer, Jaromir Hladik, is arrested by the Nazis in Prague. While awaiting his execution, he attempts to console himself in various ways, including the one mentioned by Guy. Just as the shots are about to be fired, Hladik believes that God stops time for him — the "secret miracle" of the title — and he is granted a year — in his mind — in which to complete a play that he has been working on. At the moment he finishes it, the shots fire and Hladik dies.

Guy leaves all that out of his brief allusion to the story, but the unhappy ending ensures that the psychological trick he has devised for warding off the apocalypse — dread it so intently that, given how rarely what we imagine will happen actually happens, we may avert it — is just that: a psychological trick.

Camus, Albert (1913–1960)

SEE ALSO *OUTER DARK*

Whales and Men concludes with John Western and Peter Gregory deciding, after experiencing the wonders of whales, to do very serious things. Peter becomes a member of the Irish parliament, where he begins to advocate for the save-the-whales campaign, and John opens a hospital in a war-torn Latin American country. In a letter to his ex-girlfriend Kelly McAmon, who is now married to Peter, John describes his experiences running the hospital. In the margin of the letter, a holograph note reads, "Camus Plague: (The world's condition, not just war time)."

The note suggests that McCarthy modeled John in part on Albert Camus's Dr. Bernard Rieux, who stoically treats the victims of plague in Oran, despite his sense of the ultimate futility of his efforts. John shares some of this stoic pessimism: "The universe is cold and black and silent and our loneliness becomes us," he writes to Kelly. But he adds: "I cannot believe that whales and men are alien to the universe. I believe they are arks of the covenant and the covenant is mind and mind's true nature is not rage or deceit or terror or logic or craft or even sorrow. It is longing." He ends the letter by telling Kelly that he sends "all the love my very small heart contains." In granting his Rieux such spiritual longings and tender sentiments, McCarthy departs from the tough-minded Camus and entertains leavening possibilities foreign to Camus's bracing but dispiriting plague narrative.

Cervantes, Miguel de (1547–1616)

During the "Irish Idyll," Peter and Guy have a long conversation about good and evil. At one point, Guy says, "I was just thinking," to which Peter responds, "Beware gentle knight. There is no greater monster than reason," an allusion to Cervantes's *Don Quixote*. McCarthy uses a similar allusion in *All the Pretty Horses*, when Don Hector, during a game of pool with John Grady, quotes Cervantes to express his distaste for the Madero generation's veneration of French ideas.

Many of the discussions in *Whales and Men* center on the limitations of the human intellect. Peter tells Guy, during a conversation about the nature of evil, that "the meaning of Genesis is quite clear isn't it? There was no evil in the world until man sought knowledge. We always knew that our desire to be God would kill us. It was told from the very beginning."

Dyson, Freeman (b. 1923)

McCarthy quotes physicist Freeman Dyson in a holograph marginal note written next to John Western's musings about the purpose, or lack thereof, of life—this is what these characters do. He addresses his remarks to Guy Schuler: "You say there is no purpose. But even no purpose is a purpose. In the sense that no pattern is a pattern, or that complete randomness is no longer random." More Zen koans follow these, but the gist of John's polemic seems to be that, contra Schuler, there must be purpose and meaning to existence. The reference to Dyson in the margin appears to be a thought that McCarthy intended to add to John's disquisition. McCarthy wrote, "Dyson says the universe seems to have known ... Anthropic Principle?"

I cannot find an original source for this quotation, but McCarthy may have found it in *The Anthropic Cosmological Principle* by John Barrow and Frank Tipler. Here is a quotation that the authors attribute to Dyson: "As we look out into the Universe and identify the many accidents of physics and astronomy that have worked together to our benefit, it almost seems as if the Universe must in some sense have known that we were coming" (318). According to Timothy Ferris, the Anthropic Principle is an "approach to cosmology that constrains fundamental constants of nature and other cosmic circumstances by demonstrating that were they otherwise, the universe could not support life and therefore would not be observed" (353). While this does not sound as dramatic as the notion of the universe warming up for the arrival of minds, the idea still provides scientific respectability for John Western's efforts to defend an alternative to Schuler's gloomy reductionism.

Hemingway, Ernest (1899–1961)

John Western quotes Ernest Hemingway during a disquisition on the admirable traits that human beings rightfully appreciate in predators like wolves: "Hemingway said that hawks don't share. But of course hawks do share. It's rabbits that don't share." John is being unfair to Hemingway, who was not talking about hawks, but about Zelda Fitzgerald. Hemingway uses the hawk metaphor in a hit job on Zelda in *A Moveable Feast*, accusing her of being jealous of her husband. According to Hemingway, she once told him she thought Al Jolson was "greater than Jesus." Hemingway's mockery of her too-cute-by-half bon mot insinuates that her hawk-like parsimoniousness stifled F. Scott Fitzgerald's creativity: "Nobody ... thought anything of it at the time. It was only Zelda's secret that she shared with me, as a hawk might share something with a man. But hawks do not share. Scott did not write anything any more that was good until after he knew that she was insane" (160). Figurative hawks do not share.

Hoffer, Eric (1898–1983)

One of the characters in *Whales and Men* quotes one of Eric Hoffer's most famous lines in a fragment of unattributed dialogue. One of the problems with the screenplay is that many of the long spoken parts could be spoken by any of the three principal male characters. Whoever is doing the talking in the passage is, beyond the quotation, making a claim that sounds in line with Hoffer's thesis in his most famous work, *The True Believer: Thoughts on the Nature of Mass Movements*, an inquiry into the origins of totalitarianism. Here is the relevant passage, with the loosely quoted line from Hoffer italicized. The subject is torture: "I think what we need is pain.... As if there were not enough in the normal course of events we miss no opportunity to add to the stock. But what is that we want [*sic*]? Hoffer says *we can never get enough of what we don't really want.* So what is it that we really want that blood cannot supply and only blood seems to legitimize?" (emphasis added).

The quotation comes from Hoffer's discussion of a human type he calls "the misfit," an outsider whose personal sense of dissatisfaction with life makes him vulnerable to the appeal of collective movements. According to Hoffer, "whatever they undertake becomes a passionate pursuit; but they never arrive, never pause. They demonstrate the fact that we can never have enough of that which we really do not want, and that we run fastest and farthest when we run from ourselves" (47).

Hoffer was a philosopher and social critic whose appeal rests in part on his working-class roots. He began writing while working as a longshoreman on the San Francisco docks. He is a bit like McCarthy's Ben Telfair in that his thinking was shaped by work.

Hyde, Douglas (1860–1949)

At the end of the "Irish Idyll," Peter Gregory, watching his friends depart, in a voice-over quotes from a sixteenth-century Irish poem that has been translated numerous times, including by Thomas Kinsella (Giemza 219). McCarthy's directions indicate that this version is "from the Irish of Douglas Hyde," a Gaelic scholar who influenced the Gaelic revival and became the first president of Ireland in 1938: "I shall not die for thee / Oh woman of body like a swan / I was nurtured by a cunning man / O thin palm, O white blossom." The woman Peter has in mind is John Western's girlfriend Kelly McAmon, whom he later marries.

Jeffers, Robinson (1887–1962)

A poetry reading takes place during the "Irish Idyll," and on one of these pages, McCarthy made a marginal note containing Robinson Jeffers's name and the title of a poem, "Hurt Hawks." There is no reference to Jeffers in the text of the screenplay, but the reference to the poem confirms a hunch of Edwin Arnold's related by Dianne C. Luce. In an endnote to her essay "The Vanishing World of Cormac McCarthy's Border Trilogy," Luce writes that "Edwin Arnold has suggested to me the relevance of Robinson Jeffers's 'Hurt Hawks,' in which the speaker reluctantly gives 'the lead gift' to a crippled hawk.... The poem resonates with several of the [*Border Trilogy's*] instances of animals (especially predators) killed at the hands of man out of either mercy or cruelty" (195). The instance Arnold associated with the Jeffers poem is the one in *The Crossing* in which Billy kills a hawk with an arrow. He is unable to find the hawk after it falls from the sky, but he does find a drop of its blood, which he mingles with his own by making a cut in his own hand (129–130).

Arnold is surely right in making the association. The hawk scene serves as a prelude to Billy's return, after the death of the wolf, to a more primitive state of existence, one that deeply alienates him from any human community. Billy encounters a Yaqui Indian who calls him *Huerfano*, an orphan (134). Jeffers's poem idealizes the heroic isolation of the hawk, a powerful predator with whom Billy identifies (as is symbolized by the mingling of his blood with that of the hawk). Here is how Jeffers describes the hawk whose nature Billy internalizes: "The wild God of the world is sometimes merciful to those / That ask mercy, not often to the arrogant. / You do not know him, you communal people, or you have forgotten him / Intemperate and savage, the hawk remembers him; / Beautiful and wild, the hawks, and the men that are dying, remember him" (lines 13–17). Jeffers's God is as wild as the hawk, and also very like the God who is evoked by different characters throughout *The Crossing*.

Lopez, Barry Holstun (b. 1945)

In a holograph marginal note at the bottom of a page of dialogue featuring one of the ubiquitous discussions of the wonder of whales in the screenplay, McCarthy alludes to Barry Lopez's *Arctic Dreams*. The note is enclosed in parentheses, and it was likely meant to be included in the scene. These folks are well-read and talkative, and McCarthy, having focused for the first two decades of his career on silent types, gives them opportunities to show off their literacy. McCarthy wrote, "(BIRD LANDNG ON ONE—LOPEZ)." The reference makes sense in the context of the discussion, which centers on the great physical sensitivity of whales. The passage from *Arctic Dreams* comes from a description of right whales in the prologue: "It is so sensitive to touch that at a bird's footfall a whale asleep at the surface will start wildly. The fiery pain of a harpoon strike can hardly be imagined" (3). The second sentence would also have stood out to McCarthy, concerned as he is in the screenplay with the brutality of whale hunting.

Lopez, like other writers in the naturalist tradition, such as Aldo Leopold (see entry for Leopold in *The Crossing*) and Henry Beston (whom Peter Gregory later mentions in the screenplay), has been a major influence on McCarthy, who expresses many of the same concerns about the ethics of hunting and the value of nonhuman life, not only in this screenplay but in his novels as well. Dianne Luce identifies the influence of Leopold and Lopez on McCarthy in her essay "The Vanishing World of Cormac McCarthy's Border Trilogy" (184–185).

Melville, Herman (1819–1891)

SEE ALSO *SUTTREE* AND *THE STONEMASON*

Guy Schuler is a Herman Melville fan, as is the likely real-life model for the character, the whale biologist Roger Payne, a longtime friend of McCarthy's and the source of his interest in whales. In Payne's book *Among Whales*, for which McCarthy is credited as a copy editor, Payne calls *Moby-Dick* "the greatest novel, the most inordinate book ever written" (324). Though Payne acknowledges that much of Melville's knowledge of whales was erroneous, he finds Melville to be ahead of his time in his appreciation for them, claiming that "on several occasions Melville put aside his perceptions of the 'panther heart' of the sea and of the 'dangers and affrights' of whaling and wrote lyrical passages about whales ... more along lines with which we have only recently grown comfortable ourselves" (324). Guy Schuler thinks so, too.

Payne at one point observes that our greater knowledge of whales has likely "constrained as much as it has expanded the literary possibilities of whales" (324). Would that McCarthy had paid greater heed to this statement. *Whales and Men* is exhibit A in its defense. But not only did McCarthy ignore the warning, he made his friend a character, one given to weighty, grave, and dire pontification. For instance: "I don't think you can say what death is if you don't know what life is. If I don't know what the whale is how can I talk about his nonexistence? What is it that doesn't exist? I guess sometimes I try to think not what the whale is but who he is. Maybe the way Melville did. I don't think science gets done that way, but there are times when I see the whale very differently." And again: "Melville thought the whale was not god but god's agent. 'Be the white whale principle or be the white whale agent I will wreak that vengeance upon him.' We've known for at least three thousand years, at least since the garden of Eden, that we would be destroyed by our desire to be god." These thoughts lead to his conclusion—one he claims echoes Melville—that killing whales is akin to killing God. These are fascinating ideas, as well as sound readings of *Moby-Dick*, but they come across as rather leaden and dispiriting in McCarthy's very earnest screenplay.

Montaigne, Michel Eyquem de (1533–1592)

SEE ALSO *SUTTREE*

At Le Club International, Guy Schuler asks Peter Gregory why he and John Western hit it off so well. Peter responds by quoting Montaigne's words when asked about his close friendship with Boétie: "Because it was he, because it was I." Beyond its usefulness in emphasizing how learned McCarthy's earnest intellectuals are, the reference to Montaigne's essay "Of Friendship" also emphasizes that, like Montaigne's friendship with Boétie, Peter and John's friendship is rooted in the life of the mind.

Moore, George Augustus (1852–1933)

McCarthy has Peter Gregory quote George Moore, the Irish critic, fiction writer, and memoirist, during the "Irish Idyll" at his family estate, saying, "Beautiful as it is and much as I love it I have not always been able to exclude ennui from its precincts." When asked about the source of this obvious quotation, Peter replies, "What can't be improved upon must be quoted. It's George Moore on Moore Hall." As Bryan Giemza points out, there is something fitting about Peter quoting Moore: "As an Anglo-Irish writer who wore his aristocratic origins on his sleeve and criticized them openly, George Moore would certainly resonate with Peter" (219). The quotation comes from Moore's memoir *Hail and Farewell*.

Mowat, Farley (1921–2014)

McCarthy refers to the Canadian naturalist writer Farley Mowat in a handwritten marginal note: "Wolf and old hunter (Mowat?)." Since characters in *Whales and Men* occasionally cite the work of nature writers, such as Henry Beston and Barry Lopez, the question mark suggests that McCarthy was trying to recall something from one of Mowat's books on wolves to have one of the characters quote. The most likely candidate would be *Never Cry Wolf*, Mowat's account of several weeks that he spent studying wolves at close quarters. McCarthy's note appears next to a discussion of the relationship between wolves and human beings. The Canadian writer would be congenial to McCarthy, given his interest in wilderness, animals—wolves in particular—and ecology. Mowat spent his life defending wild spaces from the encroachment of civilization and arguing for greater respect for wildlife.

In an interview, Mowat once claimed that wolves "are far less violent than man. I never saw a wolf commit a wanton act of destruction, cruelty, or maliciousness" (qtd. in "Mowat, Farley"). This notion is relevant to the passage next to McCarthy's note, where John shares his idea that "it's possible that the anthropoid experiment is a blind alley," and contrasts anthropoids with wolves in relation to violence:

> All kinds of dumb grasseating animals fight to the death. Wolves never do. The reports on chimpanzees and gorillas are just now coming in. Organized raids and battles, murder, cannibalism. We come by it honestly. That's what we're finding out. I think human society made a genuine effort to model itself on wolf society and it failed. We learned how to share food—which apes dont do—and we learned how to hunt in packs. But the third thing we needed we could never learn and that was to stop killing each other.

Mowat's work, in addition to informing the discussion of wolves in the screenplay, was a likely source of inspiration for McCarthy's depiction of the wolf that Billy attempts to rescue in *The Crossing*.

Pound, Ezra (1885–1972)

During the "Irish Idyll," Peter Gregory, with his wolfhounds at his side and a roaring fire in the hearth, reads poetry to the principal players. After a reading of Dylan Thomas, Lady Kilgore, Peter's mother, asks to hear "the Pound poem. About the river merchant's wife." Guy, apparently not as culturally literate as the others, must ask, "Pound as in Ezra?" After filling Guy in on the provenance of the poem, Peter recites it for the group. McCarthy inserted into the manuscript a photocopy of the poem.

Taylor, Gordon Rattray (1911–1981)

On a page of dialogue fragments, McCarthy wrote in the margin, "Eyes, etc. from <u>Grt Evolution Mystery</u>." He is referring to a book by the British writer and journalist Gordon Rattray Taylor. *The Great Evolution Mystery*, published in 1981, the year of Taylor's death, challenges many of the assumptions of Darwinism. In particular, Taylor argues that many of the more complex evolutionary developments, such as eyes, are hard to attribute solely to the mechanisms that Darwin identified. These are by now familiar arguments, and they are generally dismissed with sneering disdain by neo-Darwinians. However, McCarthy seems to have taken an interest in the book and to have taken its premises seriously.

A long paragraph of dialogue next to McCarthy's note articulates Taylor's general unhappiness with Darwinism, and especially neo-Darwinism, as a *complete* account of evolution—Taylor was not a creationist, and did not deny evolution altogether. The problem with the screenplay is that there is no way to tell who is speaking, since the fragments do not follow screenplay format by attributing the words to a character. Guy Schuler seems unlikely, leaving either Peter Gregory or John Western as probable speakers. The passage in McCarthy's screenplay reads:

> Darwinism explains the mechanism of an elaborate system and then burrins [Though *The Oxford English Dictionary* does not document an example of the word being used this way, McCarthy appears to be referring to a "burin," a tool used for engraving on metal.] the inventor's name from the patent plates. It is a belief system, ultimately. Its adherents tend to militancy. They brook no contradiction. And their theory is unprovable in principle. You can't rewind the universe and run it over again. Scientific proofs are reproducible proofs, that's what makes them science isn't it? Darwinism dismisses the captain and puts the stoker at the helm. The conjugations of chance that it demands to fill in its schedule beggar belief. In the end it explains nothing but itself.

This long paragraph is followed by a single sentence: "Sometimes I'm inclined to agree with you." Guy? McCarthy does not name the speaker. However, the drift of many of the other conversations between Guy and John would suggest the latter as the one questioning Darwinian premises, and the former offering grudging sympathy. In one of those conversations, John asks, "This caravan, where is it going? What is it transporting? What could it be conveying other than mind? Isn't that the grail?" His resistance to scientific reductionism makes him the probable critic of Darwinian triumphalism. The screenplay consistently balances McCarthy's equally strong commitments to a scientifically grounded understanding of the natural world—this is the guy who likes to hang out with scientists—and to religious and theological questions that take human spirituality seriously.

Teilhard de Chardin, Pierre (1881–1955)

McCarthy refers to the famous Jesuit priest and paleontologist Pierre Teilhard de Chardin in a marginal note next to one of John's long philosophical disquisitions. The note reads, "Mind a Gestalt—Chardin." Teilhard's teleological view of evolution posits that its direction is toward ever greater levels of complexity and organization (a theory very much at odds with the Second Law of Thermodynamics) and that the process of evolution will culminate at what he called the "Omega Point," the point of maximum complexity. The development of the mind is one obvious stage on that road. Presumably, the idea that the mind is a gestalt is that minds, in a holistic fashion, contain the whole of this cosmic progression within themselves as the acorn contains the tree, or that each mind contains within it the Cosmic Mind—heady stuff, at any rate. McCarthy was thinking of Teilhard in connection with the following bit of orotundity from John Western responding to Peter Gregory's cynical view of human evolution:

> I cant imagine that the purpose of the world is to evolve a creature at last capable of its destruction. You say there is no purpose. But even no purpose is a purpose much in the sense that no pattern is a pattern or that ultimate and complete randomness is no longer random. I understand you when you say there is no mind, only minds. But I dont think you can really comprehend such a thing. I think mind is what we think of when we say there is none. I think its like trying not to think of an elephant. When I look at the bones rostered in your book all I can see is a struggle for expression.... Arent they just the remnants of a caravan that patches and mends itself enroute? What other grail could it be conveying than mind? I'm satisfied that time and space are an aberration of our point of view and that there is no place to go and no time in which to get there.

All this needs to round it out is a brief *excursus* into Zeno's Paradoxes. In the old philosophical debate about the many vs. the one, McCarthy often seems to come out on the side of oneness, as in the following passage from *The Crossing*, in which the ex-priest elucidates a gestalt theory through the metaphor of storytelling:

> What does Caborca know of Huisiachepic, Huisiachepic of Caborca? They are different worlds, you must agree. Yet even so there is but one world and everything that is imaginable is necessary to it. For this world also which seems to us a thing of stone and flower and blood is not a thing at all but is a tale. And all in it is a tale and each tale the sum of all lesser tales and yet these also are the selfsame tale and contain as well all else within them. (143)

The ex-priest concludes all this by saying that "rightly heard all tales are one" (143), presumably just to eliminate any confusion about the point. McCarthy's gestalt cosmology derives from multiple sources, but the archives confirm Teilhard de Chardin as one of them.

Thomas, Dylan (1914–1953)

During the "Irish Idyll," the characters gather around a fire for an evening of urbane conversation, much of it heavily theological—Peter Gregory's brother David, a Dominican priest, has joined them. In addition, Peter reads poetry. McCarthy's directions tell us that "he is intoning the last of *Fern Hill*, much in the manner of Thomas himself."

The scene, straight out of a hackneyed Big House novel, is an example of the often heavy-handed way in which McCarthy sketches these very talkative characters. Peter reads in the manner of Dylan Thomas while his wolfhounds sleep at his side. But he is, after all, a titled Irish aristocrat. Kelly McAmon, later in the same scene, in a conversation with David, the Dominican priest, quotes Thomas while discussing God. She says that she believes in God, even if he is only "the force that through the green fuse drives the flower," the first line and title of one of Thomas's best-known poems.

Yeats, William Butler (1865–1939)

At the end of *Whales and Men* McCarthy copied a stanza from William Butler Yeats's "A Cradle Song": "The angels are stooping / Above your bed; / They weary of trooping / With the whimpering dead" (lines 1–4). Although the stanza is not included in the actual dialogue, it would presumably have been sung by Kelly to her children with Peter. The inclusion of Yeats's lullaby is one of many indications throughout McCarthy's corpus of his interest in Yeats.

McCarthy's first published novel, *The Orchard Keeper*, features an allusion to Yeats's "The Lake Isle of Innisfree" in Arthur Ownby's thoughts about yearning to return to a simple life far removed from the encroachments of the modern world: "If I was a younger man, he told himself, I would move to them mountains. I would find me a clearwater branch and build me a log house with a fireplace. And my bees would make black mountain honey. And I wouldn't care for no man" (55). These words clearly echo Yeats's poem: "I will arise and go now, and go to Innisfree, / And a small cabin build there, of clay and wattles made: / Nine bean-rows will I have there, and a hive for the honey-bee, / And live alone in the bee-loud glade" (lines 1–4). And *Suttree*, as Bryan Giemza points out in his *Irish Catholic Writers and the Invention of the American South*, contains a clear allusion to Yeats's "Easter, 1916." During his typhoid-induced hallucinations, Suttree has a vision of a new world coming into being: "It rises in one massive mutation and all is changed utterly and forever" (459). Yeats's refrain is, "All changed, changed utterly: / A terrible beauty is born" (lines 15–16). Giemza shrewdly notes that the passage from *Suttree* also evokes, with its apocalyptic forebodings, Yeats's poem "The Second Coming" (Giemza 216). The most significant allusion to Yeats is in the title of McCarthy's *No Country for Old Men*, which derives from the first line of "Sailing to Byzantium": "That is no country for old men."

Steven Frye has written about the relationship between Yeats's poem and McCarthy's novel. The closing image of Sheriff Bell's father carrying fire in a horn in *No Country for Old Men*, Frye argues, evokes Yeats's image of eternal fire in "Sailing to Byzantium," and serves to highlight a contrast in the novel that corresponds to the poem's contrast between transience and transcendence. "However," Frye adds, this is not the fire of destruction but purification, creation, and light. At his fire, his father will, in Yeats [*sic*] words "gather him into the artifice of eternity." In this sense, in *No Country for Old Men* McCarthy juxtaposes two worlds: the external and objective world of sense, of artless violence, disorder, and bloodshed, where passion vents itself in pain; and the interior world of Bell's consciousness, which is a realm infused with the same, but one that seeks and finds a stability and permanence in human love, spiritual transcendence, and a mild and mitigated acceptance. (20)

Frye is quite right to link the fire in Yeats with McCarthy's fire. Bell corresponds to Yeats's "aged man," who is likened to "a tattered coat upon a stick" (lines 9–10), and Bell's dream of his father corresponds to the speaker in the poem's vision of Byzantium:

> O sages standing in God's holy fire
> As in the gold mosaic of a wall,
> Come from the holy fire, perne in a gyre,
> And be the singing-masters of my soul.
> Consume my heart away; sick with desire
> And fastened to a dying animal
> It knows not what it is; and gather me
> Into the artifice of eternity. (lines 17–24)

The fire, the spiritual and physical weariness of old age, the yearning for transcendence and permanence, all find their analogues in the character of Bell and his dreams and yearnings. Bell's yearning for the "artifice of eternity" finds expression in his reflections on a stone water trough that he saw in France during World War II. The trough is a far cry from "such a form as Grecian goldsmiths make" (line 27), but it suits with the Shaker simplicity of McCarthy's late prose stylings. In this novel, it represents the Yeatsian celebration of artifice:

> That country had not had a time of peace much of any length at all that I knew of.... But this man had set down with a hammer and chisel and carved out a stone water trough to last ten thousand years. Why was that? What was it that he had faith in.... And I have to say that the only

thing I can think is that there was some sort of promise in his heart. And I dont have no intentions of carvin a stone water trough. But I would like to be able to make that kind of promise. (308)

The promise in his heart corresponds to the imagined Byzantium of the old man in Yeats's poem, as does Bell's dreamland in which the fire continues to burn in the darkness.

It is noteworthy that both at the beginning of McCarthy's career, with Arthur Ownby, and very late in his career, with Sheriff Bell, McCarthy imagined old men disillusioned with the modern world and yearning for Innisfree and Byzantium. Bell yearns for the same promise that Ownby seeks in the unsettled mountain country that McCarthy gives us in his lyrical description of the view of the Appalachians from Red Mountain: "From the crest on a clear day you can see the cool blue line of the watershed like a distant promise" (10). The promise in the heart and the promise of the watershed, place of unsullied beginnings, haunt McCarthy's fiction from first to last.

CHAPTER 13

Correspondence

Most of the names below come from McCarthy's correspondence with J. Howard Woolmer, a rare book dealer whose early interest in McCarthy's work led to four decades of letters between the two men. The box and folder numbers refer to the Woolmer Collection. I have recorded their "book chat" in the entries that follow. Some of the names in this chapter appear in letters McCarthy sent to Peter Greenleaf that are now part of the Wittliff Collections.

Brinnin, John Malcolm (1916–1998)

McCarthy briefly mentions John Malcolm Brinnin in a letter to Woolmer dated 28 October 1981. Brinnin was an American poet and literary critic most famous for his 1955 book *Dylan Thomas in America*. Brinnin had arranged the Welsh poet's first trip to the United States, and the book is about his experiences with him. McCarthy, whose admiration for Thomas is evident in his having characters lovingly recite his poetry during a scene in *Whales and Men* (see the entry for Dylan Thomas in *Whales and Men*), was likely familiar with this book, if not with other works by Brinnin.

In the letter to Woolmer, who seems to have been helping McCarthy to find a literary agent, he responds to Woolmer's query about whether McCarthy knows Brinnin's work: "Good to hear from you. Thank you for your inquiries on my behalf. I do indeed know Brinnin's work. I will keep his recommendation in mind and possibly go agent-shopping when I get to New York" (Box 1, Folder 4). Perhaps Brinnin had suggested a good agent's name for Woolmer to pass along to McCarthy.

Byron, George Gordon, Lord (1788–1824)

McCarthy mentions Byron in a letter to Peter Greenleaf, a correspondent who provided several letters from McCarthy to the Wittliff Collections in 2013. Greenleaf's letters to McCarthy, though not included in the collection, clearly solicit the author's views on other writers. In a letter postmarked 22 June 1981, McCarthy wrote: "I don't know if I agree about writers being the only dependable readers. I remember reading once the names of the writers Byron admired—none of whom anyone has heard of since" (Peter Greenleaf Collection, Box 1700, Folder 1). The reference suggests two things. The first is that Cormac McCarthy has read Byron, which is not surprising. The second, however, is more interesting. It suggests that McCarthy's interest in Byron is deep enough to motivate the kinds of secondary investigations into a writer's life and thought that deep admiration often engenders.

The database of the Modern Language Association (MLA) only reveals one study of Byron's influence on McCarthy, Charles Bailey's "The Last Stage of the Hero's Evolution: Cormac McCarthy's *Cities of the Plain*." In it, Bailey argues that in the last volume of *The Border Trilogy* McCarthy evokes the figure of the Byronic antihero in his depiction of John Grady Cole and Billy Parham: "And just as Byron became disillusioned and, in lament, debunked the previous heroes as incompatible with a world that is too much with us, so does McCarthy lament even the anti-hero, made finally irrelevant in a world corrupted and degraded by advancing science and nuclear technology" (294). If the letter to Greenleaf provides a genuine hint about McCarthy's influences, Bailey's essay turns out to be prescient.

Chatwin, Bruce (1940–1989)

His letters to J. Howard Woolmer and Peter Greenleaf, in addition to Garry Wallace's account of meeting McCarthy, attest to a serious interest on McCarthy's part in the work of Bruce Chatwin, the British novelist and travel writer. Indeed, this interest broadened into influence. *The Crossing* is deeply informed by McCarthy's reading of Chatwin's *The Songlines* (1987), an account of Chatwin's travels in Australia and his investigations into the culture of the Aborigines.

The earliest mention of Chatwin in the archives is in a 1984 letter to Peter Greenleaf, who had recommended that McCarthy read one of Chatwin's novels: "I haven't found any of the books you recommended. I've ordered Chatwin's book twice (On the Black Hill) but so far have not received it. A couple of other people told me they thought it was very good. I read his book—Patagonia and thought it was excellent" (Box 1700, Folder 1). In a letter dated 2 May 1985, McCarthy reports a mixed response to the novel: "I'm about halfway thru the Chatwin—started off excellent and is bogging down some but we'll see." McCarthy's interest in Chatwin's *In Patagonia* (1977) may have been inspired by his friend Roger Payne, a preeminent whale biologist, who often traveled to that region to research right whales (see chapter 2 of his *Among Whales*). McCarthy mentions traveling to Patagonia in a letter to Woolmer, a trip likely inspired by Payne.

Woolmer and McCarthy shared their enthusiasm for Chatwin in two letters from January 1988. Woolmer begins the correspondence by mentioning a meeting with Chatwin: "I ran into Bruce Chatwin in London in November and to his everlasting shame he'd never read C. McC., so I sent him a couple of paperbacks and will let you know if he replies. I liked his <u>On the Black Hill</u> very much" (Box 1, Folder 7). Chatwin's published correspondence contains a letter to Woolmer thanking him for the McCarthy books and expressing his admiration for McCarthy: "How kind to send the Cormac McCarthys. I've read *The Orchard Keeper* which is splendid, and am taking *Suttree* with me to the Caribbean next week. Hope we'll meet again soon" (497). Woolmer passed this information on to McCarthy in a letter dated 19 May 1988.

McCarthy's letters to Woolmer suggest that McCarthy not only admired Chatwin's work but may have gotten to know him in the years before his death. The first, dated 21 March 1988, is a response to Woolmer's letter quoted above: "I read <u>Songlines</u> not too long ago and thought it was very good. Recommended it to friends all about and they liked it but had reservations about the journal entry sections. Just the parts I liked best. I also liked his Patagonia book. Everyone I met in Patagonia absolutely despised it" (Box 1, Folder 7). A letter dated 8 April 1989 records McCarthy's sadness at Chatwin's death of AIDS that year: "I was very distressed over Chatwin's death. A talented and honest man and a decent human being. The perfect candidate, in other words, for the Fates to single out. I'd told every friend I have to read <u>Songlines</u> and have even read passages long distance over the phone" (Box 1, Folder 7). In the same letter McCarthy laments the death of Edward Abbey, and his phrasing suggests that McCarthy and Chatwin knew each other, perhaps through Woolmer, who seems to have made Chatwin's acquaintance some years before: "I also lost *another writer friend* two weeks ago—Ed Abbey" (emphasis added).

Finally, Garry Wallace's "Meeting McCarthy" mentions Chatwin: "Again I asked McCarthy if he could recommend any good books or authors that a beginning writer should read. . . . Upon further prodding, he mentioned several of John [McPhee's] books and *The Song Lines* [sic] by Bruce Chatwin" (136).[1] All of this confirms McCarthy's interest in Chatwin, but his influence on McCarthy is most evident in *The Crossing*.

The Chatwin book that most influenced *The Crossing* was *The Songlines*. It is written in the style of a travel book, but Chatwin usually described it as a novel. A section composed of journal entries and quotations constitutes about a third of the book, and this is the section McCarthy liked best, according to the letter quoted above. In the novel, Bruce (he is the main character) chronicles his investigation into Aboriginal songs and their relationship to their nomadic culture. It is, in fact, a celebration of nomadism, a hymn to humanity's restless need to keep moving, as well as a theory of poetry as a kind of verbal topography marking our movement through the world: "I have a vision of the Songlines stretching across the continents and ages; that wherever men have trodden they have left a trail of song (of which we may, now and then, catch an echo); and that these trails must reach back, in time and space, to an isolated pocket in the African savannah, where the First Man opening his mouth in defiance of the terrors that surrounded him, shouted the opening stanza of the World Song, 'I AM!'" (282). Throughout the book, Chatwin explores this notion that humanity's deepest nature is rooted in song. Commenting on the work of Theodor Strehlow, whose studies of Aboriginal song influenced Chatwin, he says that Strehlow wanted "to find in song a key to unravelling the mystery of the human condition" (69).

In *The Crossing*, this notion finds expression in the theme of the Mexican *corrido*, a type of folksong celebrating the exploits of a hero, as a vessel housing deep truths about the human condition, truths beyond the province of history. The ex-priest whom Billy encounters in Huisiachepic is the first of many wisdom figures in the book to articulate this view: "Things separate from their stories have no meaning. They are only shapes. Of a certain size and color. A certain weight. When their meaning has become lost to us they no longer have even a name. The story on the other hand can never be lost from its place in the world for it is that place. And that is what was to be found here. The corrido. The tale. And like all corridos it ultimately told one story only, for there is only one to tell" (142–143). The claim that the story, or corrido/song, "can never be lost from its place in the world for it is that place" sounds very much like Chatwin's reflections on Aboriginal songs and the relationship of those songs to the land. In *The Songlines* the character Arkady, "a Russian who was mapping the sacred sites of the Aboriginals" (1), as well as an alter-ego for Chatwin himself (J. Chatwin 126), tells the character "Bruce" that "each totemic ancestor, while travelling through the country, was thought to have scattered a trail of words and musical notes along the line of his footprints, and how these Dreaming-tracks lay over the land as 'ways' of communication between the most far-flung tribes" (13).

The idea that a kind of primordial song, rooted in the nomadic wanderings of primitive hunter-gatherers, constitutes an ur-language that links all human beings, as well as human beings with the natural world, appears to be deeply appealing to McCarthy. In *The Songlines*, Gypsies and Aborigines are held up as vastly superior to those who have settled in the cities of the plain. "Bruce" tells another character that Gypsies "see themselves as hunters. The world is their hunting ground. Settlers are 'sitting game.' The Gypsy word for 'settler' is the same as the word for 'meat'" (156). McCarthy also accords great dignity to hunters. This is evident in early novels, including *The Orchard Keeper*, as well as in later works, such as *No Country for Old Men*. In *The Crossing*, this dignified standing is most evident in the novel's celebration of wolves. Don Arnulfo tells Billy that the wolf "Es cazador," or a hunter, and that "the hunter was a different thing than men supposed." Moreover, according to Don Arnulfo, "men believe the blood of the slain to be of no consequence but ... the wolf knows better" (45). The knowledge the wolf/hunter possesses is rooted in a deep awareness of the transience of all things and in the knowledge that "there is no order in the world save that which death has put there" (45).

In *The Songlines*, Gypsies, like Aborigines, are suspicious of the idea of possession. This characteristic, unrelated to the kind of suspicion of private property ownership found in Marxist or anarchist political philosophies, is rooted in an existential sense of transience and the concomitant need for movement over stasis. The ex-Benedictine Dan Flynn, an expert on Aboriginal culture, tells "Bruce" that "Aboriginals, in general, had the idea that all 'goods' were potentially malign and would work against their possessors unless they were forever in motion" (57).

The Gypsies Billy encounters near the end of *The Crossing* exhibit the same kind of nobility and awareness of the transitory nature of reality that is found in Chatwin's Gypsies and Aborigines. McCarthy, following Chatwin's book, elevates the nomad to a position of purity within the hierarchy of human types: "Every representation was an idol. Every likeness a heresy. In their images [photographs] they [the Gypsies] had thought to find some small immortality but oblivion cannot be appeased ... and this was why they were men of the road" (413).

McCarthy's characters are often men of the road, as is the author himself. Richard B. Woodward commented on McCarthy's own nomadic tendencies in a piece for *The New York Times Magazine*: "Having saved enough money to leave El Paso, McCarthy may take off again soon, probably for several years in Spain. . . . 'Three moves is as good as a fire,' he says in praise of homelessness" (n.p.). Chatwin also shared this restless need to stay on the go. In an interview with Michael Ignatieff, he told Ignatieff, after commenting on his wonderful home, which he shares with his wife, Elizabeth, that "we have everything here, but I always wish I was somewhere else" (qtd. in J. Chatwin 1).[2] McCarthy and Bruce Chatwin are clearly kindred spirits, perhaps even acquaintances, and it is not surprising that they admired each other's work, or that McCarthy took inspiration from *The Songlines*.[3]

Clarke, Arthur C. (1917–2008)

Charles Bailey, in an essay on the influence of Lord Byron on McCarthy, suggests that he is proposing a "curious yoking" (293). Arthur C. Clarke would seem "curioser and curioser," but a letter to Wittliff donor Peter Greenleaf suggests that McCarthy is a reader of the great British science fiction writer. McCarthy's published work does not suggest an actual yoking, or *influence*, but the letter does confirm an *interest*. Dated 1984, the letter addresses Greenleaf's desire to travel to Sri Lanka: "I wish you'd gotten to Sri Lanka last year too, then you could tell me about it. I have a friend here who has been and he thinks it's a great place. Like you, however, I prefer not to be shot in the streets. Arthur C. Clarke lives in Sri Lanka. I think at one time he had the only television there" (Box 1700, Folder 1).

Although this mention does not confirm that McCarthy is a Clarke reader, the observation about the television seems like the kind of detail about a writer that an enthusiast would take note of. Furthermore, as Michael Chabon has persuasively argued (see entry for Carl Stephenson in *Suttree*), McCarthy's imagination is deeply imbued with the tropes and techniques of genre fiction, and many readers and critics have recognized an affinity between *The Road* and dystopian and post-apocalyptic science fiction novels.

Davenport, Guy (1927–2005)

Guy Davenport was a writer of short fiction, a critic of both the literary and visual arts, and a painter. Davenport and McCarthy were on friendly terms, as revealed by two letters from McCarthy to J. Howard Woolmer as well as a *Paris Review* interview with Davenport by John Jeremiah Sullivan. A letter to Woolmer dated 27 August 1986 reads, "Note from Guy Davenport says he has a new collection of essays coming from North Point at year's end: Every Force Evolves a Form. Do you know his essays The Geography of the Imagination? Marvelous book" (Box 1, Folder 6). In the *Paris Review* interview, Sullivan responds to Davenport's claim that "I have no life" by exclaiming, "This from no doubt the only man on earth to have known Ezra Pound, Thomas Merton, and Cormac McCarthy personally" (n.p.).

It is unclear when McCarthy and Davenport came to know each other, but Davenport was an early admirer of McCarthy, writing an insightful review of *Outer Dark* in 1968. His chief insight is contained in the following remark: "Mr. McCarthy is unashamedly an allegorist. His responsibility as a storyteller includes believing with his characters in the devil, or at least in the absolute destructiveness of evil." Though *Outer Dark* may be a particularly vivid instance of McCarthy's penchant for allegorical storytelling, reading his corpus in the light of Davenport's claim is instructive. For instance, *Child of God*, when read allegorically, can be seen as a kind of religious parable, one that concludes with the redemption of the murderous necrophiliac Lester Ballard. Whether or not that reading works for readers, the symbolic overlay makes it inescapable. Davenport saw this aspect of McCarthy's aesthetic early on.

The admiration, as the letter to Woolmer makes clear, was mutual. The book McCarthy expresses enthusiasm for, Davenport's *Geography of the Imagination*, is a first-rate work of literary criticism. The first essay, which also supplies the title of the collection, would have been of great interest to McCarthy, as it links, in a fascinating reading, two of McCarthy's favorite writers, James Joyce and Oswald Spengler. After summarizing Spengler's division of world cultures into "the Apollonian, or Graeco-Roman; the Faustian, or Western-Northern European; and the Magian, or Asian and Islamic" (10), he argues that these divisions correspond to Edgar Allan Poe's aesthetic categories of the classical, the Islamic, and the grotesque (8), and, in a more surprising turn, to Joyce's organizational patterns:

> Look at the first three stories of Joyce's *Dubliners*. The first is concerned with a violation of rites that derive from deep in Latin culture by way of the Roman Mass, the second takes its symbols from chivalry, the moral codes of Northern knighthood, and the third is named "Araby." This triad of symbolic patterns is repeated four more times, to achieve fifteen stories. The first three chapters of *Ulysses* also follow this structure ... it is about a man, Leopold Bloom, in a northern European, a Faustian-technological context, who is by heritage a Jew of Spengler's Magian culture, who is made to act out the adventures of Ulysses, exemplar of classical man. (10)

It is easy to imagine McCarthy's enthusiasm for this deft display of critical acumen. Another letter to Woolmer describes *The Geography of the Imagination* as "a first rate piece of work," and adds that "good books seem to get rarer and rarer," a comment that situates Davenport within an elite company.

Graves, John (1920–2013)

A standard trope in biographical accounts of Cormac McCarthy is that he avoids other writers. Richard B. Woodward's 1992 interview of McCarthy for *The New York Times Magazine*, McCarthy's first grudging step in the direction of wider publicity, contains a paragraph that has cemented this perception: "His hostility to the literary world seems both genuine ('teaching writing is a hustle') and a tactic to screen out distractions. At the MacArthur reunions he spends his time with scientists, like the physicist Murray Gell-Mann and the whale biologist Roger Payne, rather than other writers. One of the few he acknowledges having known at all was the novelist and ecological crusader Edward Abbey. Shortly before Abbey's death in 1989, they discussed a covert operation to reintroduce the wolf to southern Arizona" (4).[4] However, the Wittliff Collections at Texas State University reveal another literary friendship. The John Graves collection contains six letters from Graves to McCarthy and two from McCarthy to Graves. Graves, much of whose work falls into the category of American nature writing, a genre dear to McCarthy, is best known for his book *Goodbye to a River*, which recounts a canoe trip down the Brazos through north and central Texas.

McCarthy's letters to Graves focus on his love of fishing (and books about fishing) and on his travels to Mexico to research *All the Pretty Horses*. The first letter is undated, but would have been written in late 1987 or in January 1988. In it he tells Graves that he is planning to travel to Mexico soon, and though he does not mention *All the Pretty Horses*, the letter does say that he is working on a novel.

Woodward claims, in his *New York Times Magazine* piece, that "McCarthy doesn't write about places he hasn't visited, and he has made dozens of . . . scouting forays to Texas, New Mexico, Arizona and across the Rio Grande into Chihuahua, Sonora and Coahuila."

McCarthy mentions such a trip in the letter to Graves: "I enjoyed your letter and your description of canoeing on the Pecos. What I want to do this spring is get down to Sonora and check out the Bavispe river. There is a lot of country down there that is just indescribably remote. I've been back to some of those villages in the Sierras and it is really like going back a hundred years. Wonderful people too" (Graves Collection, Box 28, Folder 8).[5]

Perhaps it is just such villages McCarthy had in mind when, in *All the Pretty Horses*, John Grady sees "small villages distant on the plain that glowed a faint yellow in that incoordinate dark and he knew that the life there was unimaginable to him" (257). And he may have had those wonderful people in mind when, in *Cities of the Plain*, Billy explains why it was important to him to help a group of Mexicans with a flat tire. He tells Troy that on the worst day of his life, he and his brother "was on the run and he was hurt and there was a truckload of Mexicans just about like them back yonder appeared out of nowhere and pulled our bacon out of the fire. I wasnt even sure their old truck could outrun a horse, but it did. They didnt have no reason to stop for us. But they did. I dont guess it would of even occurred to em not to" (36). Troy suggests that Billy is a Good Samaritan. Billy denies this, but it seems clear that this sort of charity is precisely where McCarthy locates the religious life.

In the same letter, McCarthy turns to the subject of fishing, an enthusiasm both men share: "Your trip to Florida sounded great. Always wanted to fly fish for Tarpon. Do you know McGuane's book <u>A Sporting Chance</u>? Some good stories about Keys fishing in it as I recall. I'm very partial to that country down there myself. I think I could live there if I was ever banished from the desert." In his reply, dated 24 January 1988, Graves describes the quasi-religious quality many practitioners find in the "contemplative sport," and then he writes, in a passage of the letter redolent of the mellow tones of Izaac Walton: "That session with tarpon in the Keys last spring, brief though it was, rather shook me up, bringing new awareness of a whole wide realm of things, the sea and all that goes with it, whose pull was stout for me in younger years but which had deteriorated into mere memory, if good memories are ever mere." McCarthy's reply, probably written in the spring of 1988, adopts a similar tone: "God knows I used to love it. I'd hate to have to add up the hours and the days I've stood in a trout stream or a bass pond waving a fly rod back and forth." He goes on to recommend several books about fishing, including *Ted Williams Fishing "the Big Three": Tarpon, Bonefish, Atlantic Salmon*; George Reiger's *Profiles in Saltwater Angling*; and Thomas McGuane's *A Sporting Chance* (though McCarthy is conflating the titles of two McGuane books, *The Sporting Club* and *An Outside Chance*; see entry for McGuane in this chapter). McCarthy's decision to make his most autobiographical character, Cornelius Suttree, a fisherman, highlights the importance of fishing to McCarthy, and its spiritual significance finds expression in Suttree's reflection that "he might have been a fisher of men in another time but these fish now seemed task enough for him" (14).

The Graves letters reveal further connections with writers that belie the cliché about McCarthy (one he, of course, engendered) that he strictly eschews the company of other professional scribblers. McCarthy is friends with Bill Wittliff, the screenwriter and patron of the Wittliff Collection, where McCarthy's papers are housed. In a comment to Graves, McCarthy mentions discussing the television miniseries *Lonesome Dove* with Wittliff, who was working on the adaptation of Larry McMurtry's book at the time and wrote the screenplay for it. In a letter to Woolmer, McCarthy mentions his admiration for the miniseries. The letters also reveal a McCarthy connection with the Texas Institute of Letters, whose website lists him as a current member. In the first letter to Graves, he asks if Graves will be attending a meeting in Bourne, Texas, in April 1988. McCarthy indicates that he is planning to go, "unless something unforeseen arises," and that he hopes Graves will be there. This comment suggests that McCarthy's reticence about attending literary gatherings may not be as thoroughgoing as his reputation implies.

From this same letter we also gain a rare insight into McCarthy on the subject of writing: "I'm back at work on (another) novel. I finished the one I was working on and put it away for a while and started another. New projects are the most fun and rewriting is hard work—to me anyway." The novel he had put away was *All the Pretty Horses*, the new project *The Crossing*. Graves wrote to McCarthy on 3 February 1993 to express his high praise for *All the Pretty Horses*: "I will confess that a number of times while reading I had wet eyes, and the reason was not sadness or sentimentality but always the grace and power of your language and your perceptions." Graceful seems an appropriate way to describe the language of these letters as well.

Hansen, Ron (b. 1947)

Ron Hansen, one of the few contemporary novelists for whom McCarthy has expressed unabashed enthusiasm, is noted for both gritty westerns, such as *Desperadoes* and *The Assassination of Jesse James by the Coward Robert Ford*, and delicately nuanced explorations of religious and moral themes, such as *Atticus* and *Mariette in Ecstasy*. McCarthy recommends Hansen to Peter Greenleaf in a letter postmarked 16 August 1983. The reference is made in the context of a discussion of writers whom McCarthy does *not* like. After mentioning D. H. Lawrence, Marcel Proust, and Henry James, he writes, "Best new novel I've read in a long time is Desperadoes by Ron Hansen" (Box 1700, Folder 1).

McCarthy also expressed his admiration for Hansen to Mark Morrow, who photographed and interviewed McCarthy for his book *Images of the Southern Writer* (1985). When Peter Josyph interviewed Morrow for his *Cormac McCarthy's House*, Morrow commented to Josyph about what a hard sell McCarthy is where fiction is concerned (he wrote to Greenleaf in the letter quoted above that he would read "Damn near anything except bad novels"). Morrow quotes McCarthy as saying that "even people who write well can't write novels.... They assume another sort of voice and a weird, affected kind of style. They think, 'O now I'm writing a novel,' and something happens. They write really good essays ... but goddamn, the minute they start writing a novel they go crazy" (*House* 29). However, McCarthy recommended Hansen's *Desperadoes* as an exception. The novel, published in 1979, the same year as *Suttree*, recounts the violent adventures of the Dalton Gang through the reminiscences of the sixty-five-year-old Emmett Dalton. McCarthy began *Blood Meridian* around 1975, and his enthusiasm for Hansen's book can be explained in part by the literary interest in the Wild West that he shares with Hansen.

McCarthy also admires *Mariette in Ecstasy* (1992), Hansen's lyrical story about a young nun whose ecstatic religious experiences, ranging from trances to stigmata, generate controversy and confusion within her order (Hansen is Roman Catholic). Bryan Giemza, in his discussion of McCarthy's relationship to Roman Catholicism, takes note of a letter from the psychologist Robert Coles to McCarthy, thanking him for a copy of the Hansen book that he sent him (221). McCarthy's enthusiasm for Hansen's deeply religious novel provides support for readers and critics who find in McCarthy's work a sense of religious quest. McCarthy's own statements confirm the centrality, however ambiguously understood, of spirituality to his worldview. McCarthy also makes this clear in a 2009 interview for the *Wall Street Journal*:

> *WSJ*: Is the God that you grew up with in church every Sunday the same God that the man in "The Road" questions and curses?
>
> *CM*: It may be. I have a great sympathy for the spiritual view of life, and I think that it's meaningful. But am I a spiritual person? I would like to be. Not that I am thinking about some afterlife that I want to go to, but just in terms of being a better person. I have friends at the Institute. They're just really bright guys who do really difficult work solving difficult problems, who say, "It's really more important to be good than it is to be smart." And I agree it is more important to be good than it is to be smart. That is all I can offer you. (Jurgensen "Hollywood's Favorite Cowboy")

Giemza is right to find McCarthy's interest in *Mariette in Ecstasy* to be evidence of McCarthy's abiding, if tenuous, connection to his Roman Catholic upbringing (221–222). McCarthy's reticence about discussing other writers, and his apparent willingness to recommend Hansen over the course of several decades, suggest a deep appreciation for Hansen's religiously informed fiction.

Hardy, Thomas (1840–1928)

Thomas Hardy has the distinction of being one of the few English Victorian novelists whose work McCarthy likes. McCarthy mentions Hardy in a letter to Wittliff donor Peter Greenleaf postmarked 16 August 1983. The letter is interesting for its reiteration of McCarthy's literary antipathies, which are already known to readers of Richard B. Woodward's piece for *The New York Times Magazine*, and for its inclusion of a name not mentioned in that piece:

> I see I've come upon a questionnaire:
> I have read a lot of books and short of listing a few thousand titles I don't know how to answer your friend as to what I read. Damn near anything except bad novels. I have a great admiration for <u>Moby Dick</u>. If I list the writers I <u>haven't</u> gotten along with (but may in my dotage, who knows?) the list would be shorter and would include D. H. Lawrence and Proust and Henry James and quite a few English Victorian novelists—but certainly not Hardy. Best <u>new</u> novel I've read in a long time is <u>Desperadoes</u> by Ron Hansen. (Box 1700, Folder 1)

Although surface resemblances between the two authors may be few, McCarthy shares Hardy's deep-rooted pessimism about the human condition. For McCarthy, the affinity may be especially for the melancholy mood that pervades Hardy's work.

Kundera, Milan (b. 1929)

McCarthy mentions Milan Kundera in a letter to Woolmer dated 17 November 1988. He writes, "I read Kundera's book on the novel yesterday. Refreshing to find someone almost as pessimistic as myself. Or almost so" (Box 1, Folder 7). Kundera, the Czech-born novelist who in 1975 fled his Communist homeland for France, where he has resided ever since, is most famous as the author of *The Unbearable Lightness of Being*. The book McCarthy is referring to is *The Art of the Novel*, the English translation of which appeared in 1988, the year of the letter.

I agree with McCarthy that Kundera's pessimism falls short of his own bleak vision in, for example, *Blood Meridian*. But, to quote Sheriff Bell, it will do until the real thing gets here. But Kundera should know something about it—his pessimism was born out of his direct experience of Communist totalitarianism, and his aesthetic shaped by the terrifying visions of Franz Kafka. Here is a sample of what McCarthy found refreshing:

That life is a trap we've always known: we are born without having asked to be, locked in a body we never chose, and destined to die. On the other hand, the wideness of the world used to provide a constant possibility of escape.... Suddenly, in our century, the world is closing around us. The decisive event in that transformation of the world into a trap was surely the 1914 war, called (and for the first time in history) a world war.... But the adjective "world" expresses all the more eloquently the sense of horror before the fact that, henceforward, nothing that occurs on the planet will be a merely local matter, that all catastrophes concern the entire world, and that consequently we are more and more determined by external conditions, by situations that no one can escape and that more and more make us resemble one another. (26–27)

On second thought, Kundera may have McCarthy beat. As McCarthy said to Oprah Winfrey in a 2007 interview, Americans have been very lucky. McCarthy gets his pessimism via the likes of Oswald Spengler and Arthur Schopenhauer. Kundera gets his straight from the source. Nevertheless, Kundera's faith in the achievements of a high European culture—most notably the grand achievement of the European novel—creates a sense of promise that McCarthy's work rarely, if ever, entertains.

Leone, Sergio (1929–1989)

McCarthy expresses interest in Sergio Leone, an Italian filmmaker, in a letter to the film critic Robert C. Cumbow. The author of *The Films of Sergio Leone*, Cumbow initiated the correspondence with a letter stating his admiration for McCarthy's work. When McCarthy responded, Cumbow sent McCarthy a copy of his Leone book. McCarthy's reply reveals both his deep interest in the art of film and a particular interest in Sergio Leone:[6]

Thank you very much for the book. It's very good-looking as well as being very interesting. You've really studied these films haven't you? I thought the type of analysis you use here very revealing. I was particularly struck by the section on the "catholic filmmaker" and your roundup of images and scenes. Some of his films I think are very good. He really is a <u>filmmaker</u>. <u>As</u> films they are rather amazing. If they fail it is always for other reasons, usually an inability to carry the narrative to some conclusion other than the more obvious, or even the stereotypical.

I'd forgotten that he did <u>Once Upon a Time in America</u>. I saw it again about a week ago and it makes more sense. (Cumbow, Wittliff Collection)

Two things are striking about this letter. The first is that it indicates an interest in criticism—art talk—something McCarthy avoids in formal interviews, even suggesting an aversion to that sort of thing. However, this stated aversion is something of an artist's pose, like Mark Twain claiming he was not particularly well read, a pose rendered unbelievable by Alan Gribben's dense two-volume *Mark Twain's Library: A Reconsideration*. In an interview with Leon Rooke for the Canadian literary magazine *Brick* in 1986, McCarthy informed Rooke, when asked about his current reading, that he had just finished *Shakespeare and the Common Understanding*, by Norman Rabkin. McCarthy's reading of Rabkin raises questions about the degree to which McCarthy follows literary scholarship.

I suspect that McCarthy is suspicious of literary culture, understanding that culture to include writers, literary journalists, and academic scholars, all of whom hobnob with each other within the purlieus of academia. It is hard to imagine McCarthy as a writer in residence in a university English department, or even giving a reading or lecture. His ex-wife Anne DeLisle has said that even in the depths of poverty McCarthy would turn down lucrative speaking offers (Woodward). At gatherings for recipients of the MacArthur Genius Grant, McCarthy has said, he hangs out with the scientists (Woodward). But the letter to Cumbow indicates an interest in the work of those who are able to insightfully explore works of art through the art of criticism.

The second point of interest is McCarthy's expression of admiration for Cumbow's chapter on Leone as a Catholic filmmaker. This admiration is interesting because much of what Cumbow says about Leone's films in this regard could also be said of McCarthy's novels. This correspondence is no doubt what prompted Cumbow's interest in McCarthy and his successful attempt to correspond with him. As

Bryan Giemza notes in his study of McCarthy's artistic debt to Catholicism, the "Catholic mythos" that Cumbow finds at the heart of Leone's films is also present in McCarthy's novels. For instance, Giemza points out Cumbow's analysis of Leone's use of abandoned churches to symbolize a world without a moral order: "One thinks immediately of the ruined church in *The Crossing* and the abandoned church of *Blood Meridian*; as in Leone's films, churches can become a place of slaughter" (227). According to Cumbow, in Leone's films "empty churches, ruins of churches, bell towers without churches, yes—all [are] reminders of the *absence* of moral order" (215, emphasis in original).

However, Cumbow notes the presence of grace in the films as well, and the following observation might also work as a description of McCarthy's use of a Catholic or Christian mythos: "But where God no longer acts, the film director still does. Leone himself has conferred grace on certain of his characters: and by doing that he has brought back a kind of moral order to the stripped-down world of his own imagining" (216). John Wesley Rattner, Rinthy Holme, Cornelius Suttree, John Grady Cole, Billy Parham, the father and son in *The Road*—while touched to varying degrees by the tragic condition of human beings living in a world lacking an external moral order, all find some kind of moral order within themselves, and in so doing find some form of grace or redemption. Even the kid and Lester Ballard, who are much more problematic figures, do not remain untouched by grace—see the kid's response to the "eldress in the rocks" (315), and Lester Ballard's "resurrection" after his journey to the underworld (190–191). What Cumbow says about Leone—that he "confers a kind of redemption on even his most reprehensible characters" (217)—could with equal justice be said about the creator of Lester Ballard. The similarities between Leone's artistic perspective and his own grim religious vision must not have been lost on McCarthy when reading Cumbow, and it is interesting to consider the degree to which Leone's work inspired McCarthy's shift to the western genre with *Blood Meridian*.[7]

Lowry, Malcolm (1909–1957)

McCarthy mentions Malcolm Lowry in a letter to Woolmer dated 25 November 1986, in which he expresses genuine admiration for the

British novelist. Lowry is most famous for *Under the Volcano* (1947), a tragic account of the last day—the Day of the Dead—in the life of an alcoholic British ex-consul to Mexico, Geoffrey Firmin.

Lowry knew the debilitating effects of alcoholism firsthand. Albert Erskine, McCarthy's editor at Random House, also edited Lowry's novel, and McCarthy's letter to Woolmer addresses the relationship between Erskine and Lowry. He writes to Woolmer, "I think Under the Volcano is an amazing book and Lowry a genuinely tragic figure. Albert has told me some stories about him that would curl your hair" (Box 1, Folder 6). In an article detailing the relationship between Erskine and McCarthy, Daniel King quotes Joseph Blotner's account of Erskine's efforts to check Lowry's penchant for self-destruction: "Blotner ... describes Erskine's efforts whilst working with Malcolm Lowry, which frequently required the editor to 'search the bars along Third Avenue to find his wayward author'" (255). No doubt these searches provided the material for those hair-curling tales Erskine shared with McCarthy.

King points out that Erskine's efforts show "both Erskine's devotion to his editorial duties and the easy manner he seems to have had in dealing with his authors" (255). Erskine does not seem to have encountered anything hair-curling in his relationship with McCarthy, unless you count iron-like obstinancy about apostrophes and hyphens as hair-curling. King, through his research into Erskine's correspondence with McCarthy, does discover that "easy manner" that helped to make Erskine's three decades of editing McCarthy so fruitful. He also shows that the relationship was founded to a great extent upon the two men's bibliophilia. Of particular interest is King's list of books that McCarthy requested from Erskine: Robert Penn Warren's *Flood*, *Reason and Violence* by David G. Cooper and R. D. Laing, *Fiction and the Figures of Life* by William Gass, Eugen Herrigel's *Zen and the Art of Archery* (see entry for Herrigel in *Blood Meridian*), and an unnamed novel by Theodore Dreiser about which McCarthy expressed admiration (262).

McGuane, Thomas (b. 1939)

McCarthy mentions one of Thomas McGuane's fishing books to John Graves in an undated letter that reveals McCarthy's devotion to the sport of fishing: "Your trip to Florida sounded great. Always wanted to fish for Tarpon. Do you know McGuane's book <u>A Sporting Chance</u>? Some good stories about Keys fishing in it as I recall. I'm very partial to that country down there myself. I think I could live there if I was ever banished from the desert." McCarthy is conflating the titles of two of McGuane's books, one the novel *The Sporting Club*, the other a collection of essays on various sports, including fishing, entitled *An Outside Chance: Classic and New Essays on Sport* (see entry for Graves in this chapter). McCarthy's mistake with the title suggests that he has read at least those two works by McGuane, which provides insight into where McCarthy's tastes run in relation to his contemporaries.

Miller, Henry (1891–1980)

SEE ALSO *SUTTREE*

Two letters in McCarthy's correspondence with J. Howard Woolmer confirm his deep interest in Henry Miller. In the first, dated 13 December 1976, McCarthy, responding to Woolmer's request for a copy of the script for *The Gardener's Son*, asks him to look for a copy of a hard-to-find Miller title:

> I dont have another copy of the script but I can get you a Xerox. I think the cost is about six dollars. Dont go sending any money, we might work out a trade: If you can find a copy of the letters between Henry Miller and Michael (I think) Frankel [*sic*] published as <u>The Hamlet Correspondence</u> I'd love to get hold of it. I'm sure it would come to more than the $6.00 so if you can find it, send it and let me know what I owe you. (Box 1, Folder 2)

Woolmer was successful: on 26 January 1977, McCarthy wrote a thank-you note to him: "Thank you for the book. It is very exotic looking. This was the only one of Miller's books I didnt have and I've been looking forward to reading it for years. I'm happy to consider it a fair trade if you are. But I think I've out traded you." The book contains correspondence between Miller and Michael Fraenkal, who was the model for the character Boris in *Tropic of Cancer*. McCarthy's desire to have a complete Miller collection testifies to the importance of Miller to him (see also entry on Miller in *Suttree*).

Ondaatje, Michael (b. 1943)

Michael Ondaatje's novels have elicited McCarthy's enthusiastic praise, and he mentioned him in letters to both Peter Greenleaf and J. Howard Woolmer as well as in a 1986 interview with Leon Rooke for the Canadian literary journal *Brick*. Ondaatje is a Canadian novelist and poet who was born in Sri Lanka. His most famous novel, *The English Patient*, won the 1992 Booker Prize and was later made into a film, which won the Oscar for Best Picture in 1997.

It appears that Greenleaf was the one who introduced McCarthy to Ondaatje's work. In a letter to Greenleaf dated 2 May 1985, McCarthy thanks him for sending some books: "I read two of the Ondaatje's and they were both marvelous" (Box 1700, Folder 1). McCarthy's enthusiasm was apparently more than mere politeness in response to a gift. Another letter to Greenleaf, dated 25 February 1986, attests to an ongoing interest in Ondaatje, mentioning one of his novels by name: "I just got back from New Orleans where a friend of mine has been making a film. We stopped in a bookstore looking for Coming Through Slaughter—which I'd been talking about. The man didn't have the book but he knew about Buddy Bolden. I think there are a couple of books out about him. In Search of Buddy Bolden I think is one the proprietor mentioned." *Coming Through Slaughter* (1976) is a fictional account of the jazz trumpeter Buddy Bolden, one of the pioneers of jazz.[8]

In the interview with Leon Rooke, McCarthy mentions Ondaatje as a writer whose work he had been reading (n.p.). Later in 1986, in a letter dated 27 August, McCarthy mentions Ondaatje to Woolmer. Woolmer, a rare book dealer, had been collecting first editions of McCarthy's novels. McCarthy writes, "What other contemporary writers are you gathering? I'd be interested to know who you like. Have you read any good books lately? Are there any good books lately?—Don't feel obligated to answer this. Did we talk about Michael Ondaatje?" (Box 1,

Folder 6). However, in a letter to Greenleaf dated 5 January 1988, McCarthy comments, "New Ondaatje novel not an improvement on the old to my way of thinking" (Box 1700, Folder 1).

The new Ondaatje novel McCarthy is referring to here is *In the Skin of a Lion*. As for the two books by Ondaatje that McCarthy told Greenleaf he had read, one would be *Coming Through Slaughter*, but the other is unknown. Most of Ondaatje's early work is made up of poetry and odd, experimental pastiches. It is tempting to think that the other book was *The Collected Works of Billy the Kid: Left-Handed Poems* (1970), a revisionist western that would likely resonate with the author of *Blood Meridian*. A retelling of the life of Billy the Kid through poetry, prose, and historical photographs, the book foregrounds the violence of the West in ways that call to mind McCarthy's forays into the western genre.

Scarry, Elaine (b. 1946)

McCarthy mentions the scholar and literary critic Elaine Scarry in a letter to Woolmer written in the fall of 1986. Scarry is best known for her 1985 book *The Body in Pain: The Making and Unmaking of the World*. After lamenting that "good books get rarer and rarer," he reports on reading this book: "Just finished a <u>very</u> interesting book called <u>The Body in Pain</u> by Elaine Scarry. Be an interesting book to discuss with someone but I can never get anybody else to read these strange tomes" (Box 1, Folder 6, emphasis in original). Scarry's book, a complex exploration of torture, war, imagination, and creativity, is partly an analysis and critique of violence and partly a treatise on aesthetics. As McCarthy indicated, it is a strange tome. In it Scarry examines "torture as an affirmation of both the torturer's power and the victim's vulnerability," as well as of the "hellish nature of war," according to an online summary; Scarry, the summary notes, then shifts into a discussion of the imagination "as the antithesis of torture, noting that while torture leads to destruction, the imagination sparks creativity" ("Scarry, Elaine"). Given McCarthy's own explorations of violence, his interest in this book is not hard to fathom.

In fact, at least one critic noted affinities between McCarthy and Scarry many years before the Woolmer correspondence became available. Rick Wallach, in his article "From *Beowulf* to *Blood Meridian*: Cormac McCarthy's Demystification of the Martial Code," argues that McCarthy highlights the use of cultural systems to mask the horrifying reality of violence and make it palatable. Wallach looks at martial codes and how they "conventionalize destructive activity in a craftsmanly way" (199). McCarthy reveals how such martial codes achieve this end through the judge, he notes, and he even quotes Scarry's work in connection with his analysis:

> Compared to the bombastic, self-deluded orations of code heroes like Beowulf and Hrothgar, Judge Holden's proclamations indicate a sophisticated grasp of his role as antagonist and the subterfuges necessary to advance his purposes. His facile comparisons of war to dance, to religion, and to desire itself recall Elaine Scarry's observation that war "requires both the reciprocal infliction of massive injury and the eventual disowning of the injury so that its attributes can be transferred elsewhere, as they cannot if they are permitted to cling to the original site of the wound, the human body" (64). Critics who have accused McCarthy of amorality ought to bear in mind Scarry's and Kristeva's disclosure of the necessity of expelling the sites of pain. (211)

McCarthy's letter reveals the prescience of Wallach's use of Scarry's work in his explication of McCarthy's fictional exploration of violence in *Blood Meridian*.

Scarry's structuralist analysis of war certainly does echo Judge Holden's conception of war as an elaborate game. This game, in Holden's view, necessarily excludes differences in its brutal insistence on unity as a final outcome. Here is how he puts it: "Men are born for games. Nothing else. Every child knows that play is nobler than work. He knows too that the worth or merit of a game is not inherent in the game itself but rather in the value of that which is put at hazard. Games of chance require a wager to have meaning at all.... But trial of chance or trial of worth all games aspire to the condition of war for here that which is wagered swallows up game, player, all" (249).

The judge puts a fine point on this view of war when he says, in the same scene, that "war is the ultimate game because war is at last a forcing of the unity of existence. War is God" (249). Scarry's book was published in 1985, the same year as *Blood Meridian*, and we know from the letter that McCarthy read it in 1986, so there is no question of influence, but McCarthy must surely, in light of the words he put into the judge's mouth, have taken note of this passage in Scarry's book:

> In other words, in consenting to enter into war, the participants enter into a structure that is a self-cancelling duality. They enter into a formal duality, but one understood by all to be temporary and intolerable, a formal duality that, by the very force of its relentless insistence on doubleness, provides the means for eliminating and replacing itself by the condition of singularity (since in the end it will have legitimatized one side's right to determine the nature of certain issues). A first major attribute here is the transition, at the moment of the entry into war, from the condition of multiplicity to the condition of the binary; a second attribute is the transition, at the moment of ending the war, from the condition of the binary to the condition of the unitary. (87)

War is the forcing of the unity of existence. Scarry's view, conveyed in the language of structuralism, is very close to the view of the judge, though of course he delights in a reality that Scarry laments throughout her book. McCarthy must have noticed how these insights ran parallel to his.

Moreover, McCarthy was likely moved by Scarry's humane revulsion of violence, which he shares. *Blood Meridian* can be read as a fierce indictment of the human proclivity for bloodshed. However, McCarthy parts company from Scarry's clearly pacifist leanings. In his interview with Richard B. Woodward he made his opposition to pacifism plain: "There's no such thing as a life without bloodshed.... I think the notion that the species can be improved in some way, that everyone could live in harmony, is a really dangerous idea. Those who are afflicted with this notion are the first ones to give up their souls, their freedom. Your desire that it be that way will enslave you and make your life vacuous." McCarthy subscribes to the tragic vision of life, where, in the melancholy spirit of tragic irony, one can bemoan human violence while accepting it as a permanent feature of our existence, a reality that we can only deny in bad faith.

Notes

Chapter 1. Introduction: Books Out of Books

1. My source for McCarthy's biography is the introduction to *Perspectives on Cormac McCarthy*, by Edwin T. Arnold and Dianne C. Luce.

2. I had a chance to talk to McCarthy in 2007, shortly after he had won the Pulitzer. I jokingly asked him which was the greater honor: the Pulitzer or Oprah's Book Club. He said that he did not care about either, but that Oprah's paid better.

Chapter 3. *Outer Dark*

1. The marginal note appears at the bottom of a page describing the hanged corpse of the tinker. In the upper right corner of the page McCarthy wrote, "thurs Nov 26 Thanksgiving—$7.99 in pocket prospects dim writing = happiness."

Chapter 6. *Suttree*

1. McCarthy's notes consist mostly of words, phrases, sentences, and occasionally short quotations from other authors, such as the Agee quotation. Readers will sometimes come across paragraph-length passages as well, though these are rare. McCarthy thinks through his novels in language that he might use in the novel. There is almost no editorializing, exposition, or outlining. The notes become possible content for the novel. He is trying out descriptions, contemplating word choices (one often finds lists of the kinds of archaisms that constitute one of his stylistic signatures), and experimenting with dialogue. Readers will sometimes recognize something that made it into the published work, but much of it ends up being cut. Sometimes, McCarthy plays around with an idea that doesn't make it into the novel he is working on, but it shows up years later. For instance, below the Agee quotation is a description of a train going by that would find its way into print two novels and more than a decade later:

> When the train crosses the trestle you can see the long taper of the headlight come out
> of the woods to the south and run the span and then the locomotive hounds into sight

steaming and chuffing with the huge wheels chopping and the dark cars strung out behind and then the coaches and the caboose trundling along in the wake of the din and
the smoke falling down over the river and then the trestle empty once again. (The rain
falls lightly quartered in the headlong light.) (Box 19, Folder 14)

Here is that train, first imagined in the late 1970s, shooting past John Grady Cole in *All the
Pretty Horses*:

It came boring out of the east like some ribald satellite of the coming sun howling and
bellowing in the distance and the long light of the headlamp running through the tangled
mesquite brakes and creating out of the night the endless fenceline down the dead
straight right of way and sucking it back again wire and post mile on mile into the darkness after where the boilersmoke disbanded slowly along the faint new horizon. (3–4)

From the same folder containing notes from *Suttree* we find the following: "Flora's rule: At
eight the primrose closes." This quotation does not appear in *Suttree*, but it appears six novels
and nearly three decades later in *The Road*: "He sat by a gray window in the gray light in
an abandoned house in the late afternoon and read old newspapers while the boy slept. The
curious news. The quaint concerns. *At eight the primrose closes*. He watched the boy sleep-
ing. Can you do it? When the time comes? Can you?" (28–29, emphasis added). Something
about the poetry of that sentence kept it alive in McCarthy's imagination for decades before
he decided it was now time to place *that* stone in *this* place in the work under construction.

  2. Though it is not idealized, McCarthy's portrait of Knoxville's seamy side is certainly
nostalgic, as the elegiac language describing Suttree's departure from McAnally Flats confirms. Nostalgia for the rough and tumble of earlier times is evident in a letter to J. Howard
Woolmer dated 22 June 1981 in which McCarthy describes witnessing a shootout in downtown Knoxville:

Went downtown yesterday and suddenly found myself surrounded by fleeing felons
firing off revolvers, police running up the street returning the fire, several detectives
dragging another man from an alley and fastening handcuffs and leg irons to him, etc.
A news lady rushed up to me with a microphone and a tape recorder and asked me what
was going on. I told her I had no idea, but it certainly seemed like the good old days for
a few minutes. (Woolmer Collection, Box 1, Folder 4)

  3. The scene quoting *Herzog* does little to help identify what, exactly, McCarthy was
thinking about when he typed them on the page. It is a very early scene, probably written in
the mid to late 1960s, in which an early version of Gene Harrogate attends a revival meeting
led by one Reverend Green, who will finally make his way into McCarthy's fictional universe
as the tent revivalist in *Blood Meridian* whom the judge accuses of various transgressions,
including bestiality (7). In the scene from the *Suttree* manuscript, Harrogate is the character
associated with bestiality, in addition to his amours in the melon patch. The early Gene is a
grotesque without any humanizing touches, unlike the beloved "city mouse" of the published
novel. The scene is most reminiscent of the Sut Lovingood tales of George Washington Harris
(also a resident of Knoxville, also interested in country riffraff, grotesques, and bawdy humor,
and a probable influence on McCarthy). It is funny, but it does *not* resemble the novel that

McCarthy would publish approximately a decade later (the final two sentences are hand-written at the end of a typed page):

> A hush fell over the congregation. They could hear the winter wind sough through the guywires of the tabernacle. Harrogate was flapping his arms about in the hope of inspiration to continue and Green had come awakened and was motioning to the pianist but the pianist wasn't looking that way. He was watching Harrogate.
>
> Neighbors, I fell so low they warnt no hope for me atall, Harrogate said. Veering hopefully on a new tack. If I was to tell you what all I done you'd say there's a feller they wasn't no hope for atall.
>
> Tell it all, brother, a voice said from the congregation. Green shifted nervously in his chair.
>
> I started out tellin lies and went from there to stealin and drinkin whiskey. I done nastiness with my daddy's chickens till it's a wonder I aint growed feathers.
>
> The audience went upright as if the ground beneath them had shifted. Green was hissing at the pianist and searching in his pockets for something to throw at him.
>
> Time the Reverend Green here got to me I was in pitiful shape. I guess I was headed for the lectric chair is where I was headed. I'd already done time in the county and been shot in the ass … been shot. In the … I wont tell you what all I was a-doin or you might run out the door.
>
> Tell it all brother.
>
> You want to hear it sure enough?
>
> Ow, goddamn it, the piano player said. A twentyfivecent piece had taken him edgewise in the temple. Psst, Green said.
>
> Well if you don't care to hear it, I was in a watermelon patch with my britches down and it wasn't to take a dump neither. *He grinned down at the congregation. No one moved.* (Box 19, Folder 13, emphasis added)

4. The scene also features a bit of Joycean wordplay. The priest, attempting to be kind, "gave a little smile, lightly touched with censure, remonstrance gentled" (255). Surely *censer* and *monstrance* hover behind the description of the priest's benevolent countenance. Given the stylistic influence of Joyce on this novel in particular, and McCarthy's stated enthusiasm for Joyce in general, it seems likely.

5. Robert Penn Warren was an enthusiastic admirer of McCarthy's work, and the two men knew each other through their shared editor Albert Erskine. In a letter to J. Howard Woolmer dated 1 April 1980, McCarthy mentions this connection: "Warren is a very nice man. We share the same editor at Random House but I have met him (Warren) only once. We keep somewhat abreast of one another's doings through Albert. Interesting that he liked *Child of God*. Some people think it a most peculiar book, but lately it has been receiving a sort of belated enthusiasm in the form of reviews and theses and such" (Woolmer Collection, Box 1, Folder 4).

6. This strikes me as a description that might apply to Cormac McCarthy as well. In his interview with Oprah Winfrey he replied to her question about "the God thing" in the following way: "Well—it would depend on what day you ask me, you know? But, but some time, sometimes it's good to pray. I don't think you have to have a clear idea of who or what God is in order to pray. You can, you can even be quite doubtful about the whole business." In an

interview with the *Wall Street Journal*, he claimed, "I have a great sympathy for the spiritual view of life, and I think that it's meaningful. But am I a spiritual person? I would like to be. Not that I am thinking about some afterlife that I want to go to, but just in terms of being a better person." The closest thing to a creed that we are likely to get from McCarthy is found in Garry Wallace's account of meeting him in 1989:

> He said that the religious experience is always described through the symbols of a par- ticular culture and thus is somewhat misrepresented by them. He indicated that even the religious person is often uncomfortable with such experiences and accounts of them, and those who have not had a religious experience cannot comprehend it through second-hand accounts, even good ones like James's *Varieties of Religious Experience*. He went on to say that he thinks the mystical experience is a direct apprehension of reality, unmediated by symbol, and he ended with the thought that our inability to see spiritual truth is the greater mystery. (138)

However, it should be noted that the "symbols of a particular culture" that McCarthy favors tend to be the symbols of Christianity. Both *Child of God* and *Suttree* end with symbolic deaths, burials, and resurrections. And the epilogue to *Cities of the Plains* contains this ob- servation from the mysterious stranger whom Billy Parham encounters in his peregrinations: "Every man's death is a standing in for every other. And since death comes to all there is no way to abate the fear of it except to love that man who stands for us. We are not waiting for his history to be written. He passed here long ago. *That man who is all men and who stands in the dock for us* until our own time come and we must stand for him" (288, emphasis added). Without the moments of grace and even spiritual peace that punctuate McCarthy's novels (think of the beautiful description of Suttree, at the end of the novel, as having "taken for tal- isman the simple human heart within him"), their genuinely terrifying darkness might de- vour the humane meanings so many readers find in them.

   7. Here is McCarthy's Joyce parody, typed below the note referring to De Vries's parody in *The Tents of Wickedness*:

> In deckleedged drawers visible sideways through a frayed rictus in her smicket rent lat- erally from hip to the hasp of her kneehinge.
>   Standing on the floor onefooted her hand clasped to the cap of the bedpost, pine- apple finial, glueless and removable endplay and wallclearance in its socket, one knee at rest upon the bed's edge, calf in plane with the floor and foot pointed rearward and slightly curled.
>   Mouth smirked in simulated wantoness, brows arched in indefinable surprise or ex- pectation, nostrils dilating slightly with breathing, a trick of long training, like a blooded horse's.
>   Back arched like a bow cocked evocative of a pelvic thrust ready for loosing, breast high, braless and weighty in the lace cups, the cheeks of her cherryred twicecloven ham- flanks tilted upward like a mulattoe's. (Box 30, Folder 1)

This, I assume, is a description of a prostitute. Thankfully, it did not make the cut.
   8. As an example, note the different portrayal of the kid in this early draft of the scene in which he kills a Mexican bartender in a fight. The kid's language, including a saltier pro-

fanity more akin to HBO's *Deadwood* than to *Blood Meridian*, is indicative of a much talkier character, one whose consciousness is more available to the reader:

> The boy looked at the drinkers. They were not watching him and neither were they talking. He slammed the glass on the counter and held up one finger. One more, he said.
> The barman pointed to the door, Nada mas, he said. He made a little shooing gesture with the back of his hand.
> The boy pointed a finger at him. You thieving cocksucker, he said. I'll break your fucking face for you. The barman's face changed not at all. He brought up an old fashioned military pistol with a flint lock. He shoved back the cock with the heel of his hand, an enormous wooden clicking in the silence. You could hear the click of glasses along the bar. Then you could hear the scuffle of chairs being pushed back by the players at the wall.
> The bartender nodded his head toward the door and the kid stepped back from the bar. Old man, he said.
> The old man did not answer.
> Old man, you tell this fat son of a bitch that I will stomp his goddamned ass into clabber. Texas aint big enough to hide him. (Box 35, Folder 3)

That "Texas aint big enough" line jars when we try to hear it from the kid we know from the published novel. Light and equally profane banter between the kid and Toadvine also sounds dissonant, though in a cleaned-up form it sounds very much like the banter of John Grady Cole and Lacey Rawlins in *All the Pretty Horses*.

9. McCarthy's allusion to Flaubert sounds like commentary on the source of the allusion, as if the narrator is not only alluding to but verifying Flaubert's assertion. He does something similar in an allusion to Rainer Maria Rilke in *The Stonemason*. The protagonist, Ben Telfair, echoes the second of Rilke's "Duino Elegies" in the following passage: "I dont know what it means that things exist and then exist no more. Trees. Dogs. People. *Will* that namelessness into which we vanish then taste of us?" (104). The italics are in McCarthy's text and create the effect of commentary on Rilke's poem, this time not through verification, but by an emphasis on the aching rightness of the question. Here are the lines from Rilke:

> … Like dew from the morning grass,
> What is ours floats into the air, like steam from a dish
> Of hot food. O smile, where are you going? O upturned glance:
> New warm receding wave on the sea of the heart …
> Alas, but that is what we *are*. Does the infinite space
> We dissolve into, taste of us then? … (157, emphasis in original)

The line from *The Stonemason* not only alludes to Rilke but also addresses Rilke, adopting a tone of shared bewilderment over the transience of things.

10. In Garry Wallace's account of meeting McCarthy, he describes McCarthy's interest in psychotropic drugs: "McCarthy commented that some cultures used drugs to enhance the spiritual experience, and that he had tried LSD before the drug was made illegal. He said that it had helped open his eyes to these kinds of experiences" (138).

11. McCarthy likely worked on this scene in the late 1970s, as it appears in the Spring 1980 issue of *TriQuarterly*.

304 Notes to Pages 89–98

12. Right above the notes on Foucault are some observations on the art of film, one of McCarthy's serious interests. I cannot make a connection between these remarks and the Foucault quotations, or for that matter with anything in *Suttree*. They may simply be something like journal notes, McCarthy's musings on a subject of interest. Whatever the case may be, they stand out in the midst of the notes on *Suttree* by virtue of the lack of context:

> All of this has little to do with the fourcornered reality of making a film, but a filmmaker without some esthetic stance is like a businessman without an ethical stance and the end product however well intended is liable to the sweet taint of corruption. A classic work of art has no odor whatever.
> It should be possible to make a film totally flexible in its perceptions. That is, dependent upon the gifts among the perceivers
> The old man in tatters with untrimmed beard bearing a bag that read in blue stencil Davis Travel Agency. (Box 19, Folder 13)

The last sentence of the first paragraph has an epigrammatic flavor, but I cannot identify an outside source for it. The last sentence of the second paragraph sounds like a description of a scene from a film, but I cannot determine what McCarthy is referring to.

13. A possible source for McCarthy's use of the matrix concept is Annie Dillard's *Teaching a Stone to Talk*:

> In the deeps are the violence and terror of which psychology has warned us. But if you ride these monsters deeper down, if you drop with them farther over the world's rim, you find what our sciences cannot locate or name, the substrate, the ocean or matrix or ether which buoys the rest, which gives goodness its power for good, and evil its power for evil, the unified field: our complex and inexplicable caring for each other, and for our life together here. This is given. It is not learned. (19–20)

A probable source is Jacob Boehme's concept of the *unground*.

14. A variant of the scene in which Suttree dreams of his grandfather contains a slightly altered version of this quotation:

> But Suttree felt humbled to have spoken with his grandfather, deep in the inner world where there is no ego and the man was a man like all men.
> Because the nature of the world is non verbal and we are trapped into appreciations of things by endowing them with names. We cannot see the true nature of reality beyond the obfuscation of the nominal. (Box 30, Folder 1)

Following this passage, McCarthy copied a quotation from the Chinese *Dao De Jing*:

> Tao: Those who know don't speak
> Those who speak don't know

Although it is fascinating to watch McCarthy explore spiritual and philosophical issues in such a forthright way, and although such passages as we find in the drafts undermine those who impugn McCarthy with the charge of nihilism, there seems to be little question that the much more compact form these musings take in the published novel is aesthetically superior: "We spoke easily and I was humbly honored to walk with him deep in that world where he was a man like all men" (14). Like Ben Jonson on Shakespeare, "would that he had blotted thousands" is often my response to McCarthy's portentous philosophizing. He is at his best when he pares the language down to the elegant concision we see in the published version of the dream scene.

15. Another book that uses this convention and that may have served as a model for McCarthy is Meshach Browning's *Forty-Four Years of the Life of a Hunter*, which McCarthy mentions with obvious fondness in several letters to J. Howard Woolmer (Box 1, Folder 4). The section titles definitely have some of the flavor of the chapter headings in *Blood Meridian*: "Birth and Parentage—Difficulties of his widowed Mother—Moves to the West—Accident on the Road—Settles on Flintstone" (xi). Several more follow in this vein, and although the main character's adventures are less hair-raising than the events in the kid's life, the rustic air of Browning's chapter headings make the book a possible source for McCarthy's headings in *Blood Meridian*.

16. The book is both chilling and, for modern readers, sometimes unintentionally funny. For instance, chapter 9 is titled: "Whether Witches may work some Prestidigitatory Illusion so that the Male Organ appears to be entirely removed and separate from the Body." This age-old question, which Kramer and Sprenger answer with an emphatic yes, tells us much about the deep sources of men's fear of witches.

17. I, of course, have eagerly searched the nooks and crannies of McCarthy's papers for just such moments of Second Order commentary. This raises interesting questions about the nature and purpose of literature, as well as questions about, to put it bluntly, how to read a book. The academic study of literature occupies one end of a spectrum that has, at its other end, less exalted institutions, such as book clubs, including the book club of book clubs, Oprah's. What they have in common is a painfully earnest commitment to Second Order reflection on art. We *are* so proud to get at the meaning of poems, aren't we? But there is no denying the frisson that accompanies the discovery, in one of those nooks or crannies, of Cormac McCarthy, speaking in his own voice, commenting on his own books. In a cranny of an early manuscript of *Outer Dark*, I found the following explanation of the Unholy Trinity that dogs Culla Holmes: "(tribunal?) THEME: The triune kill all that Holme wants to kill—ending w/ child. ?" (Box 8, Folder 1). This sort of thing simply does not occur often in McCarthy's papers, but the same draft of *Outer Dark* also features this very direct explication: "In order for this book to make sense the *events* must assume the shape of a character and the characters themselves become mere moves, mere manifestations of the perfect, coherent, logical, and immutable *deformation* of evolving fate" (Box 8, Folder 2, emphasis in original). This comment certainly lends credibility to Guy Davenport's astute assessment of the novel when, in the *New York Times*, he described McCarthy as a "born allegorist." The reader can figure that one out, but how interesting to find McCarthy himself affirming the centrality of allegory to his narrative purposes. But the satisfaction of being able to say that, yes, in fact, and from the horse's mouth no less, this book is an allegory, that allegory is the right category, is very much of the Second Order of thinking. McCarthy, by his own account, and to all appearances, avoids it as much as possible.

18. For instance, here is a scene that takes place in a brothel.

This john wanted her to poke a knotted nylon stocking up his ass and then as he came to pull it out. Well we couldn't find any old stockings so crazy Faye cuts off a piece of cord from the venetian blinds and ties knots all in it and greases it up and pokes it up the old john's ass.

He's banging away and grunting and she's standing there with one foot on the bed holding the ripcord and this old hustler that's tricking him is enormous fat, I forget her name—the john went for her because she was so fucking fat, and I'm sitting there on the edge of the bed smoking a cigarette and old Faye keeps saying tell me when, tell me when, and the old fat hustler is humping and farting and the old boy is breathing hard and going on and pretty soon he says: Now, now. And the old fat hustler says Now, and old Faye says: Now? And I said Now and the trick says Now Now Now and she puts her foot on his ass and gets a double grip on this goddamned venetian blind cord and gives the awfulest yank on it, she looked like she was trying to start an outboard motor. The old boy let out the most bloodcurdling shriek I ever heard, she'd damn near jerked him inside out like a sock, and his ass was hanging out and he was hollerin and old Faye, she leaned over him and she said: How was that?

This is wincingly funny, but the disturbing sexual sadomasochism is present in other scenes that McCarthy also, thankfully, cut. Some are quite bizarre, and will remain unaired here. For those of stout constitution, see Box 19, Folder 13.

19. Or consider the conclusion to Lester Ballard's story in *Child of God*. After escaping the lynch mob (crucifixion), Lester escapes into a network of underground caves (burial), re-surfacing several days later to see a bus full of schoolchildren go by. He locks eyes with a child looking out the window and sees himself in the boy (resurrection). These kinds of allegorical or archetypal patterns often communicate spiritual meaning more profoundly than narra-tive exposition would, but also, bafflingly, prevent others from seeing these deeper layers of significance. Without those layers, or levels, McCarthy really does look like a thoroughgoing nihilist.

20. For an extended discussion of this topic, see Arthur Herman's excellent *The Idea of Decline in Western History*. Herman's book is informative, though decidedly critical of the kind of historical and philosophical pessimism that seems so compelling to McCarthy.

21. McCarthy's love of the gothic can be seen in the only blurb, to my knowledge, that he has ever penned. The blurb appears on the back cover of *The Strange Case of Edward Gorey*, a biography of the eccentric artist by the novelist Alexander Theroux: "Just read a few weeks ago your book on Gorey and enjoyed it very much—Cormac McCarthy, April, 2010." Gorey's illustrations simultaneously parody and delight in the trappings of the gothic.

22. A box containing notes and fragments from *Cities of the Plain* contains the following:

Chess—Schliemann gambit for black player
Maelzel's chess player (Box 76, Folder 2)

"Maelzel's Chess Player" is the title of an essay by Poe that debunks a hoax involving a chess machine. The hoax involved a chess-playing automaton called The Turk.

23. Another work in which McCarthy explores the path from sin to salvation is the play *The Sunset Limited*. Black is a Christian convert whose "testimony" includes tales of addic-tion and imprisonment (like Suttree). On the commentary track for the DVD of the HBO production of the play, McCarthy, during a discussion of Black's struggles with alcohol, men-tions *The Big Book*, as the text used by Alcoholics Anonymous is called. McCarthy's famil-

iarity with this book is a further indication of his interest in the need for redemption and salvation in this vale of tears.

24. When I met McCarthy in 2007, he told me that ours is the first civilization to try to get by without a culture. The words stuck with me, but at the time the distinction was not clear to me. What is clear to me now is that he was using the language of Spengler to describe what he sees as our own bad time.

25. This possibility was suggested to me by Dr. James Barcus in a seminar on McCarthy at Baylor University in the spring of 2012.

26. I am not a Thomas Wolfe scholar, so I offer these speculations tentatively, but my memory of *You Can't Go Home Again* prompts my suggestion that the following passage is indebted to Wolfe. In it "The Poet" records his thoughts about the Indian Michael, apparently one of the earliest characters (along with the mussel fisherman Reese) to make it all the way to the published novel:

> Perhaps the poet even suspected that the radiance of Michael's smile and the warmth of his greeting in return hinged at least somewhat on the sound of his own name which he had not heard pronounced by another human being for almost seven years. He said: Hello Michael. And something happened in Michael and seemed to make him more whole. That was not a thing that a man experienced often in one or several lifetimes and the poet whether he knew or not about the name still recognized that something had happened in history and the realization made him fearful. He said to himself: I was not ready. Not this soon I wasn't ready. (Box 19, Folder 13)

It is hard to imagine something this maudlin and purple in the *Suttree* we know.

27. McCarthy expresses a similar idea about creativity in notes grouped with his papers for *The Road*. Despite their location in the archives, they seem unrelated to that novel. Their proximity to a paragraph labeled *The Passenger* suggests that it may be part of McCarthy's notes for his unpublished novel. The quotation echoes Faulkner's suggestion that high ambition will always be accompanied by some degree of failure: "Making a poem is not like making a chair. Both require craftsmanship, but the chair to be perfect must be perfect while the poem can never attain to true excellence without incorporating some flaw. A flawless poem would be one that did not try hard enough" (Box 87, Folder 5). Compare this to Faulkner's claim that Wolfe "failed the best because he tried the hardest."

Chapter 7. *Blood Meridian*

1. The man "enkindles the stone in the hole with his steel hole by hole striking the fire out of the rock which God has put there" (*Blood Meridian* 337). There is something sinister about the man's use of God's fire to create a blind, mechanical ordering of both man and nature (since he is likely preparing to build a fence, perhaps a barbed-wire fence). It is instructive to compare this scene to Sheriff Bell's dream at the end of *No Country for Old Men*. Here, also, is an image of a man moving forward while another follows behind, and here the leader punctuates his advance by kindling a fire, but how different the meaning:

> He just rode on past and he had this blanket wrapped around him and he had his head down and when he rode past I seen he was carryin fire in a horn the way people used

to do and I could see the horn from the light inside of it. About the color of the moon. And in the dream I knew that he was goin on ahead and that he was fixin to make a fire somewhere out there in all that dark and all that cold and I knew that whenever I got there he would be there. (309)

Chapter 11. *The Road*

1. Although Ellis appreciates McCarthy's ability to make readers laugh, he also recognizes that McCarthy's seriousness can be a palate cleanser:

It would therefore seem that, especially as we only find a regular sense of humor in antagonists and secondary or tertiary characters (such as Harrogate, innocent as he otherwise remains), McCarthy is more interested in the naïveté of young men so innocent—if not ignorant—as to lack an ironic distance, a sense of humor, or indeed very much self-consciousness at all. Writing through decades when his contemporaries have so fruitfully and extensively explored well-educated navel-gazing self-referential sarcasm that many novels now collapse under such self-consciousness, we may consider McCarthy's exceptional habit here a gift to the variety of literature in our time. (267)

Chapter 13. Correspondence

1. Wallace, after mentioning McPhee and Chatwin, goes on to say that "McCarthy said that he knew Larry McMurtry; because McCarthy loved the television movie "Lonesome Dove" so much, he said that he would never read the book" (136). The screenplay for the movie was written by McCarthy's friend Bill Wittliff of the Wittliff Collections.

2. Jonathan Chatwin is no relation to Bruce Chatwin.

3. Jay Ellis's *No Place for Home* explores the rootlessness of McCarthy's characters in greater detail.

4. Ranchers in southern Arizona might have taken exception to this kind of mischief, but it certainly sounds like the MO of the author of *The Monkeywrench Gang*. It is somehow difficult to imagine McCarthy in the role of eco-monkeywrencher.

As to the claim that McCarthy prefers the company of scientists, his connection to the Santa Fe Institute, where he was formerly listed as a Fellow, and currently as a trustee, goes back two decades. However, further evidence for McCarthy's preference can be found in the number of scientists for whom he has served as a copy editor. The first was Roger Payne, a close friend of McCarthy's, and one of the world's foremost experts on whale song. The dedication page of his book *Among Whales* reads: "In token of my admiration for his genius, this book is inscribed to Cormac McCarthy." In his acknowledgments section Payne writes: "Cormac McCarthy read nearly the entire text and made innumerable improvements to it. In the margins of my most sophomoric diatribes he wrote such comments as 'Yawn, yawn,' and 'No Sale,' thus sparing me much wider embarrassment later on (though whether enough, only time will tell). I also value deeply our many discussions about biological points in the text. In my experience there is no precedent for someone not a professional biologist being so well-read and so clearly informed about biology" (9).

Other books McCarthy has edited include *The Quark and the Jaguar* by Murray Gell-Mann, *Reinventing the Sacred: A New View of Science, Reason, and Religion* by Stuart A. Kauffman, *Warped Passages: Unraveling the Mysteries of the Universe's Hidden Dimensions* and *Knocking on Heaven's Door: How Physics and Scientific Thinking Illuminate the Universe and the Modern World* by Lisa Randall, *The Ten Most Beautiful Experiments* by George Johnson, and *Quantum Man: Richard Feynman's Life in Science* by Lawrence M. Krauss. In his biography of Gell-Mann, Johnson provided further information: "The novelist Cormac McCarthy, whom Murray had met through the MacArthur Foundation, line-edited the entire manuscript, but Gell-Mann was too rushed and disorganized to take advantage of the suggestions" (344). Krauss revised the paperback edition of his book *Quantum Man*, his biography of Richard Feynman, in the light of changes suggested by McCarthy. The title page actually features the advertisement "with corrections by Cormac McCarthy" immediately below the author and title. This is surely the first instance of a copy editor receiving marquee billing.

5. In the second letter in the Graves collection, written in early 1988, McCarthy writes, "I'm leaving for Mexico in a couple of days—not for the Sierras but just to take some sun. I've got some kind of malaise I can't seem to shake. My son says it sounds like walking pneumonia." Given the date, this would be McCarthy's son Cullen from his first marriage, to Lee Holleman.

6. McCarthy's interest in film is most evident in his repeated attempts to write a successful screenplay. *The Gardener's Son* was produced by PBS in December 1976; it was directed by Richard Pearce, with whom McCarthy has maintained a long friendship. In addition to *The Gardener's Son* McCarthy has written three screenplays that are now housed in the Wittliff Collection: *Cities of the Plain*, *No Country for Old Men*, and *Whales and Men*. These three typically inspire McCarthy admirers who have read them to admonish their hero, with shuffling embarrassment, to please keep the day job.

7. While McCarthy was in Spain acting as one of the producers of *The Counselor*, the Ridley Scott film based on McCarthy's original screenplay, journalist Mario Martinez-Paul asked him about the influence of Sam Peckinpah on his work. McCarthy, while expressing admiration for *The Wild Bunch*, denies any relationship between Peckinpah's notoriously violent westerns and his own novels. Although I would certainly agree that Peckinpah's brutal nihilism is of a different order from McCarthy's often highly moral parables, it seems pointless to deny that there is at least a surface similarity in the work of the two men. Peckinpah's portrayal of violence, the importance of masculine themes and male bonding in his work, his stark sense of tragedy, his feel for the ribald and the grotesque, his use of black humor, and his gritty take on the western genre all suggest that he opened up ground through a visual medium that McCarthy exploited through the written word. That is a lot of common ground.

8. In the commentary track for the DVD of HBO's production of *The Sunset Limited*, McCarthy, commenting on the scene in which Black expresses his admiration for John Coltrane, indicates that he shares the character's love of Coltrane, also mentioning an admiration for Miles Davis's *Kind of Blue*.

The trip to New Orleans mentioned in the letter was with McCarthy's friend Richard Pearce, who directed the PBS production of McCarthy's screenplay *The Gardener's Son*. Pearce was in New Orleans filming *No Mercy*, starring Richard Gere and Kim Basinger (out of curiosity, I watched the film myself—no mercy, indeed). In a letter to Woolmer dated 25

February 1986 (the same date as the Greenleaf letter), McCarthy mentions the trip: "I'm just back from New Orleans, where a friend of mine has been filming a new movie with Richard Gere. We went out one evening along Bourbon street interviewing strippers in the clubs for parts in the film. I don't know why I mention this as it's an impossible adventure to describe" (Box 1, Folder 6). Unless reality is very much stranger than fiction, I suspect that the creator of Lester Ballard, Gene Harrogate, and Judge Holden could manage a description of the strip clubs on Bourbon Street.

Bibliography

Abbey, Edward. *Desert Solitaire: A Season in the Wilderness*. New York: Touchstone, 1990. Print.

———. "To Cormac McCarthy." 15 June 1986. In *Postcards from Ed: Dispatches and Salvos from an American Iconoclast*. Ed. David Petersen. Minneapolis: Milkweed Editions, 2006. 184–185. Print.

Abraham, Lyndy. "Philosopher's Stone." In *A Dictionary of Alchemical Imagery*. Cambridge: Cambridge University Press, 1998. Print.

———. "Rock." In *A Dictionary of Alchemical Imagery*. Cambridge: Cambridge University Press, 1998. Print.

Agee, James, and Walker Evans. *Let Us Now Praise Famous Men*. Boston: Houghton Mifflin, 1969. Print.

Algren, Nelson. *Algren at Sea*. New York: Seven Stories Press, 2008. Print.

Applebaum, Anne. "Yesterday's Man?" Review. *New York Review of Books*. 11 January 2010. Print.

Arner, Robert D. "Ebenezer Cook." In *American Colonial Writers, 1606–1734*. Ed. Emory Elliott. *Dictionary of Literary Biography*, vol. 24. Detroit: Gale, 1984. *Literature Resource Center*. Web. 24 December 2016.

Arnold, Edwin T. "'Go to Sleep': Dreams and Visions in the Border Trilogy." In *A Cormac McCarthy Companion: The Border Trilogy*. Eds. Edwin T. Arnold and Dianne C. Luce. Jackson: University Press of Mississippi, 2001. 37–72. Print.

———. "McCarthy and the Sacred: A Reading of *The Crossing*." In *Cormac McCarthy: New Directions*. Ed. James D. Lilley. Albuquerque: University of New Mexico Press, 2002. 215–238. Print.

———. "Naming, Knowing, and Nothingness: McCarthy's Moral Parables." In *Perspectives on Cormac McCarthy*. Ed. Edwin T. Arnold and Dianne C. Luce. Jackson: University Press of Mississippi, 1999. 45–69. Print.

Arnold, Edwin T., and Dianne C. Luce. "Introduction." In *Perspectives on Cormac McCarthy*. Ed. Edwin T. Arnold and Dianne C. Luce. Jackson: University Press of Mississippi, 1999. 1–16. Print.

Atlas, James. *Bellow: A Biography*. New York: Random House, 2000. Print.

Auden, W. H. "In Memory of W. B. Yeats." In *Collected Poems*. Ed. Edward Mendelson. New York: Vintage, 1991. Print.

Bailey, Charles. "The Last Stage of the Hero's Evolution: Cormac McCarthy's *Cities of the*

Plain." In *Myth, Legend, Dust: Critical Responses to Cormac McCarthy*. Ed. Rick Wallach. New York: Manchester University Press, 2000. 293–301. Print.

Bealer, Alex W. *Old Ways of Working Wood: The Techniques and Tools of a Time-Honored Craft*. Revised ed., Edison, NJ: Castle Books, 1996. Print.

Beckett, Samuel. *Endgame*. New York: Grove Press, 1958. Print.

Bell, John Stewart. "Interview." In *The Ghost in the Atom: A Discussion of the Mysteries of Quantum Physics*." Ed. P. C. W. Davies and J. R. Brown. Cambridge: Cambridge University Press, 1986. Print.

Bell, Vereen M. *The Achievement of Cormac McCarthy*. Baton Rouge: Louisiana State University Press, 1988.

Bellow, Saul. *Herzog*. Greenwich, CT: Fawcett Publications, 1964. Print.

Beowulf. Trans. Francis B. Gummere. *The Oldest English Epic*. New York: Macmillan, 1929. Print.

Beowulf. Trans. Burton Raffel. New York: Signet Classic, 1999. Print.

Berdyaev, Nicolas. "Unground and Freedom." Introduction to *Six Theosophic Points*. Jacob Boehme. Ann Arbor: University of Michigan Press, 1958. Print.

Berg, William J., and Laurey K. Martin. *Gustave Flaubert*. New York: Twayne, 1997. Print.

Beston, Henry. *The Outermost House: A Year of Life on the Great Beach of Cape Cod*. New York: Ballantine, 1971. Print.

Bevis, Richard. "*Travels in Arabia Deserta*: Overview." In *Reference Guide to English Literature*. Ed. D. L. Kirkpatrick. 2nd ed., Chicago: St. James Press, 1991. Print.

Bird, David. "Dr. Leo Kanner, 86, Child Psychologist." Obituary. *New York Times*, 7 April 1981. Web. 24 December 2016.

Boehme, Jacob. *Six Theosophic Points*. Ann Arbor: University of Michigan Press, 1958. Print.

"Brennan, Joseph Gerard." *Contemporary Authors Online*. Gale, 2002. *Literature Resource Center*. Web. 15 January 2014.

Brennan, Joseph Gerard. *Three Philosophical Novelists*. New York: Macmillan, 1968. Print.

Britton, Burt. *Self-Portrait: Book People Picture Themselves*. New York: Random House, 1976. Print.

"Brown, Christy." *Dictionary of Irish Biography Online*. Cambridge University Press and Royal Irish Academy, 2013. Web. 7 November 2013.

Brown, Christy. *Down All the Days*. London: Secker and Warburg Limited, 1970. Print.

Bucco, Martin. *Wilbur Daniel Steele*. New York: Twayne, 1972. Print.

The Cambridge Companion to Cormac McCarthy. Ed. Steven Frye. Cambridge: Cambridge University Press, 2013. Print.

Chabon, Michael. "After the Apocalypse." *New York Review of Books*, 15 February 2007. Web. 22 August 2013.

Charles, Ron. "Apocalypse Now." Review of *The Road* by Cormac McCarthy. *Washington Post*, 1 October 2006. Web. 24 December 2016.

Chatwin, Bruce. *The Songlines*. New York: Penguin, 1988. Print.

———. "To J. Howard Woolmer." 7 January 1988. In *Under the Sun: The Letters of Bruce Chatwin*. Ed. Elizabeth Chatwin and Nicholas Shakespeare. London: Jonathan Cape, 2010. Print.

Chatwin, Jonathan. *Anywhere Out of the World: The Work of Bruce Chatwin*. Manchester: Manchester University Press, 2012. Print.

Chaucer, Geoffrey. *The Canterbury Tales*. Ware, UK: Wordsworth Editions, 1995. Print.

————. *The Canterbury Tales*. Trans. into Modern English by Nevill Coghill. New York: Penguin, 2003. Print.

Christian, William A., Jr. *Person and God in a Spanish Valley*. Revised ed., Princeton, NJ: Princeton University Press, 1989. Print.

Chuang Tzu: Basic Writings. Trans. Burton Watson. New York: Columbia University Press, 1964. Print.

Cicero. "The Dream of Scipio." In *On the Good Life*. Trans. Michael Grant. New York: Penguin, 1971. Print.

Clarkson, Michael. "Catching the 'Catcher in the Rye' J. D. Salinger." In *If You Really Want to Hear About It: Writers on J. D. Salinger and His Work*. Ed. Catherine Crawford. New York: Thunder's Mouth Press, 2006. Print.

Cleve, Felix M. *The Giants of Pre-Sophistic Greek Philosophy: An Attempt to Reconstruct Their Thoughts*, vol. 1. 2nd ed., The Hague: Martinus Nijhoff, 1969. Print.

Conrad, Joseph. *Heart of Darkness*. Ed. Paul B. Armstrong. 4th ed., New York: W. W. Norton, 2006. Print.

Cooper, Lydia. "'A Howling Void': Beckett's Influence in Cormac McCarthy's 'The Sunset Limited.'" *Cormac McCarthy Journal*, 2012. Print.

Corleis, Juergen. *Always on the Other Side: A Journalist's Journey from Hitler to Howard's End*. Juergen Corleis, 2008. *Google Books*.

Cox, Martha Heasley and Wayne Chatterton. *Nelson Algren*. Boston: Twayne, 1975. Print.

Cumbow, Robert C. *The Films of Sergio Leone*. Lanham, MD: Scarecrow Press, 2008. Print.

Dao De Jing: A Philosophical Translation. Trans. Roger T. Ames. Ed. Roger T. Ames and David L. Hall. New York: Ballantine, 2003. Print.

Daugherty, Leo. "Gravers False and True: *Blood Meridian* as Gnostic Tragedy." In *Perspectives on Cormac McCarthy*. Ed. Edwin T. Arnold and Dianne C. Luce. Jackson: University Press of Mississippi, 1999. 159–174. Print.

Davenport, Guy. *The Geography of the Imagination: Forty Essays*. Boston: Nonpareil Books, 1997. Print.

————. "Outer Dark." *New York Times*, 29 September 1968. Print.

Davidson, Donald. *The Tennessee*. 1948. 2 vols. Southern Classics Series. Nashville: J. S. Sanders, 1992. Print.

Davis, David Brion. "Southern Comfort." *New York Review of Books*. 5 October 1995. Web. 29 December 2016.

Davis, Steven L. "Mining Dobie: Cormac McCarthy's Debt to J. Frank Dobie in *The Crossing*." *Southwestern American Literature* 62.5 (2013): 52–57. Print.

Delevoy, Robert L. *Bruegel*. Trans. Stuart Gilbert. Cleveland: World Publishing Company, 1959. Print.

Dempsey, Peter. "Novelist of Shades and Patches: The Fiction of David Markson." *Hollins Critic* 42.4 (2005). *Literature Resource Center*. Web.

De Vries, Peter. *The Tents of Wickedness*. Boston: Little, Brown, 1959. Print.

Dewey, John. *Art as Experience*. New York: Perigee, 1980. Print.

Dickinson, Emily. "Poem 1668." *The Poems of Emily Dickinson: Reading Edition*. Ed. R. W. Franklin. Cambridge, MA: Harvard University Press, 1999. Print.

Dillard, Annie. *The Annie Dillard Reader*. New York: HarperPerennial, 1995. Print.

————. *Pilgrim at Tinker Creek*. New York: Harper and Row, 1988. Print.

————. *Teaching a Stone to Talk*. New York: HarperCollins, 1982. Print.

Dirda, Michael. *Classics for Pleasure*. New York: Harcourt, 2007. Print.

———. *Readings: Essays and Literary Entertainments*. New York: W. W. Norton, 2000. Print.

Dobie, J. Frank. "Jim Williams and *Out Our Way*." Introduction. *Cowboys Out Our Way*. J. R. Williams. New York: Scribner, 1951. Print.

———. *Out of the Old Rock*. Boston: Little, Brown, 1972. Print.

Doughty, Charles M. *Travels in Arabia Deserta*, vols. 1 and 2. Cambridge: Cambridge University Press, 1888. Print.

Downie, Janet. "Narrative and Divination: Artemidorus and Aelius Aristides." *Archiv Für Religionsgeschichte* 15.1 (2014): 97–116. *Academic Search Complete*. Web. 30 December 2016.

Durant, Will. *The Story of Philosophy*. New York: Pocket Books, 1953. Print.

Durrell, Lawrence, and Henry Miller. In *The Durrell-Miller Letters, 1935–80*. Ed. Ian S. MacNiven. New York: New Directions, 1988. Print.

Dyson, Freeman. "Quote." In *The Anthropic Cosmological Principle*. John D. Barrow and Frank J. Tipler. Oxford: Oxford University Press, 1986. Print.

Ebeling, Florian. *The Secret History of Hermes Trismegistus: Hermeticism from Ancient to Modern Times*. Trans. David Lorton. Ithaca, NY: Cornell University Press, 2007. Print.

Eddins, Dwight. "'Everything a Hunter and Everything Hunted': Schopenhauer and Cormac McCarthy's *Blood Meridian*." *Critique: Studies in Contemporary Fiction* 1 (2003): 25–33. Print.

Edwards, Philip. "Philip Massinger." In *Jacobean and Caroline Dramatists*. Ed. Fredson Bowers. *Dictionary of Literary Biography*, vol. 58. Detroit: Gale, 1987. *Literature Resource Center*. Web. 8 January 2014.

Eliot, T. S. "Tradition and the Individual Talent." In *Selected Prose of T. S. Eliot*. Ed. Frank Kermode. New York: Farrar, Straus and Giroux, 1975. 37–44. Print.

———. "The Waste Land." In *The Complete Poems and Plays, 1909–1950*. New York: Harcourt, 1980. Print.

Ellis, Jay. *No Place for Home: Spatial Constraint and Character Flight in the Novels of Cormac McCarthy*. New York: Routledge, 2006. Print.

"Farrell, James T." *Contemporary Authors Online*. Gale, 2013. *Literature Resource Center*. Web. 28 December 2016.

Faulkner, William. *Absalom, Absalom*. New York: Vintage, 1972. Print.

———. "Barn Burning." *Collected Stories William Faulkner*. New York: Vintage, 1977. 3–25. Print.

———. *The Sound and the Fury*. New York: Vintage, 1990. Print.

Ferris, Timothy. *The Whole Shebang: A State-of-the-Universe(s) Report*. New York: Touchstone, 1998. Print.

Finnegan, Cara A. "'Liars May Photograph': Image Vernaculars and Progressive Era Child Labor Rhetoric." *POROI: Project on the Rhetoric of Inquiry*. University of Iowa, November 2008. Web. 3 June 2016.

Flaubert, Gustave. *The Temptation of St. Anthony*. Trans. and ed. Kitty Mrosovsky. New York: Penguin, 1983. Print.

Foucault, Michel. *Madness and Civilization: A History of Insanity in the Age of Reason*. Trans. Richard Howard. New York: Random House, 1965. Print.

"Frankl, Paul." *Dictionary of Art Historians*. N.d. Web. 24 December 2016.

"Fraser, Julius Thomas." *Contemporary Authors Online*. Gale, 2002. *Literature Resource Center*. Web. 20 January 2014.

Fraser, J. T. *Of Time, Passion, and Knowledge: Reflections on the Strategy of Existence*. New York: George Braziller, 1975. Print.

Frazier, Charles. "Galway Kinnell." In *American Poets Since World War II*. Ed. Donald J. Greiner. *Dictionary of Literary Biography*, vol. 5. Detroit: Gale, 1980. *Literature Resource Center*. Web. 24 December 2016.

Frost, Robert. *Collected Poems, Prose, and Plays*. New York: Library of America, 1995. Print.

Frye, Steven. "*Blood Meridian* and the Poetics of Violence." In *The Cambridge Companion to Cormac McCarthy*. Ed. Steven Frye. Cambridge: Cambridge University Press, 2013. Print.

———. "Histories, Novels, Ideas: Cormac McCarthy and the Art of Philosophy." In *The Cambridge Companion to Cormac McCarthy*. Ed. Steven Frye. Cambridge: Cambridge University Press, 2013. Print.

———. *Understanding Cormac McCarthy*. Columbia: University of South Carolina Press, 2009.

———. "Yeats' 'Sailing to Byzantium' and McCarthy's *No Country for Old Men*: Art and Artifice in the New Novel." *Cormac McCarthy Journal* 5.1 (2005): 14–20.

Gallivan, Euan. "Compassionate McCarthy? *The Road* and Schopenhauerian Ethics." *Cormac McCarthy Journal* 6.1 (2008): 100–106. Print.

Galsworthy, John. *Studies and Essays. Hardpress*, 2006. Web.

"Gard, Wayne." *Contemporary Authors Online*. Gale, 2003. *Literature Resource Center*. Web. 4 June 2016.

Garner, Dwight. "Lost in Literary History: A Tale of Courage in the South." *New York Times*, 18 April 2014. Web. 31 January 2016.

"Ghose, Aurobindo." *Contemporary Authors Online*. Gale, 2007. *Literature Resource Center*. Web. 4 June 2016.

Giemza, Bryan. *Irish Catholic Writers and the Invention of the American South*. Baton Rouge: Louisiana State University Press, 2013. Print.

Gilbert, Stuart. *James Joyce's "Ulysses: A Study."* New York: Vintage, 1955. Print.

Ginsberg, Allen. "Howl." In *Howl and Other Poems*. San Francisco: City Lights, 2001. Print.

———. Introduction. In *Jail Notes*, by Timothy Leary. New York: Grove Press, 1970. Print.

Girard, Rene. *Things Hidden Since the Foundation of the World*. Trans. Stephen Bann and Michael Metteer. Stanford: Stanford University Press, 1978. Print.

———. *Violence and the Sacred*. Trans. Patrick Gregory. Baltimore: Johns Hopkins University Press, 1977. Print.

Goethe, Johann Wolfgang von. *Faust: A Tragedy, Parts One and Two, Fully Revised*. Trans. Martin Greenberg. New Haven, CT: Yale University Press, 2014. Print.

Graves, Robert. "To Juan at the Winter Solstice." In *Collected Poems*. London: Cassell, 1975. Print.

———. *The White Goddess: A Historical Grammar of Poetic Myth*. New York: Octagon, 1972. Print.

Guillemin, Georg. *The Pastoral Vision of Cormac McCarthy*. College Station: Texas A&M University Press, 2004. Print.

Gwynn, Frederick L., and Joseph L. Blotner, eds. *Faulkner in the University*. Charlottesville: University Press of Virginia, 1995. Print.

Hall, David L. *The Uncertain Phoenix: Adventures Toward a Post-Cultural Sensibility*. New York: Fordham University Press, 1982. Print.

Hallock, Charles. "Wild Cattle Hunting on Green Island." In *Hunting in the Old South: Original Narratives of the Hunters*. Ed. Clarence Gohdes. Baton Rouge: Louisiana State University Press, 1967. Print.

Hawthorne, Nathaniel. "Ethan Brand." *Selected Tales and Sketches*. New York: Penguin, 1987. Print.

———. "My Kinsman, Major Molineux." In *The Norton Anthology of American Literature*, vol. 1. Ed. Nina Baym, et al. Shorter 8th ed., New York: W. W. Norton, 2013. Print.

———. "Young Goodman Brown." In *The Norton Anthology of American Literature*, vol. 1. Ed. Nina Baym, et al. Shorter 8th ed., New York: W. W. Norton, 2013. Print.

Heller, Joseph. *Catch-22*. New York: Simon and Schuster, 2011. Print.

Hemingway, Ernest. *A Moveable Feast*. Ed. Seán Hemingway. New York: Scribner, 2009. Print.

Heraclitus. *Fragments*. Ed. and trans. T. M. Robinson. Toronto: University of Toronto Press, 1987. Print.

"Herbert, Edward of Cherbury." *Internet Encyclopedia of Philosophy*. N.d. Web. 24 December 2016.

Herman, Arthur. *The Idea of Decline in Western History*. New York: Free Press, 1997. Print.

Herrigel, Eugen. *The Method of Zen*. New York: Vintage, 1974. Print.

Higgins, William R. "Peter De Vries." In *American Novelists Since World War II, Second Series*. Ed. James E. Kibler Jr. *Dictionary of Literary Biography*, vol. 6. Detroit: Gale, 1980. *Literature Resource Center*. Web. 13 January 2014.

Hoagland, Edward. *Notes from the Century Before: A Journal from British Columbia*. New York: Modern Library, 2002. Print.

Hoffer, Eric. *The True Believer: Thoughts on the Nature of Mass Movements*. New York: Harper, 2002. Print.

Hughes, H. Stuart. "Preface to the Present Edition." In *The Decline of the West*, by Oswald Spengler. Ed. Helmut Werner and Arthur Helps. Trans. Charles Francis Atkinson. New York: Oxford University Press, 1991. Print.

Hughes, Pennethorne. *Witchcraft*. New York: Penguin, 1965. Print.

James, William. *The Will to Believe: and Other Essays in Popular Philosophy, and Human Immortality*. New York: Dover, 1956. Print.

Jarrell, Randall. *The Third Book of Criticism*. New York: Farrar, Straus and Giroux, 1965. Print.

Jarrett, Robert L. *Cormac McCarthy*. New York: Twayne, 1997. Print.

Jeffers, Robinson. "Hurt Hawks." In *Robinson Jeffers: Selected Poems*. New York: Vintage, 1965. Print.

Johnson, George. *Strange Beauty: Murray Gell-Mann and the Revolution in Twentieth-Century Physics*. New York: Vintage, 1999. Print.

Johnson, Samuel. "Preface to Shakespeare, 1765." In *The Yale Edition of the Works of Samuel Johnson*, vol. 7: *Johnson on Shakespeare*. New Haven, CT: Yale University Press, 1968. Print.

Jonas, Hans. *The Gnostic Religion: The Message of the Alien God and the Beginnings of Christianity*. Revised 2nd ed., Boston: Beacon Press, 1991. Print.

———. "Gnosticism." *Encyclopedia of Philosophy*. Gale, 2009. *Literature Resource Center*. Web. 9 June 2015.

Jordan, Richard. "'Just Write' Says Successful Author." *UT Daily Beacon*, 28 January 1969, 16. Print.

Josyph, Peter. "Blood Music: Reading *Blood Meridian*." In *Sacred Violence: A Reader's Companion to Cormac McCarthy*, vol. 2. Ed. Wade Hall and Rick Wallach. 2nd ed., El Paso: Texas Western Press, 2002. Print.

———. *Cormac McCarthy's House: Reading McCarthy Without Walls*. Austin: University of Texas Press, 2013. Print.

Joyce, James. *Ulysses*. Ed. Hans Walter Gabler, et al. New York: Random House, 1986. Print.

Jung, C. G. *Memories, Dreams, Reflections*. Ed. Aniela Jaffe. Trans. Richard and Clara Winston. New York: Vintage, 1963. Print.

Jurgensen, John. "Cormac McCarthy on How Coca-Cola Ended Up in *The Road* and Other Musings." *Wall Street Journal*, 12 November 2009. Web. 13 November 2009.

———. "Hollywood's Favorite Cowboy." *Wall Street Journal*, 13 November 2009. Web. 13 November 2009.

King, Daniel. "Albert Erskine at Random House: The Cormac McCarthy Years." *Comparative American Studies* 9.3 (2011): 254–272. Print.

Kinnell, Galway. "The Wolves." In *The Avenue Bearing the Initial of Christ into The New World: Poems 1953–1964*. New York: Mariner, 2002. Print.

Koestler, Arthur. *The Sleepwalkers: A History of Man's Changing Vision of the Universe*. Harmondsworth, UK: Penguin, 1964. Print.

Kramer, Heinrich, and James Sprenger. *The Malleus Maleficarum*. Trans. Montague Summers. New York: Dover, 1971. Print.

Krauss, Lawrence M. *Quantum Man: Richard Feynman's Life in Science*. New York: W. W. Norton, 2011. Print.

"Krutch, Joseph Wood." *Dictionary of Literary Biography*. Detroit: Gale, 2003. *Literature Resource Center*. Web. 18 November 2013.

Krutch, Joseph Wood. *The Desert Year*. New York: Viking, 1952. Print.

Kundera, Milan. *The Art of the Novel*. Trans. Linda Asher. New York: Harper, 2003. Print.

Kushner, David. "Cormac McCarthy's Apocalypse." *Rolling Stone*, 27 December 2007: 43–53. Print.

"Lampedusa, Giuseppi Tomasi di." In *Italian Novelists Since World War II, 1945–1965*, by Augustus Pallotta. Ed. Augustus Pallotta. *Dictionary of Literary Biography*, vol. 177. Detroit: Gale, 1997. *Literature Resource Center*. Web. 28 December 2016.

Lampedusa, Giuseppe di. *The Leopard*. Trans. Archibald Colquhoun. New York: Pantheon, 2007. Print.

"Langley, Batty." *The Twickenham Museum*. N.d. Web. 24 December 2016.

Leopold, Aldo. *A Sand County Almanac, with Essays on Conservation from Round River*. Oxford: Oxford University Press, 1966. Print.

"Lewis, Wyndham." *Dictionary of Literary Biography*. Detroit: Gale, 1983. *Literature Resource Center*. Web. 24 January 2014.

Lewis, Wyndham. *Time and Western Man*. Ed. Paul Edwards. Berkeley: Gingko Press, 1993. Print.

Lissner, Ivar. *The Living Past: 7,000 Years of Civilization*. Trans. J. Maxwell Brownjohn. New York: G. P. Putnam's Sons, 1957. Print.

London, Jack. "To Build a Fire." In *The Portable Jack London*. Ed. Earle Labor. New York: Penguin, 1994. Print.

Longley, John Lewis, Jr. "Suttree and the Metaphysics of Death." *Southern Literary Journal* 17 (Spring 1985): 79–90. Print.

Lopez, Barry. *Arctic Dreams: Imagination and Desire in a Northern Landscape*. New York: Bantam Books, 1987. Print.

———. *Of Wolves and Men*. New York: Touchstone, 1995. Print.

Lowrie, Walter. *Kierkegaard*. London: Oxford University Press, 1938. Print.

Luce, Dianne C. "Cormac McCarthy in High School: 1951." *Cormac McCarthy Journal* 7.1 (2009): 5. Print.

———. *Reading the World: Cormac McCarthy's Tennessee Period*. Columbia: University of South Carolina Press, 2009. Print.

———. "The Road and the Matrix: The World as Tale in *The Crossing*." In *Perspectives on Cormac McCarthy*. Eds. Edwin T. Arnold and Dianne C. Luce. Jackson: University Press of Mississippi, 1999. 195–219. Print.

———. "The Vanishing World of Cormac McCarthy's Border Trilogy." In *A Cormac McCarthy Companion: The Border Trilogy*. Ed. Edwin T. Arnold and Dianne C. Luce. Jackson: University Press of Mississippi, 2001. Print.

Machacek, Gregory. "Allusion." *PMLA* 122.2 (March 2007): 522–536. Print.

Mailer, Norman. *Why Are We in Vietnam?: A Novel*. New York: G. P. Putnam's Sons, 1967. Print.

Maryland: A Guide to the Old Line State. Compiled by Workers of the Writer's Program of the Work Projects Administration in the State of Maryland. New York: Oxford University Press, 1940. Print.

Massinger, Philip. "The Virgin-Martyr." In *The Plays of Philip Massinger*, vol. 1. Ed. W. Gifford. 2nd ed., New York: AMS Press, 1966. Print.

McCarthy, Cormac. *All the Pretty Horses*. New York: Vintage, 1993. Print.

———. *Blood Meridian: Or the Evening Redness in the West*. New York: Vintage, 1992. Print.

———. *Child of God*. New York: Vintage, 1993. Print.

———. *Cities of the Plain*. New York: Vintage, 1999. Print.

———. "Connecting Science and Art." Discussion. *NPR*, 8 April 2011. Transcript. Web. 24 December 2016.

———. *The Gardener's Son: A Screenplay*. Hopewell: The Ecco Press, 1996. Print.

———. Interview by Oprah Winfrey. *The Oprah Winfrey Show*. ABC. 5 June 2007. Transcript.

———. *No Country for Old Men*. New York: Knopf, 2005. Print.

———. "No Hay Ninguna Razón para Pensar Que Las Cosas Van a Mejorar." Interview by Mario-Paul Martínez. *Informacion.es*, 6 October 2012. Web.

———. *The Orchard Keeper*. New York: Vintage, 1993. Print.

———. *Outer Dark*. New York: Vintage, 1993. Print.

———. *The Road*. New York: Knopf, 2006. Print.

———. *The Stonemason: A Play in Five Acts*. New York: Vintage, 1994. Print.

———. *The Sunset Limited*. New York: Vintage, 2006. Print.

———. *Suttree*. New York: Vintage, 1992. Print.

McGinniss, Joe. *Going to Extremes*. New York: Signet, 1982. Print.

Melville, Herman. *Moby-Dick*. Ed. Hershel Parker and Harrison Hayford. 2nd ed, New York: W. W. Norton, 2002. Print.

Metress, Christopher. "Via Negativa: The Way of Unknowing in Cormac McCarthy's *Outer Dark*." *Southern Review* 1 (2001): 147–154. Print.

Miller, Karl. *Doubles*. New York: Faber and Faber, 2009. Print.

Milton, John. *The Portable Milton*. Ed. Douglas Bush. New York: Penguin, 1987. Print.

Montaigne, Michel Eyquem de. "Of Friendship." In *The Complete Essays of Montaigne*. Trans. Donald M. Frame. Stanford: Stanford University Press, 1958. Print.

———. "To Flee from Sensual Pleasures at the Price of Life." In *The Complete Essays of Montaigne*. Trans. Donald M. Frame. Stanford: Stanford University Press, 1998. Print.

Morgan, Wesley G. "McCarthy's High School Years." *Cormac McCarthy Journal* 3 (2003): 6–9. Print.

Morrow, Mark. *Images of the Southern Writer: Photographs by Mark Morrow*. Athens: University of Georgia Press, 1985. Print.

"Mowat, Farley." *Contemporary Authors Online*. Gale, 2014. *Literature Resource Center*. Web. 2 June 2016.

Myers, D. G. "Peter De Vries." *Commentary*, 27 September 2011. Web. 13 January 2014.

Nalbone, Lisa. "Colonized and Colonizer Disjunction: Power and Truth in Zeno Gandía's *La Charca*." *Hispanófila* 159 (2010): 23–37. Print.

Nall, Garry L. "Foreword." In *Life in the Saddle*. Frank Collinson. Ed. Mary Whatley Clarke. Norman: University of Oklahoma Press, 1997. Print.

Nietzsche, Friedrich. *The Gay Science*. Trans. Walter Kaufmann. New York: Vintage, 1974. Print.

O'Brien, Tim. *Going After Cacciato*. New York: Broadway Books, 1999. Print.

Paine, Albert Bigelow. *Mark Twain: A Biography*, vols. 3 and 4. New York: Harper and Brothers, 1912. *Google Books*. Web. 18 January 2016.

Pater, Walter. *The Renaissance: Studies in Art and Poetry*. Ed. Adam Phillips. Oxford: Oxford University Press, 1998. Print.

Payne, Roger. *Among Whales*. New York: Scribner, 1995. Print.

Poe, Edgar Allan. "The Black Cat." In *Poe: Poetry, Tales, and Selected Essays*. Ed. Patrick F. Quinn and G. R. Thompson. New York: Library of America, 1996. 597–606. Print.

Prather, William. "Absurd Reasoning in an Existential World: A Consideration of Cormac McCarthy's *Suttree*." In *Sacred Violence*, vol. 1: *Cormac McCarthy's Appalachian Works*. Eds. Wade Hall and Rick Wallach. El Paso: Texas Western Press, 2002. 139–151. Print.

Pritchard, William H. *Wyndham Lewis*. New York: Twayne, 1968. Print.

"Rapoport, Amos." *Contemporary Authors Online*. Gale, 2001. *Literature Resource Center*. Web. 3 June 2016.

Rilke, Rainer Maria. "Second Duino Elegy." In *The Selected Poetry of Rainer Maria Rilke*. Ed. and trans. Stephen Mitchell. New York: Vintage, 1989. Print.

Rooke, Leon. "Rash Undertakings." *Brick* 27 (1986). Web. 21 January 2008.

Rosengarten, Theodore. *All God's Dangers: The Life of Nate Shaw*. Chicago: University of Chicago Press, 2000. Print.

Rykwert, Joseph. *The First Moderns: The Architects of the Eighteenth Century*. Cambridge: MIT Press, 1983. Print.

"Scarry, Elaine." *Contemporary Authors Online*. Gale, 2014. *Literature Resource Center*. Web. 1 June 2016.

Scarry, Elaine. *The Body in Pain: The Making and Unmaking of the World*. Oxford: Oxford University Press, 1985. Print.

Scholem, Gershom. "Zen-Nazism?" *Encounter* 16.2 (1961): 96. Print.

Seesholtz, Mel. "Wilbur Daniel Steele." In *American Short-Story Writers, 1910–1945: First Series*. Ed. Bobby Ellen Kimbel. *Dictionary of Literary Biography*, vol. 86. Detroit: Gale Research, 1989. *Literature Resource Center*. Web. 30 December 2016.

Sepich, John. *Notes on Blood Meridian.* Revised and Expanded ed., Austin: University of Texas Press, 2008. Print.

———. "What Kind of Indians Was Them?: Some Historical Sources in Cormac McCarthy's *Blood Meridian.*" In *Perspectives on Cormac McCarthy.* Ed. Edwin T. Arnold and Dianne C. Luce. Jackson: University Press of Mississippi, 1999. Print.

Shakespeare, William. *The Arden Shakespeare Complete Works.* Ed. Richard Proudfoot, Ann Thompson, and David Scott Kastan. Walton-on-Thames, UK: Thomas Nelson and Sons, 1998.

Shelton, Frank. "Suttree and Suicide." *Southern Quarterly: A Journal of Arts in the South* 29.1 (1990): 71–83. Print.

Spengler, Oswald. *The Decline of the West.* Ed. Helmut Werner and Arthur Helps. Trans. Charles Francis Atkinson. New York: Oxford University Press, 1991. Print.

Steele, Wilbur Daniel. "How Beautiful with Shoes." In *50 Great Short Stories.* Ed. Milton Crane. New York: Bantam, 2005. Print.

Steinbeck, John. *The Log from the Sea of Cortez.* New York: Penguin, 1976. Print.

Steiner, George. *George Steiner at the New Yorker.* New York: New Directions, 2009. Print.

Stephenson, Carl. "Leiningen Versus the Ants." In *Classic Adventure Stories: Twenty-One Tales of People Pushed to the Limit.* Ed. Stephen Brennan. Guilford: Lyons Press, 2003. *Google Books.* Web. 22 August 2013.

Sternlicht, Sanford. "John Galsworthy." In *Nobel Prize Laureates in Literature,* Part 2: *Dictionary of Literary Biography,* vol. 330. Detroit: Gale, 2007. *Literature Resource Center.* Web. 30 December 2016.

Sullivan, John Jeremiah. "Guy Davenport, The Art of Fiction No. 174." *Paris Review* 163 (Fall 2002). Web. 27 January 2014.

Theroux, Alexander. *The Strange Case of Edward Gorey.* Seattle: Fantagraphics Books, 2010. Print.

"Thompson, Francis Joseph." *Contemporary Authors Online.* Gale, 2002. *Literature Resource Center.* Web. 18 July 2013.

Thompson, Francis. *The Poems of Francis Thompson.* London: Oxford University Press, 1951. Print.

"Thorndike, Lynn." *Contemporary Authors Online.* Gale, 1998. *Literature Resource Center.* Web. June 2016.

Todd, Connie. "Cormac McCarthy: The Road to Texas State." *Hillviews* (Spring/Summer 2008). Web. 30 December 2016.

Toulmin, Stephen. "Arthur Koestler, *The Sleepwalkers.*" Review. *Journal of Philosophy* 59.18 (1962): 500–503. Print.

Trumbo, Dalton. "To Christopher Trumbo." 8 November 1958. In *Additional Dialogue: Letters of Dalton Trumbo, 1942–1962.* Ed. Helen Manfull. New York: M. Evans, 1970. 443–451. Print.

Twain, Mark. "In a Writer's Workshop." In *Mark Twain in Eruption: Hitherto Unpublished Pages About Men and Events.* Ed. Bernard DeVoto. 3rd ed., New York: Harper and Brothers, 1940. Print.

Valéry, Paul. "The Yalu." *History and Politics.* Vol. 10 of *The Collected Valéry.* Trans. Denise Folliot and Jackson Mathews. Bollingen Ser. XLV. New York: Pantheon, 1962. Print.

Vanderheide, John. "The Process of Elimination: Tracing the Prodigal's Irrevocable Passage through Cormac McCarthy's Southern and Western Novels." In *Myth, Legend, Dust:*

Critical Responses to Cormac McCarthy. Ed. Rick Wallach. Manchester, UK: Manchester University Press, 2000. Print.

Wallace, David Foster. "The Empty Plenum: David Markson's *Wittgenstein's Mistress*." *Review of Contemporary Fiction* 8.3 (1998). Print.

Wallace, Garry. "Meeting McCarthy." *Southern Quarterly* 30.4 (1992): 134–139. Print.

Wallach, Rick. "From *Beowulf* to *Blood Meridian*: Cormac McCarthy's Demystification of the Martial Code." In *Cormac McCarthy: New Directions*. Ed. James D. Lilley. Albuquerque: University of New Mexico Press, 2002. Print.

———. "Judge Holden, *Blood Meridian*'s Evil Archon." In *Sacred Violence*, vol. 2. Ed. Wade Hall and Rick Wallach. El Paso: Texas Western Press, 2002. Print.

———. "Ulysses in Knoxville: Suttree's Agean Journey." *Appalachian Heritage* 39.1 (2011): 51–61. *MLA International Bibliography*. Web. 10 January 2014.

Watson, James. "'The Only Words I Know Are the Catholic Ones': Sacramental Existentialism in Cormac McCarthy's *Suttree*." *Southwestern American Literature* 5 (2013): 7–24. Print.

West, Nathanael. *Miss Lonelyhearts & The Day of the Locust*. New York: New Directions, 1962. Print.

Weston, Jessie L. *From Ritual to Romance*. West Valley City, UT: Waking Lion Press, 2007. Print.

Whitehead, Alfred North. *Process and Reality*. Ed. David Ray Griffin and Donald W. Sherburne. New York: Free Press, 1978. Print.

Williams, Don. "Cormac McCarthy Crosses the Great Divide." *New Millennium Writings* 14 (2004–2005). Web. 19 January 2013.

Wolfe, Tom. *The Right Stuff*. New York: Bantam, 1980. Print.

Woodward, Richard B. "Cormac McCarthy's Venomous Fiction." *New York Times Magazine*, 19 April 1992. Print.

Yeats, William Butler. "A Cradle Song." In *The Collected Poems of W. B. Yeats*. Ed. Richard J. Finneran. New York: Collier, 1989. Print.

———. "Easter, 1916." In *The Collected Poems of W. B. Yeats*. Ed. Richard J. Finneran. New York: Collier, 1989. Print.

———. "The Lake Isle of Innisfree." In *The Collected Poems of W. B. Yeats*. Ed. Richard J. Finneran. New York: Collier, 1989. Print.

———. "Sailing to Byzantium." In *The Collected Poems of W. B. Yeats*. Ed. Richard J. Finneran. New York: Collier, 1989. Print.

Young, Thomas D., Jr. "The Imprisonment of Sensibility: *Suttree*." In *Perspectives on Cormac McCarthy*. Ed. Edwin T. Arnold and Dianne C. Luce. Jackson: University Press of Mississippi, 1999. Print.

Index

109, 141, 208, 238, 244, 273–274, 280,
307–308n1 (chap. 7)
Nordau, Max: influence on *Suttree*, 121–
124
Northrop, Filmer Stuart Cuckow: influence
on *The Stonemason*, 228

O'Brien, Tim: *Going After Cacciato*, 203;
influence on *Blood Meridian*, 203–204
O'Connor, Flannery, 1; "Good Country
People," 33; "Good Man Is Hard to
Find, A," 33; *Habit of Being, The*, 162,
205; influence on *Blood Meridian*, 204–
206; McCarthy on, 32–33, 204–205;
Wise Blood, 33, 204–205
Ondaatje, Michael: *English Patient, The*,
295; McCarthy on, 295–296
Orchard Keeper, The (McCarthy): archived
papers, 6–7, 16–17, 241; Davidson's influence on, 68; Eliot's influence on,
20; Faulkner's influence on, 16, 18–21;
Frost's influence on, 16, 21–23; Hawthorne's influence on, 16–17, 23–25;
marginal comments, 16–17; metaphysics
in, 23, 29, 214; nature and civilization
in, 16, 21–24, 40, 66, 67, 107, 177, 273,
280; Poe's influence on, 127; point of
view in, 260; Shakespeare's influence
on, 17, 18–21, 128; synopsis, 16; Woolmer on, 278; writing and publication
history, 4, 9, 48; Yeats's influence on,
273
Outer Dark (McCarthy), 36, 143; allegory
in, 24, 27, 30, 147, 283; archived papers,
26–27, 28; Camus's influence on, 26,
27–33; Christianity in, 27–28, 30–31,
186; Davidson's influence on, 67–68;
Faulkner's influence on, 19; Jung's influence on, 97; marginal comments, 17, 27,
28; synopsis, 26; writing and publication history, 4, 48
Ovsyanikov, Nikita: influence on *The Road*,
252; *Polar Bears: Living with the White
Bear*, 252

Pagels, Heinz: influence on *The Road*, 252–
253

Pallotta, Augustus, 104
Pater, Walter: influence on *Suttree*, 124–
126
Payne, Roger, 257, 266–267, 278, 284, 308–
309n4
Pearce, Richard, 4, 37, 41, 309n6, 309–
310n8
phraseological appropriations, 9, 20, 73.
See also literary allusions
Pirsig, Robert M.: influence on *Blood
Meridian*, 206; influence on *The Road*,
253–254; *Zen and the Art of Motorcycle
Maintenance*, 206, 244, 251, 253
Poe, Edgar Allan, 23, 283, 306n22; "Black
Cat, The," 127; influence on *Suttree*,
126–127
Pound, Ezra, 282; influence on *Whales and
Men*, 269
Prather, Frank, 28–29
Prescott, Orville, 19
Psycho (film), 35–36

Raffel, Burton, 155
Ransom, John Crowe, 66
Rapoport, Amos: *House, Form, and Culture*, 39, 45; influence on *The Gardener's
Son*, 39, 45
Rilke, Rainer Maria: influence on *The
Stonemason*, 228–229, 303n9; *Second
Duino Elegy*, 229
Road, The (McCarthy), 51, 100, 109, 141,
159, 161, 189, 232, 292; archived papers,
307n27; Beckett's influence on, 244–
246; Chabon on, 138–139; Defoe's influence on, 246; and dystopian fiction,
282; Eliot's influence on, 247; Flaubert's
influence on, 77; Frost's influence on, 21,
247; and Grail legend, 148; inspiration
for, 113–114; Kierkegaard's influence on,
249–250; London's influence on, 139,
250–251; Markson's influence on, 251–
252; Martin's influence on, 252; Oprah
Winfrey book club selection, 5; original
title, 24; Ovsyanikov's influence on, 252;
Pagels's influence on, 252–253; Pirsig's
influence on, 253–254; Pulitzer Prize
awarded to, 5, 243, 299n2; Schopen-